Church and State
in American History

Church and State in American History

The Burden of Religious Pluralism

SECOND EDITION, EXPANDED AND UPDATED

Edited by
John F. Wilson and Donald L. Drakeman

Beacon Press   Boston

Beacon Press
25 Beacon Street
Boston, Massachusetts 02108

Beacon Press books are published under the auspices
of the Unitarian Universalist Association of
Congregations in North America.

First edition published in 1965 by D. C. Heath and Company
Revised and expanded edition published in 1987 by Beacon Press
© 1987 by Beacon Press
All rights reserved
Printed in the United States of America

92 91 90 89 88 87   8 7 6 5 4 3 2 1

Library of Congress Cataloging in Publication Data

Church and state in American history.

  Bibliography: p.
  Includes index.
  1. Church and state—United States.   2. United
States—Church history.   I. Wilson, John Frederick.
II. Drakeman, Donald L.
BR516.C492   1987   322'.1'0973   86-47513
ISBN 0-8070-0409-X

Contents

Introduction *by John F. Wilson*   ix
Chronology   xxi

I. **THE LANGUAGE OF COLONIAL ESTABLISHMENTS** (-1700)   1
   1. *John Cotton:* A Discourse about Civil Government   3
   2. *Roger Williams:* Queries of Highest Consideration   8
   3. Articles, Lawes and Orders, Divine, Politic, and Martiall for
      the Colony in Virginia   11
   4. Preface to the Fundamental Orders of Connecticut   13
   5. An Act Concerning Religion in the Maryland Colony   14
   6. The Charter of Rhode Island and Providence Plantations   16
   7. *William Penn:* Preface to the Frame of Government of
      Pennsylvania   17
   8. The Fundamental Constitutions of Carolina   18
   9. *H. Richard Niebuhr:* The Sovereignty of God   20
   10. *Perry Miller:* Puritan State and Puritan Society   25

II. **ETHNIC DIVERSITY AND EVANGELICAL DIFFERENTIATION** (1700-1760)   32
   1. The Connecticut Establishment and Provision for Dissent   34
   2. The Confession of Faith of the Christians Called Mennonites . .   35
   3. Grievances against the Connecticut Establishment   37
   4. Samuel Davies on Behalf of Dissenters in Virginia   38
   5. *H. Richard Niebuhr:* The Churches of the Immigrants   42
   6. *William Warren Sweet:* Religious Minorities in the Colonies   45
   7. *Edwin S. Gaustad:* Institutional Effects of the
      Great Awakening   47

III. **THE STRUGGLE FOR INDEPENDENCE AND THE TERMS OF
   SETTLEMENT** (1760-1820)   52
      THE THREAT OF AN ANGLICAN ESTABLISHMENT
   1. Chandler's Appeal on Behalf of Anglicans in America   53
   2. Colonial Criticism of the Appeal   56
   3. *Arthur L. Cross:* The Newspaper Controversy   61
   4. *Carl Bridenbaugh:* No Bishop, No King   64

      THE FOUNDING FATHERS ON THE ISSUE OF ESTABLISHMENT
   5. Madison's Memorial and Remonstrance   68
   6. Jefferson's Act for Establishing Religious Freedom   73

Contents

7. A Petition Relating to Church Establishment. 74
8. House and Senate Debates: 1789 75
9. Occasional Letters Regarding Religion and Government 78
10. *Daniel J. Boorstin:* The Happy Variety of Minds 82
11. *Robert T. Handy:* The Magna Charta of Religious Freedom
in America. 85

IV. **THE ERA OF REPUBLICAN PROTESTANTISM** (1820-1860)   90
1. Joseph Story on the Religion Clauses of the Bill of Rights 92
2. Lyman Beecher on Disestablishment in Connecticut 94
3. A Christian Party in Politics 96
4. Beecher's Strategy for the West 100
5. A Jacksonian Criticism of the Protestant Phalanx 102
6. A Religious Liberal's Criticism of the Protestant Strategy. 105
7. Colton on the True Character of the Evangelical Enterprise . . . 110
8. *James F. Maclear:* "The True American Union" of Church
and State. 112
9. *Charles I. Foster:* Characteristics of the Evangelical
United Front. 117

V. **THE RECOGNITION OF AMERICAN PLURALISM** (1860-1920)   121
THE PUBLIC SCHOOLS AS DIVISIVE
1. *Judge Storer:* The Bible in the Common Schools 123
2. *Judge Welch:* The Bible in the Public Schools 126
3. *Samuel T. Spear:* Religion and the State 129

"AMERICANISM" PROTESTANT AND CATHOLIC
4. *Washington Gladden:* The Anti-Catholic Crusade 132
5. *Josiah Strong:* America the Embodiment of Christian
Anglo-Saxon Civilization 136
6. *E. B. Brady:* An American Catholic on Church and State 139
7. *John Ireland, D.D.:* Catholicism and Americanism 142
8. *Robert D. Cross:* Catholicism and a Non-Catholic State 143
9. *Winthrop Hudson:* The Passing of the Protestant Era in
America 148

AMERICAN GOVERNMENTS AND RELIGIOUS INSTITUTIONS
10. *Philip Schaff:* The American Theory and System 151
11. *James Bryce:* The Churches and the Clergy 154
12. *T. M. Cooley:* Constitutional Limitations Regarding Religious
Liberty 157

VI. **MAINSTREAM PLURALISM** (1920-1960)   161
CHURCH AND STATE IN RELIGIOUS PERSPECTIVES
1. *John A. Ryan:* Comments on the "Christian Constitution
of States" 163

2. *John Courtney Murray, S.J.:* Civil Unity and Religious Integrity 168
3. *John Coleman Bennett:* Patterns of Church-State Relations— Grounds for Separation. 173
4. A Presbyterian Report on Church and State 176
5. *Richard L. Rubenstein:* Church and State: the Jewish Posture . . . 181

CHURCH AND STATE AS A POLITICAL ISSUE

6. Catholic and Patriot: Governor Smith Replies 184
7. *Paul Blanshard:* The Catholic Plan for America 187
8. *John F. Kennedy:* Remarks on Church and State 190
9. *James A. Pike:* A Roman Catholic in the White House? 193

CHURCH AND STATE BEFORE THE COURT

10. Cantwell v. Connecticut 195
11. West Virginia State Board of Education v. Barnette 197
12. Everson v. Board of Education. 200
13. Illinois ex rel. McCollum v. Board of Education 205
14. Zorach v. Clauson 208
15. *Philip Kurland:* A Doctrine in Search of Authority 212
16. *Mark de Wolfe Howe:* The Constitutional Question 213
17. *Paul G. Kauper:* Church and State 218

VII. **DIMENSIONS OF INCLUSIVE PLURALISM** (1960-   )   223

RELIGION AND GOVERNMENT: SOCIAL ISSUES

Religion in the Public Schools

1. Engel v. Vitale. 225
2. School District of Abington Township v. Schempp 230
3. Epperson v. Arkansas 234
4. Stone v. Graham 236
5. Widmar v. Vincent 238
6. Wallace v. Jaffree 240
7. School Prayer Amendment. 245

Religion and Politics

8. *James E. Wood, Jr.:* Religious Fundamentalism and the New Right 246
9. National Conference of Catholic Bishops on Religion and Politics 251
10. National Council of Churches on Religion and Politics 252
11. National Jewish Community Relations Advisory Council on Religion and Politics 254

Religion and Governmental Activity

12. McGowan v. Maryland 256
13. Marsh v. Chambers 259
14. Lynch v. Donnelly 264

Contents

CHURCH AND STATE: INSTITUTIONAL ISSUES

Taxation and Regulation

15. Walz v. Tax Commission 269
16. Bob Jones University v. United States 273
17. Larson v. Valente 276
18. *William P. Thompson:* Government Intervention in Religious
    Affairs 279

Aid to Religious Schools

19. Lemon v. Kurtzman 281
20. Mueller v. Allen 286
21. *John Courtney Murray, S.J.:* Remarks on Aid to Parochial
    Schools 290
22. *Edd Doerr:* The People Speak: Parochiaid and the Voters . . . 291
23. *A. E. Dick Howard:* Up against the Wall: The Uneasy
    Separation of Church and State 292

GOD AND COUNTRY: CULTURAL ISSUES

24. *Robert N. Bellah:* Civil Religion in America 295
25. *John F. Wilson:* The Civil Religion Proposal as a Revitalization
    Movement in American Culture 301

Suggestions for Further Reading   304
Index   307

Introduction

"Church and State" currently designates a certain kind of tension implicit in our pluralistic society. Aid to parochial schools, public school prayer, tax exemption for religious institutions, religious beliefs of political candidates, abortion and the nuclear arms race—all these issues (and many others as well) are thought to involve questions of "Church and State." Some were first widely recognized in post-World War II America. Others have been long established on the American social scene. Even when applied to modern problems, however, the term "Church and State" suggests that the issue is an expression of an ancient differentiation between two kinds of institutions that have organized the life of western men and women. One authority structure has been primarily concerned with temporal life as an end in itself; the other has been concerned with temporal life as a means to "spiritual" ends. To identify certain points of tension in our common life under the rubric "Church and State" is to say that the spheres of temporal and spiritual authorities here intersect, or that conflicting claims arise in the exercise of temporal and spiritual powers.

In one respect the phrase "Church and State" is unfortunate because its connotations are excessively formalistic. It suggests that there is one spiritual authority structure confronting a single temporal authority structure as was essentially the case in some periods in western history. In fact the colonial period of our history exhibits attempts to realize classical kinds of relationships between a single spiritual authority structure—the Church—and a single temporal authority structure—the colonial State. But our colonial period also illustrates how different sorts of ingredients in American society, e.g., ethnic diversity and evangelical separatism, worked to outmode classical Church-State patterns. On the religious side of the equation, one church could not embody the manifold spiritual life of the American people. Consequently, the federal government was erected on the assumption that there should be no national establishment of religion. Although largely nominal state establishments continued, in one case until 1833, it became increasingly clear that a single spiritual authority structure was not a realistic alternative even on that level. This pattern, which has subsequently characterized American society, has often been described as "the separation of Church and State."

Some interpreters believe that the formal disengagement of these authority structures of Church and State dissolved the ancient problems of their relationship. If there is no one church recognized by the state, the argument runs, how can there be any Church-State problems? If difficulties exist, the argument continues, it is only because the separation of the two has been insufficiently rigorous. The confusion embodied in this position is produced, obviously, by the misleadingly formal character of the Church-State formula. There is no single authority structure—or combination of them—which could presume to embody the "religious" or "spiritual" life of America. In shorthand fashion this situation is usually designated as "religious pluralism," that is, many different religious movements exist in America and they pursue relatively autonomous courses. Therefore the classical term "Church"—in denotation as well as connotation—is alien to the American scene.

It ought to be equally obvious that there is no single authority structure to embody the temporal life of Americans—i.e., a single state is no more an empirical reality than a single church. Like religious pluralism, governmental pluralism involves the multiplicity of authorities that possess overlapping jurisdictions within our society. Thus federal, state, county, and local governments are juxtaposed and all contribute to the structuring of the common life. Sometimes they are mutually reinforcing; on other occasions they counterbalance each other. Although the federal government has precedence (and the federal government has a preemptive power among governmental institutions not paralleled among religious institutions), in practice there is considerable deference toward local authorities. The federal constitution was framed with the intent that there should not be an American "State" in the classical sense. Powers were divided at the national level, and manifold governments were fostered at other levels as well. In addition, the development of semi-autonomous bureaucratic structures and quasi-judicial commissions (not continuously subordinated to explicit political review) further "pluralized" the process of governing American society. Also large corporate entities exercise powers in our society that any formal "State" would reserve to itself. There simply is no classical "State" in American experience that corresponds either to the medieval or modern European uses of this term. Accordingly, the term "Church and State" breaks down completely if the attempt is made to use it in a traditional fashion.

Is "Church and State" at all useful, then, in reference to the American scene? Clearly, a variety of spiritual authority structures interact with each other and with a complex set of temporal authority structures. We have in America not "Church" and "State" but religions and governments—all interacting within our society. Consequently, it might appear desirable to give up this rubric altogether and seek one more in accord with American experience. To do so, however, would be to accept only the most formalistic definition of the term. It is as wrong to suggest that the tensions between temporal life and spiritual life in America are wholly unprecedented as it is to argue that Church-State problems disappeared with the adoption of the First Amendment, especially as applied to the states through the due process clause of the Fourteenth. The substance of the Church-State tradition is still with us but it is with us in new forms. The rubric *per se* is inexact, but the tradition designated in that rubric is very much to the point in comprehending America's past and present. By analyzing the historical development of the conception "Church and State" it may be possible, on the one hand, to modify its formalistic connotations and, on the other, to denote more precisely what it has meant in the past and may legitimately signify now.

Consequently, this introductory essay will address itself to the following problems: first, the origin, development and content of the traditional Church-State distinction in western history; second, the range of patterns that have existed in the historical relationships between Church and State; third, the relatively distinctive pattern of Church-State relations in America, its sources and significance.

I

The distinction between "Church" and "State" in western history inevitably refers back to the classic New Testament texts recurrently cited in discussions of the issue. Perhaps the chief text is Jesus' response (as reported in the synoptic gospels: Matthew 22:15–22, Mark 12:13–17, Luke 20:20–26) to the question about rendering tribute to Caesar. "Is it lawful to pay taxes to Caesar or not?" (Mark 12:14). Of course Jesus' injunction was to "Render to Caesar the things that are Caesar's, and to God the things that are God's" (Mark 12:17). Another text, scarcely less significant, is located in Saint Paul's Letter to the Romans. As a whole the section runs to seven verses (Romans 13:1–7), but its principle is expressed classically in the first verse alone: "Let every person be subject to the governing authorities. For there is no authority except from God, and those that exist have been instituted by God." Other texts are much less important than these two, and none of them refer directly to "Church and State." Rather they presuppose that faithfulness to God requires also appropriate obedience to worldly authorities since such are instituted by God. In early Christianity this might even have demanded "obedience unto death." The early Christian canonical writings did not explore the Church-State relationship in a fashion relevant to later needs because, among other reasons, the "State" did not acknowledge the legitimacy of the "Church" as another authority structure beside it. To recognize the Church as an authority structure would be in principle to say that the State should be limited to activities relating to temporal ends. Thus the possibility of a formal Church-State pattern emerged only after the emperor Constantine was converted to Christianity in the early part of the fourth century. This resulted in the Constantinian settlement in which the Christian movement was at first accepted and then favored over alternate (and generally more syncretistic) religious movements with which it had been competing. Because of its persistent obedience to God (and thus to Caesar), the Christian Church gained recognition from Caesar allowing it to possess an authority structure in some measure independent from the State. In the eastern half of the empire the Church remained closely associated with the State—even wholly subordinated to it. It was in western Christendom, therefore, that the distinction between Church and State developed its particular significance.

At the end of the fifth century Pope Gelasius I articulated the fundamental premise concerning "Church and State" that has characterized western history. The premise was simply: "There are two." "Two swords" or "two authority structures" meant a single society under two jurisdictions—one temporal and the other spiritual. From the theological point of view, the coming of Christ and the establishment of the Church had made it unlawful for both authorities to be administered by one figure. Priest and King, or Church and State, each needed the other but both were to be separate aspects of the same society. This separated double authority structure is what marked off western from eastern Christendom, and it properly locates the significance of "Church and State." A universal Christian society was presupposed that had a twofold government or rule. While the Church embodied the spiritual order of that society, the empire organized the same society in temporal terms. The persistent problem was the relationship between the ecclesiastical and civil authority structures. What should be the relationship of these two jurisdictions?

From the ninth until roughly the middle of the eleventh century the Carolingian pattern was taken for granted. Generally the pope was subordinated to the emperor, and thus the Church to the empire. In the person of Pope Gregory VII the papacy challenged the emperor (Henry IV), however, and on the immediate question at issue—lay investiture of bishops—a moderate papal victory was won in the Concordat of Worms (1122). The Gregorian ambition was to assert at once the spiritual autonomy of the Church and the monarchical rule of the Church by the pope: "If kings are to be judged by priests for their sins, by whom can they be judged with better right than by the Roman Pontiff?" By the end of the twelfth century, Innocent III made further claims, likening the papal Church to the sun and the imperial dominion to the moon which derived its light from the former. The maximum claim for papal authority in the Church and ecclesiastical authority over the empire was made by Boniface VIII, however, in his *Unam Sanctum* in 1302. It called for the subordination of the temporal to the spiritual, reversing completely the earlier Carolingian pattern. "Both the spiritual sword and the material sword are in the power of the church. The latter should be used for the church and the former by the church; the former by the priest, and the latter by kings and captains (but at the will and by the permission of the priest). Therefore the one sword should be under the other, and temporal authority subject to spiritual." Even as Boniface made such claims, however, the papacy was humiliated in its captivity at Avignon, and stirrings from England and France marked the beginnings of new nation-states that would sustain their own national churches in place of what Latin Christendom ordered in its twofold pattern. Concurrently Aristotelian naturalists, e.g., Marsilius of Padua, argued for the restriction of spiritual authority in the name of an autonomous secular realm. "Church and State" as two swords or authorities no longer meant pope and emperor as jointly quarreling trustees of a universal Christian society. The Church was no longer the spiritual structure of a universal society, but instead was either the religious expression of a national entity or an association of like-minded individuals more often than not in conflict with a repressive State. The ground was present in which the secular states of modern Europe would grow.

From this perspective, the "Protestant Reformation" was an ambiguous event, at once allied with the centrifugal national forces that were destroying what remained of universal society and concurrently attempting to repristinate the two-authority doctrine that had been so characteristic of western Christendom. Thus it was neither wholly "modern" nor wholly "reactionary" but a curious combination of both. The Lutheran branch of the Reformation identified the two authorities as two realms each dependent directly upon God so that both the faithless prince and the faithful believer had a vocation in the divine economy. The Calvinist branch, by contrast, usually sought to locate temporal authority in the hands of those saints who were responsive to the spiritual authority of the Church. In either case the recovery of universalism was impossible as Protestants (and Catholics also) discovered in the bloody religious wars.

This brief review of the developing Church-State pattern ought to indicate that it was never a static relationship in western history at least through the sixteenth century. Nor was its essence embodied, for instance, in the relationship of emperor and pope in the thirteenth century. On the contrary, the common substance of the Church-State relationship was the recognition of two authority structures in the corporate life of humanity—one essentially temporal and the other primarily spiritual. In shorthand form these were designated as "State" and "Church," but there were manifold expressions of this relationship long before the terms and the rubric were introduced into American history. Therefore "Church and State in American History" is properly a consideration of the relationships between temporal and spiritual authority structures—or religious institutions and civil governments. It is self-evident that these relationships did not end with the adoption either of the First or the Fourteenth Amendments.

II

Another type of "Church and State" analysis may help suggest the range of phenomena properly classified under this heading. This should establish in another way why the Church-State rubric must not be identified with a particular form of that relationship, e.g., papal Church and imperial magistracy within a single and inclusive Christian society. What have been the chief alternative patterns of the relationship between the temporal and spiritual authority structures? Answers to this question may be arranged schematically. One sort of answer curiously brackets bitter antagonists. Both antagonists deny that there should be two authority structures, i.e., that human life is to be comprehended under the dual aspect of temporal and spiritual concerns. The parties to this strange consensus disagree, of course, as to which of the two authority structures should absorb the other. On the one hand a "hierocratic" regime authorizes the priests to hold all power—spiritual and temporal both—in their hands. By contrast a "statist" or consistent "totalitarian" position refuses to recognize an independent spiritual authority structure, and may not only create a subservient temporal religion but also proscribe and persecute traditional religious faith. While the latter position has been a common one in the modern west (and is in some respects a return to paganism), "hierocracies" have been uncommon since the destruction of Israel. Both priest-king and commissar deny the traditional western consensus on Church and State—that an independence of the two authority structures is fundamental.

Another kind of answer to this question allows a certain independence of the two institutions, but it ultimately subordinates one to the other. Like the previous position it may also be resolved into clearly differentiated alternatives. One option involves the subordination of spiritual authority to temporal authority—at the extreme the utilization and manipulation of the Church by the State. Usually this alternative is designated as "Erastianism" after a sixteenth-century Swiss theologian, Thomas Erastus, who argued that where there is uniformity of religion, ecclesiastical jurisdiction is to be exercised under the review of the civil authorities. Although the label is usually applied only to the situation of nation-states from the sixteenth century on, the principle involved (subordination of spiritual to temporal authority) expresses the pretensions of many emperors beginning with Charlemagne. The other form of subordination argues that spiritual ends take precedence over temporal ones. Such, of course, were the classical papal claims. It was no less characteristic of Calvinism as it pursued the ideal of the holy community. It is appropriate to label such an alternative "theocratic" as long as it is distinguished from the "hierocratic" pattern, which denies all autonomy to the temporal authority. This broader theocratic tradition, whether in Rome, Geneva, or Massachusetts Bay, was not essentially the rule of "priests" (or preachers for that matter) over temporal matters. Rather it presupposed that the consciences of the lay civil authorities—autonomous in temporal matters—should be formed by, and their outward practice conformed to, the Christian faith. The whole society—in its dual aspect—was created by God, and both authorities were to be appropriately conformed to the divine intention. The "medievalism" of early Protestant ideals is apparent once again.

A third type of answer recognizes that there are separate authority structures and proposes that they should be disengaged from each other. Again, however, there are different ways in which this independence can be construed. One alternative is the segregation of the spiritual authority structure from the temporal authority structure, which was close to the Protestant Anabaptist ideal. In another way this would seem to be implied in the Jeffersonian "wall of separation" metaphor and in a great deal of contemporary rhetoric about the "separation of church and state." Another kind of independence between Church and State is a recognition of mutually supportive roles. While the spiritual authority structure or structures ought to lend their power to the civil order, the temporal authorities should recognize and assist religious institutions.

It is clear that this kind of typology has a certain artificiality, although it is sufficiently flexible to comprehend reasonably well most concrete instances of Church-State relationships. Its chief significance, however, ought to be the weight it lends to the argument of this essay that if "Church and State" is to be a useful phrase it must be broad enough to include a wide variety of historical relationships between spiritual and temporal authority structures. The rubric is relatively use-less if it is primarily identified with one particular pattern that is considered normative.

III

In studying "Church and State in American History," seven different periods may be identified. Each is distinctive because each represents a new phase in the relationship between religious institutions and civil governments in light of the changing patterns of religious pluralism in America. Through these stages ide-ological resources have been joined with social circumstances to create a series of experimental resolutions of the tensions between spiritual and temporal au-thority structures. Before briefly surveying these periods it is important to rec-ognize that the American experiments in Church-State relations have almost universally assumed that the dual authority pattern was appropriate. America has not provided congenial soil for the anti-clerical sentiment that was so wide-spread in Europe during the nineteenth century and that understandably resulted in a defensive posture on the part of religious institutions. It might be argued that the more militant forms of modern secularism effectively deny this pre-sumption of two "realms." But characteristically, American secularism is little more than indifferent toward the claim that the spiritual dimension of life has an authority of its own. Again—contrary to many interpretations of New England Puritanism—America has not witnessed very many attempts at a hierocratic meld-ing of spiritual and temporal authorities. Perhaps the most interesting, and cer-tainly the only significant, experiment with this kind of order was the early Mormon venture. In the person of Joseph Smith, Jr., the offices of prophet, priest, and king were once again united. Brigham Young and his associates received this mantle and structured the Salt Lake Valley community on this pattern. The main-stream of American experience, however, has taken for granted that there should be two authority structures—although a significant variety of interpretations has been offered.

The seventeenth-century Atlantic colonies represent a useful first period in this study. There we find the traditional Church-State terms very much present. We are introduced to the language of establishment that was simply taken for granted—for even the likes of Roger Williams, although denying the propriety of established religion, could make his case only in those same terms. It is important to grasp that—aside from the lively experiment of Rhode Island—all of the colonies erected "establishments" of some sort. No one would deny the vastly different degrees of rigor (both in the conception and execution of their establishments) that characterized, for example, Massachusetts Bay and Pennsylvania. But it is entirely wrong to so emphasize Pennsylvania's relative latitude that the common language used by both is hidden from view. The New England Puritans did not set up the hierocratic regimes so often attributed to them. John Cotton was neither a latter-day Sadducee nor a Joseph Smith, Jr., born before his time. The New

England Puritan assumptions were far more akin to the ideals of Innocent III. Theirs was to be a commonwealth, ruled in temporal affairs by Christian laymen whose consciences were formed by the preaching of the Word (if not nourished by the administration of the Eucharist). Not all of the colonies aspired to such a formally theocratic constitution of the relationship between Church and State. By virtue of economic necessity, if not ideological programs, some represented more nearly the Erastian position that the religious institution should be subordinated to (though not absorbed in) the temporal regime and its needs. Nevertheless the language of establishment was universal.

During the first six decades of the eighteenth century the establishment language that previously had been taken for granted was challenged by the diversification of religious life in the colonies. The overwhelming number of colonists were Protestant in sympathy—even if they were not allowed or willing to become active church members. But different kinds of Protestant families and groups relentlessly immigrated; even the relatively homogeneous New England settlements yielded, first on the fringes and then at the center as well: Scotch-Irish Presbyterians in Anglican Virginia, "German" Mennonites in Quaker Pennsylvania, Anglicans in Congregational Connecticut and Massachusetts. In addition, the upheavals of the "Great Awakening" split asunder the Presbyterians and Congregationalists, and served to expand the slim Baptist ranks. Given the circumstances of colonial development, this proliferation of Protestant groups made necessary the policy of toleration. Toleration of dissent is perfectly compatible with a pattern of establishment. It does not, however, make credible the theocratic subordination of state to religion, nor on the other hand does it render society religiously uniform—which is the great strength in the Erastian subordination of Church to State. Therefore the first six decades of the eighteenth century represent a transitional period during which the language of establishment was outdated. In no sense was the fundamental assumption of dualism denied—there were two realms, each with its appropriate institutional expressions. But the radical competition among the churches made it inevitable (though the illusion died hard) that a single spiritual authority structure on the traditional model would be out of the question.

During the third period of our study—which runs between 1760 and approximately 1820—direct confrontations with the problem of establishment took place. Simply to indicate some of the factors present is to make evident how a basic reevaluation of the traditional pattern had become necessary. As the colonies were drawn into a closer network, the multiplicity of Protestant groups was all the more evident. Continuing feeble efforts to regularize if not prefer the Church of England in the colonies dramatized for the proto-Americans the desirable latitude present in their religious life. Religious liberty as an ideal began to be discussed. The Enlightenment estimate of religion exerted an effect. The net result of these and other factors can be seen with particular clarity in the public newspaper debate during the 1760's over the scheme to appoint Church of England bishops in America. The colonial critics of this proposal did everything in their power to marshal public antipathy toward it through belittlement and ridicule. In the course of this argument they articulated notions about religion that would have been unthinkable a century earlier, e.g., that plural religious institutions were desirable, or that clergymen should be meagerly paid so that their pretension and power would not corrupt their exercise of spiritual functions. Such sentiments indicate how tenuous the traditional language of establishment had become. In the Virginia struggle for religious freedom and disestablishment, however, we find the first consistent political argument toward the "independence" of Church and State. Jefferson's passion for religious freedom is well known, and he later bequeathed that attractive if confusing metaphor of a "wall of separation" between Church and State, which continues to echo throughout the common life. But James Madison is probably the more significant figure, both in the Virginia struggle and in the adoption of the First Amendment, which guarantees religious freedom and prohibits congressional legislation "respecting an establishment of religion." With the debate over the bishops and with Madison's contribution, the American future in Church-State relations seemed clearly to have been pointed in the direction of an independence between spiritual and temporal authority structures.

Because of this "revolution" in the position of the churches, the next period—roughly extending to the Civil War—is significant. To be sure, many relevant events were taking place that would in their own time influence Church-State relationships in America, e.g., the influx of large contingents of Catholic immigrants as well as significant numbers of "German" Jews. While these developments were quietly setting the stage for the post-Civil War period, however, the most fascinating attempt was that of the evangelical forces in America to recover in an informal way what had been their legal position before disestablishment. During this "era of republican Protestantism" a great "united front" of interdenominational agencies developed that aspired to make America a Protestant Christian republic in substance if not in form. The reader will have to judge how profoundly this enterprise shaped and formed the common life so that even more than a century after its maximum activity our political, social and economic—as well as religious—languages testify to its vital impact. This effort had its critics, and many of its coveted projects failed; but the concept of an indirect relationship between religious and political authority structures assumed that there was no direct mutually supporting relationship between Church and State. Madison's theory had not allowed for cooperation among evangelical denominations any more than it had anticipated the development of political parties (not altogether dissimilar entities). One of the broader questions concerns the degree to which this was an indigenous American movement and how much it was part of the conservative Anglo-American response to the French Revolution.

After the Civil War the ethnic multiplication and religious diversification that had proceeded throughout the previous era could no longer remain unrecognized and unacknowledged. Even before the Civil War, the public schools became the focus of the conflicting claims of temporal and spiritual authority structures. It is interesting that where the fact (and burden) of religious pluralism was explicitly recognized, a position favoring a neutral relationship between Church and State emerged that clearly repudiated the assumption of a cultural uniformity that underlay "republican Protestantism." This anticipated, of course, more modern discussions. For the Roman Catholics this situation required dissent from European interpretations of the normative relationships between the two authority structures and led to the advocacy of an "Americanism" that appeared almost heretical to Europeans. For the Protestants a harder task was required. Beneath and behind that sense of national mission and anti-Roman animus nourished by the evangelical tradition, the Protestants had to locate more ancient resources that would equip them to comprehend other Church-State alternatives than the one so dear to them. As the eighteenth century had been a transitional period during which formal disestablishment became necessary, so this period (1860–1920) was both transitional and a period of "disestablishment"—not of state-recognized churches but of a Protestant religious consensus.

During the period from the First World War until the election of a Roman Catholic president in 1960, that ancient problem of the relationship of temporal and spiritual authority structures became widely discussed in at least three different perspectives, all in the context of an American religious pluralism encompassing the three major religions: Protestantism, Judaism and Roman Catholicism. The Church-State issue was viewed under the aspect of a theological-religious problem, in the guise of political struggles within a pluralist society, and finally as a constitutional and legal issue. A responsible consensus seemed to ensure that the United States, as a matter of necessity if not choice, must develop its particular pattern on the basis of independence between Church and State. The existence of two authority structures seems to have been recognized in principle if not always honored in practice, and the historical alternatives of subordinating one to the other were not widely viewed as plausible formal options. There was, however, no consensus as to whether the independence of Church and State should be one of segregation, neutrality or mutual support.

In the most recent period, commencing in the early 1960's, the meaning of the term "pluralism" has been expanded to include yet other, and very diverse, groups. This era has been marked by a willingness within American institutions to give unprecedented recognition to claims for equal treatment made by a variety of ethnic, racial, religious and other minority bodies. But not all Americans have welcomed the new religious and cultural pluralism, which extends well beyond the Protestant-Catholic-Jewish mainstream. As a result, a deep struggle is under way about the place of religion in society. The essential question is: Should the government disregard or take formal account of those western values (often called Judeo-Christian) thought by many to be at the foundation of our national culture? More broadly speaking, the Church-State issue of the contemporary era separates those who think that government should accommodate and encourage the sort of religion that they see as a foundation of our culture, and those who think that the government should not extend aid or support to religion in any way. In short, this is a battle between believers in what the Supreme Court has called "benevolent neutrality" and proponents of a strict separation of Church and State. While this battle over the legitimacy of governmental aid to religion continues to rage, the issue of the Church's activity in the political realm has returned in recent years as groups as diverse as the Moral Majority and the Roman Catholic bishops have lobbied in God's name for a variety of political programs. These continuing questions suggest that many Americans have not abandoned the concept that at some fundamental level there remains a single spiritual authority that should instruct the State and be supported by it despite governmental, ecclesiastical and cultural pluralism.

IV

Within the framework so sketched, this book presents primary readings that exemplify the Church-State question as it has developed in American history, along with critical interpretations of the issue. The readings demonstrate the many expressions of tension between the temporal and spiritual goals of our society. The interpretations propose some points for discussion. Introductions and suggested further readings amplify the text. Taken as a whole, this book should position its readers to understand the importance in our history of the Church-State issue and its continuing influence upon our modern culture.

Let us summarize what this book is and what it is not. This book is a collection of readings in the relationships between those authority structures dedicated to spiritual ends and those shaped primarily for temporal purposes throughout the course of American history. Understood in these terms American experience has derived from continental European civilization, although its Church-State patterns have not been identical with contemporary developments across the Atlantic. As a historical collection, the book places major emphasis upon the interrelationships of political, legal and religious phenomena in any given period and, as important, the interpretation to be placed upon these phenomena. It would be possible to construe the Church-State issue in purely legal terms, assembling the relevant legal texts from charters, constitutions, legislation and judicial decisions. In such a study the legal relationships between churches and governments would be the unifying theme. Alternatively it would be possible to develop a study of the relationships between religion and politics in American history that would be a very different book, focused by another theme. Or again, a collection of readings in ecclesiastical polities and public affairs would meet another sort of need in the present day. No one of these alternatives, however, would be a consistently historical collection in the way this book is intended to be.

A great deal of literature allegedly about "Church and State" really concerns the achievement of religious toleration as a reality and the development of religious liberty as an ideal. Toleration and religious liberty have certainly influenced the question of Church and State. But it is entirely mistaken to assume that the Church-State relationship is either resolved or dissolved by the religious latitude so characteristic of American society. Those who are concerned with toleration and religious liberty really disclose the persistence of individualistic categories in American intellectual life. Analysis of social dynamics and appreciation of collective languages are not widely present in American thought. Consequently, corporate issues—e.g., the relationships of religious and governmental authority structures—have often been discussed as if they were to be understood as the sum of individual religious and political relationships within society. From this point of view religious liberty for the individual has seemed to be the substantial goal that "separation of Church and State" guaranteed. Attractive as such a formula is, it does not accord with the empirical reality of authority structures nor with the persistent collective behavior of Americans past and present. The significance of "Church and State" as a rubric is that it requires the analysis of our social history against the background of western European history with its richer experience and traditions, and its more exact and comprehensive language. This is an illuminating point of view for readers weaned on the individualistic social discourse of American life, which is reinforced by the canned rhetoric of contemporary mass media.

"Church and State" is a phrase that has echoed throughout American history. In this sense it has been a "constant" from the colonial settlements to the present term of the Supreme Court. However, by no means has it always carried the same meaning or referred to comparable social realities. Like all words that function in political life, the Church and State "language" has undergone a metamorphosis in the last three hundred years as radical as the transformation experienced by society on the North American continent during that period. Like all words that function in religious life the Church and State "language" has retained traditional connotations even when inappropriate and clearly misleading for purposes of description. Like all words that function in legal contexts, the church and state "vocabulary" has a formalistic character insufficiently empirical for analytic usage. Thus a volume of readings titled *Church and State in American History* necessarily has a dualistic character—it must exhibit these several "languages" as they are used and concurrently analyze those special patterns to which the languages have responded. Accordingly, this is a historical study of the interrelationships between the legal, political and religious structures of American society as they have been intended to embody the temporal and spiritual dimensions of western life. For this reason this volume is not primarily concerned with exhaustively representing events and documents that may be related to the theme. *Church and State in American History* is directed toward introducing the assumptions and presuppositions in terms of which the events were shaped and the documents were framed.

Chronology

This book is primarily concerned with the kinds of relationship between religious institutions and civil governments which have developed through American history. Little emphasis falls upon institutions, events, or documents except as they illustrate or represent broader patterns. Accordingly this chronological table provides a list of relevant events to supplement the primary emphasis.

1607   Jamestown, Virginia settled with a Church of England chaplain.

1631   Franchise restricted to church members in Massachusetts Bay.

1649   An Act Concerning Religion in Maryland provides a measure of toleration.

1654   Maryland Act repealed, Catholics suppressed by Puritans.

1662   Half-way Covenant adopted in Massachusetts Bay; in effect gives franchise to those formally baptized although not necessarily having become full members of the established Congregational churches.

1663   Rhode Island and Providence Plantations receive royal charter through efforts of John Clarke; allows for "lively experiment" of complete religious toleration.

1665   Duke's Laws in New Amsterdam allow the Dutch toleration.

1669   First draft of the Fundamental Constitutions of Carolina proposes multiple establishment.

1691   New Massachusetts Bay Charter replaces the one revoked in 1684; provides liberty of conscience to all Christians except Roman Catholics.

1708   Connecticut allows non-Congregational Protestant worship but requires payment of taxes to support the standing order.

1722-27 A party, led by Timothy Cutler, Rector of Yale, defects from Connecticut Congregationalism to the Church of England. Anglicans subsequently released from supporting the establishment.

1739   First American tour by Whitefield; subsequently the Great Awakening rends the established church patterns.

1767-68 Extensive public controversy regarding the introduction of Church of England Bishops into America.

1777   Religious Freedom in New York State.

1785   Jefferson's Bill for Establishing Religious Freedom passed in the Virginia Assembly.

1789   Congress adopts Bill of Rights including the two religion clauses in the First Amendment.

1791   Bill of Rights ratified and takes effect.

1802   Jefferson's occasional letter to the Danbury Baptists mentions "wall of separation between Church and State."

1811   Massachusetts religious freedom act exempts members of non-Congregational churches from taxation for support of establishment.

1818   Disestablishment in Connecticut.

1819   Toleration Act in New Hampshire.

1833   Congregational Church disestablished in Massachusetts.

1868   Fourteenth Amendment ratified — Bill of Rights apply to States?

1879   *Reynolds* v. *U.S.:* First Mormon case in Supreme Court.

1890   *The Late Corporation of the Church of Jesus Christ of Latter-Day Saints* v. *U.S.* reviews Congressional act of 1887 which annulled Mormon charter.

1908   Roman Catholic Church given fully independent status within international Catholicism (removed from control of the Congregation of Propaganda).

1919   National Catholic Welfare Conference proposed following War Council experience with central agency.

1925   *Pierce* v. *Society of Sisters* strikes down Oregon law requiring attendance at public school; "charter" of parochial schools.

1928   Governor Alfred E. Smith Democratic candidate for president; issue of his faith present in campaign.

1940   *Cantwell* v. *Connecticut:* Jehovah's Witness case which explicitly applied religion clauses of the First Amendment to the States through the Fourteenth.

1947   *Everson* v. *Board of Education:* Reimbursement to parents of parochial as well as public school children for bus fares upheld in a 5–4 decision which explicitly considered the question of establishment.

1960   John F. Kennedy elected first Roman Catholic President of the United States in a very close election; religious issue prominent.

1962   *Engel* v. *Vitale:* Regents' Prayer Case outlaws the recitation of school prayer in New York State.

1963   *Abington School District* v. *Schempp* outlaws reading of the Bible in public school opening exercises.

1963-65 The Second Vatican Council is held in Rome.

1968   *Flast* v. *Cohen* gives taxpayers standing in federal court to challenge public expenditures on First Amendment grounds.

1973   *Roe* v. *Wade* recognizes women's constitutional right to an abortion in certain circumstances.

1979   The Moral Majority is organized by the Rev. Jerry Falwell to encourage people to vote for school prayer and a variety of conservative social issues.

1984   The United States and the Vatican establish full diplomatic relations for the first time in 117 years.

I. *The Language of Colonial Establishments (-1700)*

At one time it was fashionable to "weigh" and thus compare the alleged "motives" which contributed to the colonization of America. Accordingly, arguments erupted about the relative significance of commercial and religious impulses, partisans of each position supporting their cases with polemic as well as evidence. Unfortunately such an approach inhibits any study of seventeenth-century America. During that century, especially in the English-speaking world, theology was still a primary language. It was a fundamental mode of thought in which public endeavors were comprehended and advocated. As men of the early seventeenth century—and often Puritan English men—the prime movers and participants in the settlement of the new world, especially in the Virginia and New England ventures, as a matter of course assumed that religious authority should contribute to the structuring of their experiments. The society they intended to plant was to be a "cutting" from that English Protestant society they knew under Elizabeth and James. An example may clarify this point. Historians have often indicated the discrepancy between the settlers' expressed intentions of converting the Indians to Christianity and their achievements in this regard. To conclude that, because of their miserable failure in these programs, the colonists were hypocritical in their religious professions is to miss the crucial point. They failed because the Indians—apart from a Pocahontas—would not be refashioned after the English pattern, they would not abandon their own society for that pattern offered to them in the name of God and King. In the contemporary idiom, "civilitie of life" and "vertue" were necessarily linked with the "true worship of God." Thus failure to convert the Indians is less indicative of religious hypocrisy than it is of how alien the English Protestant Mind was in the new environment—and how stubbornly the colonists clung to their convictions and preconceptions. One of these preconceptions was that Church and State should have a correlative relationship.

Accordingly this section on "the language of colonial establishments" has two purposes. The first is to display the theological mode of thought in the terms of which trade and politics, no less than religious activities were carried on. It will be most appropriate to illustrate this mentality as it sought to articulate the relationship of Church and State as it was implied in that view of the world. The second purpose is to indicate the different patterns of religious establishment which were developed in the several colonies. It is important to recognize that although these patterns embody significant diversities the fundamental theological assumptions about society were not disrupted.

There is little doubt that theological literature and discourse is more

1

prominent in the "remains" of Massachusetts Bay, for instance, than in the legacies from other colonial endeavors. This is largely to be explained, however, in the circumstances of the various settlements. For instance, the Virginia Company and its primary officers resided in London and delegated officials managed the plantation, while the Massachusetts Bay Company transported itself and its charter across the Atlantic. Again, after achieving successful settlement the Virginia enterprise was involved in a decade-long struggle for subsistence as a garrison state while the attention of the London investors was given to their Bermuda project. By contrast, Massachusetts Bay rapidly developed during a decade of intensive immigration once the plan for a significant colony had been decided upon. It is evident that a fully developed religious establishment could not have been introduced into Virginia under these circumstances. Yet that colony relied on the mutual reinforcement of spiritual and temporal authorities as much as the New England experiments did. On the principle of intelligibility, then, special attention will be given to the literature from New England.

Thomas Hooker, clerical leader of the exodus from Newton (now Cambridge) in Massachusetts Bay to the Connecticut River settlements around Hartford, expressed the conventional presuppositions about "Church and State" in a sentence: "Men sustain a double relation."[1] They were, first, "members of the commonwealth," which was a civil relationship touching the outer man — or men's bodies. Secondly, they were "members of a Church," which was a spiritual relationship involving the souls and consciences of men. Both of these "relations" were among men and between men and God. Thus the civil life, or the life of the commonwealth, had its relationship to God which was not exclusively mediated through the institution of the Church. Hooker's was a particular version of a Calvinistic scheme which itself was a variant of a traditional Christian position. For him State and Church were coordinated and mutually dependent since both were ordained by God to support each other. Temporal life required spiritual orientation no less than spiritual life presupposed temporal order.

The point to be emphasized is that civil and religious life remained distinguished in the assumptions undergirding the various seventeenth-century efforts to colonize America. There were variations within the pattern but the dual ends of human life were never denied. Certainly a hierocracy was not established; civil polity was not subordinated to ecclesiastical direction. "Church and State" were explicitly coordinated with the exception of Rhode Island, and that exception — as will be evident in the readings — was articulated in the language of the day. Otherwise the means and degrees of correlation between civil and religious life varied among the colonies. The variety was certainly a major factor in the eventual disestablishment of the colonial Churches. But that development cannot be comprehended without appreciating the terms in which differentiation occured. The language of establishment was the language of the day.

---

[1] Thomas Hooker, *A Survey of the Summe of Church Discipline* (London, 1648), Part I, pp. 4 f.

John Cotton

1. A DISCOURSE ABOUT CIVIL GOVERNMENT

The leaders of Massachusetts Bay lavishly expounded their theory of society and their understanding of the relationship between Church and State. Enough of this literature is still available to discredit facile pronouncements that the colony was a potential democracy corrupted by clerical tyranny. One of the classic texts about the relationship between civil and religious life has not been readily available, perhaps because of a longstanding confusion over its authorship. A New Haven Colony was early projected as an improvement upon the Massachusetts experiment and its founders hoped to clarify some of the "problems" which were becoming apparent here. Apparently the Rev. John Davenport sought out the advice of his friend and mentor, the Rev. John Cotton of Boston. At issue was whether the franchise for civil government ought to be restricted to church members. In answering this question John Cotton, a dominant figure in the Bay, displayed the chief marks of Puritan scholasticism and effectively rehearsed the major assumptions about "Church and State." The "double relation" men sustained to Church and commonwealth will be evident in Cotton's exposition. On the confused question of authorship of this tract refer to "The Authorship of 'A Discourse'," by I. M. Calder in the *American Historical Review* (Volume XXXVII, pp 267 ff.).

Reverend Sir,

I have reviewed [your writing] and find, as I formerly expressed to yourself, that the question is mis-stated by you. The arguments which you produce to prove that which is not denied are (in reference to this question) spent in vain, as arrows are when they fall wide of the marks they should hit though they strike in a white which the archer is not called to shoot at.

The terms wherein you state the question are these: "Whether the right and power of choosing civil magistrates belongs to the Church of Christ?"

To omit all critical inquiries, in your stating [of] the question I utterly dislike two things.

1. You speak of the civil magistrates indefinitely and without limitation — under which notion all magistrates . . . are included, Turks and Indians and idolaters as well as Christian. Now no man, I think, holdeth or imagineth that the Church of Christ hath power and right to choose all civil magistrates throughout the world. For:

a. In some countries there is no Church of Christ, all the inhabitants being heathen men and idolaters, and among those who are called Christian, the number of Churches of Christ will be found to be so small, and the members of them so few and mean, that it is impossible that the right and power of choosing civil magistrates in all places should belong to the Churches of Christ.

b. Nor have the churches countenance of state in all countries, but [they] are under restraint and persecution in some. . . .

c. In some countries the churches are indeed under the protection of magistrates, as foreigners, permitted quietly to sit down under their wings. But neither are the members capable of magistracy there, nor have they the power of voting in the choice of magistrates. . . .

Abridged and edited to conform more nearly to current usage [Ed.]

d. In some countries sundry nations are so mingled that they have severally an equal right unto several parts of the country. . . .

Now he that should affirm that the Churches of Christ as such have right and power of choosing civil magistrates in such places seemeth to me more to need physick than arguments to recover him from his error.

2. The second thing that I dislike in your stating [of] the question is that you make the Churches of Christ to be the subject of this right and power of choosing civil magistrates. For:

a. The church so considered is a spiritual political body consisting of diverse members male and female, bond and free—sundry of which are not capable of magistracy, nor of voting in the choice of magistrates inasmuch as none have that right and power but free burgesses, among whom women and servants are not reckoned although they may be and are church members.

b. The members of the Churches of Christ are [to be considered] under a twofold respect answerable to the twofold man which is in all the members of the Church while they are in this world: the inward and the outward man (II Corinthians 4:16). Whereunto the only wise God hath fitted and appointed two sorts of administrators, ecclesiastical and civil. Hence they are capable of a twofold relation, and of action and power suitable to them both, viz., civil and spiritual, and accordingly [they] must be exercised about both in their seasons without confounding those two different states or destroying either of them. What they transact in civil affairs is done by virtue of their civil relation, their church-state only fitting them to do it according to God.

Now that the state of the question may appear I think it seasonable and necessary to premise a few distinctions to prevent all mistakes if it may be.

First let us distinguish between the two administrations or polities, ecclesiastical and civil, which men commonly call the church and commonwealth. I incline rather to those who speak of a Christian communion, [and] make the communion to be the genus and the states ecclesiastical and civil to be species of it. For in a Christian Communion there are . . . different administrations or polities or states, ecclesiastical and civil: ecclesiastical administrators are a divine order appointed to believers for holy communing of holy things, civil administrators are a human order appointed by God to men for civil fellowship of human things. . . .

1. Though both agree in this—that there is order in their administrations—yet with this difference: the guides in the Church have not a despotical but economical power only [since they are] not lords over Christ's heritage but stewards and ministers of Christ and of the Church, the dominion and law-giving power being reserved to Christ alone as the only Head of the Church. But in the other state he hath given lordly power, authority, and dominion unto men.

2. Though both agree in this—that man is the common subject of both—yet with this difference: Man by nature being a reasonable and social creature, capable of civil order, is or may be the subject of civil power and state. But man by Grace called out of the world to fellowship with Jesus Christ and with His people is the only subject of church power. Yet [even] so the outward man of church members is subject to the civil power in common with other men while their inward man is the subject of spiritual order and administrations.

3. Though they both agree in this—that God is the efficient [cause] and author of both, and that by Christ—yet not [identically]. For God as the creator and governor of the world is the author of civil order and administrations, but God as in covenant with his people in Christ is the author of church-administrations. So likewise Christ,

as the efficient Word and Wisdom of God creating and governing the world, is the efficient [cause] and fountain of civil order and administrations. But as mediator of the new covenant and Head of the Church he establishes ecclesiastical order.

4. Though they both agree in this — that they have the same last end, viz., the glory of God — yet they differ in their next ends. For the next end of civil order and administration is the preservation of human societies in outward honor, justice, and peace. But the next ends of church order and administrations are the conversions, edification, and salvation of souls, pardon of sin, power against sin, peace with God, &c.

5. Hence arises another difference about the objects of these different states. For though they both agree in this — that they have the common welfare for their aim and scope — yet the things about which the civil power is primarily conversant are bodies . . . I Corinthians 6:4, or . . . the things of this life [such] as goods, lands, honor, the liberties and peace of the outward man. The things whereabout the church power is exercised are . . . the things of God [such] as the souls and consciences of men, the doctrine and worship of God, the communion of saints. Hence also they have: (a) different laws, (b) different officers, (c) different power whereby to reduce men to order according to their different objects and ends.

Now [in order] that a just harmony may be kept between these two different orders and administrations two extremes must be avoided:

1. That they be not confounded either by giving the spiritual power — which is proper to the church — into the hand of the civil magistrate (as Erastus would have done in the matter of excommunication) . . . or [in the other case] by giving civil power to church-officers who are called to attend only to spiritual matters and the things of God, and therefore may not be distracted from them by secular entanglements. (I say church-officers, not church-members, for they — not being limited as the officers are by God — are capable of two different employments [according to the] two different men in them in different respects, as has been said. As they may be lawfully employed about things of this life so they are of all men fittest, being sanctified and dedicated to God to carry on all worldly and civil business to God's ends, as we shall declare in due time.). . .

2. The second extreme to be avoided is that these two different orders and states — ecclesiastical and civil — be not set in opposition as contraries [so] that one should destroy the other, but as coordinate states in the same place reaching forth help mutually each to [the] other for the welfare of both according to God. Both officers and members of Churches [should] be subject, in respect of the outward man, to the civil power of those who bear rule in the civil state according to God. . . . Civil magistrates and officers in regard to the outward man [ought to] subject themselves spiritually to the power of Christ in church-ordinances, and by their civil power preserve the same in outward peace and purity. This will best be attained when the pastor may say to the magistrate. . . , "Thou rulest with Christ and administerest to Christ. Thou hast the sword for him. Let this gift which thou hast received from him be kept pure for him." The civil magistrate in his church-state [should fit] Ambrose ['s] description of a good emperor: "A good magistrate is within the church, not above it." . . . So much shall serve to have been spoken concerning the first distinction.

The second distinction to be premised for clearing the true state of the question is . . . between a commonwealth already settled and a commonwealth yet to be settled wherein men are free to choose what form they shall judge best. . . . Men that profess the fear of God, if they be free to make choice of their civil judges (as in this new plantation we are), . . . should rather choose such as are members of the Church for that purpose than others who are not in that state.

The third distinction premised for clearing the truth in this point is between free burgesses and free inhabitants in a civil state. Concerning which there must be had a different consideration. This difference of people living under the same civil jurisdiction is held and observed in all countries (as well heathen as others) — as may be proven, if it were needful, out of the histories of all nations and times. And the experience of our times as well in our own native country as in other places confirms it. In all [of] which many are inhabitants that are not citizens, that are never likely to be numbered among *archontes,* or rulers. [So it is] in the case now in question. When we urge that magistrates be chosen out of such as are members of these churches we do not thereby go about to exclude those that are not in church-order from any civil right or liberty that is due unto them as inhabitants and planters, as if none should have lots in due proportion with other men, nor the benefit of justice under the government where they live [except] church-members — for this were indeed to have the commonwealth swallowed up [by] the church. But [since] there ever will be differences between the world and the church in the same place, and [since] men of the world are allowed [by] God [to have] the use and enjoyment . . . of civil government for their quiet and comfortable subsistence in the world, and [since] church members (though called out of the world unto fellowship with Christ) [will ever be] living in the world and having many worldly necessities and business in common with men of the world who live among them, [both] stand in need of the civil power to right them against civil injuries and to protect them in their right and outward orderly use of their spirituals against those who are apt to be injurious to them in the one or in the other

respect. [Those who are outside the church] are not under the church's power and yet, living within the verge of the same civil jurisdiction, [both] are under the civil power of the magistrates. Hence it is that we plead for this order to be set in civil affairs that such a course may be taken as will best secure to ourselves and our posterities the fruitful managing of civil government for the common welfare of all, as well [those] in the church as without. [This will] most certainly be effected when the public trust and power of these matters is committed to such men as are most approved according to God. These are church-members — as shall afterward, God assisting, be proved.

The fourth distinction to be premised for clearing the truth and to prevent mistakes in this question shall be between the actions of church-members. For some actions are done by them all jointly as a spiritual body in reference to spiritual ends, and some actions are done only by some of the body in reference to civil ends. . . . Members fitly chosen out of the church and made free burgesses are fitter to judge and determine according to God than other men [are]. . . .

The fifth distinction to be premised . . . is between places where all, or the most considerable part, of the first and free planters profess their desire and purpose of entering into church-fellowship according to Christ and of enjoying in that state all the ordinances in purity and peace and of securing the same unto their posterity so far as men are able, and those places where all or the most considerable part of the first and free planters are otherwise minded and profess the contrary. Our question is of the first sort, not of the second.

So much shall seem to have been spoken to the distinctions (which having been premised) we now proceed to declare the true state of the question which is as followeth:

Whether a new plantation where all or the most considerable part of free planters profess their purpose and desire of securing to themselves and to their posterity the pure and peaceable enjoyment of Christ's ordinances, whether, I say, such planters are bound in laying the foundations of church and civil state to take order that all the free burgesses be such as are in the fellowship of the church or churches which are or may be gathered according to Christ? And [further] that those free burgesses have the only power of choosing from among themselves civil magistrates and men to be entrusted with transacting all public affairs of importance according to the rules and directions of Scripture?

I hold the affirmative part of this question upon this ground, that this course will [be] most conduc[ive] to the good of both states and by consequence to the common welfare of all—[to which] all men are bound principally to attend in laying the foundation of a common-wealth lest posterity rue the first miscarriages when it will be too late to redress them.

Argument 1: Theocracy, or to make the Lord God our governor, is the best form of government in a Christian commonwealth, and . . . men who are free to choose (as in a new plantation they are) ought to establish [it]. . . . That form of government where, (a) the people who have the power of choosing their governors are in covenant with God, (b) wherein the men chosen by them are godly men and fitted with a spirit of government, (c) in which the laws they rule by are the laws of God, (d) wherein laws are executed, inheritances alloted, and civil differences are composed according to God's appointment, [and] (e) in which men of God are consulted [about] all hard cases and in matters of religion, [this] is the form which was received and established among the people of Israel while the Lord God was their governor.

Argument 2: The form of government which gives unto Christ his due preeminence is the best form of government in a Christian commonwealth. . . .

Argument 3: That form of government [in which] the best provision is made for the good both of the church and of the civil state is the best form of government in a Christian communion . . . . Junius, [who speaks] of the consent and harmony of the Church and civil state in the concurrence of their several adminstrations to the welfare of a Christian Commonwealth, . . . expresses it by the conjunction of the soul and body in a man. . . .

Argument 4: That form of government [in which] the power of civil administration is denied unto unbelievers and [is] committed to the saints is the best form of government in a Christian Commonwealth. . . .

Argument 5: That form of government [in which] the power of choosing from among themselves men to be entrusted with managing all public affairs of importance is committed to those who are furnished with the best helps for securing to a Christian state the full discharge of such a trust is the best form of government in a Christian Commonwealth. . . .

Argument 6: [There is a danger of devolving power upon those not members of the church.]

It seems to be a principle imprinted in the minds and hearts of all men in the equity of it that such a form of government as best serves to establish their religion should, by the consent of all, be established in the civil state.

2. QUERIES OF HIGHEST CONSIDERATION (1644)

As over against the rest of New England the settlements around Narragansett Bay provide vivid contrast on the issue of Church and State. To its orthodox contemporaries this minute and quarrelsome colony was a cesspool. Moderns have wished to locate vital stirrings of "democracy" in its troubled waters. Either judgment fails to distill the dual significance of Rhode Island. Modernists fail to appreciate the continuing medievalism in Roger Williams' tortuous argument with his former colleagues. The colleagues themselves recognized no more than Williams himself did the practical success which would eventually attend the segregation of religious authority from civil jurisdiction. Williams' checkered career need not be recounted here. His *Queries of Highest Considera-tion* appeared in London during 1644 when he was there seeking support in the Long Parliament for the struggling settlement. The pamphlet was not addressed to Cotton—that exchange was published separately. But if not to Cotton the *Queries* was addressed to men of his stripe on the English scene. Some of the Dissenting Brethren, indeed, counted Cotton as a spiritual father. Arguing against an established church for England (under discussion in the Westminster Assembly during the first civil war), Williams did not deny that "double-relation" which was fundamental to seventeenth-century thought about Church and State. But he did deny that a coordination of spiritual and temporal authorities logically followed from that premise. For Williams such "coordination" inevitably meant subordination of the spiritual to the temporal. For the sake of the "spiritual relation" or the "inward man" he advocated that church suste-nance be denied to the state. He argued that civil society had to be secularized in order that religious life might be authentically spiritual. The *Queries* was di-rected to participants in the Westminster Assembly but his personal quarrel was with the established church of Massachusetts Bay in which Cotton was the great ornament.

Addressed to the Dissenting Brethren and the Scottish Commissioners at the Westminster Assembly in London

Worthy sirs,

In serious examination of your late apol-ogies we shall in all due respect and ten-derness humbly query:

First, what precept or pattern hath the Lord Jesus left you in his last will and tes-tament for your Synod or Assembly of Di-vines by virtue of which you may expect his preference and assistance?

If you say (as all Popish synods and coun-cils do), the pattern is plain, Acts 15, we ask if two or three particular congregations at Antioch sent to that first mother church at Jerusalem where the Apostles were . . . [who] had power to make decrees for all churches, Acts 16, we ask whether this be a pattern for a nation or kingdom . . . to reform or form a religion, &c.?

Abridged and edited to conform more nearly to current usage. A full text may be consulted in *Publications of the Narragansett Club*, Volume II (1867), pp. 11 ff. (second so numbered) or in *The Complete Writings of Roger Williams* (New York, 1963) same volume and pages (facsimile of the former).

We pray you to consider [rather] if the golden image [of Daniel 3] be not a type and figure of the several national and state religions which all nations set up and ours hath done, for which the wrath of God is now upon us?

Query II. Whereas you both agree (though with some differences) that the civil magistrate must reform the church, establish religion, and so consequently must first judge and judicially determine which is true [and] which is false, . . . we now query—since the Parliament (being the representative commonwealth) hath no other power but what the common weale derive [unto] and betrust it with—whether it will not evidently follow that the commonweal, the nation, the kingdom, and (if it were in Augustus' time) the whole world must rule and govern the Church and [also] Christ himself as the Church is called, I Corinthians 12:12.

Furthermore if the Honourable Houses (the representative commonweal) shall erect a spiritual court for the judging of spiritual men and spiritual causes (although a new name be put upon it) [we query] whether or not such a court is not in the true nature and kind of it an High Commission? And is not this a reviving of Moses and the sanctifying of a new land of Canaan of which we hear nothing in the Testament of Jesus Christ, nor of any other holy nation but the particular Church of Christ? (I Peter 2:9)

Is not this to subject this holy nation, this heavenly Jerusalem, the wife and spouse of Jesus, the pillar and ground of truth to the uncertain and changeable mutations of this present evil world?

Query III. Whether, since you prefer to be builders, you have not cause to fear and tremble lest you be found to reject the cornerstone [i.e., Jesus Christ] in not fitting to him only living stones [i.e., true believers] . . . ?

Query IV. Whether in your consciences before God you be not persuaded—

notwithstanding your promiscuous joining with all—that few of the people of England and Scotland (and fewer of the nobles and gentry) are such spiritual matter, living stones, truly regenerate and converted? And therefore whether it be not the greatest courtesy in the world which you may possibly perform unto them to aquaint them impartially with their condition and how impossible it is for a dead stone to have fellowship with the living God, and for any man to enter the kingdom of God without a second birth? John 3.

Query VII. We query where you now find one footstep, print, or pattern in this doctrine of the Son of God for a national holy covenant and so, consequently, . . . a national church? Where find you evidence of a whole nation, country or kingdom converted to the faith, and of Christ's appointing of a whole nation or kingdom to walk in one way of religion?

Again we ask whether . . . the constitution of a national church . . . can possibly be framed without a racking and tormenting of souls as well as of the bodies of persons, for it seems not possible to fit it to every conscience?

Query VIII. We readily grant [that] the civil magistrate [is] armed by God with a civil sword (Romans 13) to execute vengeance against robbers, murderers, tyrants, &c. Yet where it concerns Christ we find [that] when his disciples desire vengeance upon offenders (Luke 9) he meekly answers, "You know not what spirit you are of. I came not to destroy men's lives but to save them." If ever there were cause for the servants of Christ Jesus to fight, it was when—not his truth, or servants, or ordinances, but—his own most holy person was in danger, Matthew 26. Yet then that Lamb of God checks Peter [who was] beginning to fight for him, telling him that all who take the sword shall perish by the sword. . . . Unto which may also be added John 18:35: "My kingdom is not of this world. If my kingdom were of this

9

world then would my servants fight that I should not be delivered, &c."

We query—if security be taken by the wisdom of the state for civil subjection—why even the Papists themselves and their consciences may not be permitted in the world? For otherwise if England's government were the government of the whole world not only they but a world of idolaters of all sorts—yea, the whole world—must be driven out of the world?

Query X. Since you report your opposing and suppressing of heresies and [your] glorious success, &c, we query whether that be a demonstrative argument from the scriptures for a truth of a church or government of it since even the Church of Rome may boast of the same against many schisms and heresies, and doth triumph with wonderful success even against the truth and the witness to it according to Daniel's and John's prophecies? Daniel 11, Revelation 13.

Query XII. Since you both profess to want more light and that a greater light is to be expected . . . we query how you can profess and swear to persecute all others as schismatics, heretics, &c, who believe they see a further light and dare not join with either of your churches? [We query] whether the Lamb's wife has received any such commission or disposition from the Lamb (her husband) so to practice? [We query] whether (as King James once wrote upon Revelation 20) it be not a true mark and character of a false church to persecute? It being the nature only of a wolf to hurt the lambs and sheep, but impossible for a lamb or sheep—or a thousand flocks of sheep—to persecute one wolf (we speak of spiritual sheep and spiritual wolves). For other wolves against the civil state we profess it to be the duty of the civil state to persecute and suppress them.

And lastly, whether the States of Holland which tolerate (though not own, as you say) the several sects among them which differ from them and are of another con-

science and worship, [we query] whether or not they come not nearer to the holy pattern and command of the Lord Jesus to permit the tares to have a civil being in the field of the world until the harvest, the end of it? (Matthew 13)

We know the allegations against this counsel [of mine]: the [archetype of such practice] is from Moses (no Christ), his pattern is the typical land of Canaan, the kings of Israel and Judah, &c. We believe [that this] will be found [to be] but one of Moses' shadows which vanished at the coming of the Lord Jesus—yet such a shadow as is directly opposite to the very testament and coming of the Lord Jesus. [It is] opposite to the very nature of a Christian Church, the only holy nation and Israel of God. [It is] opposite to the very tender bowels of humanity (and how much more Christianity?), [which] abhors to pour out the blood of men merely for their souls' belief and worship. [It is] opposite to the very essentials and fundamentals of the nature of a civil magistracy, a civil common weal or combination of men which can only respect civil things. [It is] opposite to the Jews conversion to Christ by not permitting them a civil life or being. [It is] opposite to the civil peace and the lives of millions slaughtered upon this ground in mutual persecuting of each other's consciences, especially the Protestant and the Papist. [It is] opposite to the souls of all men who by persecutions are ravished into a dissembled worship which their hearts embrace not. [It is] opposite to the best of God's servants who, in all Popish and Protestant states, have been commonly esteemed and persecuted as the only schismatics, heretics, &c. [It is] opposite to that light of scripture which is expected yet to shine [but] which must, by that doctrine, be suppressed as a new or old heresy or novelty. All this in all ages experience testifies [to], [ages] which never saw any long lived fruit of peace or righteousness grow upon that fatal tree.

3. ARTICLES, LAWES, AND ORDERS, DIVINE, POLITIC, AND MARTIALL FOR THE COLONY IN VIRGINIA (1610-1611)

From its "planting" in 1607 until 1624 when it was taken over as a royal colony, the Virginia settlement was controlled by a company which held "power and authority of government" according to several charters from James I. While the Virginia Company resided in London delegated officials actually managed the affairs of the plantation. Without exception the charters and related documents were phrased in that "language" used by Cotton and Williams and they illustrate the close association of divine and mundane authorities which reinforced each other's administrations. A full "establishment" was out of the question in the early garrison state where the ministers were really "chaplains." "Dale's Laws" embody the regimen introduced by Sir Thomas Gates, Lord Delaware, and Sir Thomas Dale which helped to rescue the faltering plantation from extinction. The complete set of thirty-seven "Laws" was to be read to the assemblies every Sunday by the clergymen. More significantly, perhaps, a long and orthodox prayer was appointed to be read twice daily on the Court of the Guard by the captain or other officer. If the "Laws" and the prayer seemed "ancient and common" it was only because "these grounds are the same constant Asterismes [constellations] and starres which must guide all that travell in these perplexed wayes and paths of publique affairs." By the middle of the seventeenth century Virginia society had developed its own pattern for the relationship between Anglican parish churches and the colonial government which gave unique authority to the local vestry in the absence of both a hereditary patron and an accessible bishop.

Whereas his Majesty like himself a most zealous prince hath in his own realms a principal care of true Religion and reverence to God, and hath always strictly commanded his generals and governors with all his forces wheresoever to let their ways be like his ends for the glory of God, . . . I have . . . adhered unto the laws divine, and orders politic and martial of his Lordship . . . an addition of such others as I have found either the necessity of the present state of the Colony to require, or the infancy and weakness of the body thereof . . . able to digest. . . .

1. First, since we owe our highest and supreme duty, our greatest and all our allegiance, to him from whom all power and authority is derived and flows as from the first and only fountain, and being special soldiers empressed in this sacred cause, we must alone expect our success from him who is only the blesser of all good attempts, the King of Kings, the commander of commanders, and Lord of Hosts, I do strictly command and charge all captains and officers, of what quality or nature soever . . . , to have a care that the Almighty God be duly and daily served, and that they call upon their people to hear sermons, as that also they diligently frequent Morning and Evening Prayer themselves by their own example and daily life and duty herein encourage others thereunto, and that such who shall often and willfully absent themselves be duly punished according to the martial law in that case provided.

2. That no man speak impiously or

Abridged and edited to conform more nearly to current usage. A full text may be consulted in *Tracts and Other Papers*, ed. Peter Force, Volume III (Washington, 1844).

maliciously against the holy and blessed Trinity or any of the three persons, that is to say, against God the Father, God the Son, and God the holy Ghost, or against the known articles of the Christian faith, upon pain of death.

3. That no man blaspheme God's holy name upon pain of death, or use unlawful oaths, taking the name of God in vain, curse or ban, upon pain of severe punishment for the first offence so committed, and for the second to have a bodkin thrust through his tongue, and if he continue the blaspheming of God's holy name, for the third time so offending, he shall be brought to a martial court and there receive censure of death for his offence.

4. No man shall use any traiterous words against his Majesty's Person, or royal authority, upon pain of death.

5. No man shall speak any word or do any act which may tend to the derision or despight of God's holy word upon pain of death. Nor shall any man unworthily demean himself unto any preacher or minister of the same but generally hold them in reverent regard. . . .

6. Every man and woman duly twice a day upon the first tolling of the bell shall upon the working days repair unto the Church to hear divine service upon pain of losing his or her days allowance for the first ommission, for the second to be whipped, and for the third to be condemned to the Gallies for six months. Likewise no man or woman shall dare to violate or break the sabbath by any gaming, public, or private abroad, or at home, but duly sanctify and observe the same, both himself and his family, by preparing themselves at home with private prayer, that they may be the better fitted for the public according to the commandments of God and the orders of our Church, as also every man and woman shall repair in the morning to the divine service and sermons preached upon the sabbath day, and in the afternoon to divine service and catechizing, upon pain for the

first fault to lose their provision and allowance for the whole week following, for the second to lose the said allowance and also to be whipped, and for the third to suffer death.

7. All preachers or ministers within this our colony or colonies shall . . . choose unto him four of the most religious and better disposed as well to inform of the abuses and neglects of the people in their duties and service to God as also to the due reparation and keeping of the church handsome and fitted with all reverent observances thereunto belonging. Likewise every minister shall keep a faithful and true record or church book of all christenings, marriages, and deaths of such [of] our people as shall happen. . . .

10. No man shall be found guilty of sacrilege which is a trespass as well committed in violating and abusing any sacred ministry, duty or office of the church irreverently or profanely as by being a church robber to filch, steal or carry away anything out of the church appertaining thereunto or unto any holy and consecrated place to the divine service of God which no man should do upon pain of death. . . .

13. No manner of person whatsoever, contrary to the word of God (which ties every particular and private man, for conscience sake, to obedience and duty [to] the magistrate and such as shall be placed in authority over them) shall detract, slander, calumnate, murmur, mutiny, resist, disobey, or neglect the commandments either of the Lord Governor . . . or any authorized . . . public officer. . . .

33. There is not one man or woman in this colony now present, or hereafter to arrive, but shall give up an account of his and their faith and religion, and repair unto the minister that by his conference with them he may understand and gather whether heretofore they have been sufficiently instructed and catechised in the principles and grounds of religion. . . .

37. . . . Every minister or preacher shall

every sabbath day before catechising read all these laws and ordinances publicly in the assembly of the congregation upon pain of his entertainment check for that week.

4. PREFACE TO THE FUNDAMENTAL ORDERS OF CONNECTICUT (1638-9)

In the case of Massachusetts Bay, suffrage had been explicitly restricted to church members as early as 1631. It is likely that this act should be understood as an expediential means, adopted by the General Court, to secure and assure its control over the separated settlements within the patent as immigration rapidly increased. The Hartford settlements did not adopt a similar restriction, a fact which is erroneously interpreted as indicating the presence of an incipient democracy in the Connecticut Valley. Actually its territory was small, its location isolated, and its population comparatively homogeneous. Thomas Hooker, dominant figure in the settlement, casually offered the following postulates which would have warranted such a restriction if it had been needed: 1. "A right opinion and worship of God should be openly professed within the territories and jurisdiction of a state . . . as that which comes within the . . . object of the state and policy to attend." and 2. "Hence the supreme magistrate hath liberty and power both to inquire and judge of professions and religions, which is true and ought to be maintained, which is false and ought to be rejected."[1] The Preamble to the Fundamental Orders indicates how intimately "Church and State" were coordinated in that venture. In the Bay Colony Church attendance was required of all inhabitants and all were required to support it. The correlation of spiritual and temporal authorities was simply an expression of the medieval principle that the unity of society was guaranteed by the uniformity of religion. The principle that heresy is treason logically followed and by 1644 Massachusetts Bay required banishment for Baptists.

[1] Thomas Hooker, *A Survey of the Summe of Church Discipline* (London, 1648), Part IV, p. 75 (57).

Forasmuch as it hath pleased the Almighty God by the wise disposition of his divine providence so to order and dispose of things that we the inhabitants and residents of Windsor, Hartford, and Wethersfield are now cohabiting and dwelling in and upon the River of Connecticut and the lands thereunto adjoining; And well knowing that where a people are gathered together the Word of God requires that to maintain the peace and union of such a people there should be an orderly and decent government established according to God to order and dispose of the affairs of the people at all seasons as occasion shall require: [we] do therefore associate and conjoin ourselves to be as one public state or commonwealth; and do, for ourselves and our successors and such as shall be adjoined to us at any time hereafter, enter

Edited to conform more nearly to current usage. Text may be consulted in *The Public Records of Connecticut*, edited by J. H. Trumbull (Hartford, 1850), pp. 20 f.

into combination and confederation together to maintain and preserve the liberty and purity of the gospel of our Lord Jesus Christ which we now profess, as also the discipline of the churches which according to the truth of the said gospel is now practised among us; As also in our civil affairs to be guided and governed according to such Laws, Rules, Orders and Decrees as shall be made, ordered & decreed, as followeth:

5. AN ACT CONCERNING RELIGION IN THE MARYLAND COLONY (1649)

The Maryland Colony represents a peculiar chapter in the records of "Church-State relationships" in colonial America. Although sponsored by Lord Baltimore in the 1630's as a refuge for English Catholics, from the beginning a significant number of Protestants joined in the venture. During the 1640's—against the background of the civil war in England—hostility between Protestants and Catholics became bitter, especially since it was encouraged by outside agitators from Virginia. In this situation Baltimore attempted to undergird his tolerant policy through "An Act Concerning Religion." Within five years it had been repealed and the Catholics outlawed by the ascendant and militant Puritan party. After a series of complex developments Maryland finally became a royal colony after the Glorious Revolution. Whether Baltimore's policy of toleration was primarily idealistic or a political calculation, times were not ready for it. It is curious that this Act has become known as the "Act of Toleration." To be sure it does authorize some latitude in religious belief and observance. Read in its entirety, however, it is yet another exercise in that "language of establishment" which was so nearly universal to the seventeenth century. An analysis and assessment of the Act may be found in M. P. Andrews, *The Founding of Maryland* (New York, 1933), pp. 143 ff.

Forasmuch as in a well governed and Christian commonwealth matters concerning religion and the honor of God ought in the first place to be taken into serious consideration and endeavoured to be settled, be it therefore ordered and enacted by the Right Honorable Cecilius Lord Baron of Baltimore absolute Lord and Proprietary of this province with the advice and consent of this General Assembly:

That whatsoever person or persons within this province . . . shall from henceforth blaspheme God, that is curse him, or deny our Saviour Jesus Christ to be the Son of God, or shall deny the holy Trinity . . . , or the Godhead of any of the said three persons of the Trinity or the Unity of the Godhead, or shall use or utter any reproachful speeches, words or language concerning the said holy Trinity, or any of the said three persons thereof, shall be punished with death and confiscation or forfeiture of all his or her lands and goods to the Lord Proprietary and his heirs.

And be it also enacted by the authority and with the advice and assent aforesaid,

---

Abridged and edited to conform more nearly to current usage. The text may be located in *The Proceedings and Acts of the General Assembly of Maryland*, January 1637/8—September 1664 (Baltimore, 1883), pp. 244 ff.

That whatsoever person or persons shall from henceforth use or utter any reproachful words or speeches concerning the blessed Virgin Mary the Mother of our Saviour or the holy Apostles or Evangelists or any of them shall in such case for the first offence forfeit to the said Lord Proprietary . . . the sum of five pound sterling or the value thereof. . . . And that every such offender or offenders for every second offence shall forfeit ten pound sterling or the value thereof. . . . And that every person or persons before mentioned offending herein the third time shall for such third offence forfeit all his lands and goods and be forever banished and expelled out of this province.

And be it also further enacted by the same authority, advice and assent that whatsoever person or persons shall from henceforth upon any occasion of offence or otherwise in a reproachful manner or way declare, call or denominate any person or persons whatsoever . . . within this province . . . an heretic, schismatic, idolator, puritan, Independent, Presbyterian, popish priest, Jesuit, Jesuited papist, Lutheran, Calvinist, Anabaptist, Brownist, Antinomian, Barrowist, Roundhead, Separatist, or any other name or term in a reproachful manner relating to matter of religion shall for every such offence forfeit and lose the sum of ten shillings sterling or the value thereof . . . , the one half thereof to be forfeited and paid unto the person and persons of whom such reproachful words are or shall be spoken or uttered, and the other half thereof to the Lord Proprietary. . . .

And be it further likewise enacted by the authority and consent aforesaid that every person and persons within this province that shall at any time hereafter profane the Sabbath or Lord's Day called Sunday by frequent swearing, drunkenness or by any uncivil or disorderly recreation, or by working on that day when absolute necessity doth not require it, shall for every first offence forfeit two shillings six pence sterling or the value thereof, and for the second offence five shillings sterling or the value thereof, and for the third offence and so for every time he shall offend in like manner afterwards ten shillings sterling or the value thereof. . . .

And whereas the enforcing of the conscience in matters of religion hath frequently fallen out to be of dangerous consequences in those commonwealths where it hath been practised, and for the more quiet and peaceable government of this province, and the better to preserve mutual love and amity among the inhabitants thereof; be it therefore also by the Lord Proprietary with the advice and consent of this Assembly ordained and enacted (except as in this present Act is before declared and set forth) that no person or persons whatsoever within this province . . . professing to believe in Jesus Christ shall from henceforth be in any ways troubled, molested or discountenanced for or in respect of his or her religion, nor in the free exercise thereof within this province of the islands thereunto belonging, nor in any way compelled to the belief or exercise of any other religion against his or her consent, so [long] as they be not unfaithful to the Lord Proprietary, or molest or conspire against the civil government established or to be established in this province under him or his heirs. . . . The freemen have assented. Tho: Hatton Enacted by the Governor. Willm Stone

6. THE CHARTER OF RHODE ISLAND AND PROVIDENCE PLANTATIONS (1663)

To actualize Williams' segregation of spiritual authority and temporal jurisdiction was also to make practically possible the social being of Providence Plantations and Rhode Island which were populated by a mixed lot according to any classification of the day. Rabid religionists of several stripes shared the meagre and marginal land with traders, adventurers, individualists, and Indians. Thus when Dr. John Clarke finally did obtain a charter from Charles II in 1663 which granted religious liberty it did mark a "lively experiment" as to whether social cohesion could be achieved apart from a common religious allegiance. Neither Williams, the "theological windmill," nor the reluctant "experiment" of the Charter make any sense, however, apart from the idiom of the seventeenth century.

Whereas his Majesty has been informed by the petition of John Clarke, on behalf of . . . the purchasers and free inhabitants of the island called Rhode Island the rest of the colony of Providence Plantations in Narragansett Bay in New England, that they, pursuing with loyal minds their serious intentions of godly edifying themselves in the holy Christian faith as they were persuaded, together with the conversion of the Indian natives, did not only with the encouragement of his Majesty's progenitors transport themselves unto America but, not being able to bear in those parts their different apprehensions in religious concernments, again left their desirable habitations and transplanted themselves into the midst of the most potent Indian people of that country where (by the good Providence of God, from whom the plantations have taken their name) they have not only been preserved to admiration, but have prospered and become possessed by purchase from the natives of lands, rivers, harbors, &c, very convenient for plantations, ship building, supply of pipe-staves, and commerce with his Majesty's southern plantations, and by their friendly society with the great body of Narragansett Indians have given them encouragement to subject themselves to his Majesty. And whereas they have declared that it is much on their hearts to hold forth a lively experiment that a flourishing civil state may best be maintained among his Majesty's subjects with full religious liberty, and that true piety will give the greatest security for sovereignty and true loyalty, His Majesty, willing to preserve to them that liberty in the worship of God which they have sought with so much travail and loyal subjection, and because some of them cannot conform to the liturgy, ceremonies, and articles of the Church of England, and hoping that the same—by reason of distance—may be no breach of the uniformity established in this nation, hereby grants and declares that no person within the said colony shall hereafter be any wise molested or called in question for any difference in opinion in matters of religion that does not disturb the civil peace of the colony, and that they shall enjoy the benefit of his Majesty's late Act of Indemnity and free pardon.

Edited to conform more nearly to current usage. The text may be consulted in *The Calendar of State Papers*, "Colonial America and West Indies, 1661–68," # 512, p. 148 (July 8, 1663).

William Penn

7. PREFACE TO THE FRAME OF GOVERNMENT OF PENNSYLVANIA (1682)

The seventeenth-century language of establishment is often overlooked by those who are concerned to locate instances of official toleration or allowance of religious liberty in colonial affairs. The Articles of Capitulation on the Reduction of New Netherland, for instance, are cited because Clause 8 allowed the Dutch the "liberty of their consciences in Divine Worship and Church Discipline." The significant implication, of course, is that a single establishment of religion seemed right and proper and that this departure from that practice was an expediential arrangement. In a similar way, while William Penn is justly celebrated for granting civil liberties to all who confessed "God as the Lord of conscience," this should not obscure the fact that such was a Quaker version of the conventional "language of establishment." Because man's "spiritual relation" was "free and mental" the church could not be "corporeal and compulsive." Yet government was said to be divinely authored—"sacred in its institution and end"—not only to restrain sin but to regulate "many other affairs," and Penn required confession of God on the part of the inhabitants and profession of Jesus Christ as Saviour on the part of the rulers. This might be contrasted with Williams' proposal that spiritual and temporal affairs be radically segregated. It is natural that we should be sympathetic toward Penn's charity in comparing him with many of his contemporaries. This does not mean, however, that the Pennsylvania experiment was more than another change rung on the medieval theme that man's double relation required coordination of his religious and civil lives.

When the great and wise God had made the world, of all his creatures it pleased him to choose man his deputy to rule it. And to fit him for so great a charge and trust he did not only qualify him with skill and power, but with integrity to use them justly. This native goodness was equally his honour and his happiness. And while he stood here all went well. There was no need of coercive or compulsive means; the precept of divine love and truth in his bosom was the guide and keeper of his innocency. But lust prevailing against duty made a lamentable breach upon it. And the law that before had no power over him took place upon him and his disobedient posterity that such as would not live conformable to the holy law within should fall under the reproof and correction of the just law without in a judicial administration.

[Saint Paul] settles the divine right of government beyond exception, and that for two ends: first, to terrify evil doers; secondly, to cherish those that do well—which gives government a life beyond corruption and makes it as durable in the world as good men shall be. So that government seems to me a part of religion itself, a thing sacred in its institution and end. For if it does not directly remove the cause it crushes the effects of evil and is as such (though a lower, yet) an emanation of the

---

Abridged and edited to conform more nearly to current usage. The text is available in *The Federal and State Constitutions*, ed. F. N. Thorpe (Washington, 1909), Volume V, pp. 3052 f.

same divine power that is both author and object of pure religion. The difference [between them lies] here: the one is more free and mental, the other more corporeal and compulsive in its operations. But that is only to evil doers, government itself being otherwise as capable of kindness, goodness, and charity as a more private society. They weakly err that think there is no other use of government than correction which is the coarsest part of it. Daily experience tells us that the care and regulation of many other affairs, more soft and daily necessary, make up much of the greatest part of government and [this] must have followed the peopling of the world had Adam never fell, and [it] will continue among men, on earth, under the highest attainments they may arrive at by the coming of the blessed Second Adam, the Lord from Heaven. Thus much of government in general, as to its rise and end.

8. THE FUNDAMENTAL CONSTITUTIONS OF CAROLINA (1669-1698)

The Fundamental Constitutions have been of antiquarian interest because John Locke is thought to have had a hand in drafting the original (1669) version. Actually it is unlikely that he was deeply involved in the project. Of far more significance is the fact that the Lords Proprietors of Carolina attempted to provide an essentially feudal civil government for their colony which they intended to be perpetual. The document — never fully in effect, apparently — passed through at least five versions. The original one contained several paragraphs which represent once again a statement of those traditional assumptions regarding "Church-State relations." This selection is from the final version (1698). Although very important changes took place in the other provisions during the revisions, the clauses relating to religion and religious institutions are substantially identical to those of the earliest draft.

25. No man shall be permitted to be a Freeman of Carolina or to have any estate or habitation within it who does not acknowledge a God, & that God is publically & solemnly to be worshipped.

26. As the country comes to be sufficiently planted & distributed into fit divisions it shall belong to the Parliament to take care for the building of churches and the public maintenance of divines to be employed in the exercise of religion according to the Church of England, which being the only true & orthodox & national religion of the King's dominions is so also of Carolina, and therefore it alone shall be allowed to receive public maintenance by grant of Parliament.

27. Any seven or more persons agreeing in any religion shall constitute a church or a profession to which they shall give some name to distinguish it from others.

28. The terms of admittance & communion with any church or profession shall be written in a book and therein be subscribed by all the members of the said church or profession which shall be kept by the public Register of the Precinct wherein they reside.

Abridged and edited to conform more nearly to current usage. The text is available in *The Colonial Records of North Carolina*, ed. W. L. Saunders, Volume II (Raleigh, 1886), pp. 852 ff. The five versions of The Fundamental Constitutions may be compared in *North Carolina Charters and Constitutions, 1578–1698* edited by M. E. E. Parker (Raleigh, 1963), pp. 128 ff.

29. The time of every ones subscription and admittance shall be dated in the said book of religious records.

3C. In the terms of communion of every church or profession these following shall be there without which no agreement or assembly of men upon pretence of religion shall be accounted a church or profession within these rules:

1st That there is a God.

2nd That God is publicly to be worshipped.

3rd That it is lawful and the duty of every man being thereunto called by those that govern to bear witness to truth, and that every church or profession shall in their terms of communion set down the external way whereby they witness a truth, as in the presence of God whether it be by laying hands on or kissing the Bible as in the Church of England or by holding up the hand or any sensible way.

31. No person above seventeen years of age shall have any benefit or protection of the law, or be capable of any place of profit or honor, who is not a member of some church or profession (having his name recorded in some one and but one religious record at once).

32. No person of any church or profession shall disturb or molest any religious assembly.

33. No person whatsoever shall speak anything in their religious assembly irreverently or seditiously of the government or governor or of state matters.

34. Any person subscribing the terms of communion in the record of the said church or profession before the precinct register and any five members of the said church or profession shall be thereby made a member of the said church or profession.

35. Any person striking out his own name out of any religious record, or his name being struck out by any officer thereunto authorized by each church or profession respectively, shall cease to be a member of that church or profession.

36. No man shall use any reproachful, reviling or abusive language against the religion of any church or profession, that being the certain way of disturbing the peace & hindering the conversion of any to the truth by engaging them in quarrels & animosities to the hatred of the professors and that profession which otherwise they may be brought to assent to.

37. Since charity obliges us to wish well to the souls of all men, and religion ought to alter nothing in any man's civil estate or right, it shall be lawful for slaves as well as others to enter themselves and be of what church or profession any of them shall think best & thereof be as fully members as any freeman. But yet no slave shall hereby be exempted from that civil dominion his master has over him, but in all other things in the same state & condition he was in before.

38. Assemblies upon what pretence soever of religion not observing & performing the abovesaid rule shall not be esteemed as churches but [as] unlawful meetings, and be punished as other riots.

39. No person whatsoever shall disturb, molest or persecute another for his speculative opinions in religion or his way of worship.

40. Every freeman of Carolina shall have absolute power & authority over his negro slaves of what opinion or religion soever.

H. Richard Niebuhr

9. THE SOVEREIGNTY OF GOD

Professor Niebuhr wrote upon a variety of subjects as a teacher of theology and ethics at the Divinity School of Yale University. *The Kingdom of God in America* has had a wide reading since its publication.

It is a platitude to say that the hope of the Puritans who came to America was the establishment of theocracy. If "theocracy" be understood in its literal meaning the statement is very true, and it epitomizes all the faith and convictions as well as the fears and perplexities, the experiments and errors, which marked the history of New England Protestantism. But, taken literally, the establishment of theocracy was not the hope of the Puritans only. It was no less the desire of Pilgrims in Plymouth, of Roger Williams and his assorted followers in Rhode Island, of the Quakers in the middle colonies of German sectarians in Pennsylvania, of the Dutch Reformed in New York, the Scotch-Irish Presbyterians of a later immigration and of many a native movement. All of these had been deeply influenced, if not directly inspired, by the faith of the Protestant renewal with its fresh insistence on the present sovereignty and initiative of God, and all of them faced the dilemma of Protestantism.

The idea of the kingdom of God was dominant in the first period of American development as it is the leading idea today. Then as now it was the property not of one group but of all the groups which, coming out of a similar past, faced a common problem. In the early period, however, Protestants did not think of the kingdom in the idealistic and utopian terms which became current later. Our time speaks of God's kingdom when it means an ideal for future human society. Such a kingdom may be a wish, a plan, a dream, an ideal or a goal. It is an "ought-to-be," in contrast to the "is." It is the blueprint of an order of life that does not exist. There are not wanting interpreters of early American faith who read back into that time this idea of the present. Parrington writes that "it was to set up a kingdom of God on earth that the Puritan leaders came to America; and the phrase should enlighten us concerning their deeper purpose." How it should enlighten us he suggests in the same essay when he says: "The more one reads in the literature of early New England the more one feels oneself in the company of men who were led by visions, and fed upon utopian dreams. It was a day and world of idealists." This is a fairer picture than the usual portrait of the dour Puritan legalist, yet it seems almost as far from being a faithful representation. Utopianism is also ascribed to the non-Puritan colonists. How often has not the "holy experiment" of William Penn been described as a venture similar in character to the New Harmonies, the Oneida communities, the Brook Farms and Amanas of a later, more romantic day?

Doubtless there is some virtue in this idealistic interpretation of the early American kingdom of God. The Protestants of the seventeenth century lived between two revolutions; they looked back to the revolutionary revelation of God in Christ and they looked forward to his full unveiling, to the ultimate redemption which faith promised them. Yet one who follows Parring-

From H. Richard Niebuhr, *The Kingdom of God in America* (New York, 1935), pp. 45–58. Copyright 1935 by H. Richard Niebuhr. Reprinted by permission of Harper & Row, Publishers, Inc.

ton's advice and goes to the pages of Bradford, Robinson, John Cotton, Hooker, Winthrop, William Penn, or to their teachers and predecessors, to Calvin, Ames, Wollebius, Fox, Barclay, Pennington, seeking there the utopian note of nineteenth century romanticism or twentieth century idealism, is likely to be disappointed. When the idealistic note occurs it is a grace note, or it is sounded by some minor player in the orchestra, such as the author of *Wonder Working Providence of Sions Saviour in New England.*

The strain carried by the first violins is realistic rather than idealistic. The leaders do not speak so much of high-flown plans as of grim necessities. It is instructive to pay attention to the reasons which they give for migration to America. Bradford writes that the Pilgrims began "to incline to this conclusion, of removall to some other place . . . not out of any newfangledness, or other such like giddie humor, by which men are often times transported to their great hurt and danger but for sundrie weightie and solid reasons." These reasons he lists as, first, "the hardnes of the place and countrie," i.e., Holland; second, the danger that old age making their lot too hard to bear, would scatter or destroy the flock; third, the hard labor to which the children were subjected and the temptations to which they were exposed; and "lastly (and which was not least), a great hope and inward zeal they had, of laying some good foundation, or at least to make some way therunto, for the propogating and advancing the gospell of the kingdom of Christ in those remote parts of the world; yea, though they should be but even as stepping stones unto others for the performing of so great a work." John Winthrop's *Conclusions for the Plantation of New England* exhibits the same strain of sober thoughtfulness with no nearer approach to the utopian idea than is suggested by the hope that the conversion of the Indians may

"help on the cominge in of fulnesse of the Gentiles," and by the further possibility that the Lord may have "some great worke in hand whiche he hath revealed to his prophets among us." In even less enthusiastic fashion John Cotton discovers *God's Promise to his Plantations* not in visions granted to them or in the fulfillment of "an American dream" but in his "designment of a place for his people," by "espieing out" or discovering the land, carrying them along to it, so that they plainly see his providence, making room for them to dwell there. Among the reasons which warrant removal to such a place there are again "solid and weightie" considerations, such as the "gaining of knowledge," "for merchandize and gaine-sake," "to plant a Colony," escape from burdens and misery, as well as the "liberty of the ordinances" and the flight from corruption and persecution. To be sure, Cotton entertains a hope, like Bradford's, that a people rooted in Christ will bring forth fruits of righteousness, but this hope is far removed from the idealistic utopianism of modern kingdoms of God. One wonders whether William Penn, if he had had foreknowledge of the future, would have allowed the phrase "holy experiment" to slip from his pen. It lies buried amid reflections as sober, practical and contemporary as those of Bradford and Cotton. If these men were not solid burghers, little capitalists who wanted to make the world safe for property, neither were they dreamers who had fed on honeydew and drunk the milk of paradise.

Seventeenth century Protestants could not be utopians or idealists in the popular sense of the words, for they did not share the fundamental presuppositions of utopianism—the beliefs that human ills are due to bad institutions, that a fresh start with good institutions will result in a perfect commonwealth, and that human reason is sufficiently wise, or human will sufficiently selfless, to make the erection of a perfect society possible. They were for the most part thoroughly convinced that mankind had somehow been corrupted; they knew that the order of glory had not yet been established; they were pilgrims all who did not expect to be satisfied in the time of their pilgrimage.

While many writers are ready to concede that this is true of Pilgrims and Puritans they like to ascribe to Roger Williams and the Quakers a more this-worldly attitude. Yet Williams' devotional meditations and letters bear witness to his longing for a nonterrestrial blessedness and to a gentle cynicism with which he observed the working out of human plans, his own included. He wrote:

Gods children, as travailers on the Land, as Passengers in a ship, must use this world and all comforts of it, with dead and weaned and mortified affections, as if they used them not. . . . O let us therefor beg grace from Heaven, that we may use earthly comforts as a stool or ladder to help us upward to heavenly comforts, profits, pleasures, which are only true, and lasting, even eternall in God himself, when these Heavens, and earth are gone.

As for the coming kingdom, it was darkness rather than light, for "with what horrours and terrours shall these Heavens and Earth passe away." "It must be so in this world's sea," he wrote to Winthrop, *"sicut fluctus fluctum sic luctus luctum sequitur.* And every day hath his sufficiency or fullness of evil to all the children of the first sinful man." Such expressions abound in his letters.

William Penn's expectations of Pennsylvania were high and his disappointment was keen, but not so keen as it would have been had he not known with Barclay that "all Adam's posterity, or mankind . . . is fallen, degenerated and dead, deprived of the sensation or feeling of this inward testimony or seed of God, and is subject unto the power, nature, and seed of the Serpent" —or with Pennington that "man is a captive, his understanding captive, his will captive, all his affections and nature in captivity." Whatever quarrels there might be about the theological definition of human depravity, the conviction of its reality was a common one.

These early American Protestants believed in the kingdom of God, but it was not a society of peace and concord to be established by men of good will; it was rather the living reality of God's present rule, not only in human spirits but also in the world of nature and of human history. His kingdom was not an ideal dependent for its realization on human effort; men and their efforts were dependent upon it; loyalty to it and obedience to its laws were the conditions of their temporal and eternal welfare. "If we would know how the Puritan felt," wrote Peter Bayne—and he might well have added, if we would know how separatists and Quakers felt—"we must resolutely divest our minds of all ideas relating to the divine Being, derived from the habit acquired by men in these last ages of sitting in judgment on the character of God and discussing the quality of scriptural ethics. The Puritans had not risen or sunk to that tender French conception of the Almighty as *'le bon Dieu.'"* Neither had they risen or sunk to the spiritualistic idea of the kind heavenly Father which their descendants often proclaimed as the necessary corollary of the ideal of human brotherhood. They did not begin with an idea of God made up out of the most amiable human characteristics, proceeding then to inquire whether a corresponding being existed; they began rather with that last being which crowns with destruction the life which proceeds from it. This being they had come to trust and to worship because of its self-revelation in Jesus Christ.

The Savoy Declaration, like the Westminster Confession which it largely repeated, is not so much a compendium of theological definitions as a mighty assertion of conviction. Its affirmation of God's sovereignty sounds like a grand *Te Deum:*

There is but one onely living and true God; who is infinite in Being and Perfection, a most pure Spirit, invisible without body, parts or passions, immutable, immense, incomprehensible, almighty, most wise, most holy, most free, most absolute, working all things according to the Counsel of his own immutable and most righteous Will, for his own Glory, most loving, gracious, merciful, long-suffering, abundant in goodness and truth, forgiving iniquity, transgression and sin, the rewarder of them that diligently seek him; and withal most just and terrible in his Judgment, hating all sin, and who will by no means clear the guilty. . . . He is the alone Fountain of all Being; of whom, through whom and to whom are all things; and hath most Soveraign dominion over them, to do by them, for them and upon them, whatsoever himself pleaseth. . . . To him is due from Angels and men, and every other Creature, whatsoever Worship, Service or Obedience, as Creatures they owe unto the Creator, and whatever he is further pleased to require of them.

If we want to know what the Puritan meant by the kingdom of God we must study that considered statement of his faith or, turning to his English cousin, let a Baxter tell us that "the World is a Kingdom whereof God is the King . . . an absolute Monarchy . . . by the title of Creation. . . . God is the end as well as the beginning of the divine monarchy of the world" and "all men as men are the subjects of God's kingdom, as to Obligations and Duty, and God will not ask the consent of any man to be so obliged." In the refrain of Hooker's *Survey of the Summe of Church Discipline* and of Cotton's *Abstract of the Laws of New England* the faith is summarized: "The Lord is our King; The Lord is our Lawgiver; He will save us."

Quakers and separatists did not differ from other English Protestants in their confession of the rule of God. Their more mystical approach led them to think of him as first of all the Lord of conscience and the inner life, yet they presupposed his dominion over all things. "If you build upon anything," Howgill wrote, "or have confidence in anything which stands in time and is on this side eternity and the Being of

beings, your foundation will be swept away, and night will come upon you, and all your gathered-in things and taken-on and imitated will all fail you." George Fox's *Journal*, like Augustine's *Confessions*, is a great affirmation of faith in the kingdom of God. "Blessed forever be the name of the Lord, and everlastingly honored, and over all exalted and magnified be the arm of his glorious power, by which he hath wrought gloriously; let the honor and praise of all his works be ascribed to him alone."

No more orthodox believer confessed the living, sovereign power of God more clearly than did Isaac Pennington:

The Lord God of heaven and earth, of glory, of majesty, of everlasting power, victory and dominion over all, who made both heaven and earth, and hath the command of all things therein, he disposeth of nations, of governments, of earthly powers according to his pleasure, and who may say unto him, what dost thou? Who may implead him for making a rich nation poor, a strong nation weak, or for bringing down the high and mighty, the strong, stout, honorable and noble in a nation, and exalting the poor, the mean, the persecuted? And if he turn his hand again and lay them flat whom he had lifted up, who can withstand him, or who can contradict him? . . . The Lord God taketh not pleasure in overturning of nations, or in breaking in pieces the power thereof: yet if they will by no means hearken, but harden their hearts, and stand in the way of his counsel and design, he cannot spare them. . . . Therefore stand not in battle against him, but bow before him, ye great ones of the earth!

How contemporaneous this kingdom of God was in the Quaker's conception, and how relevant to political affairs, his admonitions to Parliament, to Oliver Cromwell and to sundry magistrates adequately show.

Roger Williams was less deeply affected by the sense of God's dynamic character, more drawn to the vision of divine beauty, yet it is apparent that back of his protests against the compromises of Massachusetts Bay Puritans stood his firm conviction of the sovereignty of God and of the ineluctability of his rule. Persecution is contrary to that rule and will bring destruction. "Oh! how likely is the jealous Jehovah, the consuming fire, to end these present slaughters of the holy witnesses in a greater slaughter!" Doubtless these men all prayed, "Thy kingdom come, thy will be done on earth as it is in heaven" but with even greater fervor they confessed, "Thine is the kingdom and the power and the glory forever and ever."

If the kingdom of God was not utopia neither was it administration by means of special miracles of the sort in which the authors of *Wonder-Working Providences* and *Magnalia Christi Americana* took especial delight. The God of Protestant faith was not the First Cause of a later Deism, but neither was he the meddling deity of eighteenth century supernaturalism. His relation to nature was intimate and close. Nature, as a recent writer has put it, was like a glove upon his hand. Nothing happened which was not in relation to him and was not therefore a meet occasion for penitence or praise. Yet he appeared in ordinary rather than in special events. His rule was manifested, as it had been for Jesus, in the rain which fell on just and unjust, in the sun which shone on evil and good, in storms by sea and drought by land, rather than in the miraculous happenings which sanctimonious piety, adulterated with supersistion, loved to relate and embellish. The Protestants saw the law of God in the immutable ways, in the actual pattern of reality to which revelation had given the key and which reason, following upon revelation, could discern. The will of God was not unnatural in the sense that it was imposed upon a stubborn and refractory nature from without by spirit warring against flesh; it might be called supernatural, if that term implies the presence of power and purpose behind or beyond as well as within natural events. The early Protestant idea of the sovereignty was at least as closely akin to Sir Isaac Newton's conceptions of nature as it was to those of

miracle-bound supernaturalists. Yet to interpret it by sole reference to either one of the set of ideas which developed from it in the later, mechanically minded time is to misunderstand it thoroughly.

This kingdom of God was not something to be built or to be established nor something that came into the world from without; it was rather the rule which, having been established from eternity, needed to be obeyed despite the rebellion against it which flourished in the world. It may be likened to the rule of a universal Caesar against whom ignorant tribes had made vain rebellion, deluding themselves with the belief that his power was remote or that it was inimical to them. The Puritans, Pilgrims, Quakers, with their associates, were first of all loyalists. They were loyal, in Chesterton's phrase, to the "flag of the world"; they were convinced that this flag represented power and law as well as benevolence in which men could trust when they had lost confidence in their own good will and in that of their ecclesiastical and political overlords. To think of them as primarily protesters and rebels is to regard them from a point of view foreign to their own. The first thing in their minds was positive. They were nonconformists, dissenters, protesters, independents, only because they desired to be loyal to the government of God, and in that positive allegiance they were united, however much their unity was obscured for later times by their party quarrels.

We shall do well, therefore, when we look upon them, whether in England or America, to heed Carlyle's warning:

By no means to credit the widespread report that these seventeenth century Puritans were superstitious, crackbrained persons, given up to enthusiasm, the most part of them, . . . the minor part being cunning men who knew how to assume the dialect of the others and thereby as skillful "Machiavels" to dupe them. . . . This is a widespread report but an untrue one. . . . He will be wise to believe these Puritans do mean what they say, and to try unimpeded to discover what it is; gradually a very stupendous phenomenon may rise on his astonished eye, a practical world based on a belief in God.

The practical world based on belief in God seems rather impractical when attention is directed to the confusion which appeared in early American efforts at Protestant construction. The strife of parties, the divisions and persecutions connected with the founding of the New England and the Quaker colonies were an American parallel to the conflict which marked the constructive efforts of Protestantism in England and on the European continent. There was uncertainty here about the organization of the state, about the structure of the church, about the relations of church and state, and about the extent to which loyalty to the kingdom of God was compatible with concern for the temporal and passing order. No such simple principles as those which guided the constructive work of eighteenth century humanism seem to have been followed by the theocentric architects of the new social life. If we would understand their deeds and sayings we are required, it appears, to refer to private experiences, personal prejudices and interests, and to the human penchant for inventing abstract reasons to justify the inconsistencies of conduct. No logical, only a psychological or sociological description of the meaning of divine sovereignty for constructive Protestantism in America seems possible.

But the confusion and strife so apparent upon the surface were borne upon an underlying unity, nor were they really more obvious than similar appearances of conflict in the time of humanistic construction. A logical order in which divine sovereignty was the first principle runs through the disorder, and the conflict was at least as much an affair of reason as of emotion and interest. That the latter played their inevitable role the Protestants were as ready to concede as their critics have been to urge, for they knew the human mind to be darkened; they did not except themselves from that universal rule whereby all men are liars; their lips, they confessed, were "uncircumcised." Nevertheless their reason sought its way amid pitfalls and temptations, looking ever again to its first principle lest it be lost completely.

Perry Miller

10. PURITAN STATE AND PURITAN SOCIETY

The two volumes of *The New England Mind* were Professor Miller's major studies of American puritanism. This selection is taken from a collection of separate essays on the subject which he entitled *Errand into the Wilderness*.

The Puritan theory of the state began with the hypothesis of original sin. Had Adam transmitted undiminished to his descendants the image of God in which he had been created, no government would ever have been necessary among men; they would all then have done justice to each other without the supervision of a judge, they would have respected each other's rights without the intervention of a policeman. But the Bible said—and experience proved—that since the Fall, without the policeman, the judge, the jail, the law, and the magistrate, men will rob, murder, and fight among themselves; without a coercive state to restrain evil impulses and administer punishments, no life will be safe, no property secure, no honor observed. Therefore, upon Adam's apostasy, God Himself instituted governments among men. He left the particular form to be determined by circumstance—this was one important human art on which the Puritans said the Bible was *not* an absolute and imperious lawgiver—but He enacted that all men should be under some sort of corporate rule, that they should all submit to the sway of their superiors, that no man should live apart from his fellows, that the government should have full power to enforce obedience and to inflict every punishment that the crimes of men deserved.

There was, it is true, a strong element of individualism in the Puritan creed; every man had to work out his own salvation, each soul had to face his maker alone. But at the same time, the Puritan philosophy demanded that in society all men, at least all regenerate men, be marshaled into one united array. The lone horseman, the single trapper, the solitary hunter was not a figure of the Puritan frontier; Puritans moved in groups and towns, settled in whole communities, and maintained firm government over all units. Neither were the individualistic business man, the shopkeeper who seized every opportunity to enlarge his profits, the speculator who contrived to gain wealth at the expense of his fellows, neither were these typical figures of the original Puritan society. Puritan opinion was at the opposite pole from Jefferson's feeling that the best government governs as little as possible. The theorists of New England thought of society as a unit, bound together by inviolable ties; they thought of it not as an aggregation of individuals but as an organism, functioning for a definite

purpose, with all parts subordinate to the whole, all members contributing a definite share, every person occupying a particular status. "Society in all sorts of humane affaires is better then Solitariness," said John Cotton. The society of early New England was decidedly "regimented." Puritans did not think that the state was merely an umpire, standing on the side lines of a contest, limited to checking egregious fouls but otherwise allowing men free play according to their abilities and the breaks of the game. They would have expected *laissez faire* to result in a reign of rapine and horror. The state to them was an active instrument of leadership, discipline, and, wherever necessary, of coercion; it legislated over any or all aspects of human behavior, it not merely regulated misconduct but undertook to inspire and direct all conduct. The commanders were not to trim their policies by the desires of the people, but to drive ahead upon the predetermined course; the people were all to turn out as they were ordered, and together they were to crowd sail to the full capacity of the vessel. The officers were above the common men, as the quarter-deck is above the forecastle. There was no idea of the equality of all men. There was no questioning that men who would not serve the purposes of the society should be whipped into line. The objectives were clear and unmistakable; any one's disinclination to dedicate himself to them was obviously so much recalcitrancy and depravity. The government of Massachusetts, and of Connecticut as well, was a dictatorship, and never pretended to be anything else; it was a dictatorship, not of a single tyrant, or of an economic class, or of a political faction, but of the holy and regenerate. Those who did not hold with the ideals entertained by the righteous, or who believed God had preached other principles, or who desired that in religious belief, morality, and ecclesiastical preferences all men should be left at liberty to do as they wished—such persons had every liberty, as Nathaniel Ward said, to stay away from New England. If they did come, they were expected to keep their opinions to themselves; if they discussed them in public or attempted to act upon them, they were exiled; if they persisted in returning, they were cast out again; if they still came back, as did four Quakers, they were hanged on Boston Common. And from the Puritan point of view, it was good riddance.

These views of the nature and function of the state were not peculiar to the Puritans of New England; they were the heritage of the past, the ideals, if not always the actuality, of the previous centuries. That government was established by God in order to save depraved men from their own depravity had been orthodox Christian teaching for centuries; that men should be arranged in serried ranks, inferiors obeying superiors, was the essence of feudalism; that men should live a social life, that profit-making should be restrained within the limits of the "just price," that the welfare of the whole took precedence over any individual advantage, was the doctrine of the medieval church, and of the Church of England in the early seventeenth century. Furthermore, in addition to these general principles, there were two or three more doctrines in the New England philosophy which also were common to the age and the background: all the world at that moment believed with them that the church was to be maintained and protected by the civil authority, and a certain part of the world was contending that government must be limited by fundamental law and that it takes its origin from the consent of the people.

Every respectable state in the Western world assumed that it could allow only one church to exist within its borders, that every citizen should be compelled to attend it and conform to its requirements, and that all inhabitants should pay taxes for its support. When the Puritans came to New En-

gland the idea had not yet dawned that a government could safely permit several creeds to exist side by side within the confines of a single nation. They had not been fighting in England for any milk-and-water toleration, and had they been offered such religious freedom as dissenters now enjoy in Great Britain they would have scorned to accept the terms. Only a hypocrite, a person who did not really believe what he professed, would be content to practice his religion under those conditions. The Puritans were assured that they alone knew the exact truth, as it was contained in the written word of God, and they were fighting to enthrone it in England and to extirpate utterly and mercilessly all other pretended versions of Christianity. When they could not succeed at home, they came to America, where they could establish a society in which the one and only truth should reign forever. There is nothing so idle as to praise the Puritans for being in any sense conscious or deliberate pioneers of religious liberty—unless, indeed, it is still more idle to berate them because in America they persecuted dissenters for their beliefs after themselves had undergone persecution for differing with the bishops. To allow no dissent from the truth was exactly the reason they had come to America. They maintained here precisely what they had maintained in England, and if they exiled, fined, jailed, whipped, or hanged those who disagreed with them in New England, they would have done the same thing in England could they have secured the power. It is almost pathetic to trace the puzzlement of New England leaders at the end of the seventeenth century, when the idea of toleration was becoming more and more respectable in European thought. They could hardly understand what was happening in the world, and they could not for a long time be persuaded that they had any reason to be ashamed of their record of so many Quakers whipped, blasphemers punished by the amputation of ears, Antinomians exiled, Anabaptists fined, or witches executed. By all the lights which had prevailed in Europe at the time the Puritans had left, these were achievements to which any government could point with pride. In 1681 a congregation of Anabaptists, who led a stormy and precarious existence for several years in Charlestown, published an attack upon the government of Massachusetts Bay; they justified themselves by appealing to the example of the first settlers, claiming that like themselves the founders had been nonconformists and had fled to New England to establish a refuge for persecuted consciences. When Samuel Willard, minister of the Third Church in Boston, read this, he could hardly believe his eyes; he hastened to assure the authors that they did not know what they were talking about:

> I perceive they are mistaken in the design of our first Planters, whose business was not Toleration; but were professed Enemies of it, and could leave the World professing they *died no Libertines*. Their business was to settle, and (as much as in them lay) secure Religion to Posterity, according to that way which they believed was of God.

For the pamphlet in which Willard penned these lines Increase Mather wrote an approving preface. Forty years later, he and his son Cotton participated in the ordination of a Baptist minister in Boston, and he then preached on the need for harmony between differing sects. But by that time much water had gone under the bridge, the old charter had been revoked, there was danger that the Church of England might be made the established church of the colonies, theology had come to be of less importance in men's minds than morality, the tone of the eighteenth century was beginning to influence opinion — even in Boston. Increase was old and weary. Puritanism, in the true sense of the word, was dead.

Of course, the whole Puritan philosophy of church and state rested upon the as-

sumption that the Word of God was clear and explicit, that the divines had interpreted it correctly, and that no one who was not either a knave or a fool could deny their demonstrations. *Ergo,* it seemed plain, those who did deny them should be punished for being obstinate. John Cotton said that offenders should not be disciplined for their wrong opinions, but for persisting in them; he said that Roger Williams was turned out of Massachusetts not for his conscience but for sinning against his own conscience. Roger Williams and John Cotton debated the question of "persecution" through several hundred pages; after they had finished, I think it is very doubtful whether Cotton had even begun to see his adversary's point. And still today it is hard to make clear the exact grounds upon which Roger Williams became the great apostle of religious liberty. Williams was not, like Thomas Jefferson, a man to whom theology and divine grace had become stuff and nonsense; on the contrary he was pious with a fervor and passion that went beyond most of his contemporaries. So exalted was his conception of the spiritual life that he could not bear to have it polluted with earthly considerations. He did not believe that any man could determine the precise intention of Scripture with such dreadful certainty as the New England clergy claimed to possess. Furthermore, it seemed to him that even if their version were true, submission to truth itself was worth nothing at all when forced upon men by the sword. Williams evolved from an orthodox Puritan into the champion of religious liberty because he came to see spiritual truth as so rare, so elevated, so supernal a loveliness that it could not be chained to a worldly establishment and a vested interest. He was a libertarian because he contemned the world, and he wanted to separate church and state so that the church would not be contaminated by the state; Thomas Jefferson loved the world and was dubious about the spirit, and he sought to separate church and state so that the state would not be contaminated by the church. But John Cotton believed that the state and church were partners in furthering the cause of truth; he knew that the truth was clear, definite, reasonable, and undeniable; he expected all good men to live by it voluntarily, and he was sure that all men who did not do so were obviously bad men. Bad men were criminals, whether their offense was theft or a belief in the "inner light," and they should be punished. Moses and Aaron, the priest and the statesman, were equally the vice-regents of God, and the notion that one could contaminate the other was utter insanity.

The two other ideas derived from the background of the age, rule by fundamental law and the social compact, were also special tenets of English Puritanism. For three decades before the settlement of Massachusetts the Puritan party in England had been working hand in glove with the Parliament against the King. The absolutist Stuarts were allied with the bishops, and the Puritan agitator and the Parliamentary leader made common cause against them both. As a result of this combination, the Puritan theorists had taken over the essentials of the Parliamentary conception of society, the contention that the power of the ruler should be exercised in accordance with established fundamental law, and that the government should owe its existence to a compact of the governed. Because these ideas were strategically invaluable in England, they became ingrained in the Puritan consciousness; they were carried to the New England wilderness and were preached from every pulpit in the land.

The Puritans did not see any conflict between them and their religious intentions. In New England the fundamental law was the Bible. The magistrates were to have full power to rule men for the specific purposes to which the society was dedicated; but they as well as their subordinates were tied to the specific purposes, and could not go beyond the prescribed limits. The Bible was clear and definite on the form of the church, on the code of punishments for crimes, on the general purposes of social existence; its specifications were binding on all, magistrates, ministers, and citizens. Consequently, the Puritans did not find it difficult to conclude that in those matters upon which the Bible left men free to follow their own discretion, the society itself should establish basic rules. The New England leaders and the people frequently disagreed about what these rules were, or how detailed they should be made, but neither side ever doubted that the community must abide by whatever laws had been enacted, either by God or by the state. The government of New England was, as I have said, a dictatorship, but the dictators were not absolute and irresponsible. John Cotton was the clerical spokesman for the Massachusetts rulers, but he stoutly demanded "that all power that is on earth be limited."

The belief that government originated in the consent of the governed was equally congenial to the Puritan creed. The theology is often enough described as deterministic, because it held that men were predestined to Heaven or Hell; but we are always in danger of forgetting that the life of the Puritan was completely voluntaristic. The natural man was indeed bound in slavery to sin and unable to make exertions toward his own salvation; but the man into whose soul grace had been infused was liberated from that bondage and made free to undertake the responsibilities and obligations of virtue and decency. The holy society was erected upon the belief that the right sort of men could of their own free will and choice carry through the creation and administration of the right sort of community. The churches of New England were made up of "saints," who came into the church because they wanted membership, not because they were born in it, or were forced into it, or joined because of policy and convention. Though every resident was obliged to attend and to pay taxes for the support of the churches, no one became an actual member who did not signify his strong desire to be one. The saints were expected to act positively because they had in them a spirit of God that made them capable of every exertion. No doubt the Puritans maintained that government originated in the consent of the people because that theory was an implement for chastening the absolutism of the Stuarts; but they maintained it also because they did not believe that any society, civil or ecclesiastical, into which men did not enter of themselves was worthy of the name.

Consequently, the social theory of Puritanism, based upon the law of God, was posited also upon the voluntary submission of the citizens. As men exist in nature, said Thomas Hooker, no one person has any power over another; "there must of necessity be a mutuall ingagement, each of the other, by their free consent, before by any rule of God they have any right or power, or can exercise either, each towards the other." This truth appears, he argues, from all relations among men, that of husband and wife, master and servant; there must be a compact drawn up and sealed between them.

From *mutuall acts* of consenting and ingaging each of other, there is an impression of *ingagement* results, as a *relative bond*, betwixt the contractours and confederatours, wherein the *formalis ratio*, or *specificall nature* of the covenant lieth, in all the former instances especially *that of corporations*. So that however it is true, the rule bindes such to the duties of their places and relations, yet it is certain, it requires that they should *first freely ingage* themselves in such covenants, and *then* be carefull to fullfill such duties. A man is allowed freely to make choice of his wife, and she of her husband, before they need or should perform the duties of husband and wife one towards another.

The rules and regulations of society, the objectives and the duties, are erected by God; but in a healthy state the citizens must first agree to abide by those regula-

tions, must first create the society by willing consent and active participation.

These ideas, of a uniform church supported by the civil authority, of rule by explicit law, of the derivation of the state from the consent of the people, were transported to the wilderness because they were the stock ideas of the time and place. What the New England Puritans added of their own was the unique fashion in which they combined them into one coherent and rounded theory. . . .

The theory furnishes an excellent illustration of the intellectual ideal toward which all Puritan thought aspired; in the realm of government as of nature, the Puritan thinker strove to harmonize the determination of God with the exertion of men, the edicts of revelation with the counsels of reason and experience. On one side, this account exhibits the creation of society as flowing from the promptings and coaction of God; on the other side it attributes the origination to the teachings of nature and necessity. The social compact may be engineered by God, but it is also an eminently reasonable method of bringing a state into being. Delimitation of the ruler's power by basic law may be a divine ordinance to restrain the innate sinfulness of men, but it is also a very natural device to avoid oppression and despotism; the constitution may be promulgated to men from on high, but it is in fact very much the sort which, had they been left to their own devices, they might have contrived in the interests of efficiency and practicality. Men might conceivably have come upon the erection of governments through explicit compacts, in which they incorporated certain inviolable regulations and a guarantee of rights, quite as much by their own intelligence as by divine instruction. As always in Puritan thought, there was no intention to discredit either source, but rather to integrate the divine and the natural, revelation and reason, into a single inspiration. "Power of Civil Rule, by men orderly chosen, is Gods Ordinance," said John Davenport, even if "It is from the Light and Law of Nature," because "the Law of Nature is God's Law." The Puritan state was thus from one point of view purely and simply a "theocracy"; God was the sovereign; His fiats were law and His wishes took precedence over all other considerations; the magistrates and ministers were His viceroys. But from another point of view, the Puritan state was built upon reason and the law of nature; it was set up by the covenant of the people, the scope of its power was determined by the compact, and the magistrates and ministers were the commissioned servants of the people.

II. Ethnic Diversity and Evangelical Differentiation (1700-1760)

The "language of establishment" took for granted that there was a uniformity of religious life within society. Even as this "language" continued to be used in the eighteenth-century colonies, however, developments were taking place which would render it wholly obsolete. The religious life of the colonies—never completely uniform separately, let alone collectively—was becoming so pluralized that an "establishment of religion" could mean little more than public financial support and preference for one "denomination" of Christians. This was a far cry from that coordination and interpenetration of spiritual and temporal concerns which had been the earlier virtually universal ideal and which had been substantially realized particularly in several of the early New England settlements. The critical issue in this development was not so much a creedal latitudinarianism or liberalism of spirit. Nor was it a worldliness stimulated by commercial endeavors. Such attitudes were perfectly compatible with personal indifference toward "establishments" and support of them for "the public good." What rendered the older language anachronistic was the differentiation of religious life itself. Thus numerous religious groups, all of which considered themselves autonomous spiritually, were placed beside each other and together—rather than independently—they constituted the common life. This differentiation resulted in conviction confronting belief and zeal challenging prejudice. As a consequence, the colonies were set on a road to disestablishment although that destination was not at all clear in the beginning. Broadly speaking a distinction must be drawn between two sources which gave rise to this pluralization of religious life. One source was rooted in the ethnic diversity which soon became a reality in the colonies. The second source was in the evangelical energies which sought to transform the existing churches but which more often led to the formation of new ones. Frequently these "causes" acted in the same situation and contributed to the same results, but for purposes of analysis it is necessary to distinguish them.

It is no part of this study to offer a systematic consideration of how immigration has influenced American religious ideas and practices. It is appropriate to observe, however, that early in the eighteenth century the colonies, most of which had been fundamentally English in composition, began to receive an increasingly diverse population. Thus the Scots started to immigrate after the Act of Union in 1708. The Ulstermen began to arrive about 1717. "German" or

"Dutch" groups of Germans and Swiss came between 1720 and 1740. From the point of view of the religious life of the colonies this immigration introduced no form of Protestantism radically different from those already on the scene. But while the earlier pattern had been one—especially in the northern and southern colonies—of relative religious homogeneity, the new settlers juxtaposed their ethnically defined religious patterns beside the existing ones. Thus the Scottish Presbyterian in Carolina was "foreign" no less than the Irish Presbyterian was in New England. And Pennsylvania took into itself not only the calvinistic Ulstermen but also such exotic continental groups as the Moravians and the Mennonites. This pattern of ethnic-religious diversification of American life became even more significant in the nineteenth century and its effects continue to be important in mid-twentieth century American life. Nevertheless the early role of this factor in creating conditions making necessary disestablishment requires attention in the present context.

If the colonies were receiving a population which diversified their religious life, Protestant evangelicalism within the colonies was also working upon the population in such a way as to lead to that same end. The "Great Awakening" is the name usually given to the religious turmoil which troubled the east coast during the second quarter of the eighteenth century. Arising out of a desire to intensify the authentic religious life of the faithful, it broke out in New Jersey, went through a New England phase, and disturbed the southern colonies also. George Whitefield, the English evangelist, preached to great throngs up and down the settlements while lesser figures itinerated on local circuits. Where old churches could not or would not be renewed, new ones were formed. These new churches frequently represented classes of the population which had been effectively excluded from the original churches. No less than the ethnic-based churches "imported" from Europe, this domestic development made the ideal of religious homogeneity wholly irrelevant to the American scene. Accordingly "religious establishment" could only be an empty phrase signifying little more than financial support and civic preference for a particular institution. The language of establishment might still be used but its meaning had shifted.

1. THE CONNECTICUT ESTABLISHMENT AND PROVISION FOR DISSENT (1708)

Connecticut, along with Massachusetts Bay, took for granted the desirability of a rigorous and exclusive church establishment. Connecticut was able to realize this pattern more successfully, however, due chiefly to a greater insularity. The Connecticut system was incorporated in the Saybrook Platform which was adopted in 1708.[1] Contemporaneously with this legislation of an establishment, nevertheless, external circumstances made it necessary to recognize the presence of "dissenters" and to grant them the appearance if not a measure of toleration. Quakers and members of the Church of England, it was correctly feared, might influence the Crown to proceed with the intended consolidation of the New England Colonies under a governor of his appointment. England itself had recognized dissenters with its Toleration Act of 1689. Thus the dissenters' act and the related provision which qualified the Saybrook Platform were loopholes for the Baptist or Anglican who would submit to double-taxation. The Quaker—who would not submit to the oath of allegiance—was not really helped at all.

[1] Cf. Williston Walker, *The Creeds and Platforms of Congregationalism* (New York, 1893; Boston, 1960).

And it is further enacted, for the ease of such as soberly dissent from the way of worship and ministry established by the ancient laws of this government (and still continuing), That if any such persons shall at the county court of that county they belong to qualify themselves according to an act made in the first year of the late King William and Queen Mary, granting liberty of worshipping God in a way separate from that which is by law established, they shall enjoy the same liberty and priviledge in any place within this Colony, without any let, hindrance, and molestation whatsoever. Provided always that nothing herein shall be construed to the prejudice of the rights and privileges of the churches as by law established in this government, or to the excusing [of] any person from paying any such minister or town dues as are now or shall hereafter be due from them.

Edited to conform more nearly to current usage. The text is located in *The Public Records of the Colony of Connecticut*, Volume V (Hartford, 1870), p. 50. Enacted May 13, 1708. See also the legislative acceptance of the Saybrook proposals on September 9, 1708, *Ibid.*, p. 87.

2. THE CONFESSION OF FAITH OF THE CHRISTIANS CALLED MENNONITES

The Mennonites took their name from Menno Simons (d. 1561) who was an Anabaptist leader of the continental Reformation. His followers were incorrectly grouped with the revolutionaries and spiritualists by both Protestants and Catholics and all were severely persecuted. The Mennonites actually sought to recover primitive Christianity, taking the historical Jesus as the norm for their life. Accordingly they asked only to be left undisturbed, a radical request since it made religious uniformity impossible. Although chiefly from the Netherlands (which had granted a measure of toleration to them) the Mennonites who came to America in the eighteenth century were known as "Germans." In Pennsylvania they found a welcome respite from their harrassed life. In order to introduce themselves they published an English translation of their Confession of Faith along with an Appendix which includes the following passages about their view of government and magistrates. The selection discloses the spirit in which they sought to recover early Christianity while also indicating the diversity of population which outmoded religious establishments. A recent discussion of this group in its early years may be found in *The Anabaptist View of the Church* by Franklin H. Littell (Boston, 1952, 1958).

And now if some will conclude out of our doctrine and wrongfully judge us as if we cast off, dispised or set at nought the Office of the Magistrates, they may be pleased to know that we utterly deny such reproaches for we acknowledge it freely that [the office] is ordained by God, and therefore the Powers are called "The Ministers of God, and are ordained to punish the evil doers, and defend the just," according to the doctrine and testimony of Saint Paul. (Romans, Chapter 13)

And though we can find no exact rule or example in the New Testament, like as it is in the Old, after which that office should be served, or how the high and heavy worldly business should be ruled, [and though we] also cannot see that they are ruled according to the Godly commands of the Old Testament but in most places are ruled according to the Constitution or appointment of the Emperors, Kings, Lords and higher powers, their commands, laws and customs (which are diverse from one another), and yet it behoves and becomes a right and true Christian that he should be little and low in this World, and shun the greatness of the same, and keep himself like the lowly ones. And therefore we (as also because of the manifold encumberances which befall this office) think ourselves too low and find ourselves too weak to undertake the same or to rule the same. But yet we will declare herewith, and also at all times endeavor to show, that we hold it in great worth and honor as an ordinance of God, as it is written: "his work is worthy of praise and honor," or, as others translate it, "what He orders is honorable and glorious, &c." (Psalm 111) And [we] judge or account no body cursed in our hearts by reason of his office if he do walk upright in the true Christian religion and according to his duty.

Which may be taken . . . that we hold and acknowledge ourselves for conscience

"Published . . . in the Low-Dutch, and translated . . . into the English Language, 1725. (Philadelphia: . . . 1727)," Abridged and edited to conform more nearly to current usage from pp. 26–29, 35–39.

sake and duty towards God to honor them and [we] also herewith (as at other times we commonly do) very friendly and not less earnestly exhort all our fellow members . . . that they not only behave themselves with due respect to the powers, and give them all honor, but also as it becomes loyal and obedient subjects to assist them with all uprightness, truth and obedience according to the holy Gospel, and to follow their Christian calling and duty according to the doctrine of Paul as above mentioned, and to pay all required taxes, tolls, excises, and convoy charges truly and willingly without any deficiency.

This is that which our Lord and Teacher commands, "Render unto Caesar the things which are Caesar's," Matthew 22. And above that, that everyone, not only in all meetings or places of worship but also by all other opportunities both day and night, make mention of them in their ejaculations or hearty prayers to God. . . .

Thus we have thought it good to publish the here before-going Confession and also this appendix in the English Language and no longer to withhold [from] our English friends in their hearty desires. And if we find that this is welcome to them — that we Dutch learn to speak English . . . . — then we will hope that our powers (which are set by God over countries and nations) may take it in a Christian like consideration if it is not better for their countries and cities,

and also if it were not worthy of praise for their own persons, that they ruled and dealt with patience, meekness, and peaceableness with their subjects and inhabitants that are of another religion, and that they did not let themselves be moved by anybody to forcing of conscience nor hinder their subjects of their inward worship. . . .

When all this is seriously considered and weighed in the balance of God's holy Word, then we will hope and steadfastly believe that nobody will rule and deal otherwise with his subjects than he willingly would that he or his, living under the powers of another religion, should be dealt with and ruled, and to live according to that kingly command which teaches, "To do to another as we willingly would that [it] should be done to us."

And, Ah! if it might please all — who aforetime have been so zealous in these things — in time to come to deal lovingly with and patiently suffer their subjects which are of another religion, like as our eminent powers in this province do who protect and defend us, and therefore serve as an excellent example to all others to follow the same. And those that will be like them in the same shall also have the like praise and honor. They will give occasion to their subjects to bring their earnest prayers [for them] to the Lord. . . .

Soli Deo Gloria

3. GRIEVANCES AGAINST THE CONNECTICUT
ESTABLISHMENT (1751)

The following memorial addressed to the Connecticut Legislature by a separate Congregational Church at Preston, petitions for relief from the requirement that they support the stated ministry (the established Congregational Church) and that they accept the Saybrook Platform (the ideological establishment). In this regard the Connecticut pattern was probably the extreme case of an establishment seeking to preserve its prerogatives—it certainly should not be considered typical. But the plea for toleration was characteristic because such a development represented the only practicable solution to the colonial religious situation in the mid-eighteenth century. Toleration within the patterns of establishment was not sufficiently radical, however, to serve as the religious condition for a federal government—or, for that matter, for the constitutive states.

To the Honourable General Assembly of the Colony of Connecticut to be convened at New Haven In said Colony on the Second thirsday of October A. D. 1751 the Memorial of John Avery and others the Subscribers hereunto Humbly Shueth that your Memorialists live Some of us within the first, and some of us within the Second Eccleciastical Societys In the Town of Preston Some few within the Second Society In Groton and Some few within the South Society in Norwich and Some In the Second Society of Stonington, that we are that one of the Very Many Sects of Professors of Christianity that are Commonly Called Separates that we Have truly and Contientiously Desented and Separated from all the Churches and Religious Societyes within whose limits we live That we are Settled according to the Present Establishment of this Government, that our Habitations are Generally Compact none of us living more than 7 or 8 miles from the Place of our Public worship most of us within Two Miles, that the Number of families Is About forty and the Number of Souls about 300, of which there are more than fifty Church Members all belonging to our Communion and of our Profession that we Have at our own Cost Settled a Minister & built a Meet-

ing House for Divine worship & have long since been Imbodied Into Church Estate that Nevertheless we are Compelled to pay towards the Support of the Ministry & for the building of Meeting Houses In these Societies from which we have Respectively Sepperated and Desented as aforsesaid and for our Neglect to Make Payment of Such Rates we have Many of us been Imprisoned others have had their Estates Torn & sold to the almost ruining of some familyes wherefore we Intreat the attention of this Honnourable Assembly and Pray Your Honnours to Suffer us to Say that we always have & for the future most Chearfully Shall Contribute our Proportion towards the Support of Civil Government & we not only Prise & value but Humbly Claim and Challenge our Right In the Immunities of the Present Constitution.

Our Religion or Principles are no ways Subversive of Government and we are not only Inclining but Engaging to Support It—and there Is no Difference between us and other Members of the Community but what is Merely Ecclesiastical In which Respect also they Differ one from another & the whole Christian World no less.

Our Religious Sentiments and way of worship No ways affect the State.

From Leroy S. Blake, *The Separates* (Boston, 1902), pp. 118–121.

We are as Industrious In our business and as Punctual in our Contracts as If we were Anabaptists or Quakers and we Challenge to hold enjoy and Improve what Is our own by the Same Rules and Laws as all other Denominations of Christians Do.

And we Suppose there is (In the nature of things) no Reason we Should maintain & Support any Religion or way of worship but what we our Selves Embrace and Propose to receive the advantage of and that No body has right to Impede or Hinder us In that way of worship which in our Conscienses we think to be Right for us. In all matters Civil we are accountable to the State So in all Matters of worship we are accountable to him who Is the object of It. to whom alone we must stand or fall and on these Principles are founded all acts of Toleration. Your Memorialists therefore humbly Intreat the Interposition and Protection of this honnourable Assembly that your honnours would order and Grant that your Memorialists and all such as adhere to or shall be Joined & attend the Publick worship with them may for the future be Released and Exempted from Paying Taxes for the Building of Meetinghouses or for the Support of the ministry in any of the Societies from which we have Sepperated (within the compass of eight miles from the place of Publick worship or Such other Limmits as your honnours Shall See fit) or that your honnours would grant us the Same Ease and Liberty as by law is Provided for the Ease of Anabaptists and Quakers or otherwise Grant Such Relief as in your wisdom you Shall Judge Just and your Memorialists are Ready to Qualify themselves according to the act of Toleration.

And as In Duty Bound Ever Pray.

Dated the 10th Day of September A. D. 1751.

4. SAMUEL DAVIES ON BEHALF OF DISSENTERS IN VIRGINIA (1752)

Samuel Davies, who became fourth president of the College of New Jersey (Princeton) in 1759, was instrumental in organizing Presbyterianism in Virginia. His most significant contribution was to secure the right of dissent from the established Anglican Church under the English Act of Toleration. Through correspondence with Philip Doddridge — an English dissenting minister — Davies learned that the Bishop of London was concerned about dissenters in Virginia. He grasped the opportunity to address a long apology to the Bishop on behalf of his fellow colonists. The following excerpts are from that letter which was written from Hanover, Virginia during January, 1752. Although the Bishop for whom it was intended never saw it, the letter in this way failing to fulfill its intention, it does represent the theme of this chapter in a striking fashion. The ethnically-based religious complexity of the colonies was reinforced and compounded by the effects of evangelical faith which Davies equally embodied.

I hope, my lord, you will not suspect I have so much arrogance as to encounter your lordship as a disputant, if I presume to make some free and candid remarks . . . . My only design is to do justice to a misrepresented cause, which is the inalienable

The above are selected excerpts. The full text may be consulted in *Sketches of Virginia* by William Foote, Volume I, (Philadelphia, 1850), pp. 178 ff.

right of the meanest innocent; and as an impartial historical representation will be sufficient for this purpose, 'tis needless to tire your lordship with tedious argumentation.

The frontier counties of this colony, about an hundred miles west and southwest from Hanover, have been lately settled by people that chiefly came from Ireland originally, and immediately from the Northern colonies, who were educated Presbyterians, and had been under the care of the ministers belonging to the Synod of New York (of which I am a member) during their residence there. Their settling in Virginia has been many ways beneficial to it, which I am sure most of them would not have done, had they expected any restraint in the inoffensive exercise of their religion, according to their consciences. After their removal, they continued to petition the Synod of New York, and particularly the Presbytery of Newcastle, which was nearest to them, for ministers to be sent among them. But as the ministers of said Synod and Presbytery were few, and vastly disproportioned to the many congregations under their care, they could not provide these vacancies with settled pastors. . . . The only expedient in their power (was) to appoint some of their members to travel, alternately, into these destitute congregations, and officiate among them as long as would comport with their circumstances. It was this, my lord, that was the first occasion, as far as I can learn, of our being stigmatized *itinerant preachers.*

The dissenters here, my lord, are but sufficiently numerous to form two distinct organized congregations, or particular churches, and did they live contiguous, two meeting-houses would be sufficient for them, and neither they nor myself, would desire more. But they are so dispersed that they cannot convene for public worship, unless they have a considerable number of places licensed; and so few that they cannot form a particular organized church at each

place. There are seven meeting-houses licensed in five different counties. . . . But the extremes of my congregation lie eighty or ninety miles apart; and the dissenters under my care are scattered through six or seven different counties. . . . The counties here are large, generally forty or fifty miles in length, and about twenty or thirty miles in breadth; so that though they lived in one county, it might be impossible for them all to convene at one place; and much more when they are dispersed through so many. Though there are now seven places licensed, yet the nearest are twelve or fifteen miles apart; and many of the people have ten, fifteen, or twenty miles to the nearest, and thirty, forty, or sixty miles to the rest; nay, some of them have thirty or forty miles to the nearest. That this is an impartial representation of our circumstances, I dare appeal to all that know anything about them.

All the dissenters here depend entirely on me to officiate among them, as there is no other minister of their own denomination within two hundred miles, except when one of my brethren from the northern colonies is appointed to pay them a transient visit, for two or three Sabbaths, once in a year or two: and as I observed they cannot attend on my ministry at one or two places by reason of their distance; nor constitute a complete particular church at each place of meeting, by reason of the smallness of their number.

These things, my lord, being impartially considered, I dare submit it to your lordship,

Whether my itinerating in this manner in such circumstances be illegal? And whether, though I cannot live in five different counties at once, as your lordship observes, I may not lawfully officiate in them, or in as many as the peculiar circumstances of my congregation, . . . render necessary?

Whether contiguity of residence is necessary to entitle dissenters to the liberties granted by the Act of Toleration? Whether when they cannot convene at one place, they may not, according to the true intent and meaning of that Act, obtain as many houses licensed as will render public worship accessible to them all? And whether if this liberty be denied them, they can be said to be tolerated at all? i.e. Whether *dissenters are permitted to worship in their own way,*(which your lordship observes was the intent of the Act) who are prohibited from worshipping in their own way, unless they travel thirty, forty or fifty miles every Sunday?

Whether, when there are a few dissenting families in one county and a few in another, and they are not able to form a distinct congregation or particular church at each place, and yet all of them conjunctly are able to form one, though they cannot meet statedly at one place; whether, I say, they may not legally obtain sundry meeting-houses licensed, in these different counties, where their minister may divide his time according to the proportion of the people, and yet be looked upon as one organized church? And whether the minister of such a dispersed church, who alternately officiates at these sundry meeting-houses should on this account be branded as an itinerant?

Whether, when a number of dissenters, sufficient to constitute two distinct congregations, each of them able to maintain a minister, can obtain but one by reason of the scarcity of ministers, they may not legally share in the labours of that one, and have as many houses licensed for him to officiate in, as their distance renders necessary? And whether the minister of such an united congregation, though he divides his labours at seven different places, or more, if their conveniency requires it, be not as properly a *settled* minister as though he preached but at one place, to but one congregation?

I beg leave, my lord, farther to illustrate the case by a relation of a matter of fact, and a very possible supposition.

It very often happens in Virginia, that the parishes are twenty, thirty, forty, and sometimes fifty or sixty miles long, and proportionably broad; which is chiefly owing to this, that people are not so thick settled, as that the inhabitants in a small compass should be sufficient for a parish. The Legislature here has wisely made provision to remedy this inconveniency, by ordering sundry churches or chapels of ease to be erected in one parish, that one of them at least may be tolerably convenient to all the parishioners; and all these are under the care of one minister, who shares his labours at each place in proportion to the number of people there.

Now, I submit it to your lordship, whether there be not at least equal reason that a plurality of meeting-houses should be licensed for the use of the dissenters here, since they are more dispersed and fewer in number? . . . I submit it also to your lordship, whether there be not as little reason for representing me as an itinerant preacher, on account of my preaching at so many places for the conveniency of one congregation, as that the minister of a large parish, where there are sundry churches or chapels of ease, should be so called for preaching at these sundry places, for the convenience of one parish?

But I find I have been represented to your lordship as an uninvited intruder into these parts:

To justify me from this charge, my lord, it might be sufficient to observe, that the meeting-houses here were legally licensed before I preached in them, and that the licenses were petitioned for by the people,

But to give your lordship a just view of this matter, I shall present you with a brief narrative of the rise and increase of the dissenters in and about this county, and an account of the circumstances of my settling among them.

About the year 1743, upon the petition of the Presbyterians in the frontier counties of this colony, the Rev. Mr. Robinson, who now rests from his labours, was sent by order of Presbytery to officiate for some time among them. A little before this about four or five persons, heads of families, in Hanover, had dissented from the established church, not from any scruples about her ceremonial peculiarities, much less about her excellent Articles of Faith, but from a dislike of the doctrines generally delivered from the pulpit, as not savouring of experimental piety, nor suitably intermingled with the glorious peculiarities of the religion of Jesus. It does not concern me at present, my lord, to inquire or determine whether they had sufficient reason for their dislike. They concluded them sufficient; and they had a legal as well as natural right to follow their own judgment. These families were wont to meet in a private house on Sundays to hear some good books read, particularly Luther's; whose writings I can assure your lordship were the principal cause of their leaving the Church; which I hope is a presumption in their favour. After some time sundry others came to their society, and upon hearing these books, grew indifferent about going to church, and chose rather to frequent these societies for reading. At length the number became too great for a private house to contain them, and they agreed to build a meeting-house, which they accordingly did.

Thus far, my lord, they had proceeded before they had heard a dissenting minister at all. (Here again I appeal to all that know any thing of the matter to attest this account.) They had not the least thought at this time of assuming the denomination of Presbyterians, as they were wholly ignorant of that Church: but when they were called upon by the court to assign the reasons of their absenting themselves from church, and asked what denomination they professed themselves of, they declared themselves Lutherans, not in the usual sense of that denomination in Europe, but merely to intimate that they were of Luther's sentiments, particularly in the article of Justification.

Hence, my lord, it appears that neither I nor my brethren were the first instruments of their separation from the Church of England. And this leads me back to my narrative again.

While Mr. Robinson was preaching in the frontier counties, about an hundred miles from Hanover, the people here having received some information of his character and doctrines, sent him an invitation by one or two of their number to come and preach among them; which he complied with and preached four days successively to a mixed multitude; many being prompted to attend from curiosity. Tis true many after this joined with those that had formerly dissented; but their sole reason at first was, the prospect of being entertained with more profitable doctrines among the dissenters than they were wont to hear in the parish churches, and not because Mr. Robinson had poisoned them with bigoted prejudices against the established church. And permit me, my lord, to declare, . . . that I have been . . . the joyful witness of the happy effect of these four sermons. Sundry thoughtless impenitents, and sundry abandoned profligates have ever since given good evidence of a thorough conversion, not from party to party, but from sin to holiness, by an universal devotedness to God, and the conscientious practice of all the social and personal virtues.

It is true, my lord, there have been some additions made to the dissenters here since my settlement, and some of them by occasion of my preaching. They had but five meeting-houses then, in three different counties, and now they have seven in five counties, and stand in need of one or two more. But here I must again submit it to your lordship, whether the laws of England forbid men to change their opinions, and act according to them when changed? And whether the Act of Toleration was intended to tolerate such only as were dissenters by birth and education? Whether professed dissenters are prohibited to have meeting-houses licensed convenient to them, where

41

there are conformists adjacent, whose curiosity may at first prompt them to hear, and whose judgments may afterwards direct them to join with the dissenters? Or whether, to avoid the danger of gaining proselytes, the dissenters, in such circumstances, must be wholly deprived of the ministration of the gospel?

— And here, my lord, that I may unbosom myself with all the candid simplicity of a gospel minister, I must frankly own, that abstracting the consideration of the disputed peculiarities of the established church, which have little or no influence in the present case, I am verily persuaded . . . those of the Church of England in Virginia do not generally enjoy as suitable means for their conversion and edification as they might among the dissenters. I cannot help thinking that they who generally entertain their hearers with languid harangues on morality or insipid speculations, omitting or but slightly touching upon the glorious doctrines of the gospel, which will be everlastingly found the most effectual means to reform a degenerate world; such as the corruption of human nature in its present lapsed state; the nature and necessity of regeneration, and of divine influences to effect it; the nature of saving faith, evangelical repentance, &c.

I am surprised, my lord, to find any intimations in the letter from Virginia about the validity and legality of the licenses for seven meeting-houses granted by the General Court, especially if that letter came from the Commissary. These were granted by the supreme authority of this colony; and cannot be called in question by the Council without questioning the validity of their own authority, at least the legal exercise of it in this instance.

H. Richard Niebuhr

5. THE CHURCHES OF THE IMMIGRANTS

The Social Sources of Denominationalism has been a very influential sociological interpretation of religion and religious institutions in American history. The following selection is from Chapter VIII of that book. It has far wider reference than the period under immediate consideration.

The process whereby the immigrant churches have been adapted to a common environment has not been a simple one. It has met many obstacles, and synthesis has been delayed by many opposing forces. Alongside of the factors which made for accommodation other factors which brought forth competition have been present in this as in every other social complex. The process of synthesis has been accompanied by differentiation. The churches of the immigrants have grown like each other in some respects, but in other respects they have tended to differentiate themselves and to emphasize their unique individualities. They were transplanted into a common social environment but at the same time they were set into the midst of a competitive system of denominationalism. . . It was necessary for many churches which had enjoyed a virtual monopoly in their European homeland to compete actively for the loy-

From *The Social Sources of Denominationalism* by H. Richard Niebuhr (New York, 1929), excerpts from pp. 220–230. Reprinted by permission of Richard R. Niebuhr acting for Mrs. Florence M. Niebuhr.

alty of their members and for their position in the new society. The situation, as is the case in other kinds of competition, pro moted a high social self-consciousness and the emphasis of the peculiar characteristics of the group. Agreements with competitors were minimized, disagreements stressed.

The influence of competition, however, was not confined to this rivalry with other sects. The churches of the immigrants were involved in the whole complex pattern of conflict between the native and the "foreign" groups. The economic, cultural and political phases of this conflict were reflected again and again in religious rivalry and in the religious self-assertion of the immigrants. The cross-currents of such social interaction are illustrated today by the relations of Jews and Gentiles, and, especially, of Catholics and Protestants. In many of the cities of America the opposition of a Protestant, Nordic, middle-class party to a Catholic, south-European, proletarian group is the basis of political battles; and the political cleavage in turn reinforces the religious conflict.

In an earlier era the conflict between the native population and Dutch, Irish, German, and Scandinavian immigrants had similar economic, cultural, and political aspects. And it profoundly influenced the denominationalism of the immigrants by involving their religious life in the whole pattern of competition. The suspicion with which the indigenous population regarded early German and Irish immigrants had economic sources, in part, for the immigrant has ever been a threat to the native standard of living. It had cultural aspects as well. The newcomers were mostly poor, they were often illiterate, sometimes thriftless, always different in their language and customs. The sense of superiority which every native possesses had many opportunities for growth and many occasions for expression. Under the circumstances the development of hostility was natural, as it was later when Italians and Slavs supplanted Germans and

Irish in the steerages of trans-Atlantic ships. Hostility called forth hostility; the assertion of superiority by one group called forth corresponding self-assertion in the other and the whole situation of conflict issued in a sense of racial or cultural solidarity within each of the antagonistic societies. As a result of this social process the immigrants tended to become a distinct social class with a highly developed self-consciousness. They attended now to the values which the new environment threatened—to their language and their traditions. These were both the uniting bonds of the group and the symbols of its social solidarity. It was necessary, too, for the immigrants under these circumstances to find a center around which they could organize their values, a leadership which would hold together the scattered individuals of the race, a form of organization which would enable them to maintain and foster their solidarity. The only center which was available, as a rule, was religion; the only leaders, with few exceptions, who had braved the difficulties of a new orientation along with the migrating artisans and farmers were the clergy; the only organization which was readily at hand for maintaining the unity of the group was the church. Of literary culture the average immigrant had little. Neither Goethe nor Nietzsche was more than a name to him, but Luther and the German Bible or the crucifix and the mass he knew. These then became symbols of that whole past to which distance, the trials of the New World, and the exigencies of conflict lent a new enchantment. The preacher or priest, moreover, was often the only educated man in the immigrant community. To him the old culture was not merely a mass of memories but a literature and an art expressive of a national genius. He expressed for his countrymen their inarticulate loyalties and fostered their sense for these cultural values. The church with its use of the old language, with its conservative continuance of Old World customs, with its strictly racial character was the most important of the social organizations of the immigrant.

In this way many an immigrant church became more a racial and cultural than a religious institution in the New World. Its parochial schools were fostered not only that the children might receive instruction in religion but also that they might learn the mother-tongue and with it the attitudes and social ideals of the old homeland. . . . So the churches of the immigrants often found a new and additional reason for their separate existence. They now represented racial sectarianism as in the land of their birth they had represented the principle of ecclesiastical uniformity. They became competitive conflict societies, intent upon maintaining their distinction from other groups, no matter how closely these might be akin to them in doctrine, polity and piety.

The cultural or racial character of such sectarianism usually comes to light when the accommodation of a part of the immigrant population to the new civilization has proceeded so far that the language question arises. An early and interesting example of the common situation is offered by the story of a language controversy in the Dutch Reformed Church of New York in the middle of the eighteenth century. William Livingstone, one of the earliest English preachers in that church, wrote in 1754 that "to prevent the ruin of the Dutch churches common sense pointed out the absolute necessity of disuniting them from the language by translating the public Acts of devotion and worship into English." The suggestion aroused a storm of protest. "Recourse was had" by the anti-English party "to their old practice of reviling and calumniating the Presbyterians, who were charged with a design no less wicked than false and impossible, of seizing the Dutch churches and converting them and their congregations to their own use." "Who cannot see," said Livingstone, "that the grand design was to prevent the introduction of the English tongue into the Dutch churches lest the dis-

criminating badge with the vulgar, the difference of language, being removed, a coalition might ensue and Presbyterianism by that means be strengthened and supported, while the augmentation of the English by proselytes from the Dutch Church would in a great degree be interrupted. . . . The truth is that those who oppose the introduction of the English tongue into one of the Dutch churches are convinced that the different languages are the only criteria to distinguish them from each other, and this is evident from their fear that the use of the same tongue will naturally produce a union. Yet surely it cannot be so destructive of the interests of the Dutch churches to coalesce with a sect with whom they perfectly agree in doctrine, worship and government." In this instance the Dutch church sought to maintain its language largely, it seems, as symbol of prestige, which protected its membership from too intimate an association with the newly arrived "vulgar" Scotch-Irish. But in this as in many other instances the instinct of self-preservation was also clearly operative. Without the Dutch language the church, it appeared to many of its members, would lose its reason for existence since confessionally it was very similar to the Scotch Presbyterian and German Reformed Churches, the representatives of which in the U.S. far outnumbered the Dutch.

The histories of most other foreign-language immigrant churches repeat these conflicts between the language parties in the church, the emphasis on the cultural character of the religious organization, the effort to foster through the church the old customs and ideals as well as the racial tongue, and also the gradual acceptance by the immigrants of the language and the modes of the new environment. During the first period of competition and of economic conflict between immigrants and natives the churches of the immigrants tend to differentiate themselves as cultural organizations, which maintain and emphasize their separate individuality not on doctrinal but on cultural grounds. But after accommodation has set in, after the old language and the old ways have been irretrievably lost, after contacts with native churches have increased, the battle ground of competition changes. Ecclesiastical and doctrinal issues replace the cultural lines of division, and the loyalty of an English-speaking, second generation is fostered by appeal to different motives than were found effective among the immigrants themselves. The need for continued differentiation and for the self-justification of an organism which is strongly desirous of continuing its existence, are responsible now for a new emphasis. Denominational separateness in a competitive situation finds its justification under these circumstances in the accentuation of the theological or liturgical peculiarities of the group. Resistance to assimilation continues, but the immigrant church in its battle with other sects for membership and position takes up a new strategic position.

William Warren Sweet

6. RELIGIOUS MINORITIES IN THE COLONIES

Professor Sweet was author of many books on religion — and especially protestant denominations — in American history. This selection is from a chapter entitled "America and Religious Liberty" in his *Religion in Colonial America*.

Throughout the Christian centuries it has been the minority groups that have been the advocates of religious liberty; never the powerful State Churches. This does not mean that all minorities have always been tolerant. Frequently small sects are exceedingly exclusive, take pride in their exclusiveness and have developed a superiority complex as a result of it. But being minorities they do not possess the power to express their intolerance in violent programs of persecution or in the denial of political and religious rights to others. Outside New England and Virginia none of the colonies ever possessed majority religious bodies, so that the minority attitude toward religious toleration and the relation of Church and State came to be the prevailing colonial attitude.

In the American colonies, for the first time in the history of Christendom, there had come to be a group of civil States in which there was no majority religion. "Tolerance," Professor Garrison tells us, "has often been the special virtue of minorities, if that can be considered a virtue which is a method of getting something rather than a motive for giving something." In all the colonies, among the principal forces working for religious liberty were the minority groups. These bodies can be divided into two classes: first, those which advocated religious liberty from principle; second, those advocating it from policy. The Quakers and all the Baptist groups, which included the Mennonites and Dunkers, were advocates of religious liberty from principle; Catholics, Anglicans, Presbyterians, Lutherans and the Reformed churches were not opposed in principle to a State Church, but where they themselves were not the privileged Church, they were to be found in every instance on the side advocating religious liberty. It needs to be remembered that the principles and practices of religious liberty did not originate among peoples pretty solidly in control, nor under the leadership of men representing any majority religion.

The Middle Colonies particularly were the haven of large numbers of minority sects. In Pennsylvania, due to the liberal religious and land policies pursued by the Quaker Proprietor, there were to be found, besides many of the Proprietor's own co-religionists, Mennonites, Dunkers, Moravians, Schwenkfelders, Lutherans, German and Dutch Reformed, several varieties of Presbyterians, Welsh and English Baptists, Anglicans and Roman Catholics, with no one group having an actual majority. Even if there had been a desire on the part of the Proprietors to establish a State Church the very nature of the population would have made it a practical impossibility. While Pennsylvania presents the best example of the great varieties of religions, yet in every colony south of New England, with the exception of Virginia, much the same diversity was to be found from the beginning, becoming even greater as the colonial period wore on. In 1687 Governor Dongan, the liberal Catholic Governor of New York, made a report on conditions in that colony and in it is a summary of the religious situation,

New York [he states] has first a chaplain belonging to the Fort, of the Church of England; secondly, a Dutch Calvinist; thirdly a French Calvinist; fourthly a Dutch Lutheran. Here be not many of the Church of England; few Roman Catholics; abundance of Quaker preachers, men, and women especially; Singling Quakers; Ranting Quakers; Sabbatarians; Anti-Sabbatarians, some Ana-baptists; some Jews; in short, of all sorts of opinion there are some, and the most part none at all.

The great variety of religious groups in early Maryland may be inferred from the third provision of the Act of Toleration (1649), which promises punishment by fine or whipping and imprisonment for any person within the Province, who in a

reproachful manner or way declare, call or denominate, any psn [person] or psns [persons] whatsoever inhabiting, residing, traffiqueing, trading, or commerceing within this Province or within any of the Ports, Harbours, Creeks or Havens to the same belonging, an heretick, Seismatick, Idolator, puritan, Independent, Prespiterian, popish priest, Jesuite, Jesuited papast, Lutheran, Calvinist, Anabaptist, Brownist, Antinomian, Barrowist, Roundhead, Separatist, or any other name or terme in a reproachful manner relating to matters of Religion.

In Edmund Burke's well-known speech on *Conciliation with America* delivered on March 22, 1775, occurs this remarkably accurate summary of the religious situation in the colonies at the outbreak of the American Revolution:

Religion, always a principle of energy in this new people, is in no way worn out or impaired; and their mode of professing it is also one main cause of this free spirit. The people are Protestants; and of that kind which is the most adverse to all implicit submission of mind and opinion. This is a persuasion not only favorable to liberty, but built upon it.

The type of Protestantism most common in America, he states, was a "refinement on the principle of resistance"; it was the "dissidence of dissent, and the protestantism of the Protestant religion." In their religious beliefs they had advanced beyond all others "in the liberty of the Reformation." Existing in America under a variety of denominations they agree in nothing but communion of the spirit of liberty. When the colonists left England, the spirit of dissent was high and among the immigrants it was the highest of all. Of the stream of foreigners which had constantly flowed into the colonies, the greatest part was composed of dissenters from the establishments in the several countries from which they had come, and they therefore brought with them a temper and a character in harmony with the people with whom they mingled. The colonists had accustomed themselves to the freest debate on all religious questions, and so far had individualism developed in religion that even women were permitted to have opinions and it was said that "every man's hat was his Church."

As Edmund Burke has indicated, the colonial Churches had developed under conditions most favorable for the evolution of individualism in religion. All the largest dissenting Churches in the American colonies were self-governing, as were also most of the smaller bodies. Even the Church of England, though established by law in the Southern Colonies and officially tied to England, was in reality little more than a private sect controlled to a large degree by lay vestries. This not only meant freedom from Old World restraints of many kinds, but also the absence of Church officialdom. Added to this fact were the three thousand miles of tossing seas which rendered the colonials relatively safe from any punishment which Old World authorities, whether in Church or State, might impose for their disobedience. All this tended to produce an attitude of mind favorable to the development of new ways of thinking and independence of action.

This independence of thought which had come to prevail widely in Revolutionary America can be traced also to the fact that in large measure the colonial Churches had been founded by religious radicals. Many before leaving the mother country had already departed the usual and recognized ways of thought, both in politics and religion, and coming to a new land, separated as America was from the restraining influences of the old established customs and institutions, their radicalism would tend to increase rather than diminish. At the very time the English colonies were being established in America, a religious as well as a political revolution was under way in the mother country, and the old ecclesiastical as well as the old political faith was under attack from every quarter. Once having turned their backs upon the old home, the old State, the old Church, the colonists set their faces toward America to find a new heaven as well as a new earth.

Edwin S. Gaustad

7. INSTITUTIONAL EFFECTS OF THE GREAT AWAKENING

The Great Awakening in New England by Professor Edwin S. Gaustad is a recent study of that event. This selection is excerpts from Chapter Seven of the book.

The revival had set off explosive effects: that much was clear. But were the effects for good or ill? It was within Congregationalism that the aftermath was first and most keenly felt. The most immediate result of the revival was the making of new converts: this awakening power was sufficiently evident to win for the movement the name by which it is known. Nevertheless, an attempt to estimate the number of

From Edwin S. Gaustad, *The Great Awakening in New England* (New York, 1957), pp. 103–113. Reprinted by permission of Harper & Row, Publishers, Inc.

"new births" in the period is fraught with difficulty. Later writers are content to state simply and vaguely that "thousands" were added to the churches at this time, while earlier writers took refuge in that biblical generality, "multitudes." In the *Christian History*, statistics of the number of persons becoming full church members are seldom given. Where they are given, however, they reveal that the Great Awakening was not a mass movement of repentant sinners clamoring for acceptance by the churches. During 1741 and for some years after, the *Boston Gazette* noted the number of additions to the Boston churches during the preceding week. Since the total weekly number for all the churches hovered around ten or twelve during the height of the revival, it is evident that the crowded "sawdust trails" of later revivalism were absent. Joseph Seccombe, who in 1744 acclaimed the "good Fruits and Effects" of the revival in his parish at Harvard, Massachusetts, noted that since 1739 there had been nearly one hundred additions to his church, a yearly average of about twenty. At the height of the excitement Seccombe wrote, "scarce a Sacrament pass'd (which is with us once in eight Weeks) without some Additions to the Church . . . tho' twelve is the greatest Number that has been received at once." In East Lyme, which parish "consists of betwixt 60 and 70 Families, leaving out the Churchmen and Baptists," one hundred white persons and thirteen Indians were admitted to the church between April, 1741, and January, 1744. In the most successful month, July, 1741, there were thirty-two additions. Successes of similar proportion were attained in Groton, North Stonington, and Franklin, Connecticut.

Much more numerous and more frequently mentioned than the conversions were the signs of repentance and concern. William Cooper of Brattle Street Church remarked that in one week, at the height of the revival, more persons came to him in anxiety and concern than in the preceding twenty-four years of his ministry. Meanwhile, John Webb of New North Church declared "that he had five Hundred and Fifty Persons noted down in his Book (besides some Strangers) that have been with him in their Soul Troubles within a Quarter of a Year." This concern might fully awaken the sinner and it might also revive the saint. Prince noted that many of those coming to confer with their ministers about the state of their souls "had been in full communion and going on in a course of religion many years." The recurrent phrase "especially among young people," in connection with this visible concern for religion, suggests that many converts were formerly in the Half-Way Covenant. Depending upon the practice of each church, such a convert might or might not be reckoned a new church member. Visiting preachers or itinerant evangelists, as a rule, ventured only to indicate the numbers "under great Concern for their Souls," recognizing that longer observation was needed to determine the true conversions—if indeed such a determination was possible at all. It was at least apparent to most of the standing as well as to the traveling ministry that the anxiety was extensive and that many were asking, "What must I do to be saved?"

This concern, manifesting itself in more conspicuous ways than pastoral consultations and anxious queries, provoked a deeper loyalty to the externals of religion. Church attendance increased, while many agitated for more church services. If the meetinghouses did not open their doors with a frequency sufficient to satisfy the zealous and earnestly desirous, then religious exercises would be held in private homes. Cooper noted that

Religion is now much more the Subject of Conversation at Friends Houses, than ever I knew it. The Doctrines of Grace are espoused and relished. Private religious Meetings are greatly multiplied. . . . There is indeed an extraordinary Appetite after the sincere Milk of the Word.

An enterprising pastor would move from one private society to another, offering here a prayer or there a few words of exhortation. Young people formed their own groups for "Prayer and reading Books of Piety." "If at any Time Neighbours met, the great Affairs of Salvation were the Subject of Discourse." Weekly lectures, i.e., sermons on a weekday, were added to the schedule of many churches, Chauncy reporting in 1742 that "Evening-lectures were set up in one Place and another; no less than six in this Town, four weekly, and two monthly ones. . . ." The Massachusetts General Court responded to public interest by enforcing a more strict observance of the "Lords-Day." The concern of many young converts did not end with the reading of good and proper literature, but expressed itself in an earnest, if often unguided, evangelism. Itineracy and lay preaching with all their patent defects did much to destroy "puritan tribalism." When a church or minister refused to become evangelistic, a schism or secession would often result, this leading to the formation of a new and fervent group or to an alliance with some already existing ecclesiastical body whose missionary concern was obvious. Thus cells of self-commissioned ambassadors for Christ increased. The long-neglected Indian now received more attention both on the frontier and in the settled areas, two of the outstanding missionaries to the Indians being earnest friends of the revival. These were David Brainerd who labored effectively though briefly among the Indians of New Jersey, and Eleazar Wheelock whose Indian School at Lebanon was later moved to New Hampshire where it became Dartmouth College. In the days that followed the Awakening, people were not simply inquiring about salvation: they were striving to become both recipients of and agents for that gift of grace.

Had the Great Awakening never occurred, it is doubtful that Edwards would have written *An Humble Inquiry into the Rules of the Word of God, concerning The Qualifications Requisite to a Complete Standing and Full Communion in the Visible Christian Church.* This treatise was Edwards' public confession of a conviction he had long harbored: that none but the converted should be permitted to share in the privileges of full church membership and to receive communion. Reflection upon regeneration and conversion during the years of the Northampton and the New England revivals forced upon Edwards the revolt against Stoddardeanism, whatever the effects of such a revolt might be on "my own reputation, future usefulness, and my very subsistence." As he "became more studied in divinity" and "improved in experience," he grew convinced that only a negative answer was proper to the question: "Whether any adult persons but such as are in profession and appearance endued with Christian grace or piety, ought to be admitted to the Christian Sacraments; particularly whether they ought to be admitted to the Lord's Supper." Thereafter, those who presented themselves for church membership at Northampton were to be required to sign a confession of faith and to acknowledge their personal experience of divine grace.

The major result of this important step taken by Edwards is that it represented a return to the "sect ideal." To primitive Congregationalism, the church was a group of believers separated from the world, regularly purified through a careful discipline, emphasizing personal achievement in religion and in ethics. It was a "holy community," which should not lower its standards or erase its requirements in order to include the whole of society. The Cambridge Platform had without equivocation declared that "the matter of a visible church are Saints by calling." With reference to the admission of members, it decreed that "the things which are requisite to be found in all church members, are, Repentance from sin, & faith in Jesus Christ. And therefore these are the things whereof men are to be examined. . . ." Churches should exclude

49

from their fellowship those who do not continue to live as saints. And the sacrament of communion was the keystone in the structure of a pure church, for its observance was an occasion when strict examination of the communicants was possible and excommunication, if necessary, forthcoming. To achieve a visible church that conformed as nearly as possible to the invisible one was, beneath all the bitterness, self-righteousness and censoriousness of the New Lights, a major purpose of their separations. To purify the parish church and to alter its status from an established church for all society to a holy community for saints alone was the aim of the *Humble Inquiry.*

Where indifference to religion is widespread, tolerance is no problem; but when religion becomes intensely vital, bigotry becomes more pervasive. In Connecticut the immediate effect of the Great Awakening on religious liberty was detrimental. Elsewhere democracy and individualism in religion sprang ahead, and ultimately even in the land of steady habits, religion was made free. In the 1720's Connecticut had granted a measure of toleration to Anglicans, Quakers, and Baptists, allowing them freedom of worship and, upon proper registration, exemption from the support of any other form of worship. When in the divisive days of 1741 and after, Presbyterians and Congregationalists withdrew from the established churches to form new ones, they expected like other dissenters to be permitted to support their own ministry and to be released from the public taxation for support of the standing ministry. But the General Assembly, now acting in such a way as to make the Saybrook Platform obligatory, ruled "that those commonly called Presbyterians or Congregationalists should not take the benefit of that Toleration Act." When New Lights started changing the names of their churches to "Baptist" in order to come under the terms of the Toleration Act, that act was repealed. Other laws, already noted, provided for the arrest and punishment of New Light itinerants, and restricted ordination of ministers to graduates of approved schools, while New Light civil officials were deprived of their offices.

To Solomon Paine, the radical preacher of Canterbury, this alliance of church and state was all wrong.

> The cause of a just separation of the saints from their fellow men in their worship, is not that there are hypocrites in the visible church of Christ, *nor* that some fall into scandalous sins in the Church, *nor* because the minister is flat, formal, or ever saith he is a minister of Christ, and is not, and doth lie; but it is their being yoked together, or incorporated into a corrupt constitution, under the government of another supreme head than Christ, and governed by the precepts of men, put into the hands of unbelievers, which will not purge out any of the corrupt fruit, but naturally bears it and nourishes it, and decries the power of godliness, both in the government and gracious effects of it.

The Separate church gathered at Preston March 17, 1747, characterized the church from which it withdrew as one

> which caled it Self Partly Congregational & Partly Presbyterial; who submitted to the Laws of the Government to Settle articles of faith; to govern the Gathering of the Church & Settlement & Support of its ministers building of meeting houses, Preaching, Exhorting &c . . .

The Opposers, or Old Lights, were not everywhere, if anywhere, the leading exponents of a free and catholic spirit. The standing ministry was for peace, to be sure, wrote Reuben Fletcher, "an Independant," but

> upon the same terms that the Pope is for peace, for he wants to rule over all Christians throughout the whole world, and they want to rule from one town to another, throughout the whole country. If they could have their wills, separates and Baptists would have no more liberties here than the protestants have in France or Rome. What tyrant would not desire peace on the same terms that they do?

A generation after the revival Ezra Stiles was still justifying the despotism of Congregationalism in Connecticut.

Presbyterianizing died hard in Connecticut, but it died. In 1784 the Saybrook Platform was repealed, and though complete disestablishment was not achieved until 1818, long before that time both the government and the consociation had ceased to be ruling powers in local church affairs.

The problem of ecclesiastical freedom was not so complicated in Massachusetts where a more liberal charter and a more vocal Anglican minority precluded—even before the Awakening—an effective partnership of church and state. Though church schisms were not so plentiful in Massachusetts, theological division in the Bay colony was sharper than elsewhere. This diversity here as in Connecticut prevented rigid control by consociations. Finally there was in Massachusetts a strong voice for congregational polity. Nathanael Emmons, of Edwards' theological school and of the tradition of John Wise as well, strenuously opposed any step which seemed to compromise the autonomy of the local congregation. He resisted even the establishment of an association of the Massachusetts churches, concerning which he is reported to have said: "Associationism leads to Consociationism; Consociationism leads to Presbyterianism; Presbyterianism leads to Episcopacy; Episcopacy leads to Roman Catholicism; and Roman Catholicism is an ultimate fact." Over a century later, the Congregational historian Leonard Bacon rejoiced that in this period the churches learned to content themselves "with the simple and Scripture policy which rejects all ecumenical, national, provincial, and classical judicatures ruling the churches of Christ, and recognizes no church on earth save the local or parochial assembly and fellowship of believers. . . ."

With reference to freedom within the local church, the change is more difficult to trace. Several factors suggest, however, that even as greater liberties were enjoyed by the churches, so were the parishioners under less restraint. The emphasis upon a personal religious experience had then, as always, the effect of making converts less dependent on external authority—scriptural or ecclesiastical. Those to whom religion in the 1740's had suddenly become meaningful knew that the kingdom of God was within them; their private divine vocation, be it called new light, inner light, or sense of the heart, was their ultimate and occasionally their only appeal. To them only one covenant was of pressing significance: the covenant of grace. The church covenant was important, but secondary. Mediation was unnecessary, priesthood was universal. The civil covenant was obsolete, and society was shattered, but into members not classes.

Religious democratization of this sort found fullest expression, of course, in New Light churches. But in Old Light communions too the "power of the keyes" rested ultimately in the pew instead of in the pulpit, or even in an aggregate of pulpits. The breaking up of the prevailing parish system further weakened intrachurch discipline as well as interchurch control. After the Awakening it was possible, even fashionable, to leave the established chuch to join a separate society, a Baptist or Anglican church, or perhaps to hold religious services in a private home. Church minorities were now more outspoken than ever before, and could generally muster a council or committee that shared its ecclesiastical or more often its theological position. And, as Ezra Stiles ingenuously remarked, ". . . such are the circumstances of our churches, so intermixt with sects of various communion, that it is impolitic to use extreme and coercive measures—since universal liberty permits the oppressed to form into voluntary coalitions for religious worship." The "circumstance of our churches" together with the abundance of immediate personal religion in some of the churches promoted greater individual freedom from ecclesiastical control.

III. *The Struggle for Independence and the Terms of Settlement (1760-1820)*

If ethnic diversity and evangelical differentiation had set the conditions which ultimately would lead to the pattern of religious disestablishment, that consequence was by no means self-evident to the American colonists during the first half of the eighteenth century. As a result of the Church of England seeking entrance into all of the colonies, however, it became clear how jealous the colonists were in their ecclesiastical liberties. The threat of an established Church of England equipped with a resident bishop provided a rallying point for colonial solidarity. Although the campaign for an American bishop had proceeded fitfully since the late seventeenth century, by the 1760's it became an issue in the public press as a response to *An Appeal to the Public in Behalf of the Church of England in America* by Thomas Bradbury Chandler. A pamphleteering conflict ensued which was initiated by William Livingston with help from New York associates and Philadelphia friends; Chandler's colleagues answered immediately and in kind. In this exchange the colonial critics of Anglican designs introduced many of the arguments and much of the rhetoric which would become so much more significant in the next decades when a different though related sort of independence was at stake. The debate between these parties also dramatizes for us how far the conditions requiring disestablishment were already in existence, and how far a rationalistic temper toward religion had become operative in the public realm.

The actual struggle for disestablishment was pressed in Virginia with large roles being taken by Jefferson and Madison. Their classic texts have been reproduced here simply because they disclose that kind of understanding of religion and religious institutions which had become possible as well as neces-sary in the colonies among sophisticated men at the close of the eighteenth century. Religion—in a typically enlightenment point of view—had shown itself to be a *private* affair. Its public consequences were all that might concern the government. This was not to equate traditional religions with superstition and to seek to suppress them through secular cults, as happened on the continent. That sort of development presupposed a formalistic conception of the state which was deeply alien to American colonial experience. But it did suggest—as the American Whig and The Centinel had implied in the "Bishops War"—that religion was only one among several "interests" of man. Madison went so far in *Federalist* # 10 as to bracket religion as a source of faction along with a "rage for paper money" and other "improper or wicked project[s]". Religion did not provide a pattern or design for the good life or a good beyond life. Rather the "good life" proceeded from the interchange and exchange between these "interests." Thus by the end of the eighteenth century the traditional language of the "two relations" had been largely given over in substance as well as form. Whereas for John Cotton and the seventeenth century the two relations had been those of the inward spiritual man and the outward temporal man — both of concern within the common life — within a century and a half the two relations were commonly distinguished in the terms of private versus public matters. Connecticut might retain an "establishment" (meaning tax support for the Congregational Church) until 1818 and Massachusetts until 1833, but already the Danbury Connecticut Baptists had been fortified with Jefferson's "Wall of Separation" and a Treaty of Peace and Friendship with the Bey and Subjects of Tripoli had formally stated that the Federal Union was not "founded on the Christian religion."[1]

The Jeffersonian and Madisonian ideas on the subject might be counted "advanced," such an "independence of Church and State" as they worked for might be the only realistic basis on which the Federal Union could be achieved, and most of the states might quickly follow Virginia's lead in disestablishing churches and guaranteeing religious liberty. Nevertheless the neutral clauses of the First Amendment — "Congress shall make no law respecting the establishment of religion, or prohibiting the free exercise thereof" — were agreed to behind committee doors without fanfare. And both Jefferson and Madison would write numerous letters during their subsequent careers patiently explaining to well-meaning citizens what their intentions had been.

[1] 8 U.S. Statutes at Large, 155 (November 4, 1796), Article XI.

THE THREAT OF AN ANGLICAN ESTABLISHMENT

1. CHANDLER'S APPEAL ON BEHALF OF ANGLICANS IN AMERICA (1767)

Thomas Bradbury Chandler was prominent in the second generation of indigenous Anglicans who looked back to the defection of Timothy Cutler of Yale from the Connecticut establishment early in the eighteenth century for the origins of their party. In his *Appeal* Chandler was, at least on the surface, merely recalling a topic which very much concerned all members of the Church of England in America. Without a resident bishop the Anglican churches were crippled in their administration. Chandler's opponents, as the subsequent readings will make evident, saw other issues at stake in this matter.

The favourable Opportunity which has so long been waited for, in the Opinion of many wise and judicious Persons in America, now presents itself — and such, in several Respects, as the Circumstances of the Nation have never, until now, afforded.

From *An Appeal to the Public* by T. B. Chandler, (New York, 1767), pp. 54–60.

As the Tumults of War have ceased, and the public Tranquillity is restored, without any reasonable Suspicions of a speedy Interruption—so, the greatest Harmony subsists between our Mother-Country and most of the Colonies, the late Disputes having been brought, by the Wisdom and good Temper of the former, to a happy Termination—the Plan of an American Episcopate has been previously settled, and adjusted in such a Manner, that the religious Privileges of none can be violated or endangered—and, which we should ever acknowledge with all Thankfulness, we are, at this Time, so happy as to have a Prince on the Throne, from whose most unquestionable Disposition to promote the general Interest of Virtue and Religion, from whose sincere Affection for the Church, and from whose most gracious Declarations on the Subject before us, we cannot possibly doubt of the Royal Approbation and Concurrence—while a wise and virtuous Ministry cannot fail of being ready, to afford to so good a Cause, all needful Assistance. These are the Advantages, which now happily concur to favour the American Church, and which peculiarly mark the present Period.

It ought to be farther considered, that the Arguments for sending Bishops to America, were never so urgent and forcible as they are at present. When such Progress was made towards obtaining for this Country an Episcopate, in the former Part of this Century, the Number of American Clergy and Professors of the Church, . . . was small and inconsiderable, in Comparison with the Amount of their present Number. The amazing natural Increase of the Colonists, and the vast Accession of Europeans to the British America, have, in the Compass of Fifty or Sixty Years, enlarged the Number of its Inhabitants, and proportionably of the Members of the Church.

Should it be said, that the Church of England in America contains now near *a* *Million* of Members, the Assertion might be justified. It is not easy to ascertain the Number exactly, in a Country so widely extended and unequally peopled; but from general Calculations it has been frequently said of late Years, that the proper Subjects of the British Crown in America amount to *Three Millions*.

An actual Survey of the Number of Inhabitants in 1762, with a Distribution of them into Classes, according to their religious Professions, is said to have been carefully made: and it was then found, that, not including the new Colonies ceded by the last general Treaty of Peace, they amounted to between Two and Three Millions, in the Colonies and Islands. Of the *Whites*, the Professors of the Church were about a third Part—the Presbyterians, Independents and Anabaptists were not so many—the Germans, Papists and other Denominations, amounted to more.

Let this Representation be carefully considered, and it will appear in a very evident and striking Light, that the Wants of the American Church, as it has been destitute of Bishops, must have naturally increased, and can amount now to little less than an absolute Necessity. In these Circumstances, could such a Number of Christians, even under a Pagan Government, unless in a State of open Persecution, provided they had always proved themselves loyal and faithful Subjects, apply in vain for a Favour, so needful for themselves, and so harmless to others? How much less Reason then can the Church in America have to fear a Refusal in the present Case, not only from a Christian Nation, famed for its prudent Indulgence to all religious Denominations in general—but from a Nation, which is moreover disposed to befriend it, from peculiar Reasons both of Affection and Policy?

This Argument taken from the *Number* of those who belong to the Church of England in America, will receive great additional Force, from a Consideration of the State of the *Blacks* in our Islands and Colonies; who were found, in the above-mentioned Survey, to be about Eight Hundred and Forty-four Thousand. Although many of these, it is to be feared, through the Neglect of their Masters, are not Christians at all; yet, as they are connected with, and under the immediate Government of, Persons who profess Christianity, they may be said, in an imperfect Sense, to belong to the respective religious Classes of their Owners. However, their Situation is undoubtedly such, that in Proportion as a Sense of Religion prevails in their Masters, they will receive Benefit. Now as these are known chiefly to belong to the Professors of the Church, if an Episcopate will naturally tend to improve the State of Religion in the Church of England, it must consequently, . . . have a general good Effect upon more than half a Million of poor Creatures, Sharers with us of the same common Nature—sent into the World as Probationers and Candidates for the same glorious Immortality—whom Christ equally purchased by his precious blood-shedding—who notwithstanding, as they are bred up in Ignorance and Darkness, are suffered, to the eternal Disgrace of their Owners, to walk on "in the Shadow of Death," without a Ray of rational religious Hope to chear them.

Another Argument for granting an American Episcopate, arises from the Obligations of Gratitude; a national Sense of which, it is humbly conceived, ought, at this Time, to have a peculiar Efficacy in Favour of Religion in the American Plantations. By a signal Interposition of Divine Providence, the British Arms in America have triumphed over all that opposed them, our Colonies have been prodigiously extended, and our new Acquisitions, together with our old Settlements, have been secured, not only by Treaty, but by a total Annihilation of that Power on this Continent, whereby our former Safety was chiefly endangered.

Every *wise* Nation sees and acknowledges the Hand of God in the Production of such Events; and every *religious* Nation will endeavour to make some suitable Returns to him for such extraordinary Favours. And what Returns are proper to be made in such Cases, one Moment's serious Reflection will clearly discover. The Circumstances of Things evidently point out two Duties to our Governors, on this Occasion, both of them important in themselves, and of indispensible Obligation: *One* is, the farther Security and Support of the true Religion in America, in those Places where it already is; and the *other*, the Propagation of it in those Places, to which it has not hitherto been extended.

As America is the Region, wherein the Divine Goodness has been more remarkably displayed, in Favour of the British Nation; so, America is evidently the very Ground, on which some suitable Monument of religious Gratitude ought to be erected. This should be of such a Nature as to be visible to the World, and, that the Honour of the Supreme Ruler of Events may be thereby immediately promoted. Now as the Honour of God is most directly promoted by public Worship—as that Worship must be most acceptable to him, wherein the Praises and Adorations of his Creatures are regularly offered him, in the solemn Offices of the purest and best Religion—and as the national Religion must be supposed best to answer these Characters, in the national Opinion; it necessarily follows, that the State of the national Religion here has a Right, on this Occasion, to the peculiar Attention and Consideration of those, who are intrusted with the Direction of our public Affairs.

What then does the present State of this Religion in America require to be done? What is *possible* to be done for its Benefit and Advantage? These are the Questions that must naturally arise. And every one that professes it, every Witness of its suffering Condition, is able to answer:—The Church of England in America, is perishing for Want of common Necessaries. She has long been imploring Relief, under such Diseases as must prove fatal to her, if much longer neglected. She therefore earnestly requests, and she *only* requests, that proper Remedies may be provided for her present Sufferings. And she leaves it, with all due Submission to the Wisdom of her Superiors, whether any Thing farther is proper to be done, to strengthen and improve her Interests. She wishes for nothing, which shall be thought inconsistent with the Rights and Safety of others. She asks nothing, but what has been granted to others, without any ill Consequences; and she relies on the common Affection and Justice of the Nation, to raise her to this Equality. And, whether there is any Thing presumptuous or unreasonable in these Expectations, let Heaven and Earth judge!

2. COLONIAL CRITICISM OF THE APPEAL (1768)

William Livingston (d. 1791) graduated from Yale in 1740 and subsequently read law, becoming a "whig" and staunchly anti-Anglican in his religious sentiment. He later became first Governor of the state of New Jersey. Livingston is credited with chief responsibility for "The American Whig," a series published in the *New York Gazette* beginning on March 14, 1768. "The Centinel" was apparently written by a circle of Philadelphia friends including Francis Alison, John Dickinson, and others. It was published in the *Pennsylvania Journal* beginning on March 24, 1768. They exhibit both an explicit attitude toward religion and an implicit temper of mind which were wholly alien to that "language of establishment" which had been current at the time of colonial settlement.

The Centinel No. I

Dr. Chandler's *Appeal to the Public* . . ., which from his own Account, seems rather to be the united Effort of all the CLERGY in New-York and New-Jersey, perfected by the kind assistance of the CLERGY from the neighbouring Provinces, may by this time be supposed to have circulated pretty generally. And as the season advances, when we presume these clergy are again to meet in voluntary convention, this may be the proper time to propose a few Questions for their, or if the Dr. pleases, for his consideration. The performance seems replete with bold extravagant assertions of Facts, many of which have no foundation in Truth; it is pretty deficient in Christian Charity, tho' not deficient in low craft, and seems dangerous to the Civil and Religious Liberties of the Colonies in America. . . .

He begins with informing us "that application has been made to our Superiors, by the clergy of the several colonies, requesting one or more Bishops to be sent to America"; he complains of "unprecedented hardships" and "intolerable grievances," suffered by the "Church," the "American Church," the "Church of England in America" for want of "an American Episcopate," and upon this founds his Appeal to the Public.

We should be obliged to the Doctor, if he would inform us in plain terms, who are

Abridged and edited from the *Pennsylvania Journal*, March 24, 1768.

these Superiors to whom the clergy have applied; by whom these Bishops are to be sent; by what authority this American Episcopate is to be established; or who are the authors of their *intolerable Grievances* and *unprecedented Hardships*, that we may better judge whether the apprehensions on account of our civil liberties, which this avowed application has raised in the minds of many people, be well or ill founded. . . .

The claims of the Doctor, without an establishment, notwithstanding all his seeming modesty and candor, are too great not to awaken jealousies in the minds of free born Americans, if none had been conceived there before.

The "Church," the "American Church," "the Church of England in America," are the names by which he affects to distinguish that denomination of Christians to which he belongs. I wish the Doctor would please to define his terms, and tell us what he means by Church, and why that name should be applied to English Episcopalians only. Are not the Lutheran & Calvinist Churches, are not the Congregational, Consociated and Presbyterian Churches; are not the Baptist, the Quaker and all other Churches in America, of what denomination soever they be, Members of Christ's Catholic Church, if they profess faith in Christ and hold the great essentials of Christianity? Or does he mean to lay such a stress on the unbroken Succession, and on Episcopacy as established by law in England, as to make these essential to the being of a Church? . . .

We apprehend this is not a meer impropriety of speech adopted by a man who seems not to be one of the most correct writers, but a phrase artfully introduced with a sinister design.

The Doctor cannot have read so little either of Civil or Ecclesiastical History, or be so very little acquainted with mankind, as not to know the magic of words and the blind devotion paid to Names and Sounds. . . .

The "National Religion" is another phrase of the Doctors wherewith he graces the peculiar tenets of his Church. . . . We would ask him, why might not Christianity have been allowed the honor of being called the National Religion? Or why is Episcopacy alone honored with that name? Is it because it is established by law in England? Is not Presbyterianism also established by law, and was it not established in 1707 — a more enlightened age surely than that in which Episcopacy was established at the Reformation? . . .

It is not doubted but every man who wishes to be free will by all lawful ways in his power oppose the establishment of any one denomination in America, the preventing of which is the only means of securing their natural rights to all those at least who may differ from that denomination. . . .

One thing more I would beg to know from the Doctor; what assurances (besides his own, which are too weak to be relied on in so momentous an affair) are we to have that Bishops will be sent over with such limited powers? Attempts are made upon American liberty from a quarter where it ought not to be expected. A temper is shown by some leading Prelates even now in England that will not suffer us to place a confidence in them. . . .

We hope the Doctor will explain himself fully, and resolve the doubts and queries we have here propounded.

The Centinel No. III

Having opened the general tendency of Dr. Chandler's APPEAL, &c., I shall now proceed to make some remarks on the inconveniences and mischiefs of religious establishments.

Whoever peruses ecclesiastical history, ever since the time of Constantine, will find it contains little else than the follies,

Abridged and edited from the *Pennsylvania Journal*, April 7, 1768.

absurdities, frauds, rapine, pride, domination, rage, and cruelty of spiritual tyrants; who practised every artifice to persuade or cajole the temporal rulers to support their measures. . . .

I would not be understood to assert that the principles of the episcopal Churches tend more particularly to these abuses than those of others; but it is the fault of human nature [that it] cannot bear great power with equanimity, and perhaps is most apt to abuse it in religious matters. The high rank and large revenues of the Bishops in England must tempt them, however, into this error more easily than the leaders in Churches whose influence depends on personal qualifications only.

Religious establishments are very hardly kept from great corruption. But if the provision made for the clergy be large, and the leaders are enabled to live in grandeur, it is not likely they should long continue pure. Ambitious worldly-minded men, who seek the fleece and not the well being of the flock, will insinuate themselves into the chief offices; their example or influence will mislead or discourage others who in better company might have been usefully employed; the industry and vigilance of the spiritual guides in the proper business of their function will be relaxed; and that skill in their profession which practice, study, and attention alone can give will not be attained. . . . And should the evil proceed yet further, and the clergy, instead of being examples to their flock, set before them patterns of irregular living, open immorality, and daring wickedness, will it not be readily granted that there can be no religion at all among the zealots for an establishment so enormously corrupted?

But still worse than this: there is no probability of religion's being reformed under these ecclesiastical polities. Nothing less than a state convulsion effected the reformation in most of the countries where it took place. . . . But above all the most dreadful evil is the danger of persecution which

worldly minded men, to gratify their own pride and lust for power, are forward on proper occasions to practice and which weak men with better intentions are too apt to be lead into. We too readily think ourselves secure from error if we have the wise, the powerful, and the many [with us] in our opinions. Those who differ from us we conclude must be obstinate and perverse and [we are] without much difficulty brought to look on it as an act of charity as well as duty to administer some wholesome restraints and severities to such manifest heretics. Thus is the pride of supposed right opinion nourished under establishments. . . .

Such are some of the mischiefs which spring from the civil powers meddling with religion. Beware! O beware then my countrymen, of countenancing this mistake!

The Centinel No. IX

The abuse of power has, in all ages, furnished the most copious fund of materials to the moralist and to the historian and has ever given the greatest perplexity to the legislator. Private persons doubtless affect the public weal by their vices and their crimes; but standing singly and alone their transgressions are easily corrected. Whereas those who by the advantages of birth, fortune, office, or superior abilities are enabled to influence others and to direct the public views and councils, are not without difficulty and address kept within the bounds of law and justice. The passions and prejudices of men are constantly leading them into one mistake or another; and the remonstrances of reason and duty alone are but feeble restraints. In order therefore to curb the licentiousness of leading men, it has been found expedient to distribute the powers of government among the different orders of which the community is composed, as to excite and employ those of one rank and

Abridged and edited from the *Pennsylvania Journal*, May 19, 1768.

interest to correct the irregularities of another.

Although this may seem to lay a foundation for constant debate and faction, yet even this is a small inconvenience compared to the galling and oppressive yoke of absolute monarchy, or even the jealous severity of an aristocratic senate. But the common disadvantages of the mixed forms of government will be found neither very considerable nor lasting in case the distribution of power is made with judgment. . . .

The circumstances of the British colonies, just rising out of the difficulties of an infant state, do not admit of such a regular distribution of power [as the British Constitution admirably supplies.] . . .

In this state of things it behooves the People of North-America to consider fully what political consequences and effects the introduction of diocesan Bishops among them may produce. By Dr. Chandler's account of them . . . we find they are not to be merely voluntary Bishops . . . but prelates commissioned by his Majesty as Head of the Church and authorized by the nation as branching from the ecclesiastical establishment in England. . . .

In their zeal for their hierarchy these gentlemen, possibly, have not considered what they are about in this [regard]. Or if any of them have glanced so much beside their own concernments as to have perceived the obvious effects of their proposal on political affairs, they may have reconciled to themselves the pursuit of so dangerous a measure by the prospect of the spiritual advantage they expect will flow from it.

For my part I have often esteemed it a great advantage to the northern Colonies that their clergy have very little weight in government. This is owing to the moderate salaries paid them, to their debates and divisions about the modes and circumstantials of religion, and to the want of general connection among themselves and with the churches established in Britain. By their dissensions we are secured from the usurpations and encroachments they might otherwise make as a body; for one denomination carefully watches another and sounds the alarm on occasion of any schemes that may be devised to the prejudice of the public. This also keeps up a spirit of free-enquiry and prevents the ill effects of a . . . superstitious credulity.

But here is a measure proposed that directly tends to form and combine this order of men into a regular and powerful band, and to put them under the direction of superior officers invested with great powers over the rest. It is also calculated to connect them by uniformity, establishment and interest with the Church established in England.

While for civil government the British dominions on the continent are already divided into seventeen provinces, the Episcopal clergy . . . will be collected and disciplined under twenty or more Bishops, and a Primate appointed from home. What restraint or check will there be on the views and schemes of a body so well compacted, so weighty, so well established by statute, and so well allied to powerful hierarchies in Europe. Without an order of nobility to stand on equal footing with the prelates, without courts of common law (of jurisdiction extensive enough to issue prohibitions and correct the proceedings of the Archbishop and his suffragans when they exceed their proper limits . . .), without a General Assembly of the Colonies or other association for civil purposes, in what circumstances must the laity be to guard themselves against the ambitious designs of the spiritual power? In short they must lie entirely at the mercy and moderation of the clergy: And what these are let Spain, let Italy, let the history of England in the papal times (and even since the Reformation under the government of the House of Stuart) picture out to the reader. Men in all ages and of every character are much the same in regard to the abuse of power, and their conduct when they get above control loudly proclaims the necessity of attending to the proper distribution of it in every free government that would preserve its constitution.

The American Whig XV

If there be any force or conclusion in his argument, it plainly consists in this position: that episcopacy and not Christianity is the national religion. This is evidently implied in that bright chain of reasoning which, to do it full justice, my readers shall have in his own words. After having excited our gratitude and called for public testimonials in honour to the deity, he argues thus: "as this honour is most directly promoted by public worship; as that worship must be most acceptable to him wherein the praises and adorations of his creatures are regularly offered him, in the solemn offices of the purest and best religion; and as the national religion must be supposed best to answer these characters, in the national opinion;" it necessarily follows — mark the conclusion — that the state of the "national religion here has a right on this occasion to the peculiar attention and consideration of those who are entrusted with the direction of our public affairs." The same argument would doubtless be as conclusive in the mouth of a Musselman and in an address to the Grand Signor. It is not a plea for Christianity. It is a claim for distinction in favor of the national religion. For it cannot be denied that all other religious denominations among us, except Judaism, are at least as zealous possessors of the religion of Jesus as those of the Doctor's persuasion which he is pleased to call the national religion. . . . Hence also it is clear that the reason for establishing episcopacy in America is not that its doctrines are more pure, the practice of its professors more regular and uninterrupted than those of other denominations, or — in other words — that the

Abridged and edited from the *New York Gazette*, June 20, 1768.

Church of England is properly and exclusively the Church of Christ, in which alone all true Christians must allow the honour of God can be duly promoted but because it is, as the Doctor asserts, the national religion. . . .

But at all events the Doctor is involved in this dilemma: he must either be understood as asserting that the honour of God cannot be duly promoted in America for want of that Christian purity and perfection to which we are now strangers and which cannot be introduced among us [except] by the means of an episcopacy, or that the honour of God is not so much promoted by the purity and perfection of a Christian Church as by a national establishment of religion however corrupt it may appear to be if tested by the sacred oracles, the divine canon of Scripture. . . . Now to consider his reasoning in a just light it evidently amounts to this: it is the duty of the legislature of a country to promote the national religion whatever it may be. In Turkey, therefore, the lawgivers should advance Mohametanism, in France, Spain, and Portugal, Popery, in the British Empire, Protestant Episcopacy, in China Idolatry — all which in their several places are calculated to promote the honour of God because, in the national opinion, they must respectively be supposed best adapted to that purpose. This is certainly most excellent doctrine from the pen of a Church of England divine, and a Doctor too.

In truth every establishment of religion, if such establishments are in themselves justifiable, ought to be maintained (as well as those which are merely of a civil nature) by the infliction of temporal punishments on transgressors of the law. Nor, indeed, can its efficiency as an establishment consist in anything else. Hence therefore it is evident, in the Doctor's judgment . . . , that we cannot make suitable returns to the great author of all our benefits [except] by establishing English episcopacy in America, and enforcing it — for it otherwise cannot be an establishment—by pains and penalties. . . . It requires a very slender capacity to discern that the principles upon which the Doctor builds his claim to the peculiar attention of those who are entrusted with the direction of our public affairs "in favour of the national religion" lead directly and necessarily to the full and complete establishment of episcopacy.

But before I conclude it may not be amiss to enquire into the propriety of that expression upon which so much is built and by the major force of which we are taught that whoever is opposed to the establishment of episcopacy in the colonies is unmindful of those signal deliverances which have lately been wrought for us by the finger of God. To talk of a national religion of France, in Spain, or in Turkey would be to speak with propriety; but to apply this character to any Church in the British Empire is absurd. In England prelacy is established, in Scotland Presbyterianism, in New-England colonies Congregationalism, and in almost all the other colonies they have no religious establishment at all. How then—when by religion is meant not Christianity itself, but a particular denomination of Christians—how, I say, can any religion in the King's realm or dominions be called national? Truly I cannot conceive how unless by a well known figure in rhetoric which puts the part for the whole. But upon a subject of so much importance, and in an APPEAL TO THE PUBLIC, it is inexcusable to deal in figures. I am therefore rather of the opinion that the Doctor supposes that England, though a part only of the great whole, has exclusively considered a right in the plain and common sense of the words, as they are used and understood by British Protestants, to extend her ecclesiastical establishment throughout the colonies of the British Empire and to load Americans with burdens which neither they nor their forefathers could bear. And whether the sound of this doctrine is more agreeable to an American ear than the unmusical periods of the stamp-act I leave to my American readers to determine.

Arthur L. Cross

3. THE NEWSPAPER CONTROVERSY

The Anglican Episcopate and the American Colonies is an older but very thorough analysis of the attempts to achieve a resident bishop for the Church of England in America.

DISCUSSION on the subject of introducing American bishops first became general in the newspapers in 1768, and reached its height during the course of this and the following year. It was ushered in by two series of articles: one in the *New York Gazette*, under the signature of "The American Whig"; the other in the *Pennsylvania Journal*, under the signature of "The Centinel" (or "Sentinel"). Though the several numbers of each series were evidently written by different hands, the chief contributors under these respective names seem to have been William Livingston and Francis Alison. The latter, vice-provost of the College of Philadelphia, was assisted by some of

From Arthur L. Cross, *The Anglican Episcopate and the American Colonies* (New York, 1902), pp. 195–214, 270–272.

his Presbyterian brethren, particularly John Dickinson, the celebrated author of *The Farmer's Letters*. The ostensible purpose of these earlier articles was to answer Chandler's *Appeal to the Public*, though it has been conjectured that the disappointment occasioned by the failure of the New York Presbyterians in 1767 to obtain their charter of incorporation, a defeat which they attributed to the Bishop of London, may have had some influence in the matter. The "American Whig" was answered by "Timothy Tickle" in "A Whip for the American Whig," who was in turn called to account by "Sir Isaac Foot" in "A KICK for the Whipper." The chief opponent of the "Centinel" was Dr. William Smith, provost of the College of Philadelphia, who wrote a series of essays under the pseudonym of "The Anatomist."

Hitherto, though the apprehension of an ecclesiastico-political tyranny had been the essential underlying cause of the opposition to bishops, particularly in New England, the issue had been obscured by a network of theological polemics. During the period from Hobart to Chauncy, however, the political element was steadily pushing its way to the front, and now for the first time it presented itself squarely and unequivocally as the chief topic of consideration. In spite of the efforts of the Episcopalians, the Independents had at last succeeded in shifting the basis of the argument.

Not only had the controversy undergone a change of character; it had also become a matter of more general interest. The earlier discussions had been confined almost solely to pamphlets, and hence, it is safe to say, had claimed the attention of not more than a very narrow circle of readers. With the entrance of the newspapers into the lists, however, the public eye was arrested. For the first time people began to discuss the question in their homes, in the coffee-houses, on the street corners. Once a subject of purely spiritual concern, it now assumed a prominent place among the burning questions of the hour, to influence them or to be influenced by them, as the case might be.

A few days after the "Whig" opened the subject in the *New York Gazette*, the "Centinel" published his first piece in a Philadelphia newspaper. His professed purpose was to put several questions so that the people might be better able to judge "whether the apprehensions on account of our civil Liberties, which this avowed application has raised in the minds of many people, be well or ill founded." The "Centinel" shows himself more frankly uncompromising than any of his predecessors, declaring that he and those of his way of thinking will under no considerations listen to the plan for bishops, be the arguments and assurances what they may.

The whole argument of the "Centinel" is, to an even greater degree than that of the "Whig," based upon an assumption of the close connection between the two questions, the religious and the political. From the general principles of liberty, he maintains, Parliament ought not to interfere in the civil freedom of the colonies, and any application to that "august body," not only to make laws for them but also to establish among them any form of church discipline, deserves to be treated as an attack upon their civil liberties. His aim, he professes again and again, is not to combat any religious denomination or to oppugn the theological opinions of any man or set of men, but to defend the liberties of his country. The point in dispute, as he views it, is not concerning a bishop or concerning episcopal discipline as such, but as to the manner of introducing the bishop and establishing the discipline in America; and he hopes that "the friends and lovers of America" will consider themselves no further concerned in the controversy than as it relates to civil liberty. Though some of the distinctions which he formulates are a bit too fine to be appreciated, the main trend of his argument shows clearly enough that the theological aspect of the question had become thoroughly absorbed in the political.

The significance of the newspaper utterances lies in phases of public opinion which they both moulded and reflected, and in the sure evidence which they furnish, that the episcopal question, in its political aspect, had become important in the minds of the people. One certain indication of the widespread interest which the subject had aroused is the fact that a New York publisher found it a profitable investment to collect all the articles which contributed to the discussion, and to reprint them in the form of pamphlets. Certainly, if the question of the establishment of bishops did not contribute a lion's share in causing that enmity to the mother country, which was manifested mainly in a political direction, it was involved in the struggle and deserves to be regarded as an important part of it.

One more point in regard to the significance of the newspaper controversy deserves notice. It is generally admitted that, while the majority of the Puritans advocated the principle of forcible resistance to the oppressive measures of the home government, many influential members of the Church of England preached the doctrine of non-resistance and passive obedience. Upon closer examination it will be seen that most of these persons were in the Middle and Northern colonies, particularly in the latter, where the Puritan element predominated, and that almost to a man those who sought the introduction of bishops adopted this attitude. In view of these facts it is at least a tenable hypothesis that the bitterness of the controversy brought out so sharply the latent hostility between Episcopalian and Puritan, that many churchmen who might otherwise have taken the side of their country were, by the force of their injured religious convictions, driven over to the loyalist ranks.

* * *

Undoubtedly, there is something to be said in favor of the argument that the attempt to introduce bishops, and the opposition thereby excited, formed one of the causes of the Revolution. There can be no doubt that the opposition to bishops was based mainly on political grounds: this fact is indicated by the absence of any resistance to the establishment of an episcopate after the Revolution. Moreover, fear and hatred of the Church of England and all its appendages were existent in the colonies from their first foundation; and the fact that the majority of the colonists professed a religion hostile, or at least alien, to the Anglican establishment offered good ground for nourishing the seeds of political discontent. But, admitting all this, it must be apparent to one who has followed carefully the course of events religious and political, during the eighteenth century, that the strained relations which heralded the approach of the War of Independence strengthened the opposition to episcopacy, rather than that religious differences were a prime moving cause of political alienation. The religious controversies, accentuated and drawn into more public prominence, though not first called into being, by the existing political situation, had a reactionary effect, in that, once in full swing, they contributed, in combination with other causes, to embitter the minds of the patriots and thus to accelerate the impending crisis.

Those, then, who argue that the episcopal question was a cause of the Revolution, if they mean an impelling cause, are exposed to the criticism of misconstruing evidence and of confusing cause and effect. Nevertheless, religious affairs were closely involved in the political questions of the time, and if the ecclesiastical causes of the Revolution were secondary and contributory rather than primary and impelling, certainly there was an ecclesiastical phase of pre-Revolutionary history of no little interest and importance.

Carl Bridenbaugh

4. NO BISHOP, NO KING

Professor Bridenbaugh's recent study of this same historical issue is entitled *Mitre and Sceptre*. He is author of numerous other studies in aspects of colonial America.

For more than a year the Whigs and Centinels covered every aspect of the controversy with episcopacy that had been adduced since 1689. They brought wide reading to their historical argument, and forced their opponents to attempt an Anglican version of the origin of the colonies; from Hobart, Welles, and Chauncy, the dissenting scribblers drew materials for their defense of Presbyterian ordination. They questioned Chandler's "adulterated citations," which misled readers, and, levying on the statistical researches of Dr. Stiles, they pilloried the Jerseyman and the officials of the Venerable Society, who prepared the annual abstracts, for their false, or at least deceptive, use of figures. With satanic skill, both Centinels and Whigs pictured the missionaries as High-Church men and Jacobites, not always averse to alliances with the greatly feared Church of Rome. Francis Alison made canon law his concern, while Lawyer Livingston shrewdly tailored his argument for the victims of the current economic stringency and colonial concern over the Townshend Acts and drove home the high cost of episcopacy by printing a long itemized list of the articles needed for "his Lordship's palace, offices, &c.," coach and horses, cathedral edifice, elegant vestments, salaries for several episcopal officials, etc., etc., to the grand total of £21,740.0.0 annually! "If ever a bishop drives his gilded equipage in our streets, and shares in the public councils of the colony, and the missionaries are judges and justices in the counties, who, but the learned Doctor of Elizabeth-Town, cannot foresee the most tragical circumstances, from such a priestly mixture of power?"

What strikes the modern reader of these papers is the variety of literary forms employed by both sides during this prolonged debate. There are essays, letters, sermons, legal briefs, anecdotes, imaginary pieces, verses, and jingles. High seriousness suffuses most of them; Alison and Livingston frequently battened down their essays with citations of authorities, but, when the writers thought it useful, they resorted to wit, satire, mockery, raillery, bitter sarcasm, and invective. They hurled charges, they slandered, they tried assaults, they indulged in character assassination. The "Whip" once accused Livingston of forgery and on another occasion of prevarication, and "Whigs" showed how the Episcopalians made figures lie. Neither party hesitated to quibble over words or inconsequential details as it sought to put the other side in the wrong. Many of these newspaper articles were unfair; others reeked of false sweetness and reasonableness.

In handling all these weapons, the Dissenters had the great advantage. The initiative had been theirs, and they kept it. They had the largest audience, one whose already existing fears they had only to justify; they did not, like the Anglicans, have to convert men to new views. Above all,

From *Mitre and Sceptre: Transatlantic Faiths, Ideas, Personalities, and Politics 1689–1775* by Carl Bridenbaugh, pp. 304–307, 335–338. Copyright © 1962 by Carl Bridenbaugh. Reprinted by permission of Oxford University Press, Inc.

the Dissenters were rich in talents. The New York-New Jersey clergy, with only occasional assistance from their ablest penman, Provost Smith, really could not compete with Livingston, Alison, and their bench of able controversialists in literary competence, ecclesiastical learning, and forensic skill. The strongest point made against the Anglicans was the suspicion — which we have seen was not without foundation — of "some unavowed ecclesiastical machinations." The "American Whig" and the "Centinel" were contemporary with the "Letters of Junius" and compare most favorably with the papers of the undisclosed English journalist, but where the latter excelled in destructive talent, the colonial Dissenters surpassed him in constructive ideas. They were men contending for principles and ideals.

We will miss the lasting significance of this torrid newspaper debate if we regard it solely as a display of journalistic fireworks or merely as un-Christian propaganda. Read carefully, these essays disclose men groping their way amid the heat of controversy toward certain fundamental principles now recognized as American. In the fifth number of the "American Whig," dated April 11, 1768, Livingston offered his readers a glimpse of the future of their country:

The day dawns in which the foundation of this mighty empire is to be laid, by the establishment of a *regular American Constitution*. All that has hitherto been done, seems to be little besides the collection of materials for the construction of this glorious fabrick. 'Tis time to put them together. The transfer of the European part of the great family is so swift, and our growth is so vast, that before seven years roll over our heads [1775!] the first stone must be laid. —Peace or war; famine or plenty; poverty or affluence; in a word, no circumstance, whether prosperous or adverse, can happen to our parent; no, nay, no conduct of hers, whether wise or imprudent, no possible temper on her part, whether kind or cross-grained, will put a stop to this building. . . . What an era is this to America! and how loud the call to vigilance and activity! As we conduct, so will it fare with us and our children.

About this prophetic conception of a manifest destiny in or out of the British Empire, clustered a number of supporting ideas. Toleration was being, and for a half-century had been, slowly transformed into an ideal of religious freedom. Sectarianism in fact — the normal colonial ecclesiastical condition — was producing a new theory of complete separation of church and state suitable to the American environment and temper. American republicanism was emerging naturally in the politics of a society where religious republicanism had long prevailed. By inheritance and experience the colonists were anti-clerical, and they perceived the danger to their provinces of too intimate a connection between the clergy and politics. In the course of their exchanges, they fastened on the Episcopal missionaries once and for all the label of Tories, and they demonstrated to the public satisfaction that bishops represented incipient tyranny. Above all, these men sensed, if they did not openly proclaim it, that, despite many similarities, a really great difference was developing between England and America which necessitated a new solution satisfactory to the New World. This the neo-colonials of the opposite side did not grasp.

* * *

John Adams never tired of emphasizing the important distinction between the American Revolution and the War for Independence. "The revolution was in the minds and hearts of the people, and in the union of the colonies; both of which were substantially effected before hostilities commenced." This "great intellectual, moral, and political change" occurred when the designs of the British Government dawned upon the colonists during the fifteen years before the Battle of Lexington. "The rise and progress of this knowledge, the gradual expansion and diffusion of the change in the minds of the people and the growing hopes of a union . . . cannot be traced but by a diligent perusal of the pamphlets, newspapers, and handbills of both parties, and the proceedings of the legislatures from 1761 to 1774, when the union of the colonies was formed."

The issue of mitre and sceptre had been a *constant*, to use a mathematical term, in Anglo-American relations ever since 1630, even in the Episcopal colonies, where congregational polity existed in fact, whatever the theory, in the parish vestries. Specifically, for eighty-six years after 1689, Episcopal pressure increased intermittently but inexorably. This was a very long time, during which the minds and emotions of three—occasionally four—generations of dissenting colonists were unconsciously conditioned for revolt.

The Dissenters of England and America, allied in defense of what they conceived to be their natural religious liberties, worked out the first great voluntary transatlantic organization of the English-speaking peoples. On the Western shore, the dissenting ministry achieved the first effective intercolonial arrangement, one which adumbrated political union and contributed a useful device to it. Herein American dissent provides the spectacle of a genuine addition to the political organization of the emerging American people suited to the requirements of a great continental area.

In part the suspicions of the sincerity and true motives of the leaders of the Church of England grew out of the open and unabashed attempts of the Anglican missionaries to dominate America in the sphere of religion. They were constantly trying to proselyte among the Nonconformists of the thickly settled areas, to improve their own social position at the expense of humiliation of the Dissenters, or to secure political power in order to attain ultimately complete establishment (though of course this was unvoiced in America). These pursuits made an indelible impression on the American mind.

Organized Dissent in Britain and America employed the press with a thoroughness and success unknown elsewhere in that age. The Nonconformist ministers belonged to the fourth quite as much as to the first estate of the old British Empire. With some help from the laity, they built a propaganda machine with which they fixed in the minds of the English Nonconformists and almost the entire American public, once and for all, the idea of the identity of religious and civil liberty. And in the colonial mind, the members of Otis's Black Regiment firmly implanted the thought that the British Government's designs had evil potentials for religion quite as much as for politics.

Anglican intrigues in the Middle Colonies forced the Dissenting pastors into politics; in New England they were already there. Out of the frequently unseemly contests between curate and minister grew the characteristically American notion that the clergy have no place in the doings of legislative assemblies. Furthermore, the colonial Episcopal clergy, by their preaching of nonresistance, passive submission, and above all, by their almost unanimous support of the Stamp Act, became the nucleus around which the Tory Party formed. This legacy led the patriots to link those "inimical" to their cause with Episcopacy.

There appears to be little doubt that if the American rebellion had been suppressed, not only the dispatch of bishops but the establishment of the Church of England in the colonies would have ensued. As late as 1774, one who had long resided in the New World sent a scheme to Lord North and followed it up with a letter to the *Gazetteer* proposing a gradual increase in the strength of the Church in America, because the colonial troubles were caused by "the fanatics, chiefly . . . few or none of the Church of England . . . being among the refractory." Ambrose Serle encountered the Reverend Charles Inglis in 1777, and the two:

Passed an agreeable hour in Conversation . . . relative to the ecclesiastical Establishment in these Colonies [after their defeat], on the necessity and Manner of which we agreed.

One striking aspect of this history of church and state in England and her colonies was the political ineptitude of a politically minded clergy. However reasonable the pleas for bishops without political authority might be—and frequently this was conceded—they did not convince the Nonconformists that the framers had no ulterior motives, and, as we know, good reason for such doubts existed. Furthermore the Venerable Society seemed to excel in making ill-timed moves. A large majority of the episodes with which we have concerned ourselves in this volume and which engendered so much bitterness on both sides originated in the conclaves of the Anglican clergy in America. We cannot, of course, place the entire blame for the ecclesiastical strife of eighteenth-century America solely on the missionaries; they were, after all, merely understrappers.

It was the hierarchy of the Church of England, managing an ecclesiastical empire without the knowledge of the most vital facts, for they displayed an ignorance of religious conditions and systems in the colonies, that made such blunders possible. No High-Church official ever crossed to investigate the situation in America; only one person, an unknown and inconsequential layman, was ever authorized to do so. The Church of England must, therefore, share with the English political system, Parliament, and the Crown the responsibility for the loss of the colonies.

The great controversy over church and state profoundly stimulated the growth, after 1740, of a sense of American nationality. The most "American" fact about the English colonies, aside from the huge natural environment, was their varied religious composition and ecclesiastical organization, which figured far more in the lives of most of the inhabitants than government and politics, even of the local variety. One thing the missionaries did accomplish: their activities caused colonial Dissenters and most of the Southern clergy, and Anglican laity, to draw together years before the program of British politicians created a similar reaction. Republicanism in church quite as much as in state was the form of polity congenial to these people. To buttress their belief in their religious and civil institutions, they availed themselves of their historical tradition which, because of almost universal literacy, was more widely shared by the "public" than in any European country. Indubitably religion provided the foundation for early American nationalism.

5. MADISON'S MEMORIAL AND REMONSTRANCE (1785)

In a letter to George Mason written in 1826 Madison described the origin of this document and its relationship to the enactment of Jefferson's Bill for Establishing Religious Freedom.

During the session of the General Assembly, 1784–'5, a Bill was introduced into the House of Delegates, providing for the legal support of Teachers of the Christian Religion; and being patronized by the most popular talents in the House, seemed likely to obtain a majority of votes. In order to arrest its progress, it was insisted, with success, that the Bill should be postponed till the ensuing session; and, in the meantime, be printed for public consideration. That the sense of the people might be better called forth, your highly distinguished ancestor, Col. George Mason, Col. George Nicholas, also possessing much public weight, and some others, thought it advisable that a remonstrance against the Bill should be prepared for general circulation and signature; and imposed on me the task of drawing up such a paper. The draught having received their sanction, a large number of printed copies were distributed, and so extensively signed by the people of every religious denomination, that at the ensuing session, the projected measure was entirely frustrated, and under the influence of the public sentiment thus manifested, the celebrated Bill "Establishing Religious Freedom" enacted into a permanent barrier against future attempts on the rights of conscience, as declared in the great charter prefixed to the Constitution of the State.

A Memorial and Remonstrance To the Honourable the General Assembly of the Commonwealth of Virginia.

We, the subscribers, citizens of the said Commonwealth, having taken into serious consideration a Bill printed by order of the last session of the General Assembly, entitled "A Bill establishing a provision for Teachers of the Christian Religion," and conceiving that the same, if finally armed with the sanctions of a law, will be a dangerous abuse of power, are bound, as faithful members of a free State, to remonstrate against it; and to declare the reasons by which we are determined. We remonstrate against the said Bill—

Because, We hold it for a fundamental and undeniable truth, "that Religion, or the duty which we owe to our Creator, and the manner of discharging it, can be directed only by reason and conviction, not by force or violence." The Religion, then, of every man must be left to the conviction and conscience of every man; and it is the right of every man to exercise it as these may dictate. This right is in its nature an unalienable right. It is unalienable, because the opinions of men, depending only on the evidence contemplated in their own minds, cannot follow the dictates of other men: It is unalienable also, because what is here a right towards men is a duty towards the

Reprinted from "Principles of Religious Equality," printed by Rothwell and Ustick (n.p., n.d.). The *Memorial* may also be located in Volume I of the "Congress" edition of Madison's *Writings* (Philadelphia, 1865).

Creator. It is the duty of every man to render to the Creator such homage, and such only, as he believes to be acceptable to him; this duty is precedent, both in order of time and in degree of obligation, to the claims of civil society. Before any man can be considered a member of civil society, he must be considered as a subject of the Governor of the Universe: And if a member of civil society, who enters into any subordinate association, must always do it with a reservation of his duty to the general authority, much more must every man who becomes a member of any particular civil society do it with a saving of his allegiance to the Universal Sovereign. We maintain, therefore, that in matters of religion, no man's right is abridged by the institution of civil society; and that religion is wholly exempt from its cognizance. True it is, that no other rule exists by which any question which may divide a society can be ultimately determined but the will of the majority; but it is also true that the majority may trespass on the rights of the minority.

Because, If religion be exempt from the authority of the society at large, still less can it be subject to that of the legislative body. The latter are but the creatures and viceregents of the former. Their jurisdiction is both derivative and limited. It is limited with regard to the co-ordinate departments: more necessarily is it limited with regard to the constituents. The preservation of a free government requires not merely that the metes and bounds which separate each department of power be invariably maintained; but more especially, that neither of them be suffered to overleap the great barrier which defends the rights of the people. The rulers who are guilty of such an encroachment exceed the commission from which they derive their authority, and are tyrants. The people who submit to it are governed by laws made neither by themselves nor by any authority derived from them, and are slaves.

Because, It is proper to take alarm at the first experiment on our liberties. We hold this prudent jealousy to be the first duty of citizens, and one of the noblest characteristics of the late Revolution. The freemen of America did not wait till usurped power had strengthened itself by exercise, and entangled the question in precedents. They saw all the consequences in the principle, and they avoided the consequences by denying the principle. We revere this lesson too much, soon to forget it. Who does not see that the same authority which can establish Christianity, in exclusion of all other religions, may establish with the same ease any particular sect of Christians, in exclusion of all other sects? That the same authority which can force a citizen to contribute three pence only of his property for the support of any one establishment, may force him to conform to any other establishment in all cases whatsoever.

Because, The Bill violates that equality which ought to be the basis of every law, and which is more indispensable in proportion as the validity or expediency of any law is more liable to be impeached. If "all men are by nature equally free and independent," all men are to be considered as entering into society on equal conditions, as relinquishing no more, and therefore retaining no less, one than another of their rights. Above all, are they to be considered as retaining an *equal* title to the free exercise of religion according to the dictates of conscience," Whilst we assert for ourselves a freedom to embrace, to profess, and to observe, the religion which we believe to be of divine origin, we cannot deny an equal freedom to those whose minds have not yet yielded to the evidence which has convinced us. If this freedom be abused, it is an offence against God, not against man: To God, therefore, not to men, must an account of it be rendered. As the Bill violates equality by subjecting some to peculiar burdens, so it violates the same principle, by granting to others peculiar exemptions. Are the Quakers and Menonists the only sects who think a compulsive support of their religions unnecessary and unwarrantable? Can their piety alone be entrusted with the care of public worship? Ought their religions to be endowed, above all others, with extraordinary privileges, by which proselytes may be enticed from all others? We think too favorably of the justice and good sense of these denominations, to believe that they either covet pre-eminences over their fellow citizens, or that they will be seduced by them from the common opposition to the measure.

Because, The Bill implies, either that the Civil Magistrate is a competent judge of religious truth, or that he may employ religion as an engine of civil policy. The first is an arrogant pretension, falsified by the contradictory opinions of rulers in all ages, and throughout the world: The second, an unhallowed perversion of the means of salvation.

Because, The establishment proposed by the Bill is not requisite for the support of the Christian Religion. To say that it is, is a contradiction to the Christian Religion itself; for every page of it disavows a dependence on the powers of this world: It is a contradiction to fact; for it is known that this Religion both existed and flourished, not only without the support of human laws, but in spite of every opposition from them; and not only during the period of miraculous aid, but long after it had been left to its own evidence, and the ordinary care of Providence: Nay, it is a contradiction in terms: for, a Religion not invented by human policy must have pre-existed and been supported before it was established by human policy. It is moreover to weaken in those who profess this Religion, a pious confidence in its innate excellence, and the patronage of its author; and to foster in those who still reject it, a suspicion that its friends are too conscious of its fallacies to trust it to its own merits.

Because, Experience witnesseth that ecle-siastical establishments, instead of maintaining the purity and efficacy of religion, have had a contrary operation. During almost fifteen centuries, has the legal establishment of Christianity been on trial. What have been its fruits? More or less, in all places, pride and indolence in the Clergy; ignorance and servility in the laity; in both, superstition, bigotry and persecution. Inquire of the teachers of Christianity for the ages in which it appeared in its greatest lustre; those of every sect point to the ages prior to its incorporation with civil policy. Propose a restoration of this primitive state, in which its teachers depended on the voluntary rewards of their flocks; many of them predict its downfall. On which side ought their testimony to have greatest weight, when for or when against their interest?

Because, The establishment in question is not necessary for the support of civil government. If it be urged as necessary for the support of civil government only as it is a means of supporting religion, and if it be not necessary for the latter purpose, it cannot be necessary for the former. If religion be not within the cognizance of civil government, how can its legal establishment be said to be necessary to civil government? What influence, in fact, have eclesiastical establishments had on civil society? In some instances they have been seen to erect a spiritual tyranny on the ruins of the civil authority; in many instances they have civil authority; in many instances they have been seen upholding the thrones of political tyranny; in no instance have they been seen the guardians of the liberties of the people. Rulers who wished to subvert the public liberty, may have found an established clergy convenient auxiliaries. A just government, instituted to secure and perpetuate it, needs them not. Such a government will be best supported by protecting every citizen in the enjoyment of his Religion, with the same equal hand which protects his person and his property; by neither invading the equal rights of any sect, nor suffering any sect to invade those of another.

Because, The proposed establishment is a departure from that generous policy which, offering an asylum to the persecuted and oppressed of every nation and religion, promised a lustre to our country, and an accession to the number of its citizens. What a melancholy mark is the bill of sudden degeneracy? Instead of holding forth an asylum to the persecuted, it is itself a signal of persecution. It degrades from the equal rank of citizens all those whose opinions in religion do not bend to those of the legislative authority. Distant as it may be, in its present form, from the Inquisition, it differs from it only in degree. The one is the first step, the other the last, in the career of intolerance. The magnanimous sufferer under this cruel scourge in foreign regions, must view the bill as a beacon on our coast, warning him to seek some other haven, where liberty and philanthropy, in their due extent, may offer a more certain repose from his troubles.

Because, It will have a like tendency to banish our citizens. The allurements presented by other situations are every day thinning their number. To superadd a fresh motive to emigration, by revoking the liberty which they now enjoy, would be the same species of folly which has dishonored and depopulated flourishing kingdoms.

Because, It will destroy that moderation and harmony which the forbearance of our laws to intermeddle with Religion has produced amongst its several sects. Torrents of blood have been spilt in the old world, by vain attempts of the secular arm to extinguish religious discord, by proscribing all difference in religious opinions. Time has at length revealed the true remedy. Every relaxation of narrow and rigorous policy, wherever it has been tried it has been found to assuage the disease. The American theatre has exhibited proofs that equal and complete liberty, if it does not wholly eradicate it, sufficiently destroys its malignant influence on the health and prosperity of the State. If with the salutary effects of this system under our own eyes, we begin to contract the bonds of religious freedom, we know no name that will too severely reproach our folly. At least let warning be taken at the first fruits of the threatened innovation. The very appearance of the bill has transformed "that Christian forbearance, love and charity," which of late mutually prevailed, into animosities and jealousies, which may not soon be appeased. What mischiefs may not be dreaded, should this enemy to the public quiet be armed with the force of a law?

Because, The policy of the bill is adverse to the diffusion of the light of Christianity. The first wish of those who enjoy this precious gift, ought to be, that it may be imparted to the whole race of mankind. Compare the number of those who have as yet received it, with the number still remaining under the dominion of false religions; and how small is the former? Does the policy of the bill tend to lessen the disproportion? No: it at once discourages those who are strangers to the light of revelation from coming into the region of it; and countenances, by example, the nations who continue in darkness, in shutting out those who might convey it to them. Instead of levelling as far as possible every obstacle to the victorious progress of truth, the bill, with an ignoble and unchristian timidity, would circumscribe it, with a wall of defence, against the encroachments of error.

Because, Attempts to enforce by legal sanctions acts obnoxious to so great a proportion of citizens, tend to enervate the laws in general, and to slacken the bands of society. If it be difficult to execute any law which is not generally deemed necessary or salutary, what must be the case where it is deemed invalid and dangerous? And what may be the effect of so striking an example of impotency in the government, on its general authority?

71

Because, A measure of such singular magnitude and delicacy ought not to be imposed without the clearest evidence that it is called for by the majority of citizens: And no satisfactory method is yet proposed by which the voice of the majority in this case may be determined, or its influence secured. "The people of the respective counties are indeed requested to signify their opinion respecting the adoption of the Bill to the next session of Assembly." But the representation must be made equal, before the voice either of the representatives, or of the counties, will be that of the people. Our hope is, that neither of the former will, after due consideration, espouse the dangerous principle of the bill. Should the event disappoint us, it will still leave us in full confidence that a fair appeal to the latter will reverse the sentence against our liberties.

Because, Finally, "The equal right of every citizen to the free exercise of his religion, according to the dictates of conscience," is held by the same tenure with all our other rights. If we recur to its origin, it is equally the gift of nature; if we weigh its importance, it cannot be less dear to us; if we consult the "declaration of those rights which pertain to the good people of Virginia, as the basis and foundation of government," it is enumerated with equal solemnity, or rather studied emphasis. Either, then, we must say, that the will of the Legislature is the only measure of their authority, and that in the plenitude of this authority they may sweep away all our fundamental rights; or that they are bound to leave this particular right untouched and sacred. Either we must say, that they may control the freedom of the press; may abolish the trial by jury; may swallow up the executive and judiciary powers of the State; nay, that they may despoil us of our very right of suffrage, and erect themselves into an independent and hereditary Assembly; or we must say, that they have no authority to enact into law the Bill under consideration. We, the subscribers, say, that the General Assembly of this Commonwealth have no such authority. And that no effort may be omitted on our part against so dangerous an usurpation, we oppose to it this remonstrance; earnestly praying, as we are in duty bound, that the Supreme Law-giver of the Universe, by illuminating those to whom it is addressed, may, on the one hand, turn their councils from every act which would affront his holy prerogative, or violate the trust committed to them: And on the other, guide them into every measure which may be worthy of his blessing, may redound to their own praise, and may establish more firmly the liberties, the prosperity, and the happiness of the Commonwealth.

6. JEFFERSON'S ACT FOR ESTABLISHING RELIGIOUS FREEDOM (1786)

Although the Assembly received this bill in 1779, it was not enacted until 1786 in reaction against proposed assessments for the establishment which had been in part stimulated and focused by Madison's Memorial. As passed by the Assembly a clause of the Virginia Declaration of Rights was substituted in the text as here reproduced. It is widely noted that Jefferson ranked this act as one of his most significant achievements.

SECTION I. Well aware that the opinions and belief of men depend not on their own will, but follow involuntarily the evidence proposed to their minds; that Almighty God hath created the mind free, and manifested his supreme will that free it shall remain by making it altogether insusceptible of restraint; that all attempts to influence it by temporal punishments, or burthens, or by civil incapacitations, tend only to beget habits of hypocrisy and meanness, and are a departure from the plan of the holy author of our religion, who being lord both of body and mind, yet choose not to propagate it by coercions on either, as was in his Almighty power to do, but to exalt it by its influence on reason alone; that the impious presumption of legislature and ruler, civil as well as ecclesiastical, who, being themselves but fallible and uninspired men, have assumed dominion over the faith of others, setting up their own opinions and modes of thinking as the only true and infallible, and as such endeavoring to impose them on others, hath established and maintained false religions over the greatest part of the world and through all time: That to compel a man to furnish contributions of money for the propagation of opinions which he disbelieves and abhors, is sinful and tyrannical; that even the forcing him to support this or that teacher of his own religious persuasion, is depriving him of the comfortable liberty of giving his contributions to the particular pastor whose morals he would make his pattern, and whose powers he feels most persuasive to righteousness; and is withdrawing from the ministry those temporary rewards, which proceeding from an approbation of their personal conduct, are an additional incitement to earnest and unremitting labours for the instruction of mankind; that our civil rights have no dependance on our religious opinions, any more than our opinions in physics or geometry; and therefore the proscribing any citizen as unworthy the public confidence by laying upon him an incapacity of being called to offices of trust or emolument, unless he profess or renounce this or that religious opinion, is depriving him injudiciously of those privileges and advantages to which, in common with his fellow-citizens, he has a natural right; that it tends also to corrupt the principles of that very religion it is meant to encourage, by bribing with a monopoly of worldly honours and emoluments, those who will externally profess and conform to it; that though indeed these are criminals who do not withstand such temptation, yet neither are those innocent who lay the bait in their way; that the opinions of men are not the object of civil government, nor under its jurisdiction; that to suffer the civil magistrate to intrude his powers into the field of opinion and to restrain the profession or propagation of principles on supposition of their ill tendency is a dangerous

From *The Works of Thomas Jefferson*, ed. Paul L. Ford (New York, 1904), Volume II, pp. 438 ff.

falacy, which at once destroys all religious liberty, because he being of course judge of that tendency will make his opinions the rule of judgment, and approve or condemn the sentiments of others only as they shall square with or differ from his own; that it is time enough for the rightful purposes of civil government for its officers to interfere when principles break out into overt acts against peace and good order; and finally, that truth is great and will prevail if left to herself; that she is the proper and sufficient antagonist to error, and has nothing to fear from the conflict unless by human interposition disarmed of her natural weapons, free argument and debate; errors ceasing to be dangerous when it is permitted freely to contradict them.

SECTION II. We the General Assembly of Virginia do enact that no man shall be compelled to frequent or support any religious worship, place, or ministry whatsoever, nor shall be enforced, restrained, molested, or burthened in his body or goods, or shall otherwise suffer, on account of his religious opinions or belief; but that all men shall be free to profess, and by argument to maintain, their opinions in matters of religion, and that the same shall in no wise diminish, enlarge, or affect their civil capacities.

SECTION III. And though we well know that this assembly, elected by the people for their ordinary purposes of legislation only, have no power to restrain the acts of succeeding Assemblies, constituted with powers equal to our own, and that therefore to declare this act to be irrevocable would be of no effect in law; yet we are free to declare, and do declare, that the rights hereby asserted are of the natural rights of mankind, and that if any act shall be hereafter passed to repeal the present or to narrow its operations, such act will be an infringement of natural right.

7. A PETITION RELATING TO CHURCH ESTABLISHMENT (1786)

This petition is in Madison's handwriting and it is probable that he was instrumental in drafting it. A Bill for the Incorporation of the Protestant Episcopal Church was passed by the Assembly in 1785 which gave considerable autonomy to the Church. By the next session of the Assembly the statute was under attack and it was repealed early in 1787.

To the honourable the Speaker & Gentlemen The General Assembly of Virginia:

We the subscribers members of the protestant episcopal Church claim the attention of your honourable Body to our objections to the law passed at the last Session of Assembly for incorporating the protestant Episcopal church; and we remonstrate against the said law —

Because the law admits the power of the Legislative Body to interfere in matters of Religion which we think is not included in their jurisdiction.

Because the law was passed on the petition of some of the Clergy of the Protestant Episcopal Church without any application from the other members of that Church on whom the law is to operate, and we conceive it to be highly improper that the Legislature should regard as the sense of the whole Church the opinion of a few inter-

From *The Writings of James Madison*, ed. G. Hunt, Vol. II, 1783–1787 (New York, 1901), pp. 212–214.

ested members who were in most instances originally imposed on the people without their consent & who were not authorized by even the smallest part of this community to make such a proposition.

Because the law constitutes the Clergy members of a convention who are to legislate for the laity contrary to their fundamental right of chusing their own Legislators.

Because by that law the most obnoxious & unworthy Clergyman cannot be removed from a parish except by the determination of a body, one half of whom the people have no confidence in & who will always have the same interest with the minister whose conduct they are to judge of.

Because—by that law power is given to the convention to regulate matters of faith & the obsequious vestries are to engage to change their opinions as often as the convention shall alter theirs.

Because a system so absurd and servile will drive the members of the Episcopal Church over to the Sects where there will be more consistency & liberty.

We therefore hope that the wisdom & impartiality of the present assembly will incline them to repeal a law so pregnant with mischief & injustice.

8. HOUSE AND SENATE DEBATES (1789)

Adoption of the United States Constitution was very controversial. In response to concerns that the Constitution did not adequately protect individual liberties, James Madison introduced a number of amendments that he called a "bill of rights." The following excerpts from the House and Senate debates show the progress of the proposals that ultimately became the religion clauses of the First Amendment.

DEBATES IN CONGRESS
JUNE 8, 1789

Mr. MADISON . . . The amendments which have occurred to me, proper to be recommended by Congress to the State Legislatures, are these:

. . . That in article 1st, section 9, between clauses 3 and 4, be inserted these clauses, to wit: The civil rights of none shall be abridged on account of religious belief or worship, nor shall any national religion be established, nor shall the full and equal rights of conscience be in any manner, or on any pretext, infringed. . . .

That in article 1st, section 10, between clauses 1 and 2, be inserted this clause, to wit:

No State shall violate the equal rights of conscience, or the freedom of the press, or the trial by jury in criminal cases.

SATURDAY, AUGUST 15 [1789]

The House again went into a Committee of the whole on the proposed amendments to the constitution, Mr. BOUDINOT in the chair.

The fourth proposition being under consideration, as follows:

Article 1. Section 9. Between paragraphs two and three insert "no religion shall be

The text of the House debate can be found in *Annals of the Congress of the United States: The Debates and Proceedings in the Congress of the United States*, Vol. I, compiled from Authentic Materials by Joseph Gales, Sr. (Washington, D.C., 1834). The Senate debates can be found in *Documentary History of the First Federal Congress of the United States of America*, ed. Linda Grant Depauw (Baltimore, 1977).

established by law, nor shall the equal rights of conscience be infringed."

Mr. SYLVESTER had some doubts of the propriety of the mode of expression used in this paragraph. . . . He feared it might be thought to have a tendency to abolish religion altogether.

Mr. VINING suggested the propriety of transposing the two members of the sentence.

Mr. GERRY said it would read better if it was, that no religious doctrine shall be established by law.

Mr. SHERMAN thought the amendment altogether unnecessary, inasmuch as Congress had no authority whatever delegated to them by the constitution to make religious establishments; he would, therefore, move to have it struck out.

Mr. CARROLL.—As the rights of conscience are, in their nature, of peculiar delicacy, and will little bear the gentlest touch of governmental hand; and as many sects have concurred in opinion that they are not well secured under the present constitution, he said he was much in favor of adopting the words. . . . He would not contend with gentlemen about the phraseology. . . .

Mr. MADISON said, he apprehended the meaning of the words to be, that Congress should not establish a religion, and enforce the legal observation of it by law, nor compel men to worship God in any manner contrary to their conscience. Whether the words are necessary or not, he did not mean to say, but they had been required by some of the State Conventions, who seemed to entertain an opinion that under the clause of the constitution, which gave power to Congress to make all laws necessary and proper to carry into execution the constitution, and the laws made under it, enabled them to make laws of such a nature as might infringe the rights of conscience, and establish a national religion; to prevent these effects he presumed the amendment was intended, and he thought it as well expressed as the nature of the language would admit.

Mr. HUNTINGTON said that he feared, with the gentleman first up on this subject, that the words might be taken in such latitude as to be extremely hurtful to the cause of religion. He understood the amendment to mean what had been expressed by the gentleman from Virginia; but others might find it convenient to put another construction upon it. . . .

By the charter of Rhode Island, no religion could be established by law; he could give a history of the effects of such a regulation; indeed the people were now enjoying the blessed fruits of it. He hoped, therefore, the amendment would be made in such a way as to secure the rights of conscience, and a free exercise of the rights of religion, but not to patronize those who professed no religion at all.

Mr. MADISON thought, if the word national was inserted before religion, it would satisfy the minds of honorable gentlemen. He believed that the people feared one sect might obtain a pre-eminence, or two combine together, and establish a religion to which they would compel others to conform. He thought if the word national was introduced, it would point the amendment directly to the object it was intended to prevent.

Mr. LIVERMORE was not satisfied with that amendment; but he did not wish them to dwell long on the subject. He thought it would be better if it was altered, and made to read in this manner, that Congress shall make no laws touching religion, or infringing the rights of conscience.

Mr. GERRY did not like the term national, proposed by the gentleman from Virginia, and he hoped it would not be adopted by the House. . . .

Mr. MADISON withdrew his motion, but observed that the words "no national religion shall be established by law," did not imply that the Government was a national one; the question was then taken on Mr. LIVERMORE's motion, and passed in the affirmative, thirty-one for, and twenty against it. . . .

MONDAY, AUGUST 17 [1789]

The committee then proceeded to the fifth proposition:

Article 1. section 10. between the first and second paragraph, insert "no State shall infringe the equal rights of conscience, nor the freedom of speech or of the press, nor of the right of trial by jury in criminal cases."

Mr. TUCKER.—This is offered, I presume, as an amendment to the constitution of the United States, but it goes only to the alteration of the constitutions of particular States. It will be much better, I apprehend, to leave the State Governments to themselves, and not to interfere with them more than we already do; and that is thought by many to be rather too much. I therefore move, sir, to strike out these words.

Mr. MADISON conceived this to be the most valuable amendment to the whole list. If there was any reason to restrain the Government of the United States from infringing upon these essential rights, it was equally necessary that they should be secured against the State Governments. He thought that if they provided against the one, it was as necessary to provide against the other, and was satisfied that it would be equally grateful to the people.

Mr. LIVERMORE had no great objection to the sentiment, but he thought it not well expressed. He wished to make it an affirmative proposition; "the equal rights of conscience, the freedom of speech or of the press, and the right of trial by jury in criminal cases, shall not be infringed by any State."

This transposition being agreed to, and Mr. TUCKER's motion being rejected, the clause was adopted. . . .

THURSDAY, AUGUST 20 [1789]

The House resumed the consideration of the report of the Committee of the whole on the subject of amendment to the constitution. . . .

On motion of Mr. AMES, the fourth amendment was altered so as to read "Congress shall make no law establishing religion, or to prevent the free exercise thereof, or to infringe the rights of conscience." This being adopted,

The first proposition was agreed to. . . .

SENATE JOURNAL
SEPTEMBER 3, 1789

On Motion, To amend Article third, and to strike out these words, "Religion or prohibiting the free Exercise thereof," and insert, "One Religious Sect or Society in preference to others," It passed in the Negative.

On Motion, For reconsideration, It passed in the affirmative.

On Motion, That Article the third be stricken out, It passed, in the Negative.

On Motion, To adopt the following, in lieu of the third Article, "Congress shall not make any law infringing the rights of conscience, or establishing any Religious Sect or Society," It passed in the Negative.

On Motion, To amend the third Article, to read thus—"Congress shall make no law establishing any particular denomination of religion in preference to another, or prohibiting the free exercise thereof, nor shall the rights of conscience be infringed"—It passed in the Negative.

On Motion, To adopt the third Article proposed in the Resolve of the House of Representatives, amended by striking out these words—"Nor shall the rights of conscience be infringed"—It passed in the Affirmative.

[On September 7, 1789, the Senate rejected (without any record of the debates) the amendment passed by the House of Representatives that would prohibit the states from infringing the rights of conscience.]

SEPTEMBER 9, 1789

. . . [The Senate agreed] To amend Article the third, to read as follows "Congress shall make no law establishing articles of faith or a mode of worship, or prohibiting the free exercise of religion. . . .

DEBATES IN CONGRESS
SEPTEMBER 24, 1789

The House proceeded to consider the report of a Committee of Conference, on the subject matter of the amendments depending between the two Houses to the several articles of amendment to the Constitution of the United States, as proposed by this House: whereupon, it was resolved, that

they recede from their disagreement to all the amendments; provided that the two articles, which, by the amendments of the Senate, are now proposed to be inserted as the third and eighth articles, shall be amended to read as follows:

ART. 3.   Congress shall make no law respecting an establishment of religion, or prohibiting a free exercise thereof, or abridging the freedom of speech, or of the press, or the right of the people peaceably to assemble, and to petition the Government for a redress of grievances. . . .

9. OCCASIONAL LETTERS REGARDING RELIGION AND GOVERNMENT

To some extent informal letters written during the later years of Jefferson's and Madison's lives are at least as important in understanding their attitudes toward the question of "Church and State" as the formal documents they drafted or the constitutional arrangements they contrived. The following represent rather than exhaust this kind of source.

Jefferson's Letter to the Danbury Baptists

Readers will note how the letter is a wholly conventional response, and might question whether it provides a likely foundation for the "wall of separation" it allegedly supports.

MESSRS. NEHEMIAH DODGE, EPHRAIM ROBBINS, AND STEPHEN S. NELSON, A COMMITTEE OF THE DANBURY BAPTIST ASSOCIATION, IN THE STATE OF CONNECTICUT.

January 1, 1802.
Gentlemen—The affectionate sentiments of esteem and approbation which you are so good as to express towards me, on be-

half of the Danbury Baptist Association, give me the highest satisfaction. My duties dictate a faithful and zealous pursuit of the interests of my constituents, and in proportion as they are persuaded of my fidelity to those duties, the discharge of them becomes more and more pleasing.

Believing with you that religion is a matter which lies solely between man and

From *The Writings of Thomas Jefferson*, ed. H. A. Washington, Vol. VIII (New York, 1854), pp. 113 f.

his God, that he owes account to none other for his faith or his worship, that the legislative powers of government reach actions only, and not opinions, I contemplate with sovereign reverence that act of the whole American people which declared that their legislature should "make no law respecting an establishment of religion, or prohibiting the free exercise thereof," thus building a wall of separation between church and State. Adhering to this expression of the supreme will of the nation in behalf of the rights of conscience, I shall see with sincere satisfaction the progress of those sentiments which tend to restore to man all his natural rights, convinced he has no natural right in opposition to his social duties.

I reciprocate your kind prayers for the protection and blessing of the common Father and Creator of man, and tender you for yourselves and your religious association, assurances of my high respect and esteem.

Jefferson on the Question of Fast Days

TO THE REV. MR. MILLAR

WASHINGTON, January 23, 1808.

SIR,—I have duly received your favor of the 18th, and am thankful to you for having written it, because it is more agreeable to prevent than to refuse what I do not think myself authorized to comply with. I consider the government of the United States as interdicted by the Constitution from intermeddling with religious institutions, their doctrines, discipline, or exercises. This results not only from the provision that no law shall be made respecting the establishment or free exercise of religion, but from that also which reserves to the States the powers not delegated to the United States. Certainly, no power to prescribe any religious exercise, or to assume authority in religious discipline, has been delegated to the General Government. It must then rest with the States, as far as it can be in any human authority. But it is only proposed that I should *recommend*, not prescribe a day of fasting and prayer. That is, that I should *indirectly* assume to the United States an authority over religious exercises, which the Constitution has directly precluded them from. It must be meant, too, that this recommendation is to carry some authority, and to be sanctioned by some penalty on those who disregard it; not indeed of fine and imprisonment, but of some degree of proscription, perhaps in public opinion. And does the change in the nature of the penalty make the recommendation less a *law* of conduct for those to whom it is directed? I do not believe it is for the interest of religion to invite the civil magistrate to direct its exercises, its discipline, or its doctrines; nor of the religious societies; that the General Government should be invested with the power of effecting any uniformity of time or matter among them. Fasting and prayer are religious exercises; the enjoining them an act of discipline. Every religious society has a right to determine for itself the times for these exercises, and the objects proper for them, according to their own particular tenets; and this right can never be safer than in their own hands, where the Constitution has deposited it.

I am aware that the practice of my predecessors may be quoted. But I have ever believed, that the example of State executives led to the assumption of that authority by the General Government, without due examination, which would have discovered that what might be a right in a State government, was a violation of that right when assumed by another. Be this as it may, every one must act according to the dictates of his own reason, and mine tells me that civil powers alone have been given

From *The Writings of Thomas Jefferson*, ed. H. A. Washington, Vol. V (Washington, 1853), pp. 236–238.

to the President of the United States, and no authority to direct the religious exercises of his constituents.

I again express my satisfaction that you have been so good as to give me an opportunity of explaining myself in a private letter, in which I could give my reasons more in detail than might have been done in a public answer; and I pray you to accept the assurances of my high esteem and respect.

Madison on the Relation of Christianity to Civil Government

In 1832, only several years before his death, Madison took the time to comment upon a sermon which had been sent to him by an Episcopal clergyman. The Rev. Jasper Adams (d. 1841) was President of Charleston College in South Carolina.

private

TO REV. [JASPER] ADAMS

CHARLESTON, S. C.

I received in due time the printed copy of your Convention sermon on the relation of Xnity to Civil Government with a manuscript request of my opinion on the subject.

There appears to be in the nature of man what insures his belief in an invisible cause of his present existence, and anticipation of his future existence. Hence the propensities & susceptibilities in that case of religion which with a few doubtful or individual exceptions have prevailed throughout the world.

Waiving the rights of Conscience, not included in the surrender implied by the social State, and more or less invaded by all religious Establishments, the simple question to be decided is whether a support of the best & purest religion, the Xn religion itself ought not so far at least as pecuniary means are involved, to be provided for by the Government rather than be left to the voluntary provisions of those who profess it. And on this question experience will be an admitted Umpire, the more adequate as the connection between Governments & Religion have existed in such various degrees & forms, and now can be compared with examples where connection has been entirely dissolved.

In the Papal System, Government and Religion are in a manner consolidated, & that is found to be the worst of Governments.

In most of the Governments of the old world, the legal establishment of a particular religion and without or with very little toleration of others makes a part of the Political and Civil organization and there are few of the most enlightened judges who will maintain that the system has been favorable either to Religion or to Government.

Until Holland ventured on the experiment of combining a liberal toleration with the establishment of a particular creed, it was taken for granted, that an exclusive & intolerant establishment was essential, and notwithstanding the light thrown on the subject by that experiment, the prevailing opinion in Europe, England not excepted, has been that Religion could not be preserved without the support of Government nor Government be supported without an established religion that there must be at least an alliance of some sort between them.

It remained for North America to bring the great & interesting subject to a fair, and finally to a decisive test.

From *The Writings of James Madison*, ed. G. Hunt, Volume IX (1819–1836) (New York, 1910), pp. 484–488. Reprinted by permission of G. P. Putnam's Sons. *The Relation of Christianity to Civil Government in the United States* passed through several editions.

In the Colonial State of the Country, there were four examples, R. I., N. J., Pennsylvania, and Delaware, & the greater part of N. Y. where there were no religious Establishments; the support of Religion being left to the voluntary associations & contributions of individuals; and certainly the religious condition of those Colonies, will well bear a comparison with that where establishments existed.

As it may be suggested that experiments made in Colonies more or less under the Controul of a foreign Government, had not the full scope necessary to display their tendency, it is fortunate that the appeal can now be made to their effects under a compleat exemption from any such controul.

It is true that the New England States have not discontinued establishments of Religion formed under very peculiar circumstances; but they have by successive relaxations advanced towards the prevailing example; and without any evidence of disadvantage either to Religion or good Government.

And if we turn to the Southern States where there was, previous to the Declaration of independence, a legal provision for the support of Religion; and since that event a surrender of it to a spontaneous support by the people, it may be said that the difference amounts nearly to a contrast in the greater purity & industry of the Pastors and in the greater devotion of their flocks, in the latter period than in the former. In Virginia the contrast is particularly striking, to those whose memories can make the comparison. It will not be denied that causes other than the abolition of the legal establishment of Religion are to be taken into view in accounting for the change in the Religious character of the community. But the existing character, distinguished as it is by its religious features, and the lapse of time now more than 50 years since the legal support of Religion was withdrawn sufficiently prove that it does not need the support of Government

and it will scarcely be contended that Government has suffered by the exemption of Religion from its cognizance, or its pecuniary aid.

The apprehension of some seems to be that Religion left entirely to itself may run into extravagances injurious both to Religion and to social order; but besides the question whether the interference of Government *in any form* would not be more likely to increase than controul the tendency, it is a safe calculation that in this as in other cases of excessive excitement, Reason will gradually regain its ascendancey. Great excitements are less apt to be permanent than to vibrate to the opposite extreme.

Under another aspect of the subject there may be less danger that Religion, if left to itself, will suffer from a failure of the pecuniary support applicable to it than that an omission of the public authorities to limit the duration of their Charters to Religious Corporations, and the amount of property acquirable by them, may lead to an injurious accumulation of wealth from the lavish donations and bequests prompted by a pious zeal or by an atoning remorse. Some monitory examples have already appeared.

Whilst I thus frankly express my view of the subject presented in your sermon, I must do you the justice to observe that you very ably maintained yours. I must admit moreover that it may not be easy, in every possible case, to trace the line of separation between the rights of religion and the Civil authority with such distinctness as to avoid collisions & doubts on unessential points. The tendency to a usurpation on one side or the other, or to a corrupting coalition or alliance between them, will be best guarded against by an entire abstinance of the Government from interference in any way whatever, beyond the necessity of preserving public order, & protecting each sect against trespasses on its legal rights by others.

I owe you Sir an apology for the delay in complying with the request of my opinion on the subject discussed in your sermon; if not also for the brevity & it may be thought crudeness of the opinion itself. I must rest the apology on my great age now in its 83rd year, with more than the ordinary infirmities, and especially on the effect of a chronic Rheumatism, combined with both, which makes my hand & fingers as averse to the pen as they are awkward in the use of it.

Be pleased to accept Sir a tender of my cordial & respectful salutations.

Daniel J. Boorstin

10. THE HAPPY VARIETY OF MINDS

In this excerpt from *The Lost World of Thomas Jefferson* Professor Boorstin discusses the presuppositions which underlay the Jeffersonian concern with religious freedom.

In the universe as a whole the Jeffersonian philosopher . . . admired the beautiful variety established by the Creator. He could not conceive that human minds should fail to show the same manifoldness. "It is obvious," Rush remarked, "there is the same variety in the texture of the minds, that there is in the bodies of men." Jefferson agreed and drew an important conclusion: "As the Creator has made no two faces alike, so no two minds, and probably no two creeds." The experiments of Flourens had confirmed that the brain was an organ of such delicate texture that the slightest variation in its shape or the slightest lesion on its surface was immediately registered in the thoughts and sensations of the affected creature. Might not the differences in men's thoughts be explained then by physical differences in their thinking organs? To see the character of men's ideas determined by the shapes of their minds was thus to incorporate the variety of human thought into the indelible plan of the universe. "Differences of opinion . . . ," Jefferson remarked, "like differences of face, are a law of our nature, and should be viewed with the same tolerance." Again and again, when Jefferson had occasion to explain away the differences among thinking men, and when he was unwilling to assert categorically that his own opinion was the right one, he reasoned in just this manner. When John Randolph wrote him in 1803 concerning certain of their disagreements, Jefferson's friendly reply was that such explanations were not needed; for, he said, he had ceased to wonder at the differences of opinion on any subject, and acquiesced in them as readily as in the physical variations of the human form. In a letter to Rush in 1811 expressing eagerness to be reconciled to his old friend John Adams, Jefferson asked, "Why should we be dissocialized by mere differences of opinion in politics, in religion, in philosophy, or anything else? His opinions are as honestly formed as my own. Our different views of the same subject are the result of a difference in our organization and experience." Examples could be multiplied where Jefferson took refuge in the happy variety of nature: not merely in the more abstract philosophical problems, which never troubled Jefferson deeply anyway, but even in politics. "The terms of whig and tory," he often observed, "belong to natural as well as to civil history. They denote the temper and constitution of mind of different individuals."

If no man was responsible for the shape of his brain, and if that shape predetermined his opinions, there was surely no justification for praising, blaming, or punishing a man for what he thought. The standard of intellectual virtue obviously could not be the possession of "truth," for the Creator could not have required man to transcend his body. Yet the American philosopher refused to believe that there was no standard by which men's thinking could be judged. And he actually found one which seemed harmonious with his cosmology, with his belief in an orderly Creator, and even with his own unwillingness to commit himself explicitly to any absolute other than the Creator. The proper test, the Jeffersonian declared, was not what a man believed, but how accurately and honestly he avowed whatever the Creator had destined him to believe. The ideas which a man professed were less important than whether these ideas were the characteristic expression of the mind which the Creator had given him. Of course, according to a strict materialism, even a man's intellectual honesty was no choice of his own, but the simple effect of environmental influences on his thinking organ. Yet at this point the Jeffersonians were not too rigorous. "Your own reason is the only oracle given you by heaven," Jefferson advised his young friend Peter Carr, "and you are answerable, not for the rightness, but uprightness of the decision." Integrity of views more than their soundness, he told Gerry, was the proper basis of esteem. The Creator desired above all that men be true to themselves. According to the preamble of Jefferson's Act for establishing Religious Freedom in Virginia, "Almighty God hath created the mind free . . . all attempts to influence it by temporal punishments or burthens, or by civil incapacitations, tend only to beget habits of hypocrisy and meanness, and are a departure from the plan of the Holy author of our religion, who being Lord both of body and mind, yet chose not to propagate it by coercions on either, as was his Almighty power to do."

The free interaction of variegated minds had been commanded by the Creator Himself. But Jeffersonian materialism had given to the 'freedom' of the human mind a dangerous ambiguity. In what sense was a man "free" to think, if his ideas had been predetermined by the shape of his brain? Jefferson's own materialism and his theory of toleration were themselves theories. How could he prove them anything more than the product of his own peculiar brain? Yet it was by means of them that he sought to mediate among different views.

This problem did not much disturb the Jeffersonian. He was not anxious to escape the Pyrrhorist trap that awaits all materialist philosophies. As we have seen, thought from the Jeffersonian point of view was essentially a mode of action, rather than the intellectual pursuit of an absolute. Nothing could have seemed more futile than to seek a standard for thought when the Creator Himself had produced only varied ways of thinking. The task of the Jeffersonian philosopher, as he conceived it, was not to harmonize different concepts of truth, but to mediate among modes of mental action: not to bring consistency into the realm of thought but sociability into the world of thinkers.

In religion, for example, the Jeffersonian saw each man not in spiritual pursuit of a metaphysically accurate vision of the True God, but as engaging in an act of homage to his Creator. While it might have been impossible to make men's disparate theories of God logically consistent, the Jeffersonian had set himself quite another task, namely, to enable men sociably to perform their different acts of homage. There was no question of 'consistency' here: problems arose only when a clash of opinions became a clash of men. . . .

The very nature of ideas seemed to show that in the Creator's design sociability—the happy coexistence of the created variety of minds—had been more important than uniformity. For ideas had happily been made so that their discord never in itself produced physical injury: in Jefferson's succinct phrase, ideas were not like stones. "It does me no injury for my neighbor to say there are twenty gods, or no God. It neither picks my pocket nor breaks my leg." The Creator would surely not have given this peculiar undamaging quality to ideas unless He had intended each man to be free to publish the peculiar product of his brain. "When I hear another express an opinion which is not mine, I say to myself, he has a right to his opinion, as I to mine; why should I question it?" asked Jefferson. "His error does me no injury, and shall I become a Don Quixote, to bring all men by force of argument to one opinion? If a fact be misstated, it is probable he is gratified by a belief of it, and I have no right to deprive him of the gratification."

The variety of minds served the economy of nature in many ways. The Creator, who designed the human brain for activity, had insured the restlessness of all minds by enabling no single one to envisage all the qualities of the creation. Since no one by himself could aspire to a serene knowledge of the whole truth, all men had been drawn into an active, exploratory and cooperative attitude. . . . This different bias of different minds, by leading men to explore diverse aspects of nature, resulted in the whole being more thoroughly examined.

Even men's errors kept alive the spirit of inquiry. Rush urged that universities encourage differences of opinion to prevent them becoming (in Adam Smith's phrase) "the dull repositories of exploded opin-

ions." Priestley acknowledged the debt of all to those who differed from them, when he dedicated his defense of the phlogiston theory to several French opponents of the doctrine. In primitive communities, where the absence of civilization, science and religion caused a deficiency of stimuli, the wholesome variety of opinion was lacking; and this in turn re-enforced that "dull and disgusting sameness of mind," which, according to Rush, characterized all savage nations. Such lack of variety itself explained why savages knew so little of science. "Difference of opinion leads to inquiry," Jefferson observed, "and inquiry to truth."

Since successful inquiry was most important in the fundamental issues of human life, the diversity established by the Creator should, of course, be most encouraged in fundamental matters. In religion least of all would the Creator have intended uniformity of minds, for such uniformity might have prevented successful inquiry into the nature of the Creator Himself. On this most difficult of all subjects, Jefferson remarked in his *Notes on Virginia* (Query XVII), the mutual criticisms of men of honestly differing views were especially needed. "Subject opinion to coercion: whom will you make your inquisitors? . . . And why subject it to coercion? To produce uniformity. But is uniformity of opinion desirable? No more than of face and stature. Introduce the bed of Procrustes then, and as there is danger that the large men may beat the small, make us all of a size, by lopping the former and stretching the latter. Difference of opinion is advantageous in religion. The several sects perform the office of a *censor morum*." Priestley observed that unbelievers and even bigots have their use in the general plan: their assigned task, like that of the idolatrous Canaanites, was to exercise the faith of the Isralites, without having the power to drive the faithful out. It was by the objections of the obstinate, Priestley thought, that

Christianity would be forced to purge itself and return to its primitive purity. "A truth that has never been opposed," he remarked, "cannot acquire that firm and unwavering assent, which is given to that which has stood the test of a rigorous examination."

If the variety of minds was to forward the discovery of truth, there must indeed be a truth to be discovered. The Jeffersonian had actually argued that the happy variety of the mental world enabled men to discover a reality, stable and apart from the idiosyncrasy of each mind. But by declaring that the differences between brains explained the variety of ideas, he had merged ideas into the flux of the physical world and had seemingly deprived himself of criteria. This logical dilemma however could not discomfit the Jeffersonian mind in which the physical world always seemed an undeniably real and stable aspect of the cosmos. There might be many ways of doing homage to God; but there must be one right antidote to the poison of the rattlesnake. The American Philosophical Society, we must recall, existed for promoting "*useful knowledge*," and knowledge could not be useful unless it corresponded to the facts of nature. Yet the Jeffersonian significantly never felt it necessary to demonstrate the existence of the singleness of the visible material universe: the concrete and constructive tasks of life were close upon him and pressed with an urgency which he did not need to prove real. If he was to master his environment, he dared not luxuriate in the exquisite manholdness of the human mind.

Robert T. Handy

11. THE MAGNA CHARTA OF RELIGIOUS FREEDOM IN AMERICA

Robert Handy has been Professor of Church History at Union Theological Seminary, New York. His influential writings on American religious history include *A Christian America: Protestant Hopes and Historical Realities*. The following essay, which deals primarily with the constitutional guarantee of religious freedom, shows the variety of forces that joined together to enact the establishment and free exercise clauses of the First Amendment.

The spell cast over human affairs by the idea of Christendom has been a long one; many who rejected its outward forms were still drawn to its central vision. When we remember that in 1750 there were church establishments of one kind or another in nine of the 13 colonies, and recall how deeply embedded in the western tradition the idea of establishment was, the constitutional events that set the new nation on the path of religious freedom show their revolutionary significance. Most of the young nation's chosen representatives were at least nominally committed to Christianity while some of them were adherents of churches still established in a few of the states; how could such persons approve the First Amendment, and how could the state legislatures ratify it?

At least three general perspectives informed various individuals and groups as they worked for religious freedom. Some were dominated by one of these approaches, and yet were also influenced to some degree by the others. . . . The representatives of the three perspectives which guided those who shaped and passed the First Amendment can for the sake of convenience be called the enlightened, the dissenters, and the accommodationists.

The Enlightened

So much has been written about the impact of the Enlightenment on the revolutionary generation in general and on those in particular who shaped the Constitution and the Bill of Rights that the point need not be extensively elaborated here. Deeply impressed by the remarkable discoveries of science, which seemed to be sweeping mystery from the world, and repelled by the inhumanity and barbarity of the series of religious wars of the sixteenth and seventeenth centuries, the thinkers of the Enlightenment proposed to discover the truth about God and the universe by a rational examination of nature. . . .

Thomas Jefferson's great contributions to religious freedom were significantly shaped by the perspectives of Enlightenment. At various times he called himself a "Deist," a "Theist," a "Unitarian," and a "rational Christian." He distilled the Enlightenment's characteristic emphasis on natural religion in his "Bill for Establishing Religious Freedom," framed by him in 1777, and finally enacted with some minor changes early in 1786 by the Virginian House of Delegates and Senate as "An act for establishing religious freedom." In this statute, which he rated as second in importance among all his writings only to the Declaration of Independence, Jefferson insisted "that our civil rights have no dependence on our religious opinions, any more than our opinions in physics or geometry; that therefore the proscribing of any citizen as unworthy [of] the public confidence by laying upon him an incapacity

of being called to offices of trust and emolument, unless he profess or renounce this or that religious opinion, is depriving him injuriously of those privileges and advantages to which in common with his fellow citizens he has a natural right." . . .

Some of those who articulated the view of the Enlightenment on religion, such as Tom Paine and Ethan Allen, were sharper in their criticisms of organized religion than Jefferson, and they had their own spheres of influence. But probably of greater significance for the passage of the First Amendment was the way the thought of the Enlightenment pervaded the general intellectual and cultural atmosphere of the times and left its mark on those who remained otherwise devoted to the perspectives of revealed religion. . . . Hence those who cannot themselves be classed directly among the leaders of the Enlightenment were shaped, sometimes decisively, by its perspectives.

How to classify James Madison religiously is not easy, for he was reluctant to speak about such matters. His family had close connections with the Episcopal Church; he was a regular attendant, and he is usually listed as an Episcopalian. He was also strongly influenced by the Presbyterian president of the College of New Jersey at Princeton, John Witherspoon, who brought the Scottish Enlightenment to Princeton, and who was an ardent believer in religious freedom. Madison's own commitment to religious freedom had several taproots, one of which was unquestionably the social and religious thought of the Enlightenment. This was brilliantly displayed in his "Memorial and Remonstrance Against Religious Assessments," written in response to a bill "establishing a provision for teachers of the Christian religion" before the Virginia House of Delegates in 1784–1785. Insisting on the right of every person to the free exercise of religion, Madison argued that "this right is in its nature an unalienable right. . . . because the opinions of men, depending only in the evidence contemplated by their own minds, cannot follow the dictates of other men." He saw that freedom for one meant freedom for all: "Whilst we assert for ourselves a freedom to embrace, to profess and to observe the Religion which we believe to be of divine origin, we cannot deny an equal freedom to those whose minds have not yet yielded to the evidence which has convinced us." He summed up the case against the legal establishment of religion in phrases that echo the work of the philosophes: "What have been its fruits? More or less in all places, pride and indolence in the Clergy; ignorance and servility in the laity; in both, superstition, bigotry and persecution." It was Madison who presented the first draft of what became the Bill of Rights, and who participated actively in the Congressional debates that led to the final form of the First Amendment, which he also wrote. As the process of the ratification of the amendments proceeded until the Virginia approval of December 17, 1791 put them into effect, the way had been prepared by the perspectives on Enlightenment. . . .

The Dissenters

No one term can serve adequately to cover those Americans of various religious viewpoints who were positively oriented to freedom of religion largely for religious reasons. The term "dissenter" is used here to refer to those who were in disagreement with views held by the majority of Americans in the colonial period that religion should be established in some form or other. Often the dissenters believed in, worked for, and sometimes suffered for the separation of church and state. Individuals and groups whose origins can be traced back to the left wing of the Reformation (chiefly Mennonites) and to the left wing of Puritanism (primarily Baptists, Separate Congregationalists, and Quakers) were from the early decades of colonial history devoted to religious freedom.

Anabaptists in Europe refused to be part of any church-state system, often suffering intense persecution as a result. Their descendants in America continued to work and witness for religious freedom. Contributing significantly to the ferment of freedom in colonial America were such figures as John Clarke, Roger Williams, and William Penn, all of whom emerged from the left wing of Puritanism. They were involved in creating states without establishment of religion—a novel and revolutionary step in the history of European civilization. They proved it could be done. . . . The examples thus provided were frequently cited in later years, especially when the struggles to separate churches from states were going on in the late eighteenth century. So, in 1791, the colorful John Leland, that outspoken Jeffersonian Baptist, could say,

The state of Rhode Island has stood above one hundred and sixty years without any religious establishment. . . . New Jersey claims the same. Pennsylvania has also stood from its first settlement until now upon a liberal foundation; and if agriculture, the mechanical arts and commerce, have not flourished in these states, equal to any of the others, I judge wrong.

Leland was but one of the more prominent figures among the growing hosts of Baptists who struggled for religious freedom in the revolutionary era. . . . Their growth in the colonial period had been stimulated by the Great Awakening, that remarkable movement of religious revival that swept through the colonies in the half-century before the Revolution. Its force was indeed still operative in the South during the war years. The unestablished evangelical bodies profited greatly from this intercolonial movement, increasing in size and number. As Baptists participated in the Revolution, they sought every opportunity also to press for religious freedom. In 1774, they sent a memorial to the Continental Congress which read in part, "The free exercises of private judgment, and the unalienable rights of conscience, are of too high a rank and dignity to be submitted to the decrees of councils, or the imperfect laws of fallible legislatures. The merciful Father of mankind is the alone Lord of conscience." The story of the way the Baptists cooperated with Jefferson and Madison in the disestablishment drive in Virginia has been told many times.

[T]here were thousands of Baptists, and hundreds of representatives of other of the left-wing traditions of the Reformation and of Puritanism who played some part in the struggle for religious freedom and the separation of church and state. . . . [Especially in local] arenas the dissenters played major roles in the rise of religious freedom.

The Accommodationists

There were many Americans who had supported the Revolution and believed in religious liberty as they defined it but who also still were convinced that the United States was and should continue to be a Christian nation. Some of them were willing to give up establishments of religion, others to accommodate existing state or town establishments to the general trend towards freedom by letting other denominations share in them in some form of "multiple establishment." Such persons generally did not feel threatened by the First Amendment; they had been represented in the Congressional debate by those who shared their views. The Bill of Rights was ratified by the necessary number of states in the relatively short period of 26 months with a notable lack of protest or negative comment. The history of religion in America in the nineteenth century cannot be well understood without an awareness of the importance of the accommodative perspective which was clearly evident in the last quarter of the eighteenth. Mark DeWolfe Howe has asserted that "among the most important purposes of the First Amendment was the advancement of the interests of religion." Many church leaders came to believe that the Christian state for which they worked could be better realized under the

First Amendment, as they interpreted it, than under the older, coercive mechanisms of confessional states. . . .

[As one example, the] Maryland Constitution of 1776 ended the establishment of the Church of England so that "for the first time since the beginning of the century all Christian denominations were now equal before the law in Maryland." The old confessional state with its establishment was swept aside, but what emerged was a specifically Christian state. Article XXXIII of the constitution provided that "All persons professing the Christian religion are equally entitled to protection in their religious liberty." Persons did not have to declare their belief in Christianity to vote, but they did to hold office. It was not the Jews who were regarded as a threat to this Christian state, but the Deists, whom many in the Maryland constitutional convention regarded as infidels. . . . In this and in similar episodes what I have elsewhere called "the long spell of Christendom" exerted its power in modified or accommodated form in the late eighteenth and early nineteenth centuries. Three New England states clung to their form of the religious establishment of Congregationalism until the early nineteenth century, but their church leaders insisted on their devotion to freedom, especially in the way they avoided infringing on the rights of others. . . . [W]hen Massachusetts adopted a new Constitution of 1780, it accommodated the desire for religious freedom within the framework of a Christian state by allowing a form of multiple establishment. Key clauses that show the tension and its resolution are these selected from Articles II and III. Article II said in part that "no subject shall be hurt, molested, or restrained, in his person, liberty, or estate for worshipping GOD in the manner and season most agreeable to the dictates of his own conscience"; but III went on to state that

As the happiness of a people, and the good order and preservation of civil government, essentially depend upon piety, religion, and morality: Therefore, to promote their happiness, and to secure the good order and preservation of their government, the people of this commonwealth have a right to invest their legislature with power to authorize and require, the several towns, parishes, precincts, and other bodies politic, or religious societies, to make suitable provision, at their own expense, for the institution of the public worship of GOD: and for the support and maintenance of public Protestant teachers of piety, religion, and morality, in all cases where such provision shall not be made voluntarily.

It was more than a half-century before this pattern of establishment was ended.

Though Massachusetts did not finally ratify the Bill of Rights, the joint committee of the Senate and House endorsed it without any mention of religion, for the state's form of establishment appeared secure. Thus there were a considerable number of people in the late eighteenth and early nineteenth centuries who accommodated a belief in religious freedom to a form of a Christian state, which in some cases was to be maintained by establishments of religion at state or local levels.

Overlappings

There was considerable overlapping among the three main groups described here—overlapping that may seem quite inconsistent to the twentieth-century mind. It may be a bit surprising to find James Madison presenting to the Virginia legislature in 1785 "A Bill for Punishing Disturbers of Religious Worship and Sabbath Breakers"; it is even more surprising to find that the bill had been drafted by Thomas Jefferson. The measure provided that a ten-shilling fine would be levied "If any person on Sunday shall himself be found labouring at his own or any other trade or calling." The authors of *Freedom From Federal Establishment* conclude that "apparently such governmental accommodation to the interests of the Christian religion was deemed both good social policy and also constitutional under the state charter by James Madison and his fellow Virginians." The act was passed in the following year. This illustrates overlapping between enlightened and accommodationist viewpoints, overlapping which blended concerns for religious freedom with some aspects of a Christian state.

Dissenters often showed that they too sought a Christian state. . . . Even [Baptist Issac] Backus showed that he believed in a Christian state when he spoke in praise of a Massachusetts provision that stated, "No man can take a seat in our legislature till he solemnly declares, 'I believe the Christian religion and have a firm persuasion of its truth.'" Although the three general viewpoints outlined here can be distinctly discerned, they are not to be seen as mutually exclusive ideal types; they were held by persons who lived in a particular historical period, and they do overlap in certain ways. We are dealing with eighteenth-century and not twentieth-century minds.

IV. *The Era of Republican Protestantism (1820-1860)*

That same religious ardor which had been raised up on behalf of ecclesiastical independence from the Church of England was also called forth as sentiment for political independence. It has long been recognized that the preachers did yeoman service in the cause for independence, publicizing it, recruiting men, sustaining morale. Recently it has been observed that at the same time, ironically, they were undermining whatever remained of that traditional structure of life—the formal "double relation" in which the churches embodied the one side while civil governments represented the other. So wholly did the colonial "Calvinists" commit themselves to the cause of independence that the achievement of the political aspiration fulfilled a religious vision. Having supported independence as a quasi-religious goal an "establishment" on the part of the federal union (and perhaps even the constituent states) became illogical as well as impossible on practical grounds. American protestantism had effectively done itself out of that established position in the common life which had been largely taken for granted during earlier periods, until the pattern was effectively challenged in Virginia. From this perspective the significant "Church and State" development of the national period was the protestant attempt to recover that position it had lost—albeit expressed in an informal mode.[1]

This new "republican protestantism" embodied a two-fold thrust. On the one side it emphasized that evangelical concern with the individual and his salvation which had proved to be so dynamic in the "Great Awakening" a century earlier. Under nineteenth-century conditions this led to the perfection of revivalism as the nearly universal pattern of protestant religious life in America. Available energies were directed toward the conversion of souls, and at the hands of a Charles G. Finney the impulse was shaped into a system which virtually excluded any other conception of religious life. On the other side, republican protestantism utilized that principle of voluntary association which so intrigued an observer of America like de Tocqueville.[2] Technically speaking, the churches were no more than a species of association within the broader community which included many other kinds of association as well. This position constituted, in contrast to earlier periods, a great reduction in prestige

[1]Perry Miller suggests this broad interpretation in his article "From Covenant to Revival" in *The Shaping of Religion in America*, ed. James W. Smith and Leland Jamison (Princeton, 1961). He is particularly concerned in this article with the metamorphosis of the covenant concept which loomed so large in his interpretation of the "New England Mind."
[2]Cf., *Democracy in America*, Vol. I, Chapter XII (New York, Vintage, 1954), pp. 198 ff.

and position. No longer did churches represent the formal expression of the spiritual end of the whole society—this had been the traditional meaning of "establishment" as we have seen. But from another point of view, this new conception meant that the churches were liberated to work within the society in new ways. One of these ways was through vast cooperating interdenominational agencies which undertook to reform the life of the new nation. The United States might not be protestant Christian in form but republican protestantism sought to make it so in substance. Such a development was directly counter to the intention, shared by Jefferson and Madison, to disengage political and religious life. On the theoretical level it required that the evangelical groups work together for common ends rather than follow the Madisonian expectation that their mutual jealousies would hold each other's ambitions in check.

The concern of this section is not with the agencies and the goals of republican protestantism *per se*. Rather the point to be emphasized is the conception which underlay this vast protestant effort. It was no less than a vision of the United States as a protestant Christian nation conformed to the divine will, not through a formal—even a "theocratic"—establishment of religion, but through a common life renewed by evangelical religion and thus spontaneously God-oriented. The "Churches" and the "governments" might be independent but the common subject of both was that individual whose conversion the revivalistic system was designed to effect. The readings in the section include contemporary criticisms of this "republican protestantism" from a number of significantly different points of view.

1. JOSEPH STORY ON THE RELIGION CLAUSES OF THE BILL OF RIGHTS (1833)

Joseph Story (d. 1845), Associate Justice of the Supreme Court, was a colleague of Marshall's and together they were conservative pillars of a conservative institution. His *Commentaries on the Constitution* indicates how — in spite of the influence Jefferson and Madison exerted in shaping the religious "settlement" — the Christian religion might be presumed necessary to social stability. In this perspective an "informal protestant establishment" such as the evangelicals set out to create could seem to fulfil the true intention of the Constitution — and the Bill of Rights in particular — regardless of what Jefferson thought and Madison wrought.

Commentaries on the Bill of Rights

1863. Let us now enter upon the consideration of the amendments, which, it will be found, principally regard subjects properly belonging to a bill of rights.

1864. The first is, "Congress shall make no law "respecting an establishment of religion, or prohibiting the free exercise thereof; or abridging the freedom of speech, or of the press; or the right of the people peaceably to assemble, and to petition government for a redress of grievances."

1865. And first, the prohibition of any establishment of religion, and the freedom of religious opinion and worship.

How far any government has a right to interfere in matters touching religion, has been a subject much discussed by writers upon public and political law. The right and the duty of the interference of government, in matters of religion, have been maintained by many distinguished authors, as well those, who were the warmest advocates of free governments, as those, who were attached to governments of a more arbitrary character. Indeed, the right of a society or government to interfere in matters of religion will hardly be contested by any persons, who believe that piety, religion, and morality are intimately con-

nected with the well being of the state, and indispensable to the administration of civil justice. The promulgation of the great doctrines of religion, the being, and attributes, and providence of one Almighty God; the responsibility to him for all our actions, founded upon moral freedom and accountability; a future state of rewards and punishments; the cultivation of all the personal, social, and benevolent virtues; — these never can be a matter of indifference in any well ordered community. It is, indeed, difficult to conceive, how any civilized society can well exist without them. And at all events, it is impossible for those, who believe in the truth of Christianity, as a divine revelation, to doubt, that it is the especial duty of government to foster, and encourage it among all the citizens and subjects. This is a point wholly distinct from that of the right of private judgment in matters of religion, and of the freedom of public worship according to the dictates of one's conscience.

1866. The real difficulty lies in ascertaining the limits, to which government may rightfully go in fostering and encouraging religion. Three cases may easily be supposed. One, where a government affords aid to a particular religion, leaving all persons free to adopt any other; another, where it creates an ecclesiastical establish-

From Joseph Story, *Commentaries on the Constitution of the United States*, Vol. III (Boston, 1833), pp. 722 ff.

ment for the propagation of the doctrines of a particular sect of that religion, leaving a like freedom to all others; and a third, where it creates such an establishment, and excludes all persons, not belonging to it, either wholly, or in part, from any participation in the public honours, trusts, emoluments, privileges, and immunities of the state. For instance, a government may simply declare, that the Christian religion shall be the religion of the state, and shall be aided, and encouraged in all the varieties of sects belonging to it; or it may declare, that the Catholic or Protestant religion shall be the religion of the state, leaving every man to the free enjoyment of his own religious opinions; or it may establish the doctrines of a particular sect, as of Episcopalians, as the religion of the state, with a like freedom; or it may establish the doctrines of a particular sect, as exclusively the religion of the state, tolerating others to a limited extent, or excluding all, not belonging to it, from all public honours, trusts, emoluments, privileges, and immunities.

1867. Now, there will probably be found few persons in this, or any other Christian country, who would deliberately contend, that it was unreasonable, or unjust to foster and encourage the Christian religion generally, as a matter of sound policy, as well as of revealed truth. In fact, every American colony, from its foundation down to the revolution, with the exception of Rhode Island, (if, indeed, that state be an exception,) did openly, by the whole course of its laws and institutions, support and sustain, in some form, the Christian religion; and almost invariably gave a peculiar sanction to some of its fundamental doctrines. And this has continued to be the case in some of the states down to the present period, without the slightest suspicion, that it was against the principles of public law, or republican liberty. Indeed, in a republic,

there would seem to be a peculiar propriety in viewing the Christian religion, as the great basis, on which it must rest for its support and permanence, if it be, what it has ever been deemed by its truest friends to be, the religion of liberty.

1868. Probably at the time of the adoption of the constitution, and of the amendment to it, now under consideration, the general, if not the universal, sentiment in America was, that Christianity ought to receive encouragement from the state, so far as was not incompatible with the private rights of conscience, and the freedom of religious worship. An attempt to level all religions, and to make it a matter of state policy to hold all in utter indifference, would have created universal disapprobation, if not universal indignation.

1869. It yet remains a problem to be solved in human affairs, whether any free government can be permanent, where the public worship of God, and the support of religion, constitute no part of the policy or duty of the state in any assignable shape. The future experience of Christendom, and chiefly of the American states, must settle this problem, as yet new in the history of the world, abundant, as it has been, in experiments in the theory of government.

1871. The real object of the amendment was, not to countenance, much less to advance Mahometanism, or Judaism, or infidelity, by prostrating Christianity; but to exclude all rivalry among Christian sects, and to prevent any national ecclesiastical establishment, which should give to an hierarchy the exclusive patronage of the national government. It thus cut off the means of religious persecution, (the vice and pest of former ages,) and of the subversion of the rights of conscience in matters of religion, which had been trampled upon almost from the days of the Apostles to the present age.

2. LYMAN BEECHER ON DISESTABLISHMENT IN CONNECTICUT (1820)

Lyman Beecher (d. 1863) studied at Yale under Timothy Dwight and became the latter's right-hand man in the defense of the Congregational establishment — or "standing order" — in Connecticut. These reflections about the "fall of the standing order" in 1820 are from his Autobiography.

The habit of legislation from the beginning had been to favor the Congregational order and provide for it. Congregationalism was the established religion. All others were dissenters, and complained of favoritism. The ambitious minority early began to make use of the minor sects on the ground of invidious distinctions, thus making them restive. So the democracy, as it rose, included nearly all the minor sects, besides the Sabbath-breakers, rum-selling tippling folk, infidels, and ruff-scuff generally, and made a dead set at us of the standing order.

It was a long time, however, before they could accomplish any thing, so small were the sects and so united the Federal phalanx. After defeat upon defeat, and while other state delegations in Congress divided, ours, for twenty years a unit, Pierrepont Edwards, a leader of the Democrats, exclaimed, "As well attempt to revolutionize the kingdom of heaven as the State of Connecticut!"

But throwing Treadwell over in 1811 broke the charm and divided the party; persons of third-rate ability, on our side, who wanted to be somebody, deserted; all the infidels in the state had long been leading on that side; the minor sects had swollen, and complained of having to get a certificate to pay their tax where they liked; our efforts to enforce reformation of morals by law made us unpopular; they attacked the clergy unceasingly, and myself in particular, in season and out of season, with all

sorts of misrepresentation, ridicule, and abuse; and, finally, the Episcopalians, who had always been stanch Federalists, were disappointed of an appropriation for the Bishop's Fund, which they asked for, and went over to the Democrats.

That overset us. They slung us out like a stone from a sling.

C. E. B. "I remember seeing father, the day after the election, sitting on one of the old-fashioned, rush-bottomed kitchen chairs, his head dropping on his breast, and his arms hanging down. 'Father,' said I, 'what are you thinking of?' He answered, solemnly, 'THE CHURCH OF GOD.'"

It was a time of great depression and suffering. It was the worst attack I ever met in my life, except that which Wilson made. I worked as hard as mortal man could, and at the same time preached for revivals with all my might, and with success, till at last, what with domestic afflictions and all, my health and spirits began to fail. It was as dark a day as ever I saw. The odium thrown upon the ministry was inconceivable. The injury done to the cause of Christ, as we then supposed, was irreparable. For several days I suffered what no tongue can tell *for the best thing that ever happened to the State of Connecticut.* It cut the churches loose from dependence on state support. It threw them wholly on their own resources and on God.

They say ministers have lost their influence; the fact is, they have gained. By voluntary efforts, societies, missions, and

From *Autobiography, Correspondence, etc., of Lyman Beecher, D. D.,* ed. Charles Beecher, 2 volumes, (New York, 1864). Selections are from Volume I, pp. 342–344 and pp. 452–453. (A new edition edited by Barbara M. Cross was published in 1961 by the Harvard University Press, Cambridge, Mass.)

revivals, they exert a deeper influence than ever they could by queues, and shoe-buckles, and cocked hats, and gold-headed canes.

* * *

Revivals now began to pervade the state. The ministers were united, and had been consulting and praying. Political revolution had cut them off from former sources of support, and caused them to look to God. Then there came such a time of revival as never before in the state.

I remember how we all used to feel before the revolution happened. Our people thought they should be destroyed if the law should be taken away from under them. They did not think any thing about God—did not seem to. And the fact is, we all felt that our children would scatter like partridges if the tax law was lost. We saw it coming. In Goshen they raised a fund. In Litchfield the people bid off the pews, and so it has been ever since.

But the effect, when it did come, was just the reverse of the expectation. When the storm burst upon us, indeed, we thought we were dead for a while. But we found we were not dead. Our fears had magnified the danger. We were thrown on God and on ourselves, and this created that moral coercion which makes men work. Before we

had been standing on what our fathers had done, but now we were obliged to develop all our energy.

"On the other hand, the other denominations lost all the advantage they had had before, so that the very thing in which the enemy said, "Raze it—raze it to the foundations," laid the corner-stone of our prosperity to all generations. The law compelling every man to pay somewhere was repealed. The consequence unexpectedly was, first, that the occasion of animosity between us and the minor sects was removed, and infidels could no more make capital with them against us, and they then began themselves to feel the dangers of infidelity, and to react against it, and this laid the basis of cooperation and union of spirit.

And, besides, that tax law had for more than twenty years really worked to weaken us and strengthen them. All the stones that shelled off and rolled down from our eminence lodged in their swamp. Whenever a man grew disaffected, he went off and paid his rates with the minor sects; but on the repeal of the law there was no such temptation.

Take this revolution through, it was one of the most desperate battles ever fought in the United States. It was the last struggle of the separation of Church and State.

3. A CHRISTIAN PARTY IN POLITICS

The Rev. Ezra Stiles Ely delivered this sermon in Philadelphia on the fourth of July, 1827. Having gone so far as to declare, "that other things being equal, I would prefer for my chief magistrate, and judge, and ruler, a sound Presbyterian," Ely's proposal provided a convenient target for contemporary anticlericalism which was convinced that a conspiracy existed to unite Church and State.

We have assembled, fellow citizens, on the anniversary of our Nation's birth day, in a rational and religious manner, to celebrate our independence of all foreign domination, and the goodness of God in making us a free and happy people. On what subject can I, on the present occasion, insist with more propriety, than on the duty of all the rulers and citizens of these United States in the exercise and enjoyment of all their political rights, to honour the Lord Jesus Christ.

Let it then be distinctly stated and fearlessly maintained IN THE FIRST PLACE, that every member of this christian nation, from the highest to the lowest, ought to serve the Lord with fear, and yield his sincere homage to the Son of God. Every ruler *should be* an avowed and a sincere friend of Christianity. He should know and believe the doctrines of our holy religion, and act in conformity with its precepts. This *he ought* to do; because as a man he is required to serve the Lord; as a public ruler he is called upon by divine authority to "kiss the Son." The commandment contained in Proverbs iii. 6. *"in all thy ways acknowledge him,"* includes public as well as private ways, and political no less than domestic ways. It is addressed equally to the man who rules, and to the person who is subject to authority. If we may not disown our God and Saviour in *any* situation, it will follow that we are to own him in *every* situation. Infinite wisdom has taught us, that *he who ruleth over men must be just, ruling in the fear*

of God. No *Christian* can gainsay this decision. Let all then admit, that our civil rulers ought to act a religious part in all the relations which they sustain. Indeed, they ought pre-eminently to commit their way unto the Lord that he may direct their steps; delight themselves in him, and wait patiently for him; because by their example, if good, they can do more good than private, less known citizens; and if evil, more harm. Their official station is a talent entrusted to them for usefulness, for which they must give account to their Maker. They are like a city set on a hill, which cannot be hid; and it is a fact indisputable, that wickedness in high places does more harm than in obscurity.

I would guard, however, against misunderstanding and misrepresentation, when I state, that all our rulers ought in their official stations to serve the Lord Jesus Christ. I do not wish any religious test to be prescribed by constitution, and proposed to a man on his acceptance of any public trust. Neither can any intelligent friend of his country and of true religion desire the establishment of any one religious sect by civil law. Let the religion of the Bible rest on that everlasting rock, and on those spiritual laws, on which Jehovah has founded his kingdom: let Christianity by the spirit of Christ in her members support herself: let Church and State be for ever distinct: but, still, let the doctrines and precepts of Christ govern all men, in all their relations and employments. If a ruler

From Ezra Stiles Ely, *The Duty of Christian Freemen to Elect Christian Rulers* (Philadelphia, 1828), pp. 4–12.

is not a Christian he ought to be one, in this land of evangelical light, without delay; and he ought, being a follower of Jesus, to honour him even as he honours the FATHER. In this land of religious freedom, what should hinder a civil magistrate from believing the gospel, and professing faith in Christ, any more than any other man? If the Chief Magistrate of a nation may be an irreligious man, with impunity, who may not? It seems to be generally granted, that our political leaders in the national and state governments ought not to be notoriously profane, drunken, abandoned men in their moral conduct; but if they may not be injurious to themselves and their fellow men, who shall give them permission to contemn God? If they ought to be just towards men, ought they not also to abstain from robbing God, and to render unto him that honour which is HIS due?

Our rulers, like any other members of the community, who are under law to God as rational beings, and under law to Christ, since they have the light of divine revelation, ought to search the scriptures, assent to the truth, profess faith in Christ, keep the Sabbath holy to God, pray in private and in the domestic circle, attend on the public ministry of the word, be baptized, and celebrate the Lord's supper. None of our rulers have the consent of their Maker, that they should be Pagans, Socinians, Mussulmen, Deists, the opponents of Christianity; and a religious people should never think of giving them permission, as public officers, to be and do, what they might not lawfully be and do, as private individuals. If a man may not be a gambler and drink to intoxication in the western wilds, he may not at the seat of government; if he may not with the approbation of his fellow citizens, in a little village of the north, deny "the true God and eternal life," he may not countenance, abet, and support those who deny the Deity of our Lord Jesus Christ at Washington. In other words, our Presidents, Secretaries of the Government, Senators and other Representatives in Congress, Governors of States, Judges, State Legislators, Justices of the Peace, and City Magistrates, are just as much bound as any other persons in the United States, to be orthodox in their faith, and virtuous and religious in their whole deportment. They may no more lawfully be bad husbands, wicked parents, men of heretical opinions, or men of dissolute lives, than the obscure individual who would be sent to Bridewell for his blasphemy or debauchery.

God, my hearers, requires a Christian faith, a Christian profession, and a Christian practice of all our public men; and we as Christian citizens ought, by the publication of our opinions to require the same.

SECONDLY, Since it is the duty of all our rulers to serve the Lord and kiss the Son of God, it must be most manifestly the duty of all our Christian fellow-citizens to honour the Lord Jesus Christ and promote christianity by electing and supporting as public officers the friends of our blessed Saviour. Let it only be granted, that Christians have the same rights and privileges in exercising the elective franchise, which are here accorded to Jews and Infidels, and we ask no other evidence to show, that those who prefer a Christian ruler, may unite in supporting him, in preference to any one of a different character. It shall cheerfully be granted, that every citizen is eligible to every office, whatever may be his religious opinions and moral character; and that every one may constitutionally support any person whom he may *choose*; but it will not hence follow, that he is without accountability to his Divine Master for his choice; or that he may lay aside all his Christian principles and feelings when he selects his ticket and presents it at the polls. "*In all* thy ways acknowledge him," is a maxim which should dwell in a Christian's mind on the day of a public election as much as on the Sabbath; and which should govern him when conspiring with others to honour

Christ, either at the Lord's table, or in the election of a Chief Magistrate. In elucidating the duty of private Christians in relation to the choice of their civil rulers, it seems to me necessary to remark,

1. That every Christian who has the right and the opportunity of exercising the elective franchise ought to do it. Many pious people feel so much disgust at the manner in which elections are conducted, from the first nomination to the closing of the polls, that they relinquish their right of voting for years together. But if all *pious* people were to conduct thus, then our rulers would be wholly elected by the *impious*. If all *good men* are to absent themselves from elections, then the *bad* will have the entire transaction of our public business.

If the wise, the prudent, the temperate, the friends of God and of their country do not endeavour to control our elections, they will be controlled by others: and if *one* good man may, without any reasonable excuse, absent himself, then *all* may. Fellow Christians, the love of Christ and of our fellow-men should forbid us to yield the choice of our civil rulers into the hands of selfish office hunters, and the miserable tools of their party politics. If all the truly religious men of our nation would be punctual and persevering in their endeavours to have good men chosen to fill all our national and state offices of honour, power and trust, THEIR WEIGHT would soon be felt by politicians; and those who care little for the religion of the Bible, would, for their own interest, consult the reasonable wishes of the great mass of Christians throughout our land.

I propose, fellow-citizens, a new sort of union, or, if you please, *a Christian party in politics,* which I am exceedingly desirous all good men in our country should join: not by *subscribing a constitution* and the formation of a new society, to be added to the scores which now exist; but by adopting, avowing, and determining to act upon, truly religious principles in all civil matters. I am aware that the true Christians of our country are divided into many different denominations; who have, alas! too many points of jealousy and collision; still, a union to a very great extent, and for the most valuable purposes is not impracticable. For,

2. All Christians, of all denominations, may, and ought to, agree in determining, that they will never wittingly support for any public office, any person whom they know or believe to sustain, at the time of his proposed election, a bad moral character. In this, thousands of moralists, who profess no experimental acquaintance with Christianity, might unite and co-operate with *our Christian party.* And surely, it is not impossible, nor unreasonable for all classes of Christians to say within themselves, no man that we have reason to think is a liar, thief, gambler, murderer, debauchee, spendthrift, or openly immoral person in any way, shall have our support at any election. REFORMATION should not only be allowed, but encouraged; for it would be requiring too much to insist upon it, that a candidate for office *shall always have sustained an unblemished moral character,* and it would be unchristian not to forgive and support one who has proved his repentance by recantation and a considerable course of new obedience.

Some of the best of men were once vile; but they have been washed from their sins. Present good moral character should be considered as essential to every candidate for the post of honour. In this affair I know we are very much dependent on testimony, and that we may be deceived; especially in those controverted elections in which all manner of falsehoods are invented and vended, wholesale and retail, against some of the most distinguished men of our country: but after all, we must exercise our candour and best discretion, as we do in other matters of belief. We must weigh evidence, and depend most on those who appear the most competent and credible witnesses. It will be natural for us to believe a man's neighbours and acquaintances in preference to strangers. When we have employed the lights afforded us for the illumination of our minds, we shall feel peace of conscience, if we withhold our vote from every one whom we believe to be an immoral man.

Come then, fellow Christians, and friends of good morals in society, let us determine thus far to unite; for thus far we may, and ought to, and shall unite, if we duly weigh the importance of a good moral character in a ruler. Let no love of *the integrity of a party* prevent you from striking out the name of every dishonest and base man from your ticket. You have a right to choose, and you glory in your freedom: make then your own election: and when all good men act on this principle it will not be a vain thing. Candidates then, must be moral men, or seem to be, or they will not secure an election.

3. All who profess to be Christians of any denomination ought to agree that they will support no man as a candidate for any office, who is not professedly friendly to Christianity, and a believer in divine Revelation. We do not say that true or even pretended Christianity shall be made a constitutional test of admission to office; but we do affirm that Christians may in their elections lawfully prefer the avowed friends of the Christian religion to Turks, Jews, and Infidels. Turks, indeed, might naturally prefer Turks, if they could elect them; and Infidels might prefer Infidels; and I should not wonder if a conscientious Jew should prefer a ruler of his own religious faith; but it would be passing strange if a Christian should not desire the election of one friendly to his own system of religion. While every religious system is tolerated in our country, and no one is established by law, it is still possible for me to think, that the friend of Christianity will make a much better governor of this commonwealth or President of the United States, than the advocate of Theism or Polytheism. We will not pretend to search the heart; but surely all sects of Christians may agree in opinion, that it is more desirable to have a Christian than a Jew, Mohammedan, or Pagan, in any civil office; and they may accordingly settle it in their minds, that they will never vote for any one to fill any office in the nation or state, who does not profess to receive the Bible as the rule of his faith. If three or four of the most numerous denominations of Christians in the United States, the Presbyterians, the Baptists, the Methodists and Congregationalists for instance, should act upon this principle, our country would never be dishonoured with an *avowed infidel* in her national cabinet or capitol. The Presbyterians alone could bring *half a million of electors* into the field, in opposition to any known advocate of Deism, Socinianism, or any species of avowed hostility to the truth of Christianity. If to the denominations above named we add the members of the Protestant Episcopal church in our country, the electors of these five classes of true Christians, united in the sole requisition of apparent friendship to Christianity in every candidate for office whom they will support, could govern every public election in our country, without infringing in the least upon the charter of our civil liberties. To these might be added, in this State and in Ohio, the numerous German Christians, and in New York and New Jersey the members of the Reformed Dutch Church, who are all zealous for the fundamental truths of Christianity. What should prevent us from co-operating in such a union as this? Let a man be of good moral character, and let him profess to believe in and advocate the Christian religion, and we can all support him. At one time he will be a Baptist, at another an Episcopalian, at another a Methodist, at another a Presbyterian of the American, Scotch, Irish, Dutch, or German stamp, and always a friend to our common Christianity. Why then should we ever suffer an enemy, an open and known en-

emy of the true religion of Christ, to enact our laws or fill the executive chair? Our Christian rulers will not oppress Jews or Infidels; they will *kiss the Son and serve the Lord;* while we have the best security for their fidelity to our republican, and I may say scriptural forms of government.

It deprives no man of his right for me to prefer a Christian to an Infidel. If Infidels were the most numerous electors, they would doubtless elect men of their own sentiments; and unhappily such men not unfrequently get into power in this country, in which ninety-nine hundredths of the people are believers in the divine origin and authority of the Christian religion.

If hundreds of thousands of our fellow citizens should agree with us in an effort to elect men to public office who read the Bible, profess to believe it, reverence the Sabbath, attend public worship, and sustain a good moral character, who could complain? Have we not as much liberty to be the supporters of the Christian cause by our votes, as others have to support antichristian men and measures?

Let us awake, then, fellow Christians, to our sacred duty to our Divine Master; and let us have no rulers, with our consent and co-operation, who are not known to be avowedly Christians.

4. BEECHER'S STRATEGY FOR THE WEST (1835)

After his conversion to the "voluntary principle" Lyman Beecher moved to a parish in Boston and subsequently agreed to head up the Lane Theological Seminary in Cincinnati—a strategically placed institution in the campaign to win the West for protestantism. *A Plea for the West* is the published version of fund raising lectures which Beecher delivered to east coast audiences to gain support for Lane Seminary. In these brief excerpts it is clear that republican protestantism embodied a great deal of anti-Roman Catholic sentiment and fear of despotic government—often failing to distinguish the two issues.

The great experiment is now making . . . in the West, whether the perpetuity of our republican institutions can be reconciled with universal suffrage. Without the education of the head and heart of the nation, they cannot be; and the question to be decided is, can the nation, or the vast balance power of it be so imbued with intelligence and virtue, as to bring out, in laws and their administration, a perpetual self-preserving energy? We know that the work is a vast one, and of great difficulty; and yet we believe it can be done.

We know that we have reached an appalling crisis; that the work is vast and difficult, and is accumulating upon us beyond our sense of danger and deliberate efforts to meet it. It is a work that no legislation alone can reach, and nothing but an undivided, earnest, decided public sentiment can achieve; and that, too, not by anniversary resolutions and fourth of July orations, but by well systematized voluntary associations; counting the worth of our institutions, the perils that surround them, and the means and the cost of their preservation, and making up our minds to meet the exigency.

It is a union of church and state, which

From Lyman Beecher, *A Plea for the West*, Second Edition (Cincinnati, New York, 1835), pp. 42–87 (excerpts).

we fear, and to prevent which we lift up our voice: a union which never existed without corrupting the church and enslaving the people, by making the ministry independent of them and dependent on the state, and to a great extent a sinecure aristocracy of indolence and secular ambition, auxiliary to the throne and inimical to liberty. No treason against our free institutions would be more fatal than a union of church and state; none, when perceived would bring on itself a more overwhelming public indignation, and which all Protestant denominations would resist with more loathing and abhorrence.

And is there, therefore, no danger of a church and state union, because all denominations cannot unite, and no one can elude the vigilant resistance of the rest? Is there no other door at which the innovation can come in? How has the union been constituted in times past? Not as coveted by the church, and secured by her artifice or power; but as coveted by the state, and sought for purposes of secular ambition to strengthen the arm of despotic power.

But in republics the temptation and the facilities of courting an alliance with church power may be as great as in governments of less fluctuation. Amid the competitions of party and the struggles of ambition, it is scarcely possible that the clergy of a large denomination should be able to give a direction to the suffrage of their whole people, and not become for the time being the most favored denomination, and in balanced elections the dominant sect, whose influence in times of discontent may perpetuate power against the unbiased verdict of public opinion. The free circulation of the blood is not more essential to bodily health, than the easy, unobstructed movement of public sentiment in a republic. All combinations to forestall and baffle its movements tend to the destruction of liberty. Its fluctuations are indeed an evil; but the power to arrest its fluctuations and chain it down is despotism; and when it is accomplished by the bribed alliance of ecclesiastical influence in the control of suffrage, it appears in its most hateful and alarming form.

We say, then, . . . only keep the church and state apart, and there will be no danger. But while you watch the door at which the alliance never did come, do not forget to watch the door at which it always has entered—the door of the state, inviting the alliance of church power to sustain its own weakness, and nerve its arm for despotic dominion.

But why so much excitement about the Catholic religion? Is not one religion just as good as another?

It is an anti-republican charity . . . which would shield the Catholics, or any other religious denomination, from the animadversion of impartial criticism. Denominations, as really as books, are public property, and demand and are benefited by criticism. And if ever the Catholic religion is liberalized and assimilated to our institutions, it must be done, not by a sickly sentimentalism screening it from animadversion, but by subjecting it to the tug of controversy, and turning upon it the searching inspection of the public eye, and compelling it, like all other religions among us, to pass the ordeal of an enlightened public sentiment.

101

5. A JACKSONIAN CRITICISM OF THE PROTESTANT PHALANX (1829)

Richard M. Johnson (d. 1850) served in the House and the Senate as well as in the Vice-Presidency under Martin van Buren. His nomination to this latter position was according to the wishes of President Jackson with whom he had been close. His report to the Senate "on the subject of mails on the Sabbath" is significant in indicating one kind of resistance to the evangelicals' pressure within the common life. It is the more significant when compared with the report presented to the House on the same issue, which recommended that mails be neither transported nor delivered on Sunday: "It is believed that the history of legislation in this country affords no instance in which a stronger expression has been made, if regard be had to the numbers, the wealth or the intelligence of the petitioners." [1]

That some respite is required from the ordinary vocations of life, is an established principle, sanctioned by the usages of all nations, whether Christian or Pagan. One day in seven has also been determined upon as the proportion of time; and in conformity with the wishes of the great majority of citizens of this country, the first day of the week, commonly called Sunday, has been set apart to that object. The principle has received the sanction of the national legislature, so far as to admit a suspension of all public business on that day, except in cases of absolute necessity, or of great public utility. This principle, the committee would not wish to disturb. If kept within its legitimate sphere of action, no injury can result from its observance. It should, however, be kept in mind, that the proper object of government is, to protect all persons in the enjoyment of their religious, as well as civil rights; and not to determine for any, whether they shall esteem one day above another, or esteem all days alike holy.

We are aware, that a variety of sentiment exists among the good citizens of this nation, on the subject of the Sabbath day; and

our government is designed for the protection of one, as much as for another. The Jews, who, in this country are as free as Christians, and entitled to the same protection from the laws, derive their obligation to keep the Sabbath day from the fourth commandment of their decalogue, and in conformity with that injunction, pay religious homage to the seventh day of the week, which we call Saturday. One denomination of Christians among us, justly celebrated for their piety, and certainly as good citizens as any other class, agree with the Jews in the moral obligation of the Sabbath, and observe the same day. There are also many Christians among us, who derive not their obligation to observe the Sabbath from the decalogue, but regard the Jewish Sabbath as abrogated. From the example of the Apostles of Christ, they have chosen the first day of the week, instead of that day set apart in the decalogue, for their religious devotions. These have generally regarded the observance of the day as a devotional exercise, and would not more readily enforce it upon others, than they would enforce secret prayer or devout meditations. Urging the fact, that neither their Lord nor his disciples, though often censured by their accusers for a violation of

[1] Report from the Committee on the Post Office and Post Roads, Twentieth Congress, 2nd Session (1828–9) House of Representatives Report No. 65 (Feb. 3, 1829).

From *Public Documents* (Printed by order of the Senate of the U.S. at the 2nd Session—20th Congress, 1828–29), No. [46], January 19, 1829, abridged.

the Sabbath, ever enjoined its observance, they regard it as a subject on which every person should be fully persuaded in his own mind, and not coerce others to act upon his persuasion. Many Christians again differ from these, professing to derive their obligation to observe the Sabbath from the fourth commandment of the Jewish decalogue, and bring the example of the Apostles, who appear to have held their public meetings for worship on the first day of the week, as authority for so far changing the decalogue, as to substitute that day for the seventh. The Jewish government was a theocracy, which enforced religious observances; and though the committee would hope that no portion of the citizens of our country could willingly introduce a system of religious coercion in our civil institutions, the example of other nations should admonish us to watch carefully against its earliest indication.

With these different religious views, the committee are of opinion that Congress cannot interfere. It is not the legitimate province of the legislature to determine what religion is true, or what false. Our government is a civil, and not a religious institution. Our Constitution recognises in every person, the right to choose his own religion, and to enjoy it freely, without molestation. Whatever may be the religious sentiments of citizens, and however variant, they are alike entitled to protection from the government, so long as they do not invade the rights of others.

The transportation of the mail on the first day of the week, it is believed, does not interfere with the rights of conscience. The petitioners for its discontinuance appear to be actuated from a religious zeal, which may be commendable if confined to its proper sphere; but they assume a position better suited to an ecclesiastical than to a civil institution. They appear, in many instances, to lay it down as an axiom, that the practice is a violation of the law of God. Should Congress, in their legislative ca-

pacity, adopt the sentiment, it would establish the principle, that the Legislature is a proper tribunal to determine what are the laws of God. It would involve a legislative decision in a religious controversy; and on a point in which good citizens may honestly differ in opinion, without disturbing the peace of society, or endangering its liberties. If this principle is once introduced, it will be impossible to define its bounds. Among all the religious persecutions with which almost every page of modern history is stained, no victim ever suffered, but for the violation of what government denominated the law of God. To prevent a similar train of evils in this country, the Constitution has wisely withheld from our government the power of defining the Divine Law. It is a right reserved to each citizen; and while he respects the equal rights of others, he cannot be held amenable to any human tribunal for his conclusions.

Extensive religious combinations, to effect a political object, are, in the opinion of the committee, always dangerous. This first effort of the kind, calls for the establishment of a principle, which, in the opinion of the committee, would lay the foundation for dangerous innovations upon the spirit of the Constitution, and upon the religious rights of the citizens. If admitted, it may be justly apprehended, that the future measures of government will be strongly marked, if not eventually controlled, by the same influence. All religious despotism commences by combination and influence; and when that influence begins to operate upon the political institutions of a country, the civil power soon bends under it; and the catastrophe of other nations furnishes an awful warning of the consequence.

Under the present regulations of the Post Office Department, the rights of conscience are not invaded. Every agent enters voluntarily, and it is presumed conscientiously, into the discharge of his duties, without intermeddling with the conscience of another. Post offices are so regulated, as that but a small proportion of the first day of the week is required to be occupied in official business. In the transportation of the mail on that day, no one agent is employed many hours. Religious persons enter into the business without violating their own consciences, or imposing any restraints upon others. Passengers in the mail stages are free to rest during the first day of the week, or to pursue their journeys at their own pleasure. While the mail is transported on Saturday, the Jew and the Sabbatarian may abstain from any agency in carrying it, from conscientious scruples. While it is transported on the first day of the week, another class may abstain, from the same religious scruples. The obligation of government is the same to both of these classes; and the committee can discover no principle on which the claims of one should be more respected than those of the other, unless it should be admitted that the consciences of the minority are less sacred than those of the majority.

It is the opinion of the committee, that the subject should be regarded simply as a question of expediency, irrespective of its religious bearing. In this light, it has hitherto been considered. Congress have never legislated upon the subject. It rests, as it ever has done, in the legal discretion of the Postmaster General, under the repeated refusals of Congress to discontinue the Sabbath mails. His knowledge and judgment in all the concerns of that department, will not be questioned. His intense labors and assiduity have resulted in the highest improvement of every branch of his department. It is practised only on the great leading mail routes, and such others as are necessary to maintain their connexions. To prevent this, would, in the opinion of the committee, be productive of immense injury, both in its commercial, political, and in its moral bearings.

Nor can the committee discover where the system could consistently end. If the observance of a holyday becomes incorpo-rated in our institutions, shall we not forbid the movement of an army; prohibit an assault in time of war; and lay an injunction upon our naval officers to lie in the wind while upon the ocean on that day? Consistency would seem to require it. Nor is it certain that we should stop here. If the principle is once established, that religion, or religious observances, shall be interwoven with our legislative acts, we must pursue it to its ultimatum. We shall, if consistent, provide for the erection of edifices for the worship of the Creator, and for the support of Christian ministers, if we believe such measures will promote the interests of Christianity. It is the settled conviction of the committee, that the only method of avoiding these consequences, with their attendant train of evils, is to adhere strictly to the spirit of the Constitution, which regards the general government in no other light than that of a civil institution, wholly destitute of religious authority.

What other nations call religious toleration, we call religious rights. They are not exercised in virtue of governmental indulgence, but as rights, of which government cannot deprive any portion of citizens, however small. Despotic power may invade those rights, but justice still confirms them. Let the national legislature once perform an act which involves the decision of a religious controversy, and it will have passed its legitimate bounds. The precedent will then be established, and the foundation laid for that usurpation of the Divine prerogative in this country, which has been the desolating scourge to the fairest portions of the old world. Our Constitution recognises no other power than that of persuasion, for enforcing religious observances. Let the professors of Christianity recommend their religion by deeds of benevolence—by Christian meekness—by lives of temperance and holiness. Let them combine their efforts to instruct the ignorant—to relieve the widow and the orphan—to promulgate to the world the gospel of their Saviour, recommending its precepts by their habitual example: government will find its legitimate object in protecting them. It cannot oppose them, and they will not need its aid. Their moral influence will then do infinitely more to advance the true interests of religion, than any measures which they may call on Congress to enact.

The petitioners do not complain of any infringement upon their own rights. They enjoy all that Christians ought to ask at the hand of any government—protection from all molestation in the exercise of their religious sentiments.

Resolved, That the Committee be discharged from the further consideration of the subject.

6. A RELIGIOUS LIBERAL'S CRITICISM OF THE PROTESTANT STRATEGY (1829)

William Ellery Channing (d. 1842) was a broad churchman within Boston Congregationalism who was instrumental in the emergence of American "Unitarianism" during the 1820's. It is wrong to see Channing as a philosophic radical—rather he was a liberal Christian with a social conscience. His moral concern for the social life is evident in this criticism of the evangelical program.

In truth, one of the most remarkable circumstances or features of our age is the energy with which the principle of combination, or of action by joint forces, by associated numbers, is manifesting itself. It may be said, without much exaggeration, that every thing is done now by societies. Men have learned what wonders can be accomplished in certain cases by union, and seem to think that union is competent to every thing. You can scarcely name an object for which some institution has not been formed. Would men spread one set of opinions or crush another? They make a society. Would they improve the penal code, or relieve poor debtors? They make societies. Would they encourage agriculture, or manufactures or science? They make societies. Would one class encourage horse-racing, and another discourage travelling on Sunday? They form societies. We have immense institutions spreading over the country, combining hosts for particular objects. We have minute ramifications of these societies, penetrating everywhere except through the poor-house, and conveying resources from the domestic, the laborer, and even the child, to the central treasury. This principle of association is worthy the attention of the philosopher, who simply aims to understand society and its most powerful springs. To the philanthropist and the Christian it is exceedingly interesting, for it is a mighty engine, and must act either for good or for evil, to an extent which no man can foresee or comprehend.

That this mode of action has advantages and recommendations is very obvious. The principal arguments in its favor may be stated in a few words. Men, it is justly said, can do jointly what they cannot do singly. The union of minds and hands works wonders. Men grow efficient by concentrating their powers. Joint effort conquers nature, hews through mountains, rears pyramids,

From *The Works of William E. Channing, D. D.* (Boston, 1878), pp. 138–149.

dikes out the ocean. Man, left to himself, living without a fellow, — if he could indeed so live, — would be one of the weakest of creatures. Associated with his kind, he gains dominion over the strongest animals, over the earth and the sea, and, by his growing knowledge, may be said to obtain a kind of property in the universe.

The great principle from which we start in this preliminary discussion, and in which all our views of the topics above proposed are involved, may be briefly expressed. It is this: — Society is chiefly important as it ministers to, and calls forth, intellectual and moral energy and freedom. Its action on the individual is beneficial in proportion as it awakens in him a power to act on himself, and to control or withstand the social influences to which he is at first subjected. Society serves us by furnishing objects, occasions, materials, excitements, through which the whole soul may be brought into vigorous exercise, may acquire a consciousness of its free and responsible nature, may become a law to itself, and may rise to the happiness and dignity of framing and improving itself without limit or end. Inward, creative energy is the highest good which accrues to us from our social principles and connections. The mind is enriched, not by what it passively receives from others, but by its own action on what it receives. We would especially affirm of virtue that it does not consist in what we inherit, or what comes to us from abroad. It is of inward growth, and it grows by nothing so much as by resistance of foreign influences, by acting from our deliberate convictions, in opposition to the principles of sympathy and imitation. According to these views, our social nature and connections are means. Inward power is the end, — a power which is to triumph over and control the influence of society.

The truth is, and we need to feel it most deeply, that our connection with society, as it is our greatest aid, so it is our greatest peril. We are in constant danger of being spoiled of our moral judgment, and of our power over ourselves; and in losing these, we lose the chief prerogatives of spiritual beings. We sink, as far as mind can sink, into the world of matter, the chief distinction of which is, that it wants self-motion, or moves only from foreign impulse. The propensity in our fellow-creatures which we have most to dread is that which, though most severely condemned by Jesus, is yet the most frequent infirmity of his followers, — we mean the propensity to rule, to tyrannize, to war with the freedom of their equals, to make themselves standards for other minds, to be lawgivers, instead of brethren and friends, to their race. Our great and most difficult duty, as social beings, is, to derive constant aid from society without taking its yoke; to open our minds to the thoughts, reasonings, and persuasions of others, and yet to hold fast the sacred right of private judgment; to receive impulses from our fellow-beings, and yet to act from our own souls; to sympathize with others, and yet to determine our own feelings; to act with others, and yet to follow our own consciences; to unite social deference and self-dominion; to join moral self-subsistence with social dependence; to respect others without losing self-respect; to love our friends and to reverence our superiors, whilst our supreme homage is given to that moral perfection which no friend and no superior has realized, and which, if faithfully pursued, will often demand separation from all around us. Such is our great work as social beings, and to perform it, we should look habitually to Jesus Christ, who was distinguished by nothing more than by moral independence, — than by resisting and overcoming the world.

It is interesting and encouraging to observe, that the enslaving power of society over the mind is decreasing, through what would seem at first to threaten its enlargement; — we mean, through the extension of social intercourse. . . .

We regret that religion has not done more to promote this enlarged intercourse of minds, — the great means, as we have seen, of reconciling social aids with personal independence. As yet, religion has generally assumed a sectarian form, and its disciples, making narrowness a matter of conscience, have too often shunned connection with men of different views as a pestilence, and yielded their minds to the exclusive influences of the leaders and teachers of their separate factions. Indeed, we fear that in no department of life has the social principle been perverted more into an instrument of intellectual thraldom than in religion. We could multiply proofs without end, but will content ourselves with a single illustration drawn from what are called "revivals of religion." We have many objections to these as commonly conducted; but nothing offends us more than their direct and striking tendency to overwhelm the mind with foreign influences, and to strip it of all self-direction. In these feverish seasons, religion, or what bears the name, is spread, as by contagion, and to escape it is almost as difficult as to avoid a raging epidemic. Whoever knows any thing of human nature, knows the effect of excitement in a crowd. When systematically prolonged and urged onward, it subverts deliberation and self-control. The individual is lost in the mass, and borne away as in a whirlwind. The prevalent emotion, be it love or hatred, terror or enthusiasm, masters every mind which is not fortified by a rare energy, or secured by a rare insensibility. In revivals, a multitude are subjected at once to strong emotions, which are swelled and perpetuated by the most skilful management. The individual is never suffered to escape the grasp of the leading or subordinate agents in the work. A machinery of social influences, of "inquiry meetings," of "anxious meetings," of conferences, of prayer meetings, of perpetual private or public impulses, is brought to bear on the diseased subject, until, exhausted in body and mind, he becomes the passive, powerless recipient of whatever form or impressions it may be thought fit to give him.

Our first remark is, that we should beware of confounding together, as of equal importance, those associations which are formed by our Creator, which spring from our very constitution, and are inseparable from our being, and those of which we are now treating, which man invents for particular times and exigencies. Let us never place our weak, short-sighted contrivances on a level with the arrangements of God. We have acknowledged the infinite importance of society to the development of human powers and affections. But when we speak thus of society, we mean chiefly the relations in which God has placed us; we mean the connections of family, of neighborhood, of country, and the great bond of humanity, uniting us with our whole kind, and not missionary societies, peace societies, or charitable societies, which men have contrived. These last have their uses, and some do great good; but they are no more to be compared with the societies in which nature places us, than the torches which we kindle on earth in the darkness of night are to be paralleled with the all-pervading and all-glorifying light of the sun. We make these remarks, because nothing is more common than for men to forget the value of what is familiar, natural, and universal, and to ascribe undue importance to what is extraordinary, forced, and rare, and therefore striking. Artificial associations have their use, but are not to be named with those of nature; and to these last, therefore, we are to give our chief regard.

We now proceed to our second remark, in which we proposed to suggest a principle by which the claims of different associations may be estimated. It is this: The value of associations is to be measured by the energy, the freedom, the activity, the moral power, which they encourage and diffuse. In truth, the great object of all benevolence is to give power, activity, and freedom to others. We cannot, in the strict sense of the word, *make* any being happy. We can give others the *means* of happiness, together with motives to the faithful use of them; but on this faithfulness, on the free and full exercise of their own powers, their happiness depends. There is thus a fixed, impassable limit to human benevolence. It can only make men happy through themselves, through their own freedom and energy. We go further. We believe that God has set the same limit to his own benevolence. He makes no being happy in any other sense than in that of giving him means, powers, motives, and a field for exertion. We have here, we think, the great consideration to guide us in judging of associations.

. . . We beg our readers to carry with them the principle now laid down in judging of associations; to inquire how far they are fitted to call forth energy, active talent, religious inquiry, a free and manly virtue. We insist on these remarks, because not a few associations seem to us exceedingly exceptionable, on account of their tendency to fetter men, to repress energy, to injure the free action of individuals and society, and because this tendency lurks, and is to be guarded against, even in good institutions. On this point we cannot but enlarge, for we deem it of the highest importance.

Associations often injure free action by a very plain and obvious operation. They accumulate power in a few hands, and this takes place just in proportion to the surface over which they spread. In a large institution, a few men rule, a few do every thing; and, if the institution happens to be directed to objects about which conflict and controversy exist, a few are able to excite in the mass strong and bitter passions, and by these to obtain an immense ascendency. Through such an association, widely spread, yet closely connected by party feeling, a few leaders can send their voices and spirit far and wide, and, where great funds are accumulated, can league a host of instruments, and by menace and appeals to interest can silence opposition. Accordingly, we fear that in this country an influence is growing up, through widely spread societies, altogether at war with the spirit of our institutions, and which, unless jealously watched, will gradually but surely encroach on freedom of thought, of speech, and of the press. It is very striking to observe how, by such combinations, the very means of encouraging a free action of men's minds may be turned against it. We all esteem the press as the safeguard of our liberties, as the power which is to quicken intellect by giving to all minds an opportunity to act on all. Now, by means of tract societies spread over a whole community, and acting under a central body, a few individuals, perhaps not more than twenty, may determine the chief reading for a great part of the children of the community, and for a majority of the adults, and may deluge our country with worthless sectarian writings, fitted only to pervert its taste, degrade its intellect, and madden it with intolerance. Let associations devoted to any objects which excite the passions be everywhere spread and leagued together for mutual support, and nothing is easier than to establish a control over newspapers. We are persuaded that, by an artful multiplication of societies, devoted apparently to different objects, but all swayed by the same leaders, and all intended to bear against a hated party, as cruel a persecution may be carried on in a free country as in a despotism. Public opinion may be so combined, and inflamed, and brought to bear on odious individuals or opinions, that it will be as perilous to think and speak with manly freedom as if an inquisition were open before us. It is now discovered that the way to rule in this country is by an array of numbers which a prudent man will not like to face. Of consequence, all associations aiming or tending to establish sway by numbers ought to be opposed. They create tyrants as effectually as standing armies. Let them be withstood from the beginning. No matter whether the opinions which they intend to put down be true or false. Let no opinion be put down by such means. Let no error be suppressed by an instrument which will be equally powerful against truth, and which must subvert that freedom of thought on which all truth depends. Let the best end fail if it cannot be accomplished by right and just means. For example, we would have criminals punished, but punished in the proper way, and by a proper authority. It were better that they should escape than be imprisoned or executed by any man who may think fit to assume the office; for sure we are that, by this summary justice, the innocent would soon suffer more than the guilty; and, on the same principle, we cannot consent that what we deem error should be crushed by the joint cries and denunciations of vast societies directed by the tyranny of a few; for truth has more to dread from such weapons than falsehood, and we know no truth against which they may not be successfully turned. In this country, few things are more to be dreaded than organizations or institutions by which public opinion may be brought to bear tyrannically against individuals or sects. From the nature of things, public opinion is often unjust; but, when it is not embodied and fixed by pledged societies, it easily relents, it may receive new impulses, it is opened to influences from the injured. On the contrary, when shackled and stimulated by vast associations, it is in danger of becoming a steady, unrelenting tyrant, brow-beating the timid, proscribing the resolute, silencing free speech, and virtually denying the dearest religious and civil rights. We say not that all great associations *must* be thus abused. We know that some are useful. We know, too, that there are cases in which it is important that public opinion should be condensed, or act in a mass. We feel, however, that the danger of great associations is increased by the very fact that they are sometimes useful. They are perilous instruments. They ought to be suspected. They are a kind of irregular government created within our constitutional government. Let them be watched closely. As soon as we find them resolved or disposed to bear down a respectable man or set of men, or to force on the community measures about which wise and good men differ, let us feel that a dangerous engine is at work among us, and oppose to it our steady and stern disapprobation.

7. COLTON ON THE TRUE CHARACTER OF THE EVANGELICAL ENTERPRISE (1836)

Calvin Colton went from Yale to Andover Seminary and thereafter into a Presbyterian Church until his voice failed him. Later he became an Episcopal clergyman for a short period although already journalistic ambition had become evident. At one point he attacked the separation of Church and State in America. The book from which this selection is taken is a criticism initially directed at the Temperance Movement. His comments apply, however, to the whole protestant enterprise which sought to refashion the common life through the voluntary societies. After writing significant political and biographical pieces he held a chair of political economy at Trinity College, Hartford, Connecticut until his death.

It is a remarkable fact, that in less than the period that belongs to a single generation, the economy of society in this country, in all that pertains to moral reform and religious enterprise, has been formed on a model entirely new to ourselves, but not without type in history. It is the assumption of a controlling influence by a few, who stand at the head of moral and religious organizations of various names. The public generally are simple, honest, confiding; and do not note operations of this kind. That is, they do not understand when and how the whole frame of society is getting into a new structure, leaving the great mass in subjection to the will and control of select, and often self-elected, combinations of individuals. They do not even suspect, that societies, formed for such good purposes, could have in them the leaven of ambition; and they allow themselves to be formed into minor and subsidiary organizations, comprehending the whole mass of the community, to uphold these supervisory establishments by contributions drawn from every source and from every hand. Most extraordinary measures are devised to obtain funds; itinerating mendicants are flying in all directions, traversing the country from east to west, and from north to south; every part of the complicated machinery is well contrived to answer the end; the system is thorough and perfect; and at the head of all sit a few eminent individuals, looking down upon and managing this work of their own hands, themselves independent and secure in their places by provisions which cannot fail while their influence lasts.

The process of corruption—for such we think proper to call it, without pretending to measure its degrees—in these high officers, and in the societies under their control, is always gradual. The men come into these places ordinarily under the influence of very pure designs; it was, perhaps, an unexpected elevation; certainly there was neither experience nor custom in it; they are transplanted from a circumscribed to a wide sphere of action and influence; their views are expanded; their duties require them to travel, and to form extensive acquaintances with the public; they see the world in constantly new and shifting forms; are ever concerting and scheming for the attainment of their objects; the economy of social organization for these purposes becomes a study, and themselves adepts; practice makes perfect; they enlarge their plans, and attempt to improve them;

From *Protestant Jesuitism* by A Protestant (New York, 1836), pp. 107–112.

they attain, finally, not only a high and commanding position in society, but an almost unlimited influence; and "who," think they, at last, "can govern the world better than we? We have discovered how it can be done; we are competent; and we think it will be safest in our hands." And they set themselves about it, on the principle that all men have a right to that influence which they can command. They have no scruples; they have found out that the world must be governed by a few; that it is all effected by scheming; that perfect honesty and openness are inconsistent with such an art, and impolitic; that the secrets of government must be in the keeping of governors; that the wide public are to be informed only on points which concern them to know, and as they may be convenient instruments of power; that, in view of rival institutions, sects, or parties, all plans are to be formed and executed on principles of policy; and policy becomes, at last, the reigning principle. In spite of themselves, they and their work are transformed; they are not the things they were when they first set out. It is the unavoidable, the irresistible tendency of such organizations in such relations. It can no more be prevented than the course of nature, because it is identical with that course. These men will as necessarily become ambitious and aspiring, grasping at power and loving to wield it, and will as certainly scheme for themselves, as the infant will come to be a man; and observing the scope, and feeling the motives, of the wide field before him, will make the most of it. And never was a community more effectually brought under this dominion than we are at this moment. It is a new form indeed; but it is the operation of the same principle. A few irresponsible societies, with a few men at their head, govern this land in all that relates to our moral and religious interests; and they govern it for themselves. At least, they govern it in a way that is agreeable to themselves; and such is the ascendency of their influence, that their will is irresistible. It is a revival of the reign of Jesuitism, adapted to our time and circumstances.

We think it fair to say, that the clergy generally, and the religious public, who have been drawn into these schemes, are most remote from any participation in unworthy motives. It is the perfection of such policies, that a few lead the many, and ride upon their shoulders—while the many are persuaded that their leaders are as uncorrupt as themselves. Nor would we intimate that, for the most part, these societies have not espoused interests of importance, and most worthy of support. Our diffidence relates entirely to the character of the organizations, and their inherent tendencies to corruption and abuse. The change we desire to see is not the abandonment of these interests, but that they should be restored to the control of that public that is called upon to support them.

If the clergy of this land and the Christian public will open their eyes, they will see that the interests of moral and religious reform in the country are, almost entirely, in the hands and under the control of a few combinations of individuals, who are themselves not only above any suitable control, and irresponsible, but who have devised and put in operation a system of measures, which, by their own supervision and that of their sub-agents, force the wide community, socially and individually, into their schemes, while the public have no voice in concerting them. The measures are not submitted, but imposed. In the present posture of these affairs, there is no chance for that general control which is the only safety of a community of rights and privileges. And the ascendency of these combinations is perpetually rising; this control is becoming more uncontrollable; by a consciousness of power they are growing more confident; and no man can openly oppose them without the risk of being crushed by their influence. Their eyes are everywhere; they see and understand all movements; and not a whisper of discontent can be breathed, but that the bold remonstrant will feel the weight of their displeasure. The whole community, on whom they rely, are marshalled and disciplined to their will.

However important, therefore, those interests may be which have thus accidentally fallen into such hands, and for the very reason that they are important, it becomes the solemn duty of the public to see that they do not receive detriment on that account. Some of them have already been grossly mismanaged, and threatened with a complete wreck—such, for example, as the Temperance reformation. We do not desire to expose the faults we have noticed in the management of other enterprises, because we indulge the hope that they may yet be corrected; nor are we willing to diminish public confidence in them so long as that hope remains. Our principal aim has been to point out the defects and dangerous tendencies of organizations of a specific character, in the hands of which these interests are extensively vested, believing that they are radically and essentially Jesuitical.

James F. Maclear

8. "THE TRUE AMERICAN UNION" OF CHURCH AND STATE

Professor Maclear, in the article from which this selection is taken, views the same phenomenon as a "reconstruction of the theocratic tradition" which was the legacy of the American Puritans.

By the end of the 1780's . . . the ecclesiastical crisis of New England had become acute. And in the next decade the appearance of the Republican party brought the church question to sharpest focus. Here the fusion of political radicals with dissenters was completed, the antitheocratic traditions made politically relevant, and disestablishment transformed from a visionary ideal into an imminent possibility. Jeffersonian Baptists like John Leland expressed the new militancy: "The very idea of toleration is despicable. . . . All should be equally free, Jews, Turks, Pagans and Christians. . . . A general assessment (forcing all to pay some preacher) amounts to an establishment." Thus the stage was set for a final assault on the ancient New England ideal of a Christian republic. Could the Puritans' heirs so restate this ideal that it might again become relevant to the vision of an altered New England and to the wider American destiny to which New England had become committed?

* * *

"For several days I suffered what no tongue can tell *for the best thing that ever happened to the State of Connecticut.*" This often-quoted statement of Lyman Beecher suggests both the painfulness and the thoroughness of conservative readjustment, but not the eventual acceptance of the liberal philosophy of church-state separation, as has sometimes been said. Instead, the

Reprinted with permission from the American Society of Church History from James Fulton Maclear, "The True American Union of Church and State: The Reconstruction of the Theocratic Tradition," *Church History* 28 (1959): 41–62.

year after Connecticut disestablishment Beecher was lecturing civil magistrates on their duties to the church as if nothing had happened. This constancy to the old loyalties was general, even though the necessity of accepting legal separation was gradually being recognized. The sermon preached before the Connecticut legislature in 1823 by Nathaniel W. Taylor, Beecher's closest friend and late pastor of the Center Church, New Haven, was typical. "There were dangers and evils without the change, it is believed, greater than exist with it," was Taylor's unenthusiastic judgment. But he then went on to repeat most of the essentials of Dwight's argument:

Why should not legislators, judges, magistrates of every description, with every friend of his country, uphold those institutions which are its strength and its glory? . . . Shall clamors about the rights of conscience induce us to throw away Heaven's richest legacy to earth? . . . But you will make men Christians. And what if we do? . . . But you will make sectarians. God forbid. We plead for no such influence. We only ask for those provisions of law, and that patronage from every member of the community in behalf of a common Christianity, which are its due as a nation's strength and a nation's glory.

The continuity displayed here was consciously promoted through later decades. Nowhere was there apology for New England's past. Seventeenth-century religious persecution was dismissed as a subordinate theme and the historic religious qualification for office justified as "a necessary measure, to prevent the ascendency of new adventurers, having different principles, who might, had they been allowed to vote, have destroyed the foundations on which all our invaluable institutions now rest." . . .

Yet disestablishment gravely affected the Puritan tradition. And as Beecher suggested, its effect was ultimately beneficial. . . . Specifically, what were the services of disestablishment to this revival of the theocratic tradition?

First, constitutional separation stimulated the completion of a radical reformulation of principles. The encumbrance of political alliances, emphasizing an older and now untenable theory of church-state relations and vitiating Congregational pretensions to denominational equalitarianism, was cast off. Accordingly, by 1823 Beecher had come to oppose any direct entanglement in the political process, though one of his reasons—that no party can "in a popular government, be sufficiently secure from change to render it safe"—indicated that his thinking on this issue was only partially reformed. Indeed, it was now not only possible but essential to explore new theoretical alternatives, for in the altered circumstances a convincing justification of theocracy depended on exploiting new departures.

Moreover, disestablishment now made it possible to disarm opposition by adopting the semblance of antitheocratic principles without actually embracing their meaning. For one thing, sectarian opposition was quieted by the apparent acceptance of voluntaryism. Congregationalism no longer made exclusive claims to christianize the entire community. Indeed, the Second Awakening, promoted by Dwight and his party at least partly to strengthen the Standing Order, had already restored the insistence on the "gathered church." With disestablishment, Congregationalism's last tie with the more churchly conception of its mission seemingly was gone. Similarly, the opposition from the American liberal tradition was undermined. For New England clergy now uniformly spoke the language of religious freedom and discoursed on the "deadly embrace" of state churches. . . . And yet, despite this apparent conversion, the essentials of underlying Puritan assumptions were maintained intact.

Lastly and perhaps most significantly for future American history, church-state separation emancipated the Puritan tradition from its purely local reference. At last the

New England ecclesiastical situation was constitutionally identical with that in the remainder of the Union. Consequently, any reconstruction undertaken for New England would also apply to the rest of the United States. Leading Congregational writers were soon aware of this too. By the 1820's provincialism had been shed, and references were ordinarily being made to the general American scene. Hence the theocratic tradition was no longer on the defensive. Just as New England's political conservatism was changing from a moribund Federalism to the vigorous Whiggery of the 1840's so also the Puritan heritage was preparing to awaken as the gospel of the "true American union" of church and people—a gospel which was to flourish in the Puritan homeland and successfully invade other denominations and sections.

This further reformulation preserved every essential element of the Puritan concept of a Christian commonwealth. State support to a national religious faith which in turn would keep the United States a Christian nation, a government informed by the light of Christianity, the organic union and interdependence of church and state—all were maintained. Only such adjustments were made as were required by the new constitutional situation. What were these adjustments?

Public support for a national church was still considered essential, but both the national church and the character of support were differently conceived. Enlarging on the concept of comprehension developed earlier, writers now demanded state support to a church coextensive with the national community of Christians. In effect, the idea of a denominational grand alliance, so alarming to many Americans, was here being replaced by the more politically prudent concept of the church invisible in America. . . . In addition, the nature of the support which rulers were to bestow was different. This became clear in the 1830's when Channing ascribed political ambi-

tions to the orthodox and Moses Stuart replied, admitting, "We do fully believe that no good government on earth can be long maintained" without piety, "but this is an influence of religion on government and a connection with it which are *indirect*." Emphasis on indirection was now conventional in discussions of the subject. The day might be gone when governors could call synods, recommend creeds, and force attendance at public worship, but they were not thereby emancipated from duties to the gospel. "Our civil rulers owe to God and their country now, the same illustrious piety, the same estimation of the doctrines of God's Word, the same attendance upon the ordinances of the Gospel and co-operation for their support, and the same strict and pure morality, which rendered the civil Fathers of our land so illustrious."

As this has already suggested, the religious character of the state was also retained. Though not so closely identified with confessionalism as formerly, rulers were still to be visibly sympathetic with the Christian cause. "There are certain guarantees of integrity, and of security to the general interests of religion, which as Christians, we are bound to require," said Beecher. . . . Of magistracy, as distinct from particular magistrates, even more was required. Government was still founded on divine institution, not civil compact. It was still obliged to heed revelation. . . . The state's religious commitment even limited the freedom which it could legitimately offer. Moses Stuart thought that Jews, Mohammedans, pagans, and Deists might enjoy liberty in America, but not to the extent of showing contempt for Christians or blaspheming the Christian religion. Daniel Webster argued at law against the right of a Philadelphia philanthropist to establish a secular orphanage: "Christianity—general, tolerant Christianity—Christianity independent of sects and parties—that Christianity to which the sword and the fagot are unknown—general, tolerant Christianity is the law of the land!" Because of this adjustment to an indirect connection of church and state New England leaders felt that they had digested disestablishment without injury. . . .

But the work of reconstruction was not yet completed. It was necessary also to deal with that organic inter-relationship of church and state which Puritans had assumed and Dwight had made explicit as the state's dependence on morality and religion. Now a further dimension of relevance appeared. Specific emphasis was placed on the services of religion to republics and particularly to the American republic. Conceivably, Old World monarchies and despotisms might rule by force and terror, but a free republic depended solely upon mass moral restraint. Thus "there is no form of government better than our own for a virtuous community; and none worse for a vicious community." The problem was especially great since immigration and electoral reforms had placed government "within the reach of a perverted and profligate suffrage." Beecher in 1829 could not be optimistic, but he knew that in Christianity rested the only hope of saving the American experiment: "It is hard to elevate the mass, and harder to sustain it; and none but by the help of God and his institutions have been able to do it."

Throughout the decades leading to the Civil War this argument was repeated with variations for each of the perils confronting America. Was the United States becoming huger in territory and population with every passing year? Heman Humphrey's solution was "an immense moral power to control twenty, thirty, *fifty* millions of daring and enterprising republicans, spread over a vast territory." Did sectional passions raise the specter of coming storms and bloody conflict? Beecher's recourse was to "God's government and the institutions of Christianity" inculcating the intelligence and moral principle capable of maintaining national unity. Were increasingly bitter partisan battles destroying the fraternal bonds of republican unity? Bushnell cited Christianity as an integrating center, for "if we go to the same churches and tables of communion, receiving there the common principles and lessons of God's truth, and thence go forth to bless our country, as citizens . . . we may differ warmly and earnestly as to the mode, but we cannot be sundered into state factions." Lastly, were the American people moving apart in class and wealth? Was the republic threatened with bitter social division? Beecher admitted the situation: "There is pervading the entire class of relative poverty a strong feeling of dissatisfaction, as if they were injured, and as if the rich were the aggressors, and were revelling on the spoils which had been wrested from them." But he also knew where salvation lay. "Explosion and revolution" would never erupt, despite political radicals and universal suffrage, so long as Christianity fortified the mind and conscience. Thus the Christian gospel and its institutions were the real sustaining powers of American democracy. "On this influence depends our rise or fall—our glorious immortality or our hasty dissolution." It is not surprising that the result should have been that fusion of patriotism, republicanism, and religion which was noted by foreign visitors. Here, in this complex, the triumph of the theocratic element over its alienation from the American liberal faith was revealed. At the death of Jefferson Heman Humphrey complained of the tendency to call every American statesman a Christian, but he had himself contributed not a little to the blurring of the distinction.

To safeguard this invisible union of church and state, Beecher, it will be recalled, had experimented with techniques for re-establishing the church influence in politics, even before the collapse of the Standing Order in Connecticut. These techniques were now further developed. In a democracy, Taylor warned, public opinion is "absolutely paramount." According to Beecher, the contest for its control was already raging, "and by this generation, in the city and in country, it is to be decided whether an evangelical or a worldly influence shall prevail." Hence it was necessary for Christians to close ranks and face the task together. "Religious principle must be applied throughout the nation, and no *one* denomination *can* do it." Revivals must be encouraged and the suffrage exploited. Every freeman must "inquire concerning the candidate for whom he is solicited to vote — is he an enemy of the Bible, or the doctrines and institutions of the Gospel; — is he a duellist, or an intemperate man, or a sabbath-breaker or dissolute, or dishonest?" The ultimate goal was a "public opinion which shall accord with the morality of the Gospel."

To implement this purpose organization was needed. Therefore, coincident with the fall of the New England Establishments, an expansion of interdenominational voluntary societies was undertaken. The Connecticut Moral Society of 1812 was the beginning of many such foundations, spreading from New England to New York and the Middle West. These moral societies were seconded by organizations for allied purposes — tract societies, Bible societies, temperance societies, missionary societies, Sabbath School societies — all striving to extend "that influence which the law could no longer apply." Concerning the motivation behind such foundations, Beecher was candid: "These are the providential substitutes for those legal provisions of our fathers, which are now inapplicable by change of circumstances." By the 1830's the seriousness of such professions was being illustrated in effective political action. The General Union for Promoting the Observance of the Christian Sabbath had already launched a national campaign, deluging Congressmen with petitions against the carrying of the mails on Sundays, and in the next decade temperance societies were to begin winning public opinion to a program of legal action which secured its first striking victory in the Maine Prohibition Law. The re-establishment of the Christian interest in the politics of American democracy was taking place.

* * *

The idea of a Christian commonwealth was once again a force in American intellectual history. Toward the end of his life a melancholy John Leland looked back to note that the menace of religious oppression "in the old way" had been vanquished only to have it return with the increased strength of a "Christian Phalanx." "If my painful fears on this head are ever realized, the glory of America will depart — the blood and treasure expended in the revolution will all be lost." Though his understanding of the "new way" was confused, Leland did have a correct intuition of the restored vitality of the theocratic challenge. For these ideas now flourished outside the region and denomination where this rejuvenation had taken place.

Charles I. Foster

9. CHARACTERISTICS OF THE EVANGELICAL UNITED FRONT

An Errand of Mercy, from which this selection is taken, is a study of the conservative American social reaction to native radicalism in the context of the French Revolution. The author argues that this "united front" must be understood as an ideological structure pioneered by the British evangelicals and transposed to America in the services of republican protestantism.

The most sweeping generalization that the history of the movement will justify is that it was a united front supported by American Protestants to achieve ends far beyond the powers of their separate denominations, a united front of individual Christians and of those who, for some reason or other, wished to identify themselves with the Evangelical cause. It was not a united front composed of assorted ecclesiastical bodies. Some denominations endorsed all united-front work; some blessed certain ventures but withheld the nod from others. In each sect there were some clerical leaders who devoted their principal energies to the general societies, while others jealously guarded the prestige and power of their particular persuasions.

A certain impulse toward fusion was inevitable in these circumstances. At the core of the united front lay a cordial cooperation among the Presbyterians and Congregationalists, who formed their Plan of Union in 1800 for operations in New York state. There they encountered kindred spirits in the Reformed Dutch, and membership in these churches became quite interchangeable. The informal alliance thus attained a geographical coverage of the eastern United States. It included many leaders in business and professional life ready to supply both energy and guidance to benevolent societies; these men had influential friends among the Episcopalians, Baptists, and Methodists. Around them could rally a host who for various reasons would not want to be left out.

Once underway in their holy endeavor, the people in these organizations would naturally focus on what was common to all. And the societies, like churches, built up loyalty and devotion to their united effort. Not only did the benevolent societies absorb money and energy to which the separate denominations might have some claim, but they tended to exercise church functions. They did not administer sacraments, unless preaching is considered a sacrament. With this exception there was little that the churches had to offer which did not find duplication in the ritual of society meetings. The American Sunday-School Union was explicit: "when there should not be public worship and preaching, it should be the duty of the Superintendent so to arrange the closing exercises of the school, as to supply the place of it, and to preserve something of a similar form." What is here explicit for Sunday-school operations was implicit in the meetings of other benevolent groups, which were, after all, religious organizations conducting their proceedings in a religious atmosphere. In such circumstances it was inevitable that societies should share with the churches the emotional experience of revival and conversion.

From Charles I. Foster, *An Errand of Mercy* (Chapel Hill, 1960), pp. 123–130. Reprinted by permission of University of North Carolina Press.

At an evening meeting of tract distributors in New York city,

> ... the Superintendent, distracted with the cares of the business of the day, entered the room, fearing that the Spirit of God was withdrawn. He confessed his own spiritual deficiencies and stated how just he thought it would be of God to depart from them. After prayer and singing, he took up the Distributer's written reports, as they had been laid on the table promiscuously; and the first gave delightful evidence of *two souls converted to God.* The meeting paused and blessed the Author of conversion. His presence seemed to fill the room. Breathless silence prevailed, interrupted occasionally by sounds of weeping.

There is abundant evidence that the Evangelical united front was more than a co-operative effort of Protestant denominations or of individual Christians with their assorted sectarian prejudices. Some claimed that the movement constituted a suprachurch embracing particular churches but not owing its existence to them: "The church, in her benevolent movements, seems to be circumscribed within no limits save those of the habitable globe." The foundation of the suprachurch rested on a ground that its membership would have repudiated violently had they been aware of it—the deism of the Enlightenment. Deism espoused a basic, "natural" religion of which all formal religions were faulty human variants. And to the deists, as to the Evangelical suprachurch, the most valid expression of true religion was "benevolence."

However, the active expression of "benevolence" as Evangelical propaganda by a mystical, universal "church" was possible only in an era of good feelings which paralleled in religion a similar aspect of politics. This era in American Protestantism found encouragement in the progressive disestablishment of churches. As the principle of voluntaryism swept through the country, placing all sects on a par before the law, it relieved a situation such as Lyman Beecher wryly described in Connecticut in 1811: "So the democracy, as it rose, included nearly all the minor sects, besides the Sabbath-breakers, rum-selling tippling folk, infidels, and ruff-scuff generally, and made a dead set at us of the standing order."

Along with the elimination of legal discrimination with all its bitterness came the general impact of the Enlightenment, of which disestablishment was only one aspect. With its attack upon revealed religion and its promotion of natural religion, the Enlightenment was stressing what was common to all at the expense of peculiarity. That is, even those who fought the Enlightenment in its political and social aspects were imbued with its philosophy.

Into this relaxed atmosphere the Evangelical united front moved as a positive force to advance the concept of Protestant unity. In 1816, the Rev. J. M. Mason of New York wanted to go as far as "a sacramental communion on catholick principles." He noted: "Within a few years there has been a manifest relaxation of sectarian rigour in several denominations. And the spirit of the Gospel, in the culture of fraternal charity, has gained, upon a respectable scale, a visible and growing ascendancy. This happy alteration may be attributed, in a great degree, to the influence of Missionary and Bible Societies." There was much the same spirit in Philadelphia, where the Sunday and Adult School Union at its first anniversary in 1818 heard the Rev. Parker voice identical sentiments: "The primitive spirit of harmony and union is reviving; and I believe that Missionary societies, Bible societies, and Sabbath school societies are to be honorably instrumental in bringing about that enlarged, cheerful and universal co-operation in the work of the Lord, which is so devoutly to be wished."

On every hand there is abundant evidence of the good temper of those years. In 1819 a society for promoting the gospel among seamen opened a mariners' nonsectarian church on Roosevelt St. in New York near the East River docks. A Presbyterian minister presided at the dedication, which treated its audience to three sermons delivered in turn by Protestant Episcopal, Reformed Dutch, and Methodist Episcopal clergymen.

A considerable factor in this genial era of good feelings, one affecting both politics and religion to subdue factional differences, was the rising tide of nationalism. The Evangelical united front was one expression of this general emotion and probably could not have prevailed without it. A disgruntled Methodist, writing tongue in cheek to the editor of his religious journal, stated the case clearly enough:

Mr. Editor:—I am a national man, and therefore cannot understand what you mean by complaining of *national societies.* Sir, it is the order of the day to be national. We have our national theaters, national lottery offices, national hotels, national steam boats, and national grog shops. We have our United States shoe blacks, U.S. corset makers, U.S. infirmaries, and U.S. manufactories of every kind, from our match makers up to our carpet factories. I see no reason why we should not have national societies, since this character gives those societies a popularity and influence they could not otherwise sustain. Besides, sir, to be an officer in a national society, sounds abroad like being an officer in a national government, and will, by and by, give those societies an influence with the national government; and if this be a good thing, the sooner the better. We have already our American Bible Society, American Tract Society, American Missionary Society, American Temperance Society, American Sunday School Union, American Prison Discipline Society, American Jews' Society, &c. &c. and we are in a fair way to have an American Sabbath Society, and I know not how many more. . . . The fact is, sir, it is time that some national effort was made to create some religion as the law of the land; and unless you Methodists become "national" too, you will stand a poor chance among so many American Societies.

In this situation the threat of an enforced Protestant uniformity was, perhaps, something more than a joke. The most aggressive of the united-front societies was unquestionably the American Sunday-School Union. It managed repeatedly to blurt out fighting words, confident of general support. In 1830 it acknowledged, "the more recent forms of Christian effort were not designed to supersede the division of Christian effort into different communions. . . ." But "The Churches of Christ have slumbered for ages over the miseries of the world; and now, while individuals are associating to relieve these miseries, the Churches, with here and there an exception, are slumbering still. . . ."

To the extent that a genuine revolution threatened American Protestantism, it was not so much the danger that the independent lay societies would replace the multidenominational structure as that they might absorb it. The individual churches were the working units of the societies; agents in ever greater numbers demanded and received pulpit time for their causes. With increasing skill the agents organized congregations for their own purposes, diverting energies and money to the benefit of their independent societies. They used church property for their meetings, usually for a two-dollar fee. The agents also worked at the highest level: at every ecclesiastical assembly there was a line of them waiting to present their pleas.

Within the churches themselves a number of factors operated in favor of the work of the united front. As in Great Britain, benevolent activity was the only way open to American women for participation in public affairs. The churches were not providing outlets for tremendous energies at their disposal. At that time, too, there was political trouble in practically all of the denominations. The clergy, extremely conservative in their bias and intent upon ministerial dignity and authority, were holding the line against an earnest attempt on the part of influential laity to obtain a voice in policy-making at ecclesiastical assemblies. Probably this effort was one expression of American pride in political maturity. There were republican movements of one sort or another in the Methodist, Presbyterian, and Congregational Churches, and in the

American Catholic Church, too, for that matter. The spirit was in the air. At the price of a few small schisms, the clergy stood fast, yielding nothing to the laity. But there was a hidden cost for the victory of clerical pride. Business leaders had power and money at their command, with a healthy appetite for good works and public recognition. The Evangelical united front welcomed them with open arms, took what they had to offer, as shown by the statistics at the beginning of this chapter, and gave them what they wanted. Agents and missionaries knew that the independent societies not only paid better wages but really paid them.

Clerical conservatism in the highly organized denominations and the limitations of parish activity in those more loosely constructed affected the relationships between the churches and the benevolent societies. After all, it was a time of change, a time for speculation, a chance to get ahead. In the ministry a goodly number of energetic, ambitious clergymen either had no place to go or no chance of getting there. Some denominations such as the Baptists and Congregationalists offered no ladders at all. In others, the path to power seemed barred by unbearably stodgy denominational politics. For these frustrated clergy, the united-front societies opened the door to nationwide activity and fame. Lyman Beecher of Connecticut was an example of both effects at work. The Congregational Church had no more structure than its general associations. Real power stemmed from "Pope" Dwight at Yale and a conservative faculty at Andover, positions Beecher could not hope to challenge. He tried Presbyterianism, only to find himself too far from the center of influence at Princeton, but in the united front he found release for his tremendous enthusiasm as well as a path to national fame: missions, Bibles, tracts, Sunday schools, temperance, and education for the ministry. Another example was the Rev. James Milnor, Episcopal clergyman of New York city. He came late to the ministry; he was not in the line of succession or in favor with the young and vigorous Bishop John Henry Hobart. His progress blocked on the ecclesiastical front, he achieved national renown as the leading spirit of the American Tract Society.

Clearly there was much in the Evangelical united front to threaten the existing order of American Protestantism and with it the separation of church and state, but not enough to justify the hopes of the fusion radicals, such as the Rev. Ezra Stiles Ely, or the fears of sectarian stalwarts, such as Bishop Hobart. Several causes, however, operated to make the total scheme complementary and co-operative in its nature rather than competitive. In the first place, the various denominations could not do the massive job of revitalizing American Protestantism. They were too weak, divided, conservative, and lacking in imagination to make the Evangelical faith the important force in American culture which it later became. And, just as obviously, the denominations grew in strength with every advance of the united front. The object of the united front was the conversion of every American and, beyond that, of every non-Evangelical person in the entire world. Those conversions could be signed, sealed, and delivered only in the sacraments of some Evangelical sect. The united front might have the power and the glory of battle in the great cause, but when the dust settled, the denominations were in possession of the field.

So it was with the general prestige of religion in America. Right and left the united front fought for Bible-reading, prayer, sobriety, Sabbath observance, and church attendance as the only respectable American ways of life. It raised the prestige of Christianity to the point where belief or at least the pretense of belief was the norm of American behavior. The direct beneficiaries of that prestige were the denominational churches.

V. *The Recognition of American Pluralism (1860–1920)*

While the evangelical forces had labored to realize their "true American Union of Church and State" vast changes had been taking place within American society. Large contingents of hitherto unrepresented ethnic groups—frequently locating their identities through their Roman Catholic or Jewish religious practices—were arriving year after year. The frontier was relentlessly conquered and urban areas were developed concurrently. Inventions and investments transformed the American economy and with it American society. Also a fratricidal conflict disclosed deep conflicts within the United States. Thus, although the protestant revivalistic endeavors continued and the united front activities proceeded, the premise on which they had originated did not have continuing validity. The United States was no longer overwhelmingly Protestant. It was ceasing to be in large part rural. It could never again be potentially a "Christian Republic"—that vision which had inspired the evangelical efforts. Thus the years between the Civil War and World War I represent a period of transition in some ways analogous to the first half of the eighteenth century—at least when viewed in the perspective of "Church and State." The responses of Protestantism during these years to the changes in American society were manifold, and no such nearly universal consensus as "republican protestantism" began to develop. In this section our concern is primarily with the kinds of tension between the religiously plural society which was coming into existence and the older paradigms of Church-State relations—especially "republican protestantism" but also continental Roman Catholicism—which could not comprehend either the situation of post-Civil War America or the legacy of the Constitutional epoch.

Understandably an early and continuing issue was built into the development of the public school systems. Usually, in the East at least, the common schools were direct outgrowths of schools which had originated under religious auspices, and their conventions as well as their curriculum—both protestant in character—were bitterly resented by "foreigners" and especially "catholic foreigners." Although, for instance, the Massachusetts public schools were allegedly purged of sectarian practices well before the Civil War, and these reforms influenced other systems, the issue continued to trouble the common life—even as it does today. One of the better known conflicts—representing many more—occurred in Cincinnati, Ohio during the early 1870's. The local school board had been responsive to pressures for making the schools less obnoxiously "protestant" to Roman Catholic children. Specifically at issue was the reading of the "protestant version" of the Bible as an opening exercise.

121

Although the lower court upheld the traditional practice which the school board had modified, the State Supreme Court reversed that decision and reaffirmed the board's action. This incident—or ones substantially identical—occurred frequently as the burden of religious pluralism became a reality in the common life. That it took such issues to recall the Jeffersonian and Madisonian ideal indicates how successful the evangelical protestants had been in establishing their own conception of the relationship between religious and civil authority structures.

Generally the Roman Catholic Church found it quite possible to be reconciled to an independence of Church and State as it grew in numbers and power. Some American Roman Catholics became such partisans of the American circumstances that their orthodoxy was suspect in Europe. The Vatican actually went so far as to warn the faithful about the errors of "Americanism." European Roman Catholics, for whom separation of Church and State meant facing a hostile state and perhaps even civil penalties, were understandably uneasy about the enthusiasm of their co-religionists across the Atlantic for the pattern in which the two authority structures were disengaged—also known as a "separation." By contrast to the actual—if not ideological—acceptance of the American pattern on the part of Roman Catholics, the protestant response often took the form of a strident re-affirmation of the evangelical dream of a protestant America. Whether expressed in the scurrilous literature surveyed by Washington Gladden or embodied in the more sophisticated tract of a Josiah Strong, protestant "Americanism" could not easily accept that substantive independence of Church and State as the prerequisite to the life of a religiously plural community. In this perspective the prohibition era of the 1920's was a last major victory for that anachronistic protestant mentality.

Despite the tensions in the common life during this period Church and State were not directly linked, as the estimates of Lord Bryce, Thomas Cooley, and Philip Schaff all indicate. Along with the growing perception of the burden went recognition of that formal framework for a religiously plural community which was becoming a reality. In the years since World War I this framework has been articulated or, to change the figure, the rules of the game have been under discussion.

Judge Storer

1. THE BIBLE IN THE COMMON SCHOOLS

From their organization in 1829 the common schools of Cincinnati had opening exercises in which teachers or "scholars" read parts of the "Holy Scriptures." In 1842 it was provided that a pupil might be excused from reading the "Protestant Testament and Bible" if his parents or guardians wished it. By 1852 it was decided that, at the desire of their parents, pupils might read from the version of their preference. Finally in 1869 a majority of the Board of Education resolved to exclude religious instruction and the reading of religious books, and to terminate Bible reading at the opening exercises. The minority of the Board protested the decision and the issue went to the Superior Court of Cincinnati where Judge Storer rendered the decision of a 2 to 1 court—an injunction against the majority's resolutions.

Separated . . . from the mass of irrelevant matter in which the question before us has been involved by the learning and the industry of the counsel who have addressed us, if we regard the different standpoints from which they have argued, the propositions to be solved are simply these: Had the defendants, in the exercise of the discretion given them to direct the course of study and decide upon the text books to be used, the legal right to declare the Bible should no longer be read in the schools, where for nearly half a century it had been used as the daily exercise, and, coupled with its exclusion, the denial of all religious instruction and the reading of religious books shall be prohibited.

If no such power existed, may we not adjudge the board has acted *"ultra vires,"* and their resolutions are void. What, then, does our present Constitution prescribe. By sec. 7, art. 1, it is ordained that "Religion, morality and knowledge being essential to good government, it shall be the duty of the General Assembly to pass suitable laws to protect all religious denominations in the peaceable enjoyment of their own mode of public worship, and to encourage schools and the means of instruction." The section commences with the assertion that "all men have a natural and indefeasible right to worship Almighty God according to the dictates of their own conscience. No persons shall be compelled to, erect or support any place of worship, or maintain any form of worship, and no preference shall be given by law to any religious society, nor shall any interference with the rights of conscience be permitted." This may be said to be a literal transcript of sec. 3, art. 8, of the Constitution of 1802, and that in substance is borrowed from art. 3 of the Ordinance of 1787. These are the affirmations of a great truth, and to vindicate which we believe they were inserted in our organic law.

They recognize the existence of a Supreme Being, and the fact is judicially ad-

Published as *The Bible in the Common Schools* (Cincinnati, 1870) The case was *John D. Minor, et al. v. Board of Education of Cincinnati, et al.* It was decided in the General Term, February 1870, of the Superior Court of Cincinnati. Excerpts are from pp. 373–389.

mitted that religion, as well as morality and knowledge, are essential to good government, and consequently, make it imperative that schools and the means of education shall be regulated by the Legislature.

Now it will be admitted that no preference can be given to religious sects, as such, as difference of opinion upon religious subjects is not only tolerated, but the right to enjoy it is given to its fullest extent. There is a manifest distinction, however, between religion and religious denominations, as they present all shades of theoretic as well as practical belief. Hence it is we may recur to the clause so prominently presented in the section of our Bill of Rights that secures to all the worship of Almighty God, as the exponent of what we may rationally conclude the founders of the Constitution intended by the general term religion. . . .

The whole argument that seems to us reaches the real question before us is predicated upon the supposition that the Bible is a volume whose teachings lead to sectarianism, and which ought not, therefore, to remain in the schools.

We do not admit the assertion, either in whole or in part. What we understand by sectarianism is the work of man, not of the Almighty. We are taught in the Scriptures that we are all the children of a common Parent, who is our Father and our Friend, that we are all of the same blood, a common unity pervading the race. Such, however, is not the human lesson. Learned men are not satisfied with the plain statement of revelation. They have divided the human family into distinct parts, giving to each a separate origin. We learn from the Bible to forgive injuries, to deal justly, to elevate our conceptions above the objects that surround us, and feel we were born to be immortal. Not so are we thoroughly taught by the profoundest system of human philosophy.

A volume that unfolds the origin of men, the beginning of time, and the assurance of an eternity when the present dispensation shall end, can not, upon any rational principle, be said to indicate religious exclusiveness. It has, we admit, seen its dark days, and has contended with bitter foes, yet it has suffered as much, if it could suffer at all, from the mistaken zeal, or the dogmatism and intolerance, of its professed friends. . . .

We marvel not that the mixtures and devices of men have obscured revelation when scarcely a week passes by without the annunciation of some new annotation or analysis, or the defence of some peculiar dogma.

All these, we admit, tend to the same result, which is necessarily a devotion to a sect. But we can not admit that the Bible necessarily induces any such consequences.

If it is candidly examined, studied without preconceived prejudice, its truths admitted to the test of enlightened conscience, we doubt not the answer always will be as it ever has been, the acknowledgement of its sacred character, and a veneration for its truthfulness.

It is urged, however, that the conscience of the Catholic parent can not permit the ordinary version to be read as an exercise, as no religious teaching is permitted by his church, unless it is directed by the clergy or authorized by the church itself, and it is, therefore, offensive to the moral sense of those who are compelled to listen when any portion of the Bible is read; but the rule has long since been abolished requiring children to be present, or to read from the version now in use, if it should be the expressed wish of the parents first communicated to the teachers.

The reason of the objection, then, would seem to have ceased. More than this, it is in evidence before us that our Catholic friends have their own separate schools, and very few of their children attend the common schools, while in one of these schools the Douay translation of the Bible is read as a daily exercise.

But is it consistent with this claim of

counsel that, even if the Bible should be prohibited, Catholic children would not attend the common schools, unless subject to the teachings of their spiritual guides? The schools have been denominated godless, while the Scriptures are yet read as a daily exercise. What must they become, and what will they be termed, when the Scriptures are forbidden?

What appears to us to underlie this view of the case, is the alleged injustice that Catholic parents, in common with other property-holders, should be taxed for the support of schools that are independent of the control of the Church, and consequently, opposed to its whole economy.

This has been pressed in argument, though no one of the counsel for the plaintiffs or defendants have intimated there should be a division of the school fund. With the justice or injustice, therefore, of the mode of taxation, we have nothing to do in deciding the questions submitted to us. If the point should ever arise, we trust we shall attentively consider all the objections that may be raised to the present organization of the schools; but it furnishes no ground of argument against the reading of the Bible that the taxes for the support of the schools are not equally assessed or properly distributed. We can not believe that any portion of the community, either from prejudice or the belief of wrong done, when the judicial tribunals are open, and their complaints may be heard, would imitate the strong man of old by laying their hands upon the pillars which support the temple, when the inevitable result would be a common ruin.

We therefore conclude upon this branch of the case, that the premises upon which the whole argument of the defendants depends as to the rights of conscience being violated, have been assumed, and not proved to exist. On the other hand, we may well suppose the consciences of the many thousands who protest against the resolutions of the Board of Education, if any wrong may have been done, have equal cause to complain.

Nor do we think that the mere reading of the Scriptures without note or comment, and in detached sentences, can be deemed an act of worship, in its commonly received definition. The lessons selected are, in all probability, those which elevate the mind and soften the heart—an exercise not only proper, but desirable to calm the temper of children, while it impresses the truth of personal responsibility for good or evil conduct. It furnishes a perfect standard of moral rectitude not to be found elsewhere, which is immutable as it is authoritative. No prayer is required of the teacher or the scholar, though the simple and beautiful *pater noster* would not, we believe, be out of place.

If, then, "no religious test," to use the language of the Bill of Rights, is required of teacher or scholar, if no act of worship, in a sectarian sense, is performed, if no sectarian or denominational teaching is introduced, and even the possibility of either is prevented by the resolution long since promulgated, that those who desire it may be exempted from the general rule, we can not see how the defendants can justify the exclusion from the schools of what has been permitted there for nearly half a century without rebuke. It can not be that a new revelation has been received by the Board of Education of what is their responsibility to the public, or that they, as a body, have become wiser, better informed, or have a clearer perception of moral duty than their predecessors, for these suppositions were not made, much less suggested, and we are consequently led to believe that there has been hasty, unnecessary and unauthorized legislation, neither demanded by the state of fact upon which that legislation is said to be based, nor yet the wish of those whose sons and daughters have heretofore been or are now being educated in the public schools.

On the whole case we are satisfied that

we have complete jurisdiction of the subject before us, and of the parties; that the matters alleged by the plaintiffs and admitted by the defendants present just and equitable grounds for our interference. We so decide, because we are satisfied that the powers conferred on the defendants have been transcended; that the resolutions prohibiting the Bible and all religious instruction are *ultra vires,* and therefore void.

We have not referred to any adjudicated case, as those quoted by one of our colleagues fully justify us. We stand upon the admitted principle, as true in law as in equity, that the unauthorized acts of a corporate body or trustees, whose powers are prescribed by law, may be restrained. While we hold that every form of religious worship is to be alike protected by law, and the conscience of every man can not be questioned; while the broad shield of the Constitution is over all our citizens, without distinction of race or sect, we can not ignore the right of the petitioners to the relief they have sought, nor can we, with our views of legal duty, sustain the action of the defendants.

A majority of the Court are of this opinion, and a perpetual injunction will be therefore decreed, as prayed for in the petition.

Judge Welch

2. THE BIBLE IN THE PUBLIC SCHOOLS

The judgment of the Superior Court was appealed and the Supreme Court of Ohio reversed the decision: the original petition was dismissed and the majority of the Board was upheld.

The arguments in this case have taken a wide range, and counsel have elaborately discussed questions of state policy, morality, and religion, which, in our judgment, do not belong to the case. We are not called upon as a court, nor are we authorized to say whether the Christian religion is the best and only true religion. There is no question before us of the wisdom or unwisdom of having "the Bible in the schools," or of withdrawing it therefrom. Nor can we, without usurping legislative functions, undertake to decide what religious doctrines, if any, ought to be taught, or where, when, by whom, or to whom it would be best they should be taught. These are questions which belong to the people and to other departments of the government.

The case, as we view it, presents merely or mainly a question of the courts' rightful authority to interfere in the management and control of the public schools of the state. In other words, the real question is, has the court jurisdiction to interfere in the management and control of such schools, to the extent of enforcing religious instructions, or the reading of religious books therein?

There is a total absence . . . of any legislation looking to the enforcement of religious instruction, or the reading of religious books in the public schools; and we are brought back to the question, what is

Published as *The Bible in the Public Schools* (Cincinnati, 1873) This was extracted from Volume 23 of the Ohio State Reports, pp. 238–254.

the true meaning and effect of these constitutional provisions on this subject? Do they enjoin religious instructions in the schools? and does this injunction bind the courts, in the absence of legislation? We are unanimous in the opinion that both these questions must be answered in the negative.

The truth is that these are matters left to legislative discretion, subject to the limitations on legislative power, regarding religious freedom, contained in the bill of rights; and subject also to the injunction that laws shall be passed, such as in the judgment of the legislature are "suitable" to encourage general means of instruction, including, among other means, a system of common schools.

Equally plain is it to us, that if the supposed injunction to provide for religious instructions is to be found in the clauses of the constitution in question, it is one that rests exclusively upon the legislature. In both sections the duty is expressly imposed upon the "general assembly." The injunction is, to "pass suitable laws." Until these "laws" are passed, it is quite clear to us that the courts have no power to interpose. The courts can only execute the laws when passed. They can not compel the general assembly to pass them.

This opinion might well end here. Were the subject of controversy any other branch of instructions in the schools than religion, I have no doubt it might safely end here, and the unanimous opinion of the court thus rendered be satisfactory to all. The case is of peculiar importance, however, in the fact that it touches our religious convictions and prejudices, and threatens to disturb the harmonious working of the state government, and particularly of the public schools of the state. I deem it not improper, therefore, to consider briefly some of the points and matters so ably and elaborately argued by counsel, although really lying outside of the case proper, or only bearing on it remotely.

The real claim here is, that by "religion," in this clause of the constitution, is meant "Christian religion," and that by "religious denomination" in the same clause is meant "Christian denomination." If this claim is well founded, I do not see how we can consistently avoid giving a like meaning to the same words and their cognates, "worship," "religious society," "sect," "conscience," "religious belief," throughout the entire section. To do so, it will readily be seen, would be to withdraw from every person not of Christian belief the guaranties therein vouchsafed, and to withdraw many of them from Christians themselves. . . .

If, by this generic word "religion," was really meant "the Christian religion," or "Bible religion," why was it not plainly so written? Surely the subject was of importance enough to justify the pains, and surely it was of interest enough to exclude the supposition that it was written in haste, or thoughtlessly slurred over. At the time of adopting our present constitution, this word "religion" had had a place in our old constitution for half a century, which was surely ample time for studying its meaning and effect, in order to make the necessary correction or alteration, so as to render its true meaning definite and certain. The same word "religion," and in much the same connection, is found in the constitution of the United States. The latter constitution, at least, if not our own also, in a sense, speaks to *mankind,* and speaks of the rights of *man.* Neither the word "Christianity," "Christian," nor "Bible," is to be found in either. When they speak of "religion," they must mean the religion of man, and not the religion of any *class* of men. When they speak of "all men" having certain rights, they can not mean merely "all Christian men." Some of the very men who helped to frame these constitutions were themselves not Christian men.

We are told that this word "religion" must mean "Christian religion," because "Christianity is a part of the common law of this country," lying behind and above its constitutions. Those who make this assertion can hardly be serious, and intend the real import of their language. If Christianity is a *law* of the state, like every other law, it must have a *sanction.* Adequate penalties must be provided to enforce obedience to all its requirements and precepts. No one seriously contends for any such doctrine in this country, or, I might almost say, in this age of the world. The only foundation—rather, the only excuse—for the proposition, that Christianity is part of the law of this country, is the fact that it is a Christian country, and that its constitutions and laws are made by a Christian people. And is not the very fact that those laws do *not* attempt to *enforce* Christianity, or to place it upon exceptional or vantage ground, itself a strong evidence that they *are* the laws of a Christian people, and that their religion is the best and purest of religions? It is strong evidence that their religion is indeed a religion "without partiality," and *therefore* a religion "without hypocrisy." True Christianity asks no aid from the sword of civil authority. It began without the sword, and wherever it has taken the sword it has perished by the sword. . . .

But it will be asked, how can religion, in this general sense, be essential to good government? Is atheism, is the religion of Buddha, of Zoroaster, of Lao-tse, conducive to good government? Does not the best government require the best religion? Certainly the best government requires the best religion. It is the child of true religion, or of truth on the subject of religion, as well as on all other subjects. But the real question here is, not what is the best religion, but how shall this best religion be secured? I answer, it can best be secured by adopting the doctrine of this 7th section in our own bill of rights, and which I summarize in two words, by calling it the doctrine of "hands off." Let the state not only keep its own hands off, but let it also see to it that religious sects keep their hands off each other. Let religious doctrines have a fair field, and a free, intellectual, moral, and

spiritual conflict. The weakest—that is, the intellectually, morally, and spiritually weakest—will go to the wall, and the best will triumph in the end. This is the golden truth which it has taken the world eighteen centuries to learn, and which has at last solved the terrible enigma of "church and state." Among the many forms of stating this truth, as a principle of government, to my mind it is nowhere more fairly and beautifully set forth than in our own constitution. Were it in my power, I would not alter a syllable of the form in which it is there put down. It is the true republican doctrine. It is simple and easily understood. It means a free conflict of opinions as to things divine; and it means masterly inactivity on the part of the state, except for the purpose of keeping the conflict free, and preventing the violation of private rights or of the public peace. Meantime, the state will impartially aid all parties in their struggles after religious truth, by providing means for the increase of general knowledge, which is the handmaid of good government, as well as of true religion and morality. It means that a man's right to his own religious convictions, and to impart them to his own children, and his and their right to engage, in conformity thereto, in harmless acts of worship toward the Almighty, are as sacred in the eye of the law as his rights of person or property, and that although in the minority, he shall be protected in the full and unrestricted enjoyment thereof. The "protection" guaranteed by the section in question, means protection to the minority. The majority can protect itself. Constitutions are enacted for the very purpose of protecting the weak against the strong; the few against the many.

* * *

It follows that the judgment of the Superior Court will be reversed, and the original petition dismissed.

Judgment accordingly.

Samuel T. Spear

3. RELIGION AND THE STATE

Samuel T. Spear was an Episcopalian clergyman in Brooklyn, N.Y. His book *Religion and the State* (1876) was first published as a series of articles in *The Independent*. They arose out of what he called "the much debated school question," and were intended to contribute "some help to the public mind in arriving at [its] true solution."

The direct and immediate issue before the American people is not the general question of Church and State, but the specific question of Bible reading and religious instruction and worship in our public schools. This question is merely a branch of the larger one that relates to the attitude which civil government should assume and maintain with reference to religion. All the general principles that are applicable to the latter are equally so to the former.

The conclusion reached from the survey of the more extended field is that civil government, as such, should have nothing to do with the work of administering, sustaining, or teaching religion, and that on this subject its only legitimate function consists in affording an impartial protection to all the people in the exercise of their religious liberty, while so limiting this exercise as to make it compatible with the peace and good order of civil society. It has taken the world a long time to discover and embody this elementary truth; and even now the discovery and embodiment are limited to a small portion of the race. It is practically an unknown truth to the greater part of mankind.

The acceptance of this general doctrine in regard to the province of civil government settles the School question and all other questions that come within the range of its application. The public school, as an institution of the State, exists and is regulated by its authority, and is, moreover, supported by compulsory taxation. To prescribe for it a religious system to be taught therein, or forms of worship to be there observed, is to determine by the authority of the State what the system or forms of worship shall be, and then to compel the people to pay the expenses thereof. Such a coerced support of religion is equivalent to a State religion in the public school, and that, too, whether the religion and the worship accord with the views and wishes of the majority or not.

All this and much more would be very proper, provided the administration or teaching of religion comes within the rightful province of civil government. But, if this province be simply that of impartial protection, and not at all that of administration or teaching, then besides being highly improper, it is a trespass upon the rights and religious liberty of the people. It is such because it compels them by law to do what should be left to their own discretion. It is especially such in a country where there is great diversity in the religious faith of the people. A school system in which a specific form of religion shall be taught or practiced at the public expense, is among such a people unjust to all who dissent from that religion, but are, nevertheless, compelled to contribute to its support. It puts civil government in a false attitude. It invests it with a function that does not belong to it. On this generic ground we

From *Religion and the State, or, the Bible and the Public Schools* (New York, 1876), pp. 377–387.

believe it both impolitic and wrong to employ our public school system as the means of propagating any form of religion.

We have in this country a system of *secular* governments, established by the authority of the people for secular and not for religious purposes, which, when coming in contact with religion, are planned to afford protection to the people in the peaceable exercise and enjoyment of their religion, but not to regulate, support, or teach that religion, or to make any discriminations on religious grounds. The Constitution of the United States, so far as applicable to the subject at all, is constructed on this general principle; and the same is for the most part true of the constitutions of the several States.

Any divergence from this great principle, as is the fact in some of the State constitutions, is merely exceptional to the general spirit and purpose of our governmental system. A religious test as a qualification to hold office, or to perform any political or civil duty, or to enjoy any political or civil right, is such an exception. In two of the States the power of taxation for the support of religion is granted by their constitutions; yet this, too, is an exception. So, also, in most of the States religious corporations are exempted from taxation; yet this, while an inconsistency surviving by the force of habit and usage after the theory which gave it birth is dead, is not based on religious grounds. Notwithstanding the exceptions that mar the absolute unity and harmony of the system, considered in relation to religion, it is, nevertheless, true that the system, taken as a whole, disclaims all jurisdiction over religion, all right to discriminate among the people for religious reasons, and all right to impose any tax burdens for the support or propagation of religion. We express this general fact by the oft-repeated declaration that in this country we have no union between Church and State. One need but to study its fundamental laws to see this truth.

The proper solution of the School question. That solution is clearly the one which grows out of and accords with the fundamental principles of our national and State organization. We can accept no other, and put no other into practice, without contradicting these principles. The Puritan public school, with the religious catechism and the Bible in it — which was once the public school of New England as New England then was — does not conform to the standard furnished by the American doctrine of civil government. It gave preference to a religious sect, and at the public expense inculcated the special ideas of that sect; and this is plainly contrary to the doctrine.

The same objection applies with equal force to the Protestant public school, in which King James's version of the Sacred Scriptures and religious exercises, Protestant in their type and tendency, are incorporated into its educational system. The Catholic, the Jew, the Infidel, and, indeed, all who dissent from Protestantism, being citizens in common with Protestants and having precisely the same rights, complain of the injustice done to them in taxing them for the support of such a school. Their complaint is a valid one. We do not see how it is possible to answer it without ignoring the cardinal principles upon which our national and State life is founded. The same method of reasoning is equally applicable to a Catholic public school, a Jewish public school, or any public school which is made the organ of religious instruction or worship in any form.

The fatal difficulty with all such schools consists in the fact that, while they assign to civil government functions that do not belong to it, they come into direct collision with the American doctrine as to the nature and scope of its functions. They make the State a religious teacher at the public expense, and this is just what it cannot be in consistency with its own doctrine. Shall, then, the doctrine, when applied to popular education, be abandoned as false, or shall our public school system be adjusted to it? Shall all religious and all anti-religious sects be placed on a common ground in the full and impartial enjoyment of their citizen-rights, with no discrimination against or in favor of any class? Shall the public school be the *common* school of the people, of *all* the people, and *for* all the people, and in this respect be like the government that authorizes it, and taxes the people for its support? Shall it, by a wise and just omission, remit the subject of religion in all the forms of the idea, and in all the processes of its propagation, to other agencies, neither controlled nor supported by the State, but left entirely free at their own charges to consult their own pleasure?

. . . The true answer to these questions is this: — THE PUBLIC SCHOOL, LIKE THE STATE, UNDER WHOSE AUTHORITY IT EXISTS, AND BY WHOSE TAXING POWER IT IS SUPPORTED, SHOULD BE SIMPLY A CIVIL INSTITUTION, ABSOLUTELY SECULAR AND NOT AT ALL RELIGIOUS IN ITS PURPOSES, AND ALL PRACTICAL QUESTIONS INVOLVING THIS PRINCIPLE SHOULD BE SETTLED IN ACCORDANCE THEREWITH.

Protestants who, as Protestants, fight Catholics and seek to resist their demands in respect to the public school, are handling very dangerous weapons, though many of them do not seem to know it. They conduct the war upon a principle which may at any time be turned against themselves.

The true ground, whether for attack or defense, is the one that places the Protestant and the Catholic on an equal footing; and the moment the former takes this position, the whole power of our system of government at once comes to his support. The position is impregnable; and taking it, the Protestant is sure of a victory, not as a Protestant, but as a citizen. He concedes to the Catholic all his rights and simply claims his own. He demands for himself no more than he is willing to grant to others. This position is a strong one, because it is just and because it exactly accords with the letter and spirit of our civil constitutions.

Washington Gladden

4. THE ANTI-CATHOLIC CRUSADE

Washington Gladden was a Congregational clergyman in Columbus, Ohio from 1882 until his death in 1918. He is best known for his "social Christianity" or his concern to make Christianity relevant to the common life. This assessment of anti-Roman Catholic agitation in the A. P. A. indicates the author's liberal sympathies no less than it reports upon the bias against "Rome" which was so deep-seated in American Protestantism. This sort of agitation, among other things, was one expression of Protestant frustration in an America which was becoming so religiously plural.

The year of the Parliament of Religions witnessed a most discouraging outbreak of religious rancor in the United States. It is the ancient feud of Protestant and Romanist, and the new form which it has taken is worse than the old Know-nothingism. The animus of that party was ostensibly its opposition to foreigners; the present movement is directed solely against Roman Catholics.

The time seems inopportune for such an outbreak. The occupant of the papal throne is perhaps the most enlightened and the most progressive pontiff who has ever occupied that throne: the whole policy of the Church under his administration has been tending toward a reconciliation with modern civilization, thus in effect reversing the tendencies of the preceding reign; the right of the people to govern themselves under republican forms has been distinctly affirmed by Pope Leo XIII.; his deliverances upon the social question have manifested a large intelligence and quick human sympathy; and we are told by those who ought to know that the Pope is not alone in this liberalism — that he is heartily supported by the whole Curia, and by public sentiment at Rome. This is the administration which the anti-Catholic zealots have chosen to attack; it is in the presence of these hopeful movements of the Roman ecclesiasticism that they are seeking to uncover the smoldering embers of religious animosity.

Several secret orders are taking part in this crusade. Just now they are very strong in Ohio and in Michigan, and in all the States farther West. I learn that many of the local governments in eastern Michigan are in their possession; in some portions of Ohio they have been able to control municipal elections. In my own county, at the last election, every man but one upon the county ticket of one of the parties was reputed to be a member of one of these orders. It was also said, during the campaign, that a large proportion of the legislative candidates of one of the parties belonged to this order.

The methods employed by these orders in gathering their adherents seem to be tolerably uniform. The campaign opens with the furtive circulation of certain documents. . . .

When the ground has been well prepared by the dissemination of such dreadful doc-

From *The Century*, Vol. XLVII, No. 5 (March 1894), pp. 789–795.

uments and such harrowing tales, the work of organization proceeds. The meeting-places of these orders are intended to be secret; all their operations are carried on in the most stealthy manner. It will be readily seen, however, that a class of persons who could accept as genuine the documents which I have described would not be likely to preserve such secrets, and the existence and the main purpose of these orders speedily transpire.

Chief among these anti-Catholic secret orders is the American Protective Association, better known by its initials. The platform of principles which this order publishes in the newspapers sounds well; most platforms do. It is not, however, always easy to find in its platform the animus of a political party; much less safe is it to accept those statements of its designs which a secret political society publishes in the newspapers. If its real purposes could be published in the newspapers, there would appear to be no reason for secrecy.

The platform of the A. P. A. makes these declarations:

We attack no man's religion so long as he does not attempt to make his religion an element of politicial power.
We are in favor of preserving constitutional liberty and maintaining the government of the United States.
We regard all religio-political organizations as the enemies of civil and religious liberty.

This is the exoteric doctrine. The esoteric differs widely, as may be seen by comparing these statements with the oath taken at their initiation by all members of the order. This oath has been published in several places, having been derived, apparently, from independent sources. Some verbal differences appear in these versions, but their substantial identity is conclusive evidence of their essential genuineness. The cardinal obligations of this oath are two: (1) A promise never to favor or aid the nomination, election, or appointment of a Roman Catholic to any political office. (2) A promise never to employ a Roman Catholic in any capacity if the services of a Protestant can be obtained. The evidence that the oath of the order contains these two obligations is abundant and conclusive. Sane and reputable men, members of the order, in controversy with me upon the subject, have acknowledged this; and the challenge to men of known veracity to come forward and deny it has not been accepted. If the oath is not substantially as published, such a denial would violate no obligation.

In the light of this oath, which every member of the A. P. A. takes with his hand upon his heart, we must interpret those outgivings printed in the newspapers. When he says that he attacks no man's religion so long as he does not intrude it into politics, we explain his saying as well as we can, in view of his oath that he will not employ a Roman Catholic in any capacity if he can obtain the services of a Protestant, and that he will never countenance or aid the nomination, election, or appointment to public office by any Roman Catholic. Not a word is said in this oath about any distinction between Roman Catholics who attempt to make their religion an element of political power and Roman Catholics who do not; Roman Catholics, as such, are sweepingly proscribed. And when the champion of this order tells us in the newspapers that he is "in favor of preserving constitutional liberty," we must bear in mind that he has sworn to violate the first principle of American constitutional liberty, which forbids discrimination against men on account of their religious belief. The Constitution of the United States declares that "no religious test shall ever be required as a qualification to any office or public trust under the United States." All the State constitutions embody the same principle. The oath of the A. P. A. binds its members to apply a religious test to every candidate for office—to give political office to none but Protestants. This is what they mean when they say that they are "in favor of preserving constitutional liberty."

What may be done by secret conclaves of men, bound together by such an oath as this, meeting at night in concealed places, and carefully hiding all their operations from the public eye, any man is at liberty to conjecture. It is evident that these assemblies will be hotbeds of malicious rumor. The men who have accepted as genuine the "Instructions to Catholics" and the pseudo-encyclical are prepared to believe anything. The most preposterous lies can be started in these conclaves, for there is no one there to challenge them; and thence they can pass from mouth to mouth until they have filled the whole community with their malarious influence. A system of espionage falls in with this scheme, and spies are detailed to attend Catholic churches to watch the priests and the bishops, and to dog the footsteps of those who are supposed to be friendly to the Roman Catholics. Suspicions and fears are thus plentifully engendered, and many communities have been filled with terror. . . .

The people of . . . rural neighborhoods are told the most lurid tales of what is going on in the cities. My correspondent had heard that a year ago all the public-school teachers in Columbus were Roman Catholics; the fact was that out of 349 teachers not more than 12 were Roman Catholics. The most blood-curdling reports had also reached that hamlet of the preparations for war which the Catholics in Columbus were making. Thus the secret propaganda is able to work very effectively in the rural districts. A large proportion of these councils are found in country places.

But credulity is not confined to the country. A minister of the gospel in Columbus told me that *all* our county officers were Roman Catholics, and that 95 per cent. of the police of our city were Catholics. The fact was that at that time 5 out of 20 county officials were of that faith, and 45 out of 112 policemen.

That in this year of grace a secret political society, built on such foundations of forgery, and bound together with such an oath, should be sweeping over the land like the Russian epidemic, is certainly a fact for patriots and Christians to ponder. The depth and density of that popular ignorance which permits the use of such documents as I have cited is certainly appalling.

The silence of the pulpit in many instances is explained by the fact that members of the church are members of the order, and the pastor is unwilling to alienate any of his supporters. There are few churches, I suppose, in the Western cities in which members of this order are not found. But a more influential reason for this silence is a feeling which is shared by the great majority of Protestant ministers, that Roman Catholics, as such, are a very dangerous class of persons, and that any kind of opposition to them is therefore to be welcomed. The extermination or repression of the Roman Catholic Church seems to these pious men a desirable end, and they are therefore inclined to argue that any means to that end are justifiable.

The political proscription of Roman Catholics which the oath requires is justified on the plea that Roman Catholics are not and cannot be loyal Americans; that their doctrine of the papal supremacy puts them completely under the power of a foreign potentate. Roman Catholic scholars dispute this interpretation of their allegiance, and insist that they owe no obedience to the Pope which can interfere with their duty to their country. I will not argue this question. Let us admit for the sake of the argument that the logic of the papal theory would require the Roman Catholic to disobey, at the Pope's command, the laws of his country. But is it true that we all follow our theories to their logical results? The logic of his doctrine requires every Presbyterian to believe in infant damnation; do Presbyterians generally believe in infant damnation? The logic of his theory requires the Baptist to unchurch all other Christians. Does the Baptist follow his logic? "That good dose of inconsistency which," as Cousin says, "common sense often prescribes for philosophy" is all that saves a good many of us from being fanatics or fools. That good dose of inconsistency has been well shaken and taken by millions of Roman Catholics. They are not really any more consistent than the rest of us, and the attempt to include them in the condemnation of alienism and treason is not a sane procedure. Roman Catholics have proved their loyalty to this nation on many a bloody battle-field; and those who imagine that the Pope's orders always find them tame, spiritless subjects of his will should read of his attempted interference with the recent "Plan of Campaign" in Ireland.

The relation of the oath of this order to the oath of office taken by all high officials under our Government demands consideration. It is evident that the contradiction between the two is absolute. The oath of office promises obedience to the constitution of the State and of the nation, and these constitutions forbid any distinction or preference among men on account of their religious belief. The oath of the order binds a man to make precisely these distinctions. . . .

That the prevalence of this insanity will be brief is certain; but it may spread widely enough and last long enough to do incalculable mischief. May I not venture to call upon all intelligent Protestants, and especially upon Protestant clergymen, to consider well their responsibilities in relation to this epidemic? Can we afford, as Protestants, to approve, by our silence, such methods of warfare against Roman Catholics as this society is employing? For the honor of Protestantism, is it not high time to separate ourselves from this class of "patriots?" In any large town, if the leading Protestant clergymen will speak out clearly, the plague will be stayed or abated.

5. AMERICA THE EMBODIMENT OF CHRISTIAN ANGLO-SAXON CIVILIZATION

Josiah Strong (d. 1916) was a Congregational minister and agent throughout the middle West until, with the publication of *Our Country* (1885), he became an author with a national following. In one sense he should be seen as trying to rally a new protestant evangelical alliance which would do for the last years of the nineteenth and the first years of the twentieth centuries what the "evangelical united front" had done in the National period. But it was a program in the mode of its own time reflecting social darwinism and suggestive of John Fiske. This "vision" indicates no less than the A. P. A. how deep protestant frustrations ran, and how incapable the broad movement had become of comprehending the Church-State, or dual-authority structure, problem in American society. Republican protestantism so dominated the protestant past that the denominations were alienated from their own more classical past, i.e., puritanism and the continental reformation, which could have provided ideological resources for coming to terms with an increasingly religiously-plural society.

It is not necessary to argue to those for whom I write that the two great needs of mankind, that all men may be lifted up into the light of the highest Christian civilization, are, first, a pure, spiritual Christianity, and, second, civil liberty. Without controversy, these are the forces which, in the past, have contributed most to the elevation of the human race, and they must continue to be, in the future, the most efficient ministers to its progress. It follows, then, that the Anglo-Saxon, as the great representative of these two ideas, the depository of these two greatest blessings, sustains peculiar relations to the world's future, is divinely commissioned to be, in a peculiar sense, his brother's keeper. Add to this the fact of his rapidly increasing strength in modern times, and we have well nigh a demonstration of his destiny. In 1700 this race numbered less than 6,000,000 souls. In 1800, Anglo-Saxons (I use the term somewhat broadly to include all English-speaking peoples) had increased to about 20,-500,000, and in 1880 they numbered nearly 100,000,000, having multiplied almost five-fold in eighty years. At the end of the reign of Charles II. the English colonists in America numbered 200,000. During these two hundred years, our population has increased two hundred and fifty-fold. And the expansion of this race has been no less remarkable than its multiplication. In one century the United States has increased its territory ten-fold, while the enormous acquisition of foreign territory by Great Britain — and chiefly within the last hundred years — is wholly unparalleled in history. . . . It is not unlikely that, before the close of the next century, this race will outnumber all the other civilized races of the world. Does it not look as if God were not only preparing in our Anglo-Saxon civilization the die with which to stamp the peoples of the earth, but as if he were also massing behind that die the mighty power with which to press it? My confidence that this race is eventually to give its civilization to mankind is not based on mere numbers — China forbid! I look forward to what

From Josiah Strong, *Our Country: Its Possible Future and Its Present Crises* (New York, 1885), Chap. XIII, pp. 161 ff.

the world has never yet seen united in the same race; viz., the greatest numbers, *and* the highest civilization.

There can be no reasonable doubt that North America is to be the great home of the Anglo-Saxon, the principal seat of his power, the center of his life and influence. Not only does it constitute seven-elevenths of his possessions, but his empire is unsevered, while the remaining four-elevenths are fragmentary and scattered over the earth. Australia will have a great population; but its disadvantages, as compared with North America, are too manifest to need mention. Our continent has room and resources and climate, it lies in the pathway of the nations, it belongs to the zone of power, and already, among Anglo-Saxons, do we lead in population and wealth. . . .

It may be easily shown, and is of no small significance, that the two great ideas of which the Anglo-Saxon is the exponent are having a fuller development in the United States than in Great Britain. There the union of Church and State tends strongly to paralyze some of the members of the body of Christ. Here there is no such influence to destroy spiritual life and power. Here, also, has been evolved the form of government consistent with the largest possible civil liberty. Furthermore, it is significant that the marked characteristics of this race are being here emphasized most. Among the most striking features of the Anglo-Saxon is his money-making power—a power of increasing importance in the widening commerce of the world's future. . . .

Again, another marked characteristic of the Anglo-Saxon is what may be called an instinct or genius for colonizing. His unequaled energy, his indomitable perseverance, and his personal independence, made him a pioneer. He excels all others in pushing his way into new countries. . . .

Again, nothing more manifestly distinguishes the Anglo-Saxon than his intense and persistent energy; and he is developing in the United States an energy which, in eager activity and effectiveness, is peculiarly American. This is due partly to the fact that Americans are much better fed than Europeans, and partly to the undeveloped resources of a new country, but more largely to our climate, which acts as a constant stimulus. . . . Moreover, our social institutions are stimulating. In Europe the various ranks of society are, like the strata of the earth, fixed and fossilized. There can be no great change without a terrible upheaval, a social earthquake. . . . Thus many causes co-operate to produce here the most forceful and tremendous energy in the world.

What is the significance of such facts? These tendencies infold the future; they are the mighty alphabet with which God writes his prophecies. May we not, by a careful laying together of the letters, spell out something of his meaning? *It seems to me that God, with infinite wisdom and skill, is training the Anglo-Saxon race for an hour sure to come in the world's future.* Heretofore there has always been in the history of the world a comparatively unoccupied land westward, into which the crowded countries of the East have poured their surplus populations. But the widening waves of migration, which millenniums ago rolled east and west from the valley of the Euphrates meet to-day on our Pacific coast. There are no more new worlds. The unoccupied arable lands of the earth are limited, and will soon be taken. The time is coming when the pressure of population on the means of subsistence will be felt here as it is now felt in Europe and Asia. Then will the world enter upon a new stage of its history—*the final competition of races, for which the Anglo-Saxon is being schooled.* Long before the thousand millions are here, the mighty *centrifugal* tendency, inherent in this stock and strengthened in the United States, will assert itself. Then this race of unequaled energy, with all the majesty of numbers and the might of wealth behind it—the representative, let us hope, of the largest liberty, the purest Christianity, the

137

highest civilization—having developed peculiarly aggressive traits calculated to impress its institutions upon mankind, will spread itself over the earth. If I read not amiss, this powerful race will move down upon Mexico, down upon Central and South America, out upon the islands of the sea, over upon Africa and beyond. And can any one doubt that the result of this competition of races will be the "survival of the fittest"? . . . "In every corner of the world," says Mr. Froude, "there is the same phenomenon of the decay of established religions. . . . Among Mohammedans, Jews, Buddhists, Brahmins, traditionary creeds are losing their hold. An intellectual revolution is sweeping over the world, breaking down established opinions, dissolving foundations on which historical faiths have been built up." The contact of Christian with heathen nations is awaking the latter to new life. Old superstitions are loosening their grasp. The dead crust of fossil faiths is being shattered by the movements of life underneath. In Catholic countries, Catholicism is losing its influence over educated minds, and in some cases the masses have already lost all faith in it. Thus, while on this continent God is training the Anglo-Saxon race for its mission, a complemental work has been in progress in the great world beyond. God has two hands. Not only is he preparing in our civilization the die with which to stamp the nations, but, by what Southey called the "timing of Providence," he is preparing mankind to receive our impress.

Is there room for reasonable doubt that this race, unless devitalized by alcohol and tobacco, is destined to dispossess many weaker races, assimilate others, and mold the remainder, until, in a very true and important sense, it has Anglo-Saxonized mankind? Already "the English language, saturated with Christian ideas, gathering up into itself the best thought of all the ages, is the great agent of Christian civilization throughout the world; at this moment affecting the destinies and molding the character of half the human race." . . .

In my own mind, there is no doubt that the Anglo-Saxon is to exercise the commanding influence in the world's future; but the exact nature of that influence is, as yet, undetermined. How far his civilization will be materialistic and atheistic, and how long it will take thoroughly to Christianize and sweeten it, how rapidly he will hasten the coming of the kingdom wherein dwelleth righteousness, or how many ages he may retard it, is still uncertain; but *it is now being swiftly determined.* Let us weld together in a chain the various links of our logic which we have endeavored to forge. Is it manifest that the Anglo-Saxon holds in his hands the destinies of mankind for ages to come? Is it evident that the United States is to be the home of this race, the principal seat of his power, the great center of his influence? Is it true that the great West is to dominate the nation's future? Has it been shown that this generation is to determine the character, and hence the destiny, of the West? Then may God open the eyes of this generation! . . .

E. B. Brady

6. AN AMERICAN CATHOLIC ON CHURCH AND STATE

Protestant responses to its loss of "place" in the national life included the actions of the A.P.A. and the fantasies of a Josiah Strong (as well as more moderate and relevant activities). By contrast Roman Catholic acclimation to post-Civil War America was not so stormy. For one thing Catholics were concentrated in urban ghettos and had contrived mutually satisfactory relationships between the religious and political institutions within their communities. But at the same time a tradition within American Roman Catholicism—from the Revolutionary period on—had fully appreciated the independence of Church and State and the substantial congruence of this pattern with the classical Catholic position. Edward Brady, a Paulist Father, was among the American Roman Catholic "Liberals" of the later nineteenth century.

The church . . . does claim due recognition in the Christian state, and she holds that the best interests of Christian society are secured by an *entente cordiale* between the civil power and the ecclesiastical authority. And Pius IX., in his famous *Syllabus*, condemns as false the proposition which asserts that there should be absolutely no union between church and state. But the most earnest and the most enlightened defenders of the church and her rights in the world to-day disclaim all idea of such political union as sometimes existed in the past, and which had bequeathed a legacy of weakness to the church the evil effects of which are felt in some countries even to this day. The march of mankind, though halting and circuitous, is ever onward, and we must not turn backwards. Not to restore the past, but to try to improve the present and save the future, should be the aim of all enlightened zeal. The political ideas and methods of the mediæval age would be as much out of place in the nineteenth century as its dungeons and its cumberous coats of mail, and the church would no more think of restoring the politicial conditions of that bygone time than of resuscitating the dust of its dead kings and warriors from their long-forgotten graves. The most intense churchman has no yearning to see the past restored in this particular; such a reactionary spirit would be the height of folly. The church, like everything else in the world, must accommodate herself to her changed surroundings, and she has always done so. Her power of adaptation to the circumstances of all times and places and races is not the least evidence of her divine organization. While her doctrines are unchangeable her discipline is ever changing. But the Catholic Church has her rights in the nineteenth century as well as in the twelfth, and she never hesitates to assert them, though the ages of faith and chivalry have passed away.

From the very beginning the church claimed the right to determine the "things of God"; she made this claim when hid away in the catacombs as well as when she stood uncovered in the palace of the Cæsars. Her very existence is founded upon this right, for her mission in the world is to point out the divine law and secure its observance, and without at least the negative co-operation of the state she cannot fulfil her mission. The legislation of

From E. B. Brady, C. S. P., "Church and State," in *The Catholic World*, Vol. LIV, No. 321 (December 1891) (New York, 1892), pp. 391–396.

the civil power must be in harmony with the divine law, or at all events not opposed to it; otherwise there must necessarily be conflict between the church and the state.

The church never has questioned and never can question the absolute authority of the state in its own proper sphere, and she deprecates all idea of interference in the functions of the state. The words of Pope Leo XIII., in his encyclical on the "Christian Character of States," ought to be sufficient evidence of the church's teaching on this subject. "God," he says, "has divided the care of the human race between two powers, the ecclesiastical and the civil; the one placed over divine things, the other over human. Each is without *superior* in its own sphere; each has fixed bounds in which it is contained, and these defined by the nature and proximate cause of each one, so that a kind of circle is drawn within which the acts proper to each, each does of its own right." But while the church thus maintains the absolute authority of the state within its own sphere, she holds, with St. Paul, that "there is no power except from God," and hence "in every kind of government those who rule should keep their eyes fixed on God, the Sovereign Ruler of the world, and have him before them in executing their civil duties as their example and law." Rulers and law-makers as well as private individuals must recognize the principles of divine right and justice, and be guided by them in their official conduct and in the enactment of laws. This much the church insists upon. As the exponent of the higher law of God to Christian legislators, she demands that the laws of Cæsar shall not interfere with "the things of God," but shall render due homage to them; and, on the other hand, she commands full obedience to the laws of the state, and a strict rendering to Cæsar "the things that are Cæsar's."

This is the absolute claim of the church in her relation to the state and its laws, and a careful examination of her past history will show that this has been her real attitude all along. No doubt there have been ambitious churchmen who in their relations with the civil power contended for much more than this, as there have been ambitious statesmen who wanted to rule over spiritual as well as temporal affairs; but individuals, however high their office, are not the church, and their aims must not be confounded with those of the church, which are *essentially spiritual;* and just as grasping, unscrupulous statesmen have brought and still bring odium upon their government or their party by their abuse of power, so misguided churchmen have brought odium upon the church by trying to make her the instrument of their own personal schemes and ignoble ambitions.

But if this be the actual state of the case, if the church admits that she has no right or title to interfere in the remotest manner with the affairs of the state except where the things of God are clearly concerned, why the constant friction between church and state all adown the ages? Simply because the state has all along tried to ignore the rights of God where they actually exist, and the church has tried to enforce them. Let us take a few examples. Is not marriage a sacrament, a divine institution, in the eyes of the church, and do not the laws relating to civil marriage and divorce concern the things of God? Does not the observance of Sunday concern them? Does not Christian education concern them? Does not the maintenance of public decency and morality concern them? If the church have no right to a hearing on such matters as these, her mission is a mere mockery, and her power and her authority in the world at large is null and void. She is only a dumb dog that cannot bark.

Those and those only who hold to the purely pagan idea of a state supreme in all things and over all things can deny the rights of religion here. No one with a particle of Christian faith or feeling can question them. If Christianity is true, the claims of the church in this particular are also true. Every Catholic, I had almost said every Christian, must needs unite with Leo XIII. in saying that "to exclude the church from influence on life, from law, from the education of youth, from the family, is a great and pernicious error. A state cannot be moral if you take away religion." The experiment of a purely secular state has never yet succeeded, and certainly the results of recent attempts in this direction do not give any sufficient evidence to show that it ever will succeed. There can be no stability in human affairs without some recognition of the divine order of things. When the civil and religious elements are in full accord and move harmoniously together the best interests of society are secured.

There may be abuses, there have been abuses on both sides; but is there anything in this world that is not subject to abuse, and has there ever been any arrangement of human society that worked perfectly? Conservative governments are liable to curtail the just rights of the people, liberal governments are liable to fail in the enforcement of law; so there is some danger in every form of government. A very common, but none the less a very erroneous idea is that the Catholic Church is in favor of extreme conservatism, or even absolutism, in government, and is the uncompromising foe of all liberal constitutions. The truth is the church is not wedded to any particular form of government; all forms that fulfil the functions of government and promote the public welfare and the common good are alike to her, and she loyally supports all just constitutions, whether monarchical or republican. . . .

The rabid, unreasoning opponents of Catholicity sometimes amuse us by prophesying what the church would do should she ever gain the ascendency in this country. Their prophetic fears are not only groundless, but to us they seem supremely absurd. We know very well what the church would do under the circumstances. She would do away with divorce; she would establish a system of Christian education for her own children (she would not impose it upon others); she would try to root out public as well as private corruption; she would endeavor to secure an honest ballot and anathematize any party or individual that should by bribery or other methods pollute the sources of our political life; but she would not touch a single stone in the noble fabric of our constitution — nay, she would safeguard to the utmost of her power our free institutions, and teach her children to be willing at any moment to die in their defence.

It were a grievous injustice to the church to suppose that the few Catholic politicians who from time to time become prominent in public life represent Catholic principles in their political action. Most of them represent nothing but themselves; some there are who carry their Catholic consciences into their official conduct, and they are an honor to us and a blessing to the state; but unhappily the majority go with the tide and recognize no principle but expediency, and the church must not be held responsible for them. As for the low and venal crew of pot-house politicians who batten on bribery and the perjured spoils of office, they are a libel on humanity as well as on Christianity. The true, consistent Christian, the man who brings his Christian principles everywhere with him and acts upon them, is always the best citizen, and the words of St. Augustine on this subject are as true to-day as when they were first written, nearly fourteen centuries ago. "Let those who say the teaching of Christ is opposed to the republic," exclaims the great doctor, "give it soldiers such as the teaching of Christ bids them to be; let them give such governors of provinces, such husbands, such wives, such parents, such children, such masters, such servants, such kings, such judges—finally, such payers and exactors of the debts due the revenue itself, the very agent of the government; all these such as Christian principles com-mend them to be, and let them dare to say the church is hostile to the republic; nay, let them acknowledge that she is, if obeyed, the great source of safety to the state."

John Ireland, D.D.

7. CATHOLICISM AND AMERICANISM

The Rev. John Ireland (d. 1918), Archbishop of Saint Paul, Minnesota, was a very colorful figure in the ranks of those American Catholic clergy who were at the same time loyal Catholics and loyal Americans. The following short excerpt from a relatively late address indicates the terms in which "separation" or "independence" of Church and State was congenial to many Americans who were also members of the Roman Catholic Church.

My religious faith is that of the Catholic Church—Catholicism, integral and unalloyed—Catholicism, unswerving and soul swaying—the Catholicism, if I am to put it into more positive and concrete form, taught by the supreme chieftain of the Catholic Church, the Bishop, the Pope of Rome.

My civil and political faith is that of the Republic of the United States of America—Americanism, purest and brightest; yielding in strength and loyalty to the Americanism of none other American; surpassed in spirit of obedience and sacrifice by that of none other citizen, none other soldier; sworn to uphold in peace and in war America's Star Spangled Banner.

Between my religious faith and my civil and political faith, between my creed and my country, it has been said, there is discord and contradiction, so that I must smother something of the one when I bid the other burst forth into ardent burning, that I must subtract something from my allegiance to the one when I bend my full energy to service to the other. Those who so speak misunderstand either my creed or my country; they belie either the one or the other. The accord of one with the other is the theme of the address I am privileged this evening to make.

No room is there for discord or contradiction. Church and State cover separate and distinct zones of thought and action: The Church busies itself with the spiritual, the State with the temporal. The Church and the State are built for different purposes, the Church for Heaven, the State for earth. The line of demarcation between the two jurisdictions was traced by the unerring finger of Him who is the master of both. The law of God is—"Render to Cæsar the things that are Cæsar's; and to God the things that are God's."

The partition of jurisdiction into the spiritual and the temporal is a principle of

From *The State and the Church*, ed. John A. Ryan and M. F. X. Millar (New York, 1924), pp. 282–3, 285. Reprinted by permission. © 1922 by the National Catholic Welfare Conference, published by the Macmillan Company.

Catholicism; no less is it a principle of Americanism. Catholicism and Americanism are in complete agreement.

The Constitution of the United States reads: "Congress shall make no law respecting an establishment of religion, or prohibiting the free exercise thereof." It was a great forward leap on the part of the new nation towards personal liberty and the consecration of the rights of conscience. Not so had it heretofore been on the soil of America. Save in Maryland while reigned there the spirit of the Catholic Lord Baltimore, and in Pennsylvania under the sweet-tempered rule of William Penn, religious freedom was barred by law in the Colonies,—Protestant creeds warring one with the other, all warring with the Catholic. But it was decreed that the new flag must be unsullied by religious persecution, the new nation must be, on every score, the daughter of freedom, the guardian angel of personal rights in each and every American.

Robert D. Cross

8. CATHOLICISM AND A NON-CATHOLIC STATE

This selection is from a recent and highly regarded study of *The Emergence of Liberal Catholicism in America* by Professor Cross.

In theory, the appearance of the modern state required no alteration in the traditional Catholic argument that all authority flowed from God, was subject to His laws, and therefore required the superintendence or instruction of the Church. It had always been necessary for the Church to decide what authority could be delegated to the secular power, what methods of control to employ, and what role the individual Catholic should play in supporting and perfecting the state. But as the state changed from being a bare preponderance of force, remote from the lives of most people, and became a monopoly of force which daily affected the lives of everyone, and as it assumed forms and adopted techniques unknown to theologians of the past, Catholics found that questions of "Church and State" constituted some of the most perplexing problems in the relationship of Christianity and culture.

Traditionalists, looking longingly back to the states of the past whose kings considered themselves the particular defenders of Catholicism, found it hard to believe that the newly declared sovereign people would respect the Church's teachings as conscientiously as would a prince religiously trained and especially consecrated. Conservative suspicions deepened as nineteenth-century radicals, identifying republicanism with the drastic curtailment of the Church's influence, found an ideal of statesmanship in Cavour's attempt to construct a free state wholly separate from the Church. Like Cavour, they were willing to despoil the Church of much of its property and privilege. In bitter condemnation, Father Thébaud admitted that the modern

Reprinted by permission of the publishers from Robert D. Cross, *The Emergence of Liberal Catholicism in America* (Cambridge, Mass.: Harvard University Press), pp. 71–78. Copyright 1958 by the President and Fellows of Harvard College.

state was not yet completely the "incarnation of Antichrist," but it was in such "a great degree ruled over by really anti-Christian ideas" that the Church and the state "are evidently now arrayed against each other and engaged in a deadly conflict." The Syllabus vigorously denounced all attempts to limit the Church's control over the state.

America, as one of the first republics of the age, had always been an object of admiration for European radicals; and non-Catholic Americans proclaimed to all who would listen that the states, both federal and local, were completely separated from the control of any church. To many Catholics, the states seemed to behave that way. Immigrant groups did not need theological demonstrations to conclude that the state was no helpmate, at least to the True Church. Through favoritism to Protestant clergymen, by the enforcement of Protestant ideals of public morals, by legal restrictions on the Church's property-holding powers, by the support of "godless" public schools, it seemed as much the enemy of the Church as the governments of Francesco Crispi and Jules Ferry. "The truth is," the conservative Church Progress of St. Louis complained, "that in the whole world there is not a Catholic country with a non-Catholic population of any importance which does not show more respect for the conscience of the non-Catholic minority than the United States manifests for the conscience of Catholics there." To American Catholics of these convictions, the censures of the Syllabus were badly needed condemnations of the political system under which they lived.

The liberal Catholics resented the innuendo that the American polity was as deeply undesirable as the laicizing states of Europe. Usually taking care not to contradict explicitly the traditional Catholic teaching, they proudly declared, nevertheless, their deepfelt satisfaction with the relations between the Church and the American "state." In their testimonials they seldom bothered to distinguish between the federal government—prohibited by the Bill of Rights from directly supporting any church—and the state governments, still theoretically free to create a full-fledged Establishment. It was in this genial spirit that Cardinal Gibbons declared "'America, with all thy faults I love thee still.'" Like the other liberals he never doubted that the "state" in all its divisions was every year growing more responsive to Catholic rights and interests.

The state's unwillingness to provide direct financial aid was, the liberals devoutly believed, a blessing. The laity had responded with a generous enthusiasm that contrasted strikingly with the sullenness and outright disinterest that characterized lay activities in many "Catholic" countries. "Liberty has, indeed, its inconveniences, its dangers even," Bishop Spalding said, "but the atmosphere it creates is the native air of generous, fair, and noble souls; and where it is not, man's proper good and honor are not found." All the liberals asked was a fair field and no favor. "We are content," Father Hewit wrote, "with the total separation of Church and state . . . leaving us at liberty to propagate our religion. . . . We are content that all Christian sects, Jews, and in general all associations which do not conspire against the laws, should enjoy equal liberty." "None love more ardently" than do Catholics, Bishop Stephen Ryan insisted, "the freedom they enjoy; none have profited more by the liberty of conscience and equality of rights guaranteed to all."

Conversely, the liberals were sure that a closer connection between church and state than existed in America inevitably harmed religion by committing its interests to the whim of political officials. The filiations with the state during the Middle Ages were only "accident," Spalding wrote, not the Catholic ideal; and they had cost the Church the liberty to appoint whom it wished, at the same time that they allowed the clergy and laity to grow lax and indifferent. "The outward honor shown to the Church has generally been at the expense of her inward force," the bishop concluded. Dependence on the state made the Middle Ages "a nightmare" for the Church, Father Joseph Tracy of Boston maintained; dependence today would surely have the same sad result. Father McGlynn announced that he was "willing to go in for perfect, absolute union of Church and State in the Kingdom of Heaven beyond the grave, or in the communities of angelic men," but nowhere else. And Professor Thomas O'Gorman, in his history of the American Church, noted that "if the close union of church and state in the early Christianity of California was of some advantage to the church . . . it was also productive of some disadvantages. It cannot be otherwise . . . so long as human nature is what it is." The liberals rejoiced that the American Church was "free and unshackled by concordats," which necessarily limited her "action," and cramped her "energy."

In a dominantly Protestant America, it was relatively easy for the liberal Catholics to accept the "separation of church and state." It was a bolder step to assert, as unambiguously as they did, that closer relations had always been harmful. Yet some of the liberals went even further and happily forecast that when Catholics predominated in America, the separation would be maintained. Such avowals were highly reassuring to the many Protestants who suspected that the Church was libertarian only when Catholics were in a minority. Bishop Keane promised that, however much of America was converted, so long as real disagreement on questions of social and political morality existed, the Church was too tolerant to impose its beliefs by coercive laws. Keane cited the Church's approval of the charter of liberties granted in the Catholic France of Louis XVIII, and in Catholic Belgium. And he repeated Cardi-

nal Manning's assurances to Gladstone that, should Catholics gain controlling political power, there would be no laws of constraint or privation enacted against dissenters. The Paulist Father Edward Brady amplified Keane's reply. Should virtually all Americans become Catholic, divorce would be abolished, and the Church would insist on a Christian education for Catholic children, — "(she would not impose it upon others)." She would try to provide an honest ballot and an upright administration of justice. But "she would not touch a single stone in the noble fabric of our constitution — nay, she would safeguard to the utmost of her power our free institutions, and teach her children to be willing at any moment to die in their defense."

The liberals claimed that American Catholics had demonstrated fine tolerance even when local conditions made it possible for them to have acted otherwise. Richard Clarke testified that the several Protestant boys cared for in the Catholic Protectory he managed were respectfully escorted to a Protestant church every Sunday. Cardinal Gibbons used his personal influence to prevent the city of Baltimore from suppressing an atheistical "Sunday School." And the cardinal liked to praise Lord Baltimore for voluntarily establishing religious freedom in his personal colony. His "noble stature" would "reflect unfading glory" on himself, on his state, and on his Church.

The liberals regularly asserted that the Spanish Inquisition had been primarily a political institution, and that American Catholics wished one no more than did American politicians. One Catholic writer maintained that an inquisition would never reappear, because "all history is a record of progress from ignorance to knowledge, from weakness to strength, from bondage to freedom." Cardinal Gibbons, claiming the backing of "every Catholic Priest and layman in the land," emphatically renounced "every species of violence" in religious affairs, and asserted that in the future, doctrinal orthodoxy would be preserved, not by physically coercive means, but by the sword of the spirit, and the fire of the love of Christ.

Even such traditional methods of control as the *imprimatur* and the Index might well, the liberals suggested, be dispensed with. The *Catholic World* cited with approval an English Jesuit's opinion that, in the ideal state of the future, censorship of opinion might well be less necessary and less desirable. "The *imprimatur* might be either . . . obligatory or merely a matter of counsel to obtain it. We are not to adopt promiscuously all the praiseworthy customs of our forefathers." When conservatives in Europe and America demanded that Henry George's *Progress and Poverty* be placed on the Index, the liberals were able to block the move, and their protests implied grave doubts whether such censorship was any longer a useful practice. Canon William Barry, an English ally, stated flatly that the Index was an anachronism.

The liberals made their professions of perpetual loyalty to the American system, serene in the conviction that America had long enjoyed far better relations between churches and the state than either Catholic ultramontanes or American secularists would acknowledge. To the saturnine John Gilmary Shea, many of the founding fathers seemed no better than "base drivelling slaves of the old anti-Catholic bigotry and fanaticism, shutting their eyes to the light and full of fiendish hatred." Even Hecker was, on occasion, less than flattering in his estimate of the religious instincts of the founding fathers. But McGlynn declared firmly that it was a "calumny" to assert that the founders were "irreligious men," and Richard Clarke concluded that Washington's "relations with Catholics were friendly and intimate . . . , always just and sympathetic, characterized by . . . a particular leaning towards them." Bishop Stephen Ryan wrote his clergy on the hundredth anniversary of Washing-

ton's inauguration that "when we contrast a Washington, and the illustrious founders of our great Republic—men of deep religious convictions, men of broad, liberal minds, of genuine Christian instincts . . . with the pigmy statesmen, pretended liberals, and radical revolutionaries of other lands," it became obvious why the revolution they led and the government they established were more acceptable to Catholics than anything in Europe. In fact, one layman insisted, the Revolution did not seek to destroy religion, but only to eliminate religious bigotry. The revolt was so certainly "providential," that Gibbons rejoiced in the mistaken notion that no Catholics served with the Tories.

The "governmental spirit of the United States" from the first was not, of course, Christian in the traditional mode, and so the French Canadian Jules Tardivel intransigently concluded that it had always been "by every necessity" dominated by an "anti-Christian spirit." This kind of logic disgusted the *Catholic World*. Relations between church and state were established in America by righteous men dealing wisely with existing conditions, "not by a frantic advocacy of antique methods, or of a state of things which ought to be in the abstract, or of what emotional or traditional temperaments might desire—all legitimate enough, but barred out of here by the sovereign rule" of what the *World* was frank to call "providential conditions." A great deal of "unmistakably Christian sentiment" was "infused into our institutions," the journal continued, as would be obvious to anyone who dispassionately considered the actual operations of the state today.

In salient contrast to conditions in France and Italy, the Church in America could hold all the property it wished. Conservatives remained indignant that civil law regulated the transfer of property titles, as if the Church could be rightfully treated as the creature or subject of the state. But liberals like John Ireland concentrated on the fact that most states had dropped requirements common in mid-century that laymen of the vicinity share in Church property holding. Most bishops were now permitted to designate themselves corporations sole, and where this privilege was not available, Ireland blamed Catholics for not having made clear to the state their desire for it.

Though states did not directly finance the work of the Church, some granted aid to Catholic hospitals and asylums, ostensibly on the grounds of material interest, but often in the desire to help churches in any way constitutional. It was true that some Americans noisily denounced such subsidies, but a proposed amendment to the Federal Constitution "to perfect the cleavage between church and state" never mustered much popular support. Protests made against tax exemption of church property were similarly ineffectual.

The state deferred to the church by recognizing her clergy as civil officials for such functions as marriage. It appointed and paid chaplains to the armed services; during the Civil War, enough Catholic chaplains had been selected to weaken the old tradition that the faith was discriminated against. The custom of asking clergymen, including Catholics on occasion, to offer prayers at important public meetings had virtually acquired the sanction of law. Most officials took a solemn oath upon the Bible before assuming office. And the proclamation of a day of thanksgiving to God impressed both Americans and foreigners; "what difference is there," a visiting French cleric asked, after reading Cleveland's declaration of Thanksgiving Day, "between this beautiful proclamation of a state leader and the decree of a Catholic bishop?"

Despite these quasi-religious activities, none of the states could be deemed "Catholic," since none explicitly acknowledged the authority of the Church or carried out all its recommendations. One conservative protested that even the Christianity implicit in the common law had been eroded away by the courts; in its place, the legislatures, oblivious of their obligations to enforce the natural law, were "attempting to fabricate a crude religious and moral code, without the guidance of inspiration and influenced solely by temporary prejudice or a mistaken view of public policy." Hecker, on the other hand, was sure that the courts would continue to punish not only violations of the natural law, but also clear transgressions of revealed religious duty as crimes "against good government." Cardinal Gibbons declared that statute laws were almost invariably so "intimately interwoven with the Christian religion," that the faith had nothing to fear from their application. He was confident that the common law still virtually guaranteed the Christianity of the states."

By appealing to practices rather than to principles, the American liberals tried hard to mediate between the demands of a traditionalist Catholicism and those of contemporary culture. When a popular movement developed to put "God in the Constitution," Gibbons pleased ardent defenders of the separation of church and state by declaring his opposition; at the same time, he placated Catholics by stating that he was not agitated over constitutional phrases so long as the government continued to be guided in so much of its work by a manifestly Christian spirit. A Paulist advised fellow Catholics to work not for union, but rather a more perfect "*entente cordiale*" between church and state.

Winthrop Hudson

9. THE PASSING OF THE PROTESTANT ERA IN AMERICA

In his recent study of *American Protestantism* Professor Hudson discussed the many factors present in the protestant contribution to—and response to—the pluralization of religious life in America. In the situation so described it is clear why American protestantism was unable to reach a realistic and relevant consensus on the relationship between religious and governmental authority structures within the one society.

The shift from a Protestant to a post-Protestant era in America, . . . is not to be explained solely in numerical terms. The Protestant churches continued to claim almost twice as many members as the Roman Catholic church. Furthermore, the projection of a United States Census Bureau study in 1958 indicated that two-thirds of all Americans thought of themselves as Protestants, whereas only one-fourth thought of themselves as Roman Catholics. There are few informed observers, however, who would regard these figures as an accurate indication of the actual balance of influence exerted by these two religious traditions. Before the turn of the century the death of Phillips Brooks plunged the whole nation into mourning, but it was noted by a discerning interpreter in 1958 that it was no longer possible to imagine that "the death of any national Protestant leader or political figure other than the President himself would command the massive 'interfaith' attention which accompanied the death of Samuel Cardinal Stritch in 1958." Illustrations of this type could be multiplied, and they serve to document the fact that a more marked realignment of religious forces in the United States had taken place than the bare statistics suggest.

One of the factors contributing to the relative decline—in proportion to its numerical strength—of Protestant influence was the fact that Roman Catholic strength was centered in the cities, whereas the great stronghold of Protestantism had been centered in the small towns and villages of the countryside. Since the cities were the real power centers of twentieth-century America, these differing strongholds of the two traditions spell out in part the difference of impact they were able to exert. It was the concentration of strength in a few key cities which also explains to a considerable degree why the influence of the Jewish community was far out of proportion to its numbers. The relative weakness of Protestantism in the new situation is not to be understood solely by its dependence upon a dwindling farm and village civilization. It was due quite as much to internal factors which were the product of its peculiar historical development in the United States.

For a variety of reasons, Protestants did not find it easy to adjust to the necessities of a pluralistic society. They had possessed a near monopoly for so long that it came as a shock to discover that they were henceforth to live in a highly competitive situation in which many of the things they had taken for granted would be sharply challenged. This discovery alone was to be sufficiently demoralizing, but there were other factors that made it difficult for American Protestants to respond vigorously to the demands of a pluralistic society.

For one thing, Protestantism had become

From Winthrop Hudson, *American Protestantism* (Chicago, 1961), pp. 130–134. Reprinted by permission of University of Chicago Press.

complacent. In a very real sense, it had become a victim of its own success. Throughout the nineteenth century the Protestant churches had been on the march, seeking to win men and women to the Christian faith, to penetrate the institutions of society with Christian principles, and to keep abreast of the retreating frontier. They had succeeded remarkably well and had brought into being a society and a culture that was recognizably Christian. By the end of the century, the final frontier areas had been "churched," and the American people seemed to be settling down to a stable churchgoing existence defined in Protestant terms. There were, as has been noted, non-Protestant enclaves in the cities, but given time it was assumed that these would be assimilated. Thus, at this critical juncture, the Protestant churches — pleased with the past and confident of the future — tended to relax. A mood of complacency was scarcely appropriate for the situation in which they were to find themselves as they moved forward into the new century, and it heightened the sense of shock they were to experience when they discovered just how inappropriate it was. But American Protestantism was suffering from a deeper malady.

The deeper malady was the theological erosion which had taken place during the nineteenth century. As has been suggested, a pluralistic society is a highly competitive society — a society in which various traditions are locked in debate. In such a situation, presuppositions must be clearly defined and their implications carefully articulated, if a particular religious grouping is to survive and make its influence felt. This means that the adherents of the several traditions must be knowledgeable and informed. They must be able to give both an account of and a reasoned defense for their faith, and they must be able to spell out its implications with clarity and persuasiveness. Otherwise they are not equipped to participate effectively in the discussion. It was precisely at this point that American Protestantism had become weak.

The theological erosion that had taken place was the product of several factors. It was in part the result of the absence of any sharp challenge to the Protestant understanding of the Christian faith, for in this situation fundamental assumptions tend to be taken for granted. Consequently the Protestant community had become increasingly composed of adherents whose religious affiliation was determined more by accident of birth and persistence of custom than by conscious conviction. It was also in part the product of the attrition to which every religious movement is subject. There is always an alternation between periods of spiritual quickening and vitality and periods of decline and lethargy. Any great surge of religious life and spiritual renewal is always followed by a gradual diminution of zeal and a fading of earlier imperatives. But there were other features of nineteenth-century Protestant life which accentuated and hastened the process.

Nineteenth-century Protestantism in America, as we have seen, was the heir of the great tide of Evangelical religion, stemming from the Great Awakening, which contributed the aggressive missionary spirit that gave to nineteenth-century Protestant Action its dynamic thrust. While the restless energy released by Evangelicalism succeeded in placing a Christian stamp on much of American culture, Evangelicalism by itself was not an unmixed blessing. Doctrinal definitions tended to be neglected in the stress that was placed upon "heart religion" and the "conversion experience." The demands of the Christian life, to be sure, continued to be spelled out within the framework of an earlier theological understanding, and so long as this theological structure persisted a formative influence was exerted upon society. But since the appeal of Evangelicalism was directed more to the emotions than to the intellect, the tendency was for the inherited capital to be lost.

The theological erosion was also accelerated by the particular technique — revivalism — which Evangelicalism developed as a means of winning men and women to Christian obedience. The revivalist faced at least two temptations. First, he was tempted to reduce the ambiguities of human life and the complexities of the Christian faith to simple alternatives so that he could issue a clear-cut call for decision. Second, he was tempted to stress results and to justify whatever tended to produce them. As a result of these two pressures, the tendency of the revivalist was to over simplify the issues, and the ultimate consequence as the century moved toward its close was to contribute to those forces which were emptying the faith of American Protestantism of its content. It should be acknowledged that the temptations implicit in revivalism were resisted with varying degrees of success by the greater revivalists, for they were men acutely sensitive to the hazards and uncertainties of the road to salvation. But often this sensitivity was lacking.

The energetic busyness of the churches during the latter part of the century had done little to arrest the erosion. Members were added to the churches. Moral idealism was generated, enthusiasm elicited, and people were put to work. But the basic theological task continued to be neglected. While a cluster of relatively vague and ill-defined folk beliefs survived in most of the churches and were perpetuated by the Uniform Lessons of the Sunday schools, few Protestants were aware of possessing a comprehensive, coherent, and clearly defined intellectual structure which would help to preserve their identity within the general culture and provide them with an independent perspective of their own. Stripped of this type of self-definition, Protestantism was in no position to meet either the challenge of the world or the challenge of other religious traditions with a sharp challenge of its own. Indeed, its tendency was to lose itself within the larger society which it had helped fashion.

Philip Schaff

10. THE AMERICAN THEORY AND SYSTEM

Philip Schaff (d. 1893), originally Swiss, came to Mercersburg Seminary (Pennsylvania) in 1843 having been trained as a church historian in Germany. Schaff's contribution to the American scene was many-sided—including attempts to "explain" America and American ways to Europe. This selection is from an essay on "Church and State in the United States" which Schaff prepared for publication in the studies of the recently founded American Historical Association.

The relationship of church and state in the United States secures full liberty of religious thought, speech, and action, within the limits of the public peace and order. It makes persecution impossible.

Religion and liberty are inseparable. Religion is voluntary, and cannot, and ought not to be forced.

This is a fundamental article of the American creed, without distinction of sect or party. Liberty, both civil and religious, is an American instinct. All natives suck it in with the mother's milk; all immigrants accept it as a happy boon, especially those who flee from oppression and persecution abroad. Even those who reject the modern theory of liberty enjoy the practice, and would defend it in their own interest against any attempt to overthrow it.

Such liberty is impossible on the basis of a union of church and state, where the one of necessity restricts or controls the other. It requires a friendly separation, where each power is entirely independent in its own sphere. The church, as such, has nothing to do with the state except to obey its laws and to strengthen its moral foundations; the state has nothing to do with the church except to protect her in her property and liberty; and the state must be equally just to all forms of belief and unbelief which do not endanger the public safety.

* * *

The American relationship of church and state differs from all previous relationships in Europe and in the colonial period of our history; and yet it rests upon them and reaps the benefit of them all. For history is an organic unit, and American history has its roots in Europe.

1. The American system differs from the ante-Nicene or pre-Constantinian separation of church and state, when the church was indeed, as with us, self-supporting and self-governing, and so far free within, but under persecution from without, being treated as a forbidden religion by the then heathen state. In America the government protects the church in her property and rights without interfering with her internal affairs. By the power of truth and the moral heroism of martyrdom the church converted the Roman Empire and became the mother of Christian states.

2. The American system differs from the hierarchical control of the church over the

From Philip Schaff, "Church and State in the United States," in *Papers of the American Historical Association*, Vol. II, No. 4 (New York, 1888), 9–10 and 12–16 [391–392 and 394–398].

state, or from priest government, which prevailed in the Middle Ages down to the Reformation, and reached its culmination in the Papacy. It confines the church to her proper spiritual vocation, and leaves the state independent in all the temporal affairs of the nation. The hierarchical theory was suited to the times after the fall of the Roman Empire and the ancient civilization, when the state was a rude military despotism, when the church was the refuge of the people, when the Christian priesthood was in sole possession of learning and had to civilize as well as to evangelize the barbarians of northern and western Europe. By her influence over legislation the church abolished bad laws and customs, introduced benevolent institutions, and created a Christian state controlled by the spirit of justice and humanity, and fit for self-government.

3. The American system differs from the Erastian or Cæsaro-Papal control of the state over the church, which obtained in the old Byzantine Empire, and prevails in modern Russia, and in the Protestant states of Europe, where the civil government protects and supports the church, but at the expense of her dignity and independence, and deprives her of the power of self-government. The Erastian system was based on the assumption that all citizens are also Christians of one creed, but is abnormal in the mixed character of government and people in the modern state. In America, the state has no right whatever to interfere with the affairs of the church, her doctrine, discipline, and worship, and the appointment of ministers. It would be a great calamity if religion were to become subject to our ever-changing politics.

4. The American system differs from the system of toleration, which began in Germany with the Westphalia Treaty, 1648; in England with the Act of Toleration, 1689, and which now prevails over nearly all Europe; of late years, nominally at least, even in Roman Catholic countries, to the very gates of the Vatican, in spite of the protest of the Pope. Toleration exists where the government supports one or more churches, and permits other religious communities under the name of sects (as on the continent), or dissenters and nonconformists (as in England), under certain conditions. In America, there are no such distinctions, but only churches or denominations on a footing of perfect equality before the law. To talk about any particular denomination as *the* church, or *the American* church, has no meaning, and betrays ignorance or conceit. Such exclusiveness is natural and logical in Romanism, but unnatural, illogical, and contemptible in any other church. The American laws know no such institution as "the church," but only separate and independent organizations.

Toleration is an important step from state-churchism to free-churchism. But it is only a step. There is a very great difference between toleration and liberty. Toleration is a concession, which may be withdrawn; it implies a preference for the ruling form of faith and worship, and a practical disapproval of all other forms. It may be coupled with many restrictions and disabilities. We tolerate what we dislike, but cannot alter; we tolerate even a nuisance if we must. Acts of toleration are wrung from a government by the force of circumstances and the power of a minority too influential to be disregarded. In this way even the most despotic governments, as those of Turkey and of Russia, are tolerant; the one toward Christians and Jews, the other toward Mohammedans and dissenters from the orthodox Greek Church; but both deny the right of self-extension and missionary operations except in favor of the state religion, and both forbid and punish apostasy from it. . . .

In our country we ask no toleration for religion and its free exercise, but we claim it as an inalienable right. "It is not toleration," says Judge Cooley, "which is established in our system, but religious equality." Freedom of religion is one of the greatest gifts of God to man, without distinction of race and color. He is the author and lord of conscience, and no power on earth has a right to stand between God and the conscience. A violation of this divine law written in the heart is an assault upon the majesty of God and the image of God in man. Granting the freedom of conscience, we must, by logical necessity, also grant the freedom of its manifestation and exercise in public worship. To concede the first and to deny the second, after the manner of despotic governments, is to imprison the conscience. To be just, the state must either support all or none of the religions of its citizens. Our government supports none, but protects all.

5. Finally—and this we would emphasize as especially important in our time,— the American system differs radically and fundamentally fom the infidel and red-republican theory of religious freedom. The word freedom is one of the most abused words in the vocabulary. True liberty is a positive force, regulated by law; false liberty is a negative force, a release from restraint. True liberty is the moral power of self-government; the liberty of infidels and anarchists is carnal licentiousness. The American separation of church and state rests on respect for the church; the infidel separation, on indifference and hatred of the church, and of religion itself.

The infidel theory was tried and failed in the first Revolution of France. It began with toleration, and ended with the abolition of Christianity, and with the reign of terror, which in turn prepared the way for military despotism as the only means of saving society from anarchy and ruin. Our infidels and anarchists would re-enact this tragedy if they should ever get the power. They openly profess their hatred and contempt of our Sunday-laws, our Sabbaths,

our churches, and all our religious institutions and societies. Let us beware of them! The American system grants freedom also to irreligion and infidelity, but only within the limits of the order and safety of society. The destruction of religion would be the destruction of morality and the ruin of the state. Civil liberty requires for its support religious liberty, and cannot prosper without it. Religious liberty is not an empty sound, but an orderly exercise of religious duties and enjoyment of all its privileges. It is freedom *in* religion, not freedom *from* religion; as true civil liberty is freedom *in* law, and not freedom *from* law. . . .

Republican institutions in the hands of a virtuous and God-fearing nation are the very best in the world, but in the hands of a corrupt and irreligious people they are the very worst, and the most effective weapons of destruction. An indignant people may rise in rebellion against a cruel tyrant; but who will rise against the tyranny of the people in possession of the ballot-box and the whole machinery of government? Here lies our great danger, and it is increasing every year.

Destroy our churches, close our Sunday-schools, abolish the Lord's Day, and our republic would become an empty shell, and our people would tend to heathenism and barbarism. Christianity is the most powerful factor in our society and the pillar of our institutions. It regulates the family; it enjoins private and public virtue; it builds up moral character; it teaches us to love God supremely, and our neighbor as ourselves; it makes good men and useful citizens; it denounces every vice; it encourages every virtue; it promotes and serves the public welfare; it upholds peace and order. Christianity is the only possible religion for the American people, and with Christianity are bound up all our hopes for the future.

James Bryce

11. THE CHURCHES AND THE CLERGY

Lord Bryce (d. 1922) published *The American Commonwealth* on the basis of three visits to the United States. Since publication it has been accepted as a valuable estimate of American society. In this selection it will be seen that his assessment of the relationships between governments and religious institutions is close to those of Schaff and Cooley which were roughly contemporaneous.

It is accepted as an axiom by all Americans that the civil power ought to be not only neutral and impartial as between different forms of faith, but ought to leave these matters entirely on one side, regarding them no more than it regards the artistic or literary pursuits of the citizens. There seem to be no two opinions on this subject in the United States. Even the Protestant Episcopalian clergy, who are in many ways disposed to admire and envy their brethren in England; even the Roman Catholic bishops, whose creed justifies the enforcement of the true faith by the secular arm, assure the European visitor that if State establishment were offered them they would decline it, preferring the freedom they enjoy to any advantages the State could confer. Every religious community can now organize itself in whatever way it pleases, lay down its own rules of faith and discipline, create and administer its own system of judicature, raise and apply its funds at its uncontrolled discretion. A church established by the State would not be able to do all these things, because it would also be controlled by the State, and it would be exposed to the envy and jealousy of other sects.

The only controversies that have arisen regarding State action in religious matters have turned upon the appropriation of public funds to charitable institutions managed by some particular denomination. Such appropriations are expressly prohibited in the constitutions of some States. But it may happen that the readiest way of promoting some benevolent public purpose is to make a grant of money to an institution already at work, and successfully serving that purpose. As this reason may sometimes be truly given, so it is also sometimes advanced where the real motive is to purchase the political support of the denomination to which the institution belongs, or at least of its clergy. In some States, and particularly in New York, State or city legislatures are often charged with giving money to Roman Catholic institutions for the sake of securing the Catholic vote. In these cases, however, the money always purports to be voted not for a religious but for a philanthropic or educational purpose. No ecclesiastical body would be strong enough to obtain any grant to its general funds, or any special immunity for its ministers. The passion for equality in religious as well as secular matters is everywhere in America far too strong to be braved, and nothing excites more general disapprobation than any attempt by an ecclesiastical organization to interfere in politics. The suspicion that the Roman Catholic church uses its power over its members to guide their votes for its purposes has more than once given rise to strong anti-Catholic or (as they would be called in Canada) Orange movements, such as that which has recently figured so large-

From James Bryce, *The American Commonwealth*, 3rd ed., 2 vols. (New York, 1894), Vol. II, pp. 698–704.

ly in Ohio, Indiana, Michigan, and Illinois under the name of the American Protective Association. So the hostility to Mormonism was due not merely to the practice of polygamy, but also to the notion that the hierarchy of the Latter Day Saints constitutes a secret and tyrannical *imperium in imperio* opposed to the genius of democratic institutions.

The refusal of the civil power to protect or endow any form of religion is commonly represented in Europe as equivalent to a declaration of contemptuous indifference on the part of the State to the spiritual interests of its people. A State recognizing no church is called a godless State; the disestablishment of a church is described as an act of national impiety. Nothing can be farther from the American view, to an explanation of which it may be well to devote a few lines.

The abstention of the State from interference in matters of faith and worship may be advocated on two principles, which may be called the political and the religious. The former sets out from the principles of liberty and equality. It holds any attempt at compulsion by the civil power to be an infringement on liberty of thought, as well as on liberty of action, which could be justified only when a practice claiming to be religious is so obviously anti-social or immoral as to threaten the well-being of the community. Religious persecution, even in its milder forms, such as disqualifying the members of a particular sect for public office, is, it conceives, inconsistent with the conception of individual freedom and the respect due to the primordial rights of the citizen which modern thought has embraced. Even if State action stops short of the imposition of disabilities, and confines itself to favouring a particular church, whether by grants of money or by giving special immunities to its clergy, this is an infringement on equality, putting one man at a disadvantage compared with others in respect of matters which are (according to the view I am stating) not fit subjects for State cognizance.

The second principle, embodying the more purely religious view of the question, starts from the conception of the church as a spiritual body existing for spiritual purposes, and moving along spiritual paths. It is an assemblage of men who are united by their devotion to an unseen Being, their memory of a past divine life, their belief in the possibility of imitating that life, so far as human frailty allows, their hopes for an illimitable future. Compulsion of any kind is contrary to the nature of such a body, which lives by love and reverence, not by law. It desires no State help, feeling that its strength comes from above, and that its kingdom is not of this world. It does not seek for exclusive privileges, conceiving that these would not only create bitterness between itself and other religious bodies, but might attract persons who did not really share its sentiments, while corrupting the simplicity of those who are already its members. Least of all can it submit to be controlled by the State, for the State, in such a world as the present, means persons many or most of whom are alien to its beliefs and cold to its emotions. The conclusion follows that the church as a spiritual entity will be happiest and strongest when it is left absolutely to itself, not patronized by the civil power, not restrained by law except when and in so far as it may attempt to quit its proper sphere and intermeddle in secular affairs.

Of these two views it is the former much more than the latter that has moved the American mind. The latter would doubtless be now generally accepted by religious people. But when the question arose in a practical shape in the earlier days of the Republic, arguments of the former or political order were found amply sufficient to settle it, and no practical purpose has since then compelled men either to examine the spiritual basis of the church, or to inquire by the light of history how far State action

155

has during fifteen centuries helped or marred her usefulness. There has, however, been another cause at work, I mean the comparatively limited conception of the State itself which Americans have formed. The State is not to them, as to Germans or Frenchmen, and even to some English thinkers, an ideal moral power, charged with the duty of forming the characters and guiding the lives of its subjects. It is more like a commercial company, or perhaps a huge municipality created for the management of certain business in which all who reside within its bounds are interested, levying contributions and expending them on this business of common interest, but for the most part leaving the shareholders or burgesses to themselves. That an organization of this kind should trouble itself, otherwise than as matter of policy, with the opinions or conduct of its members, would be as unnatural as for a railway company to inquire how many of the shareholders were total abstainers. Accordingly it never occurs to the average American that there is any reason why State churches should exist, and he stands amazed at the warmth of European feeling on the matter.

Just because these questions have been long since disposed of, and excite no present passion, and perhaps also because the Americans are more practically easygoing than pedantically exact, the National government and the State governments do give to Christianity a species of recognition inconsistent with the view that civil government should be absolutely neutral in religious matters. Each House of Congress has a chaplain, and opens its proceedings each day with prayers. The President annually after the end of harvest issues a proclamation ordering a general thanksgiving, and occasionally appoints a day of fasting and humiliation. So prayers are offered in the State legislatures, and State governors issue proclamations for days of religious observance. Congress in the crisis of the Civil War (July, 1863) requested the Presi-

dent to appoint a day for humiliation and prayer. In the army and navy provision is made for religious services, conducted by chaplains of various denominations, and no difficulty seems to have been found in reconciling their claims. In most States there exist laws punishing blasphemy or profane swearing by the name of God (laws which, however, are in some places openly transgressed and in few or none enforced), laws restricting or forbidding trade or labour on the Sabbath, as well as laws protecting assemblages for religious purposes, such as camp-meetings or religious processions, from being disturbed. The Bible is (in most States) read in the public State-supported schools, and though controversies have arisen on this head, the practice is evidently in accord with the general sentiment of the people.

The matter may be summed up by saying that Christianity is in fact understood to be, though not the legally established religion, yet the national religion. So far from thinking their commonwealth godless, the Americans conceive that the religious character of a government consists in nothing but the religious belief of the individual citizens, and the conformity of their conduct to that belief. They deem the general acceptance of Christianity to be one of the main sources of their national prosperity, and their nation a special object of the Divine favour.

The legal position of a Christian church is in the United States simply that of a voluntary association, or group of associations, corporate or unincorporate, under the ordinary law. There is no such thing as a special ecclesiastical law; all questions, not only of property but of church discipline and jurisdiction, are, if brought before the courts of the land, dealt with as questions of contract; and the court, where it is obliged to examine a question of theology, as for instance whether a clergyman has advanced opinions inconsistent with any creed or formula to which he has bound himself—for it will prefer, if possible, to leave such matters to the proper ecclesiastical authority—will treat the point as one of pure legal interpretation, neither assuming to itself theological knowledge, nor suffering considerations of policy to intervene.

As a rule, every religious body can organize itself in any way it pleases. The State does not require its leave to be asked, but permits any form of church government, any ecclesiastical order, to be created and endowed, any method to be adopted of vesting church property, either simply in trustees or in corporate bodies formed either under the general law of the State or under some special statute. Sometimes a limit is imposed on the amount of property, or of real estate, which an ecclesiastical corporation can hold; but, on the whole, it may be said that the civil power manifests no jealousy of the spiritual, but allows the latter a perfectly free field for expansion. Of course if any ecclesiastical author-

ity were to become formidable either by its wealth or by its control over the members of its body, this easy tolerance would disappear; all I observe is that the difficulties often experienced, and still more often feared, in Europe, from the growth of organizations exercising tremendous spiritual powers, have in the United States never proved serious. No church has anywhere a power approaching that of the Roman Catholic Church in Lower Canada. Religious bodies are in so far the objects of special favour that their property is in most States exempt from taxation; and this is reconciled to theory by the argument that they are serviceable as moral agencies, and diminish the expenses incurred in respect of police administration. Two or three States impose restrictions on the creation of religious corporations, and one, Maryland, requires the sanction of the legislature to dispositions of property to religious uses. But, speaking generally, religious bodies are the objects of legislative favour.

T. M. Cooley

12. CONSTITUTIONAL LIMITATIONS REGARDING RELIGIOUS LIBERTY

Thomas McIntyre Cooley (d. 1898) served on the Michigan State Supreme Court for twenty years while also teaching law at the University of Michigan. *A Treatise on the Constitutional Limitations Which Rest upon the Legislative Power of the States of the American Union* was his most important work and continued to be issued in revised editions even after his death. This selection summarizes the pattern of "Church-State relationships" existing in the legal provisions of the States.

A careful examination of the American constitutions will disclose the fact that nothing is more fully set forth or more

plainly expressed than the determination of their authors to preserve and perpetuate religious liberty, and to guard against the

From T. M. Cooley, *A Treatise on the Constitutional Limitations Which Rest upon the Legislative Power of the States of the American Union,* the chapter "Of Religious Liberty," as printed in the seventh edition (Boston, 1903) which followed the last text revised by Cooley dated in 1896. This section—regarding text—was substantially unchanged from at least the fourth edition (Boston, 1878).

157

slightest approach towards the establishment of an inequality in the civil and political rights of citizens, which shall have for its basis only their differences of religious belief. The American people came to the work of framing their fundamental laws, after centuries of religious oppression and persecution, sometimes by one party or sect and sometimes by another, had taught them the utter futility of all attempts to propagate religious opinions by the rewards, penalties, or terrors of human laws. They could not fail to perceive, also, that a union of Church and State, like that which existed in England, if not wholly impracticable in America, was certainly opposed to the spirit of our institutions, and that any domineering of one sect over another was repressing to the energies of the people, and must necessarily tend to discontent and disorder. Whatever, therefore, may have been their individual sentiments upon religious questions, or upon the propriety of the State assuming supervision and control of religious affairs under other circumstances, the general voice has been, that persons of every religious persuasion should be made equal before the law, and that questions of religious belief and religious worship should be questions between each individual man and his Maker. Of these questions human tribunals, so long as the public order is not disturbed, are not to take cognizance, except as the individual, by his voluntary action in associating himself with a religious organization, may have conferred upon such organization a jurisdiction over him in ecclesiastical matters. These constitutions, therefore, have not established religious toleration merely, but religious equality; in that particular being far in advance not only of the mother country, but also of much of the colonial legislation, which, though more liberal than that of other civilized countries, nevertheless exhibited features of discrimination based upon religious beliefs or professions.

Considerable differences will appear in the provisions in the State constitutions on the general subject of the present chapter; some of them being confined to declarations and prohibitions whose purpose is to secure the most perfect equality before the law of all shades of religious belief, while some exhibit a jealousy of ecclesiastical authority by making persons who exercise the functions of clergyman, priest, or teacher of any religious persuasion, society, or sect, ineligible to civil office; and still others show some traces of the old notion, that truth and a sense of duty do not consort with skepticism in religion. There are exceptional clauses, however, though not many in number; and it is believed that, where they exist, they are not often made use of to deprive any person of the civil or political rights or privileges which are placed by law within the reach of his fellows.

Those things which are not lawful under any of the American constitutions may be stated thus:

1. Any law respecting an establishment of religion. The legislatures have not been left at liberty to effect a union of Church and State, or to establish preferences by law in favor of any one religious persuasion or mode of worship. There is not complete religious liberty where any one sect is favored by the State and given an advantage by law over other sects. . . .

2. Compulsory support, by taxation or otherwise, of religious instruction. Not only is no one denomination to be favored at the expense of the rest, but all support of religious instruction must be entirely voluntary. It is not within the sphere of government to coerce it.

3. Compulsory attendance upon religious worship. Whoever is not led by choice or a sense of duty to attend upon the ordinances of religion is not to be compelled to do so by the State. . . .

4. Restraints upon the free exercise of religion according to the dictates of the

conscience. No external authority is to place itself between the finite being and the Infinite when the former is seeking to render the homage that is due, and in a mode which commends itself to his conscience and judgment as being suitable for him to render, and acceptable to its object.

5. Restraints upon the expression of religious belief. An earnest believer usually regards it as his duty to propagate his opinions, and to bring others to his views. To deprive him of this right is to take from him the power to perform what he considers a most sacred obligation.

These are the prohibitions which in some form of words are to be found in the American constitutions, and which secure freedom of conscience and of religious worship. No man in religious matters is to be subjected to the censorship of the State or of any public authority; and the State is not to inquire into or take notice of religious belief, when the citizen performs his duty to the State and to his fellows, and is guilty of no breach of public morals or public decorum.

But while thus careful to establish, protect, and defend religious freedom and equality, the American constitutions contain no provisions which prohibit the authorities from such solemn recognition of a superintending Providence in public transactions and exercises as the general religious sentiment of mankind inspires, and as seems meet and proper in finite and dependent beings. Whatever may be the shades of religious belief, all must acknowledge the fitness of recognizing in important human affairs the superintending care and control of the great Governor of the Universe, and of acknowledging with thanksgiving His boundless favors, of bowing in contrition when visited with the penalties of His broken laws. No principle of constitutional law is violated when thanksgiving or fast days are appointed; when chaplains are designated for the army and navy; when legislative sessions are opened with prayer or the reading of the Scriptures, or when religious teaching is encouraged by a general exemption of the houses of religious worship from taxation for the support of State government. Undoubtedly the spirit of the constitution will require, in all these cases, that care be taken to avoid discrimination in favor of or against any one religious denomination or sect; but the power to do any of these things does not become unconstitutional simply because of its susceptibility to abuse. . . .

Nor, while recognizing a superintending Providence, are we always precluded from recognizing also, in the rules prescribed for the conduct of the citizen, the notorious fact that the prevailing religion in the States is Christian. . . . The moral sense is largely regulated and controlled by the religious belief; and therefore it is that those things which, estimated by a Christian standard, are profane and blasphemous, are properly punished as crimes against society, since they are offensive in the highest degree to the general public sense, and have a direct tendency to undermine the moral support of the laws, and to corrupt the community.

It is frequently said that Christianity is a part of the law of the land. In a certain sense and for certain purposes this is true. The best features of the common law, and especially those which regard the family and social relations; which compel the parent to support the child, the husband to support the wife; which make the marriage tie permanent and forbid polygamy, — if not derived from, have at least been improved and strengthened by the prevailing religion and the teachings of its sacred Book. But the law does not attempt to enforce the precepts of Christianity on the ground of their sacred character or divine origin. . . .

Whatever deference the constitution or the laws may require to be paid in some cases to the conscientious scruples or religious convictions of the majority, the general policy always is, to avoid with care any compulsion which infringes on the religious scruples of any, however little reason may seem to others to underlie them. Even in the important matter of bearing arms for the public defense, those who cannot in conscience take part are excused, and their proportion of this great and sometimes imperative burden is borne by the rest of the community.

VI. *Mainstream Pluralism* (1920-1960)

The years between 1920 and 1960 witnessed continuing attempts to define "independence of Church and State" in a society self-conscious of its religious pluralism—at least to the extent of its three major faiths. Each of these religious communities rethought its traditions in light of its American experiences. The spirit that led to the nineteenth-century liberal American Catholic "heresy" of Americanism (even if the heresy *per se* never existed) found new expression in liberating Catholic self-understanding from outdated European categories. Many Protestants also rethought their positions on the "Church-State issue," conscious that their pre-Civil War aspirations should not (or could not) necessarily prevail in a more modern and pluralistic era. The Jewish community—vocal out of proportion to its numbers—frequently contributed to this discussion. Sharing with the Roman Catholics a sense of tradition and a sense of outrage at the second-class status they both experienced for so long, the Jews have been most articulate in defending their substantial religious freedom in America. In particular, they have championed the "separation of Church and State" with fervor akin to that typically associated with the Baptists. Thus the Jews have nicely mediated between the far larger Protestant and Catholic communities.

As the religious communities sought to define "Church and State," another facet of the ancient problem received considerable public attention—the relationship between religion and politics—which is enormously complex. The relationship includes such issues as ecclesiastical pressure on political processes, the "religious vote," and selection of candidates according to the religious vote they may be expected to "pull" (if not a *de facto* religious test for office). Understandably, primary interest in these questions has been focused at the level of national politics, but religious authority structures and political behavior interact at all levels of community life. Twice during this period the question arose of whether a Roman Catholic could be elected president. It is probably wrong to attribute the defeat of Al Smith in the 1928 campaign to his Roman Catholic faith. It is quite possible that the "religious issue" had more to do with the outcome of the 1960 election, which John F. Kennedy safely won in the electoral college while failing to receive a majority of the popular vote. Some have argued that religion is an entirely "private affair" and thus it should have no significant relationship to the realm of politics, yet others assert with equal vehemence that religious and political views are inseparable.

During this period, the United States Supreme Court became an important force in Church-State matters. Guided both by the historical roots of the religion clauses of the First Amendment and by the need to address contemporary questions, the

Court has had an increasingly influential role in defining the American Church-State question. Starting at least with the *Everson* case in 1947, almost every issue involving religion and government became a potential source of litigation under either the free exercise clause or the establishment clause.

It can be argued that the rubric "Church and State" has application only where a religious institution and a political institution express the twofold life of a single community. If that is the case the phrase would seem to have little relevance for much of twentieth-century American history. But if it designates the manifold interaction between religious and political authority structures—where each is presumed to have a certain autonomy—then the term continues to be appropriate to an America self-conscious of its religious pluralism and eager to preserve its traditions of cooperation and limited civil governments.

John A. Ryan

1. COMMENTS ON THE "CHRISTIAN CONSTITUTION OF STATES"

John A. Ryan, Professor of Moral Theology at Catholic University of America, was at once traditionalistic in his interpretation of Roman Catholic Church-State thought and a liberal in social issues. His "exegesis" of Pope Leo XIII's encyclical *Immortale Dei* (November 1, 1885) was an important statement of the "conservative" Roman Catholic position.

Public Profession of Religion by the State

To the present generation this is undoubtedly "a hard saying." The separation of Church and State, which obtains substantially in the majority of countries, is generally understood as forbidding the State to make "a public profession of religion." Nevertheless, the logic of Pope Leo's argument is unassailable. Men are obliged to worship God, not only as individuals, but also as organized groups. Societies have existence and functions over and above the existence and functions of their individual members. Therefore, they are dependent upon God for their corporate existence and functions, and as moral persons owe corporate obedience to His laws, formal recognition of His authority, and appropriate acts of worship. To deny these propositions is to maintain the illogical position that man owes God religious worship under only one aspect of his life, in only one department of his life.

Since the State is by far the most important of the secular societies to which man belongs, its obligation to recognize and profess religion is considerably greater and stricter than is the case with the lesser societies. And the failure of the State to discharge this obligation produces evil results of corresponding gravity. It exhibits in most extensive proportions the destructive power of bad example.

Attitude of the State Toward the Church

But Pope Leo goes further. He declares that the State must not only "have care for religion," but recognize the *true* religion. This means the form of religion professed by the Catholic Church. It is a thoroughly logical position. If the State is under moral compulsion to profess and promote religion, it is obviously obliged to profess and promote only the religion that is true; for no individual, no group of individuals, no society, no State is justified in supporting error or in according to error the same recognition as to truth.

Those who deny this principle may practically all be included within three classes: First, those who hold that truth will by its own power speedily overcome error, and that the State should consequently assume an attitude of impartiality toward both; second, those who assume that all forms of religion are equally good and true; third, those who hold that it is impossible to know which is the true one. The first

From *The State and the Church*, ed. John A. Ryan and M. F. X. Millar (New York, 1924), pp. 29–39. Reprinted by permission. © 1922 by the National Catholic Welfare Conference, published by the Macmillan Company.

theory is contradicted and refuted by the persistence of a hundred errors side by side with truth for centuries. In the long run and with sufficient enlightenment, truth will be sufficiently mighty to prevail by its own force and momentum, but its victory can be greatly hastened by judicious assistance from the State and, indeed, from every other kind of organized social power. The successful opposition of the Church to the Protestant Reformation in those countries where the Church had the sympathy and assistance of the State, is but one of a vast number of historical illustrations. Against the theory that all forms of religion are equally sound, it is sufficient to cite the principle of contradiction; two contradictory propositions cannot be true, any more than yes can be identified with no. Finally, it is not impossible to know which religion is the right one, inasmuch as the Church of Christ comes before men with credentials sufficient to convince all those who will deliberately examine the evidence with a will to believe. The argument and the proofs are summarized by Pope Leo in the paragraphs immediately following the one now under consideration. Such is the objective logic of the situation. In a particular case the public authorities can reject and frequently have rejected the evidence for the divinity of the Catholic Church.

It is not of such rulers or such States that Pope Leo is speaking in this part of the encyclical. The principle that he is here defending has complete and unconditional application only to Catholic States. Between these and the Catholic Church the normal relation is that of formal agreement and mutual support; in other words, what is generally known as the union of Church and State. In his encyclical on "Catholicity in the United States," the same Pope gave generous praise to the attitude of our government and laws toward religion, but immediately added:

"Yet, though all this is true, it would be very erroneous to draw the conclusion that in America is to be sought the type of the most desirable status of the Church, or that it would be universally lawful or expedient for State and Church, to be, as in America, dissevered and divorced. The fact that Catholicity with you is in good condition, nay, is even enjoying a prosperous growth, is by all means to be attributed to the fecundity with which God has endowed His Church, in virtue of which unless men or circumstances interfere, she spontaneously expands and propagates herself; but she would bring forth more abundant fruits if, in addition to liberty, she enjoyed the favor of the laws and the patronage of public authority."

Occasionally some Catholics are found who reject this doctrine on the ground that alliances between Church and State have done more harm than good. Space is wanting here for an adequate discussion and refutation of this contention. Nor is a formal criticism necessary. Men who take this position are indulging in what the logicians call "the fallacy of the particular instance." Because they find some forms of union between Church and State working badly in some countries for certain periods of time, they rush to the conclusion that all forms are bad, at all times, in all countries. An adequate evaluation of the arrangement, a judicious weighing of the good effects against the bad effects, supposes a knowledge of history far more comprehensive than is possessed by any of these critics. Men who lack this knowledge ought to show a becoming modesty and hesitancy in making any general pronouncement on the complex effects of this policy.

One observation may be made which is calculated to prevent much misconception and false reasoning on this subject. It is that the *principle* of union between Church and State is not necessarily dependent upon *any particular form of union that has actually been in operation.* When men condemn the principle because they see that State support of the clergy, or State nomination of bishops, has in certain cases been harmful to the Church, they are laboring under a false assumption. Neither of these particular arrangements is required by the principle. Other critics identify the principle with the particular application of it that obtained in the Middle Ages. This assumption is likewise illogical and incorrect. The distinguished German theologian, Father Pohle, writes thus: "The intimate connection of both powers during the Middle Ages was only a passing and temporary phenomenon, arising neither from the essential nature of the State nor from that of the Church." In the same article, he points out three grave evil results of this intimate connection; namely, excessive meddling by ecclesiastical authorities in political affairs, conflicts between the two powers which produced diminished popular respect for both, and "the danger that the clergy, trusting blindly to the interference of the secular arm in their behalf, may easily sink into dull resignation and spiritual torpor, while the laity, owing to the religious surveillance of the State, may develop rather into a race of religious hypocrites and pietists than into inwardly convinced Christians."

All that is essentially comprised in the union of Church and State can be thus formulated: The State should officially recognize the Catholic religion as the religion of the commonwealth; accordingly it should invite the blessing and the ceremonial participation of the Church for certain important public functions, as the opening of legislative sessions, the erection of public buildings, etc., and delegate its officials to attend certain of the more important festival celebrations of the Church; it should recognize and sanction the laws of the Church; and it should protect the rights of the Church, and the religious as well as the other rights of the Church's members.

Does State recognition of the Catholic religion necessarily imply that no other religion should be tolerated? Much depends upon circumstances and much depends upon what is meant by toleration. Neither unbaptized persons nor those born into a non-Catholic sect, should ever be coerced into the Catholic Church. This would be fundamentally irrational, for belief depends upon the will and the will is not subject to physical compulsion. Should such persons be permitted to practice their own form of worship? If these are carried on within the family, or in such an inconspicuous manner as to be an occasion neither of scandal nor of perversion to the faithful, they may properly be tolerated by the State. At least, this is the approved Catholic doctrine concerning the religious rites of the non-baptized. Only those religious practices of unbelievers which are contrary to the natural law, such as idolatry, human sacrifice and debauchery, should be repressed. The best indication of the Church's attitude on this question is the toleration and protection accorded all through the Middle Ages to Judaism and Jewish worship by the Popes in their capacity of civil rulers of the Papal States. The same principle regarding freedom of worship seems fairly applicable to baptized persons who were born into a non-Catholic sect. For their participation in false worship does not necessarily imply a wilful affront to the true Church nor a menace to public order or social welfare. In a Catholic State which protects and favors the Catholic religion and whose citizens are in great majority adherents of the true faith, the religious performances of an insignificant and ostracized sect will constitute neither a scandal nor an occasion of perversion to Catholics. Hence there exists no sufficient reason to justify the State in restricting the liberty of individuals.

Quite distinct from the performance of false religious worship and preaching to the members of the erring sect, is the propagation of the false doctrine among Catholics. This could become a source of injury, a positive menace, to the religious welfare of true believers. Against such an evil they have a right of protection by the Catholic State. On the one hand, this propaganda is harmful to the citizens and contrary to public welfare; on the other hand, it is not among the natural rights of the propagandists. Rights are merely means to rational ends. Since no rational end is promoted by the dissemination of false doctrine, there exists no right to indulge in this practice. The fact that the individual may in good faith think that his false religion is true gives no more right to propagate it than the sincerity of the alien anarchist entitles him to advocate his abominable political theories in the United States, or than the perverted ethical notions of the dealer in obscene literature confer upon him a right to corrupt the morals of the community. No State could endure on the basis of the theory that the citizen must always be accorded the prerogative of doing whatever he thinks right. Now the actions of preaching and writing are at once capable of becoming quite as injurious to the community as any other actions and quite as subject to rational restraint.

Superficial champions of religious liberty will promptly and indignantly denounce the foregoing propositions as the essence of intolerance. They are intolerant, but not therefore unreasonable. Error has not the same rights as truth. Since the profession and practice of error are contrary to human welfare, how can error have rights? How can the voluntary toleration of error be justified? As we have already pointed out, the men who defend the principle of toleration for all varieties of religious opinion, assume either that all religions are equally true or that the true cannot be distinguished from the false. On no other ground is it logically possible to accept the theory of indiscriminate and universal toleration.

To the objection that the foregoing argument can be turned against Catholics by a non-Catholic State, there are two replies. First, if such a State should prohibit Catholic worship or preaching on the plea that it was wrong and injurious to the community, the assumption would be false; therefore, the two cases are not parallel. Second, a Protestant State could not logically take such an attitude (although many of them did so in former centuries) because no Protestant sect claims to be infallible. Besides, the Protestant principle of private judgment logically implies that Catholics may be right in their religious convictions, and that they have a right to hold and preach them without molestation.

Such in its ultimate rigor and complete implications is the Catholic position concerning the alliance that should exist between the Church and a Catholic State. While its doctrinal premises will be rejected by convinced non-Catholics, its logic cannot be denied by anyone who accepts the unity of religious truth. If there is only one true religion, and if its possession is the most important good in life for States as well as individuals, then the public profession, protection, and promotion of this religion and the legal prohibition of all direct assaults upon it, becomes one of the most obvious and fundamental duties of the State. For it is the business of the State to safeguard and promote human welfare in all departments of life. In the words of Pope Leo, "civil society, established for the common welfare, should not only safeguard the well-being of the community, but have also at heart the interests of its individual members, in such mode as not in any way to hinder, but in every manner to render as easy as may be, the possession of that highest and unchangeable good for which all should seek."

In practice, however, the foregoing propositions have full application only to the completely Catholic State. This means a political community that is either exclusively, or almost exclusively, made up of Catholics. In the opinion of Father Pohle, "there is good reason to doubt if there still exists a purely Catholic State in the world." The propositions of Pope Pius IX condemning the toleration of non-Catholic sects do not now, says Father Pohle, "apply even to Spain or the South American republics, to say nothing of countries possessing a greatly mixed population." He lays down the following general rule: "When several religions have firmly established themselves and taken root in the same territory, nothing else remains for the State than either to exercise tolerance towards them all, or, as conditions exist today, to make complete religious liberty for individuals and religious bodies a principle of government." Father Moulart makes substantially the same statement: "In a word, it is necessary to extend political toleration to dissenting sects which exist in virtue of a fact historically accomplished."

The reasons which justify this complete religious liberty fall under two heads: First, rational expediency, inasmuch as the attempt to proscribe or hamper the peaceful activities of established religious groups would be productive of more harm than good; second, the positive provisions of religious liberty found in the constitutions of most modern States. To quote Father Pohle once more: "If religious freedom has been accepted and sworn to as a fundamental law in a constitution, the obligation to show this tolerance is binding in conscience." The principle of tolerance, he continues, cannot be disregarded even by Catholic States "without violation of oaths and loyalty, and without violent internal convulsions."

But constitutions can be changed, and non-Catholic sects may decline to such a point that the political proscription of them may become feasible and expedient. What protection would they then have against a Catholic State? The latter could logically tolerate only such religious activities as were confined to the members of the dissenting group. It could not permit them to carry on general propaganda nor accord their organization certain privileges that had formerly been extended to all religious corporations, for example, exemption from taxation. While all this is very true in logic and in theory, the event of its practical realization in any State or country is so remote in time and in probability that no practical man will let it disturb his equanimity or affect his attitude toward those who differ from him in religious faith. It is true, indeed, that some zealots and bigots will continue to attack the Church because they fear that some five thousand years hence the United States may become overwhelmingly Catholic and may then restrict the freedom of non-Catholic denominations. Nevertheless, we cannot yield up the principles of eternal and unchangeable truth in order to avoid the enmity of such unreasonable persons. Moreover, it would be a futile policy; for they would not think us sincere.

Therefore, we shall continue to profess the true principles of the relations between Church and State, confident that the great majority of our fellow citizens will be sufficiently honorable to respect our devotion to truth, and sufficiently realistic to see that the danger of religious intolerance toward non-Catholics in the United States is so improbable and so far in the future that it should not occupy their time or attention.

John Courtney Murray, S.J.

2. CIVIL UNITY AND RELIGIOUS INTEGRITY

Father John Courtney Murray, S.J. was Professor of Theology at Woodstock College. He is best known for his re-expression of the Roman Catholic position on Church and State in terms which take account of the American political and social scene. Many of his articles were brought together in *We Hold These Truths* from which the following selection was taken.

The Distinction of Church and State

If the demands of social necessity account for the emergence in America of religious freedom as a fact, they hardly account for certain peculiarities of the first of our prejudices and for the depth of feeling that it evokes. Another powerful historical force must be considered, namely, the dominant impulse toward self-government, government by the people in the most earnest sense of the word. Above all else the early Americans wanted political freedom. And the force of this impulse necessarily acted as a corrosive upon the illegitimate "unions" of church and state which the post-Reformation era had brought forth. The establishments of the time were, by and large, either theocratic, wherein the state was absorbed in the church, or Erastian, wherein the church was absorbed in the state. In both cases the result was some limitation upon freedom, either in the form of civil disabilities imposed in the name of the established religion, or in the form of religious disabilities imposed in the name of the civil law of the covenanted community. The drive toward popular freedom would with a certain inevitability sweep away such establishments. Men might share the fear of Roger Williams, that the state would corrupt the church, or the fear of Thomas Jefferson, that the church would corrupt the state. In either case their

thought converged to the one important conclusion, that an end had to be put to the current confusions of the religious and political orders. The ancient distinction between church and state had to be newly reaffirmed in a manner adapted to the American scene. Calvinist theocracy, Anglican Erastianism, Gallican absolutism—all were vitiated by the same taint: they violated in one way or another this traditional distinction.

The dualism of mankind's two hierarchically ordered forms of social life had been Christianity's cardinal contribution to the Western political tradition, as everyone knows who has looked into the monumental work of the two Carlyles, *Medieval Political Thought in the West*. Perhaps equally with the very idea of law itself it had been the most fecund force for freedom in society. The distinction had always been difficult to maintain in practice, even when it was affirmed in theory. But when it was formally denied the result was an infringement of man's freedom of religious faith or of his freedom as a citizen—an infringement of either or both. Hence the generalized American impulse toward freedom inevitably led to a new and specially emphatic affirmation of the traditional distinction.

The distinction lay readily within the reach of the early American lawyers and statesmen; for it was part of the English legal heritage, part of the patrimony of the common law. One can see it appearing, for instance, in Madison's famous *Memorial and Remonstrance*, where it is interpreted in a manner conformable to the anti-ecclesiasticism which he had in common with Jefferson. But the interesting figure here is again Roger Williams. Reading him, the Catholic theorist is inclined to agree with those "juditious persons" whose verdict was reluctantly and belatedly recorded by Cotton Mather. They "judged him," said Mather, "to have the root of the matter in him."

In the present question the root of the matter is this distinction of the spiritual and temporal orders and their respective jurisdictions. One is tempted to think that he got hold of this root at least partly because of his early acquaintance with English law. He was for a time secretary to the great Sir Edward Coke and it is at least not unlikely that he continued his legal interests at Cambridge. In any event, this distinction was a key principle with Williams. He had his own special understanding of it, but at least he understood it. What is more, in 1636 he felt in his own flesh, so to speak, the effects of its violations in the Massachusetts colony. Of his banishment from Massachusetts in that year he later wrote: "Secondly, if he (John Cotton) means this civil act of banishing, why should he call a civil sentence from a civil state, within a few weeks execution in so sharp a time of New England's cold, why should he call this a banishment from the churches except he silently confess that the frame or constitution of their churches is implicitly national (which yet they profess against)? For otherwise, why was I not yet permitted to live in the world or commonweal except for this reason, that the commonweal and church is yet but one, and he that is banished from the one must necessarily be banished from the other also?" This was his constant accusation against the New England Way. He says on another oc-

casion: "First, it will appear that in spiritual things they make the garden and the wilderness (as I often have intimated), I say, the garden and the wilderness, the church and the world are all one." The same charge is lodged against "holy men, emperors and bishops" throughout history, that "they made the garden of the church and the field of the world to be all one. . . ."

However erroneously Williams may have understood the "garden," the church, as having no relation whatsoever to the "wilderness," at least he knew that church and civil society are not one but two. To make them "all one" is to violate the nature of the church and also the nature of civil society, as this latter had been understood in the liberal Christian political tradition.

As has been said, Roger Williams was not a Father of the Federal Constitution. He is adduced here only as a witness, in his own way, to the genuine Western tradition of politics. The point is that the distinction of church and state, one of the central assertions of this tradition, found its way into the Constitution. There it received a special embodiment, adapted to the peculiar genius of American government and to the concrete conditions of American society.

How this happened need not concern us here. Certainly it was in part because the artisans of the Constitution had a clear grasp of the distinction between state and society, which had been the historical product of the distinction between church and state, inasmuch as the latter distinction asserted the existence of a whole wide area of human concerns which were remote from the competence of government. Calhoun's "force of circumstances" also had a great deal of influence; here again it was a matter of the Fathers building better than they knew. Their major concern was sharply to circumscribe the powers of government. The area of state—that is, legal—concern was limited to the pursuit of certain enumerated secular purposes (to say that the purposes are secular is not to deny that many of them are also moral; so for instance the establishment of justice and peace, the promotion of the general welfare, etc). Thus made autonomous in its own sphere, government was denied all competence in the field of religion. In this field freedom was to be the rule and method; government was powerless to legislate respecting an establishment of religion and likewise powerless to prohibit the free exercise of religion. Its single office was to take legal or judicial steps necessary on given occasions to make effective the general guarantee of freedom.

The concrete applications of this, in itself quite simple, solution have presented great historical and legal difficulties. This has been inevitable, given the intimacy with which religion is woven into the whole social fabric, and given, too, the evolution of government from John Adams' "plain, simple, intelligible thing, quite comprehensible by common sense," to the enormously complicated and sprawling thing which now organizes a great part of our lives, handles almost all education, and much social welfare. In particular, we have not yet found an answer to the question whether government can make effective the primary intention of the First Amendment, the guarantee of freedom of religion, simply by attempting to make more and more "impregnable" what is called, in Rogers Williams' fateful metaphor, the "wall of separation" between church and state. However, what concerns us here is the root of the matter, the fact that the American Constitution embodies in a special way the traditional principle of the distinction between church and state.

For Catholics this fact is of great and providential importance for one major reason. It serves sharply to set off our constitutional system from the system against which the Church waged its long-drawn-out fight in the nineteenth century, namely, Jacobinism, or (in Carlton Hayes's term) sectarian Liberalism, or (in the more definitive term used today) totalitarian democracy.

It is now coming to be recognized that the Church opposed the "separation of church and state" of the sectarian Liberals because in theory and in fact it did not mean separation at all but perhaps the most drastic unification of church and state which history had known. The Jacobin "free state" was as regalist as the *ancien régime*, and even more so. Writing as a historian, de Tocqueville long ago made this plain. And the detailed descriptions which Leo XIII, writing as a theologian and political moralist, gave of the Church's "enemy" make the fact even more plain. Within this "free state" the so-called "free church" was subject to a political control more complete than the Tudor or Stuart or Bourbon monarchies dreamed of. The evidence stretches all the way from the Civil Constitution of the Clergy in 1790 to the Law of Separation in 1905.

In the system sponsored by the sectarian Liberals, as has been well said, "The state pretends to ignore the Church; in reality it never took more cognizance of her." In the law of 1905, the climactic development, the Church was arrogantly assigned a juridical statute articulated in forty-four articles, whereby almost every aspect of her organization and action was minutely regulated. Moreover, this was done on principle — the principle of the primacy of the political, the principle of "everything within the state, nothing above the state." This was the cardinal thesis of sectarian Liberalism, whose full historical development is now being witnessed in the totalitarian "people's democracies" behind the Iron Curtain. As the Syllabus and its explicatory documents — as well as the multitudinous writings of Leo XIII — make entirely clear, it was this thesis of the juridical omnipotence and omnicompetence of the state which was the central object of the Church's condemnation of the Jacobin development. It was because freedom of religion and separation of church and state were predicated on this thesis that the Church refused to accept them as a thesis.

This thesis was utterly rejected by the founders of the American Republic. The rejection was as warranted as it was providential, because this thesis is not only theologically heterodox, as denying the reality of the Church; it is also politically revolutionary, as denying the substance of the liberal tradition. The American thesis is that government is not juridically omnipotent. Its powers are limited, and one of the principles of limitation is the distinction between state and church, in their purposes, methods, and manner of organization. The Jacobin thesis was basically philosophical; it derived from a sectarian concept of the autonomy of reason. It was also theological, as implying a sectarian concept of religion and of the church. In contrast, the American thesis is simply political. It asserts the theory of a free people under a limited government, a theory that is recognizably part of the Christian political tradition, and altogether defensible in the manner of its realization under American circumstances.

It may indeed be said that the American constitutional system exaggerates the distinction between church and state by its self-denying ordinances. However, it must also be said that government rarely appears to better advantage than when passing self-denying ordinances. In any event, it is one thing to exaggerate a traditional distinction along the lines of its inherent tendency; it is quite another thing to abolish the distinction. In the latter case the result is a vicious monistic society; in the former, a faultily dualistic one. The vice in the Jacobin system could only be condemned by the Church, not in any way condoned. The fault in the American system can be recognized as such, without condemnation. There are times and circumstances, Chesterton jocosely said, when it is

necessary to exaggerate in order to tell the truth. There are also times and circumstances, one may more seriously say, when some exaggeration of the restrictions placed on government is necessary in order to insure freedom. These circumstances of social necessity were and are present in America.

The Freedom of the Church

Here then is the second leading reason why the American solution to the problem of religious pluralism commends itself to the Catholic conscience. In the discourse already cited Pius XII states, as the two cardinal purposes of a Concordat, first, "to assure to the Church a stable condition of right and of fact within society," and second, "to guarantee to her a full independence in the fulfillment of her divine mission." It may be maintained that both of these objectives are sufficiently achieved by the religious provisions of the First Amendment. It is obvious that the Church in America enjoys a stable condition in fact. That her status at law is not less stable ought to be hardly less obvious, if only one has clearly in mind the peculiarity of the American affirmation of the distinction between church and state. This affirmation is made through the imposition of limits on government, which is confined to its own proper ends, those of temporal society. In contrast to the Jacobin system in all its forms, the American Constitution does not presume to define the Church or in any way to supervise her exercise of authority in pursuit of her own distinct ends. The Church is entirely free to define herself and to exercise to the full her spiritual jurisdiction. It is legally recognized that there is an area which lies outside the competence of government. This area coincides with the area of the divine mission of the Church, and within this area the Church is fully independent, immune from interference by political authority.

The juridical result of the American limitation of governmental powers is the guarantee to the Church of a stable condition of freedom as a matter of law and right. It should be added that this guarantee is made not only to the individual Catholic but to the Church as an organized society with its own law and jurisdiction. The reason is that the American state is not erected on the principle of the unity and indivisibility of sovereignty which was the post-Renaissance European development. Nowhere in the American structure is there accumulated the plenitude of legal sovereignty possessed in England by the Queen in Parliament. In fact, the term "legal sovereignty" makes no sense in America, where sovereignty (if the alien term must be used) is purely political. The United States has a government, or better, a structure of governments operating on different levels. The American state has no sovereignty in the classic Continental sense. Within society, as distinct from the state, there is room for the independent exercise of an authority which is not that of the state. This principle has more than once been affirmed by American courts, most recently by the Supreme Court in the *Kedroff* case. The validity of this principle strengthens the stability of the Church's condition at law.

Perhaps the root of the matter, as hitherto described, might be seen summed up in an incident of early American and Church history. This is Leo Pfeffer's account of it in his book, *Church, State and Freedom:*

> In 1783 the papal nuncio at Paris addressed a note to Benjamin Franklin suggesting that, since it was no longer possible to maintain the previous status whereunder American Catholics were subject to the Vicar Apostolic at London, the Holy See proposed to Congress that a Catholic bishopric be established in one of the American cities, Franklin transmitted the note to the [Continental] Congress, which directed Franklin to notify the nuncio that "the subject of his application to Doctor Franklin being purely spiritual, it is without the jurisdiction and powers of Congress, who have no authority to permit or refuse it, these powers being reserved to the several states individually." (Not many years later the several states would likewise declare themselves to "have no authority to permit or refuse" such a purely spiritual exercise of ecclesiastical jurisdiction.)

The good nuncio must have been mightily surprised on receiving this communication. Not for centuries had the Holy See been free to erect a bishopric and appoint a bishop without the prior consent of government, without prior exercise of the governmental right of presentation, without all the legal formalities with which Catholic states had fettered the freedom of the Church. In the United States the freedom of the Church was completely unfettered; she could organize herself with the full independence which is her native right. This, it may be confidently said, was a turning point in the long and complicated history of church-state relations.

John Coleman Bennett

3. PATTERNS OF CHURCH-STATE RELATIONS— GROUNDS FOR SEPARATION

The Rev. John C. Bennett was President of Union Theological Seminary in New York City. He had been a close associate of Reinhold Niebuhr both as a colleague and in editing a lively journal *Christianity and Crisis*. Mr. Bennett has written widely on social, political, and religious problems from the point of view of Christian ethics.

There is no Protestant doctrine concerning Church-State relations. There is a Baptist doctrine that is very clear and that has always had great influence in this country. There is an American doctrine which has been developing since the beginning of the Republic and some aspects of it are still being clarified by the courts.

When the Federal Government was formed, it was possible to begin with a clean slate so far as its relation to Churches was concerned. Today the idea of separation of Church and state is so much taken for granted in this country that it is difficult to realize what an adventurous step it was. The Constitution itself prohibits all religious tests for federal office holders and this was an important start in separating the Church from the state though of itself this is not inconsistent with some forms of religious establishment. Religious tests were abandoned in Britain over a century ago. The very general words of the First Amendment to the Constitution laid down the lines along which our institutions were to develop: "Congress shall make no law respecting an establishment of religion, or prohibiting the free exercise thereof." This amendment did not apply to the states but only to the actions of Congress, and it was not until 1923 that in matters of religious liberty the guarantee of liberty by the Fourteenth Amendment ("Nor shall any State deprive any person of life, liberty, or property, without due process of law") was extended to actions by the states.

It should be noted that the word "separation" is not in the Constitution. It was Jefferson's word and it came to be the popular American word for this constitutional provision; later the Supreme Court was to use Jefferson's metaphor, "wall of separation," as a fitting description of the American Church-State pattern. I agree with those who believe that this is an unfortunate metaphor because there can be no such wall between institutions which have to so large an extent the same constituency and which share many of the same concerns for the same national community. I also believe that it would have been better if the popular word for the American system were "independence" rather than "separation." But, I am not quibbling over that and in what follows I shall speak of the separation of Church and state. . . . There are three reasons why I believe that this general pattern of "separation" is best for both Church and state and that changes in other countries which have established Churches should be (and, in fact, are) in this direction.

(1) The first reason for emphasizing the separation of Church and state is that it is the only way of assuring the complete freedom of the Church: Established

Churches in Europe are all attempting to gain the substance of freedom but this still remains a difficult struggle. Anglican leaders now declare that if the British Parliament ever again uses its acknowledged legal right to interfere with the doctrine or worship of the Church, the Church must insist on its freedom even at the cost of disestablishment.

In this country the freedom of the Church from state control is not a real problem. Freedom of the Church from control by the community or by movements of public opinion is a problem, but I am not discussing that here. The Church-State problems that call for solution in this country are basically in a different area, but they usually raise the question as to whether the Church should relate any of its efforts or its institutions to the state in such a way that the state might come to exercise control over them. But no one suspects any agency of the state in this country of trying to dictate to the Churches. I remember how great a furor there was when Mayor La Guardia of New York, who was in charge of civil defense during the Second World War, sent around to the clergy some very innocent suggestions concerning a sermon that might be preached. This was a blunder on his part, as he soon learned, but he obviously had no intention of trying to dictate to the clergy. The American Churches are extremely sensitive on matters of this sort. For example, it took a long time for enough of them to agree to have the Federal Social Security made *optional* for ministers on the basis of self-employment to enable this to become law, though it is difficult to see how this can threaten the freedom of the Church. If any Churches become lax on matters affecting their freedom they get a strong reminder from the Baptists who are in a special way watch-dogs concerning the freedom of the Church, and it is good to have them perform this function.

In this country the Churches live independently with a friendly state and the American form of separation is in the first instance as good a guarantee of the freedom of the Church as Churches have ever had in their long history.

(2) The second reason for believing in the separation of Church and State is the preservation of the state from control by the Church. This freedom from control by the Church takes two forms. One is freedom from ecclesiastical pressure on the state itself on matters of public policy. In a later chapter I shall discuss what forms of influence or even pressure by the Churches upon the state are not open to objection. Much of this influence or pressure is a part of the democratic process itself. When the constituencies of Churches express their views on public questions, this is a part of the process of the formation of public opinion. There is nothing about the role of the Church here that need be regarded as unfair pressure or ecclesiastical manipulation. . . .

There is another aspect of this freedom of the state from Church control which is related to the ecclesiastical pressure upon government but it is in itself so central in the concern of Americans that I shall lift it up for special emphasis: the freedom of all religious minorities, and of those who reject all forms of religious faith, from pressure from any Church or group of Churches of the kind that comes through the use of the power of the state.

Today when Church-State problems are discussed in this country the one concern that ranks above all others is the fear that one Church or a group of Churches may finally be able to use the state to bring about discrimination against citizens on grounds of religion or to limit the freedom of any religious bodies. The people who belong to no religious body are afraid that all religious bodies may combine against them. The Jewish community usually takes their part because it fears that if there is any such combining of religious bodies, the Christians will control the combination.

So, Jews take their position with the Baptists as watch-dogs in all matters that affect religious liberty. Both in practice often make common cause with the various forms of secularists. . . .

The religious liberty which we have in this country and which we should seek to preserve here and to encourage in every country is, of course, not only liberty within the walls of the church. Religious liberty should include in addition to this the liberty of public witness, of evangelism. It should be the liberty not only to convert, but also to be converted in the sense of changing one's religious affiliation. It should be the liberty of public teaching not only about religious matters in the narrow sense, but also about all social, economic and political questions concerning which there is a religious judgment. It should include the liberty of Churches and other religious institutions to do all that is necessary to preserve their freedom as organizations, to hold property, to choose their own leaders. It is significant that the First Amendment in the very sentence that speaks of religious liberty also mentions freedom of speech, of the press, of "the right of people peaceably to assemble, and to petition the government for redress of grievances." It is fitting that religious liberty should be related so closely to these other liberties for there can be no religious liberty unless there is religious freedom to speak, unless there is freedom for religious books and periodicals, unless there is freedom for congregations and many other religious groups to assemble, and unless there is freedom to petition on all matters that affect the rights of Churches or of the individual conscience. Whenever any state clamps down on these rights of citizens on political grounds, religious liberty even in the narrowest sense is in danger for there is always the possibility of claiming that religious teaching is politically subversive. And when governments clamp down on religious liberty, any group of citizens who express political ideas that are regarded as subversive may be accused of religious heresy. So interdependent are all these freedoms of the mind and spirit.

(3) The third reason for emphasizing the separation of Church and state is that it is best for the Church to be on its own. Here we can distinguish between two considerations.

The first is that in contrast to the experience of the national Church, it is important to have a Christian body that is distinguishable from the national community. Where the national Church does include almost the whole nation it is difficult to find any such body at all except the clergy. They in their training and function are set apart; they are the visible churchmen. I have referred to the fact that there is in some national Churches no synod representing clergy and laymen and the reason for this is that the national parliament is supposed to act in that capacity for most of its members are baptized churchmen. Once there was reality behind this arrangement, but now it is fictional and very bad for the Church. I should emphasize the fact that most national Churches are fully aware of the problems to which I refer and changes are rapidly taking place.

The second consideration which is involved in the proposition that it is best for the Church to be on its own is that a free Church must support itself. It cannot rely on funds from the state or on the remarkable system of church-taxes which are compulsory for all who acknowledge membership in the Church even though such membership is not compulsory. It is our experience in the United States that the activity of the laymen in their financial support of the Church has created an extraordinary momentum of lay interest in the Church. It is significant that the Churches that have to support themselves have the greatest resources available for missions and other benevolences. At the present time, the vitality of the American Churches

175

amaze all who observe it and this vitality is in considerable measure the result of the very active and often sacrificial interest of the laymen. The Church's use of laymen increases their sense of responsibility and their loyalty to the Church. I realize that there is much debate as to how much depth or how much understanding of the Gospel or how much distinctively Christian commitment there is in all of this lay activity. Certainly it is all very mixed. The popularity of the Church does tend to lead to the secularizing of the Church and it is ironical that Churches that are not national Churches in this country actually seem more organic to the community as a whole than do national Churches. But after all of the criticisms of this vitality in the American Churches, one can hardly deny that it provides a tremendous opportunity for the Churches to mediate the truth and the grace of the Gospel to people.

In this chapter I have set forth the main reasons for believing in the separation of Church and state. I have always kept in mind the fact that these reasons have a special application to the United States but, while they do not necessarily suggest that the American form of separation is good for all countries, they do suggest that older forms of the national Church should everywhere give way to new patterns which do justice to the freedom of the Church, to the religious liberty of all citizens and to the need of developing distinctively Christian communities characterized by lay initiative.

4. A PRESBYTERIAN REPORT ON CHURCH AND STATE

The General Assembly of the United Presbyterian Church in the U.S.A. several years ago created a special committee to study the issue of Church and State. The 175th General Assembly (1963) received and accepted a report from that committee which supported "the principle of organic separation of Church and State." The following "guidelines for study and action" were also adopted which define that organic separation.

The celebration of religious holidays, Bible reading and prayer in public schools

Public schools are creations of the whole society operating through civil authority and justify their existence solely in terms of their usefulness to the society. Their role is to nurture the cultural, social, and material advancement of all citizens by a special system of instruction through intellectual and social disciplines and to stimulate a free search for truth within this discipline.

In the fulfillment of this role, public schools should not ignore the personal beliefs in God which are a part of the life of its pupils, but should recognize and respect such beliefs. Public schools should neither be hostile to religious beliefs nor act in any manner which tends to favor one religion or church over another.

The use of public property for religious displays and pageants

"Report of the Special Committee on Church and State" submitted to the 175th General Assembly of the United Presbyterian Church in the U.S.A. It may be located in the Minutes, Sixth Series, Volume VI (1963), Part I, Journal, pp. 185 ff. It is also available as a pamphlet, "Relations between Church and State" from the Office of the General Assembly, Witherspoon Building, Philadelphia, Pennsylvania.

The occasions under which public property is used for religious displays and pageants typically come during the Christian holiday seasons, as for example, in the setting up of creches on court house or school lawns. Such presentations, which are rightly resented by many persons in a religiously pluralistic community, need to be sharply distinguished from those in which a religious group or groups, through the use of procedures prescribed by law, arrange with public authorities for the holding of services of worship commemorative parades, or pageants, as for example, an Easter Sunrise Service.

The evaluation of fitness of candidates for public office on the basis of religious affiliation

The position taken by the 172nd General Assembly on this question now needs to be expanded. A candidate's religious conviction is relevant to the question of his competence to govern. But since religious affiliation may not accurately reflect a candidate's conviction, questions in this area must be sharply focused, lest religious bigotry blur the issue.

The specific form in which this question most often arises for Protestants today concerns members of the Roman Catholic communion running for public office at every level of political life. One of the factors in the current situation is the emergence of what seems to be an indigenously American type of Roman Catholic thought. This change would adapt the traditional view of Roman Catholicism on matters of church and state to the American scene. The United Presbyterian Church welcomes this development and the possibility of new conversations with Roman Catholics which it seems to imply. At the same time, it is sensitive to the fact that this development is both recent and, as yet, by no means representative of the authorities of the Roman Catholic Church in this country.

The dispensing of birth control information in tax-supported health and welfare agencies and other problems relating to medicine and public health

Insofar as the modern development of public heath is concerned, United Presbyterians are particularly sensitive to problems generated by the current conflict between Protestants, Roman Catholics, and others over the issue of birth control. With regard to this specific issue, Presbyterians see the Roman Catholic attitude toward birth control as rooted in a Biblically untenable view of sexuality. Another problem raised is the question of the relationship between public health activities and generally acceptable medical practices. The United Presbyterian Church favors carefully defined government action in this area; at the same time it is unalterably opposed to the utilization of public health structures for the furtherance of views peculiar to a particular religious community.

The passage, strengthening, or challenging of Sunday closing laws

Since the 172nd General Assembly remitted its mandate on church and state, the United States Supreme Court has ruled that Sunday closing laws of three states primarily protect social and humanitarian, rather than ecclesiastical, pursuits and therefore do not violate the Federal Constitution. Most states presently have some kind of Sunday laws on their statute books. Some of these laws exempt persons who celebrate the Sabbath on a day other than Sunday. The Supreme Court, by its decisions, has declared existing laws to be constitutional.

Without expressing either favor or disfavor toward the Court's ruling, this Committee affirms its conviction that the church itself bears sole and vital responsibility for securing from its members a voluntary observance of the Lord's Day. The

177

church should not seek, or even appear to seek, the coercive power of the state in order to facilitate Christians' observance of the Lord's Day.

The church is also concerned about persons who suffer economic injustice because of the inner constraint of religious conscience and the external coercion of the law. The church is aware that many who press for the seven-day commercial week care little for the integrity of the family, a day of rest for the working man, or the celebration of the Sabbath or the Lord's Day, and appear to be motivated primarily by economic self-interest. The church does not wish to strengthen the hand of those whose hostility to Sunday closing laws arises from motivations inconsistent with the general welfare. However, any efforts by the church to strengthen existing Sunday closing laws would almost certainly be widely construed as the church's seeking its own interest.

The provision of public funds, directly or indirectly, to parochial schools

All citizens, of whatever religious conviction or none, share responsibility for the general education of all children in our society. As of now the public school, supported by taxes of all citizens, is the main agency for this purpose and is indispensable. Private and parochial schools, however valuable to their patrons and society, cannot adequately fulfill this total social obligation in the absence of a strong public school system.

While we affirm the right of parents, citizens, and churches to establish and maintain non-public schools whose ethos and curriculum differ from that of the community as a whole, our main concern must at this time be directed to the support of the public system of elementary and secondary schools since these schools must be freely and everywhere available to all children to the extent that society decides education is compulsory.

United Presbyterians, historically committed to the general support of public education because of their Lord's concern for the poor, handicapped, and outcast, should also recognize that private and parochial schools now educate a significant number of our nations' children. We, therefore, share with those who maintain these non-public school systems a stake in the quality of the education they provide to their children, who one day will take up their responsibilities as adult citizens in our society. Some of these non-public school systems, and notably the Roman Catholic, are subject to critical financial problems not dissimilar to those that face our nation's public schools.

Historically, United Presbyterians have been, and still are, in principle opposed to the use of public funds to aid these non-public schools, since this constitutes a violation of the separation principle and might well lead to a further fragmentation of general education which could eventually destroy our society. We believe that many Roman Catholics, without giving up their commitment to their parochial schools, also share this apprehension. Certainly Roman Catholics have in some cases worked side by side with Protestants, Jews, and others to strengthen public education. It, therefore, ill-behooves United Presbyterians to stand by without concern for what happens to the parochial school system of their Roman Catholic brethren.

Censorship, either by public or private agencies, of material offensive to one or more religious groups

We believe that the vitality and integrity of any religious group is not, in the long run, served by the suppression of privately promulgated material that is offensive to it or critical of it. The authenticity of a particular theological tradition, moral code, or way of life is confirmed by the vigor with which its people live out their commitment, and further by its ability to tolerate verbal and pictorial expressions from persons or groups hostile to it.

Hence efforts to stamp out such expressions by the offended group itself do not appear to us to be symptoms of health or grace. Further, we are convinced that no human being or agency has the wisdom to decide on religious grounds what the general public may see and hear. When the only sources of art, literature, history, public information, etc., are those that must satisfy the religious and moral requirements of a specific religious group or coalition of such groups, both religious and non-religious persons have cause for alarm. Efforts to enlist the power of the state or any of its agencies to censor religiously offensive material are clearly dangerous not only to the cause of true religion, but to the survival of a free society. It ought to be as obvious now as in any other period of history that the same governmental authority which today can prescribe what is religiously prohibited by law may tomorrow prescribe what is religiously required by law.

The interpretation of marriage, divorce, and adoption laws

The laws of the state concerning marriage, divorce, and adoption, since the primitive church became a force in the Roman Empire, have become increasingly involved with religious concepts. During medieval times the state, coincidentally with a decline in its power, all but surrendered its legislative and judicial rule in family law to the church. Ecclesiastical courts had almost complete authority. With the rise of Protestantism and the resurgent growth of the state power, governments and courts took control of family law from the church. But, in so doing, they acquired most of the religious concepts on which the laws were based. This cast the state in a fundamentally impossible position, particularly in the area of divorce law. The state became concerned with religious concepts of sin and guilt which are the proper functions of the church. This created a basic infringement by the state on a province of the church. The effect caused the state to convert sin into something resembling a civil crime.

The state's primary concern with family law should be to create and maintain an orderly and stable family unit which is basic to the welfare of the society. Thus, the state's proper area of involvement is the social and material welfare of the family; the keeping of records and statistics; and concern that family units do not produce wards of the society, adult or children. In the light of these primary concerns, and from the church's viewpoint, the current state of family law is disgraceful. In addition tragic confusion arises from the disparity of the laws of the several states.

The church, as well as the state, should be vitally concerned with the well-being of the family. Within the fellowship of the church the family teaches faith and life. The proper constitution and preservation of the family and, where necessary, the basis of its dissolution, is of vital concern to the church. In the light of the separation principle, Christians should be deeply concerned about laws which use the power of the state to enforce religious concepts which are not the state's proper concern.

Tax exemption for religious agencies

The church has no theological ground for laying any claim upon the state for special favors. The church must regard special status or favored position as a hindrance to the fulfilling of its mission. As a matter of contemporary fact, various levels of government give the church and many of its agencies a wide variety of tax exemptions. The church would find it difficult to obtain the abrogation of these laws and administrative practices. In the face of this situation, two points need to be made abundantly clear by the church, the first directed to itself and its membership and the second to the state and its representatives.

First, to itself as the agent of the ministry of Jesus Christ to the world, the church should know that it renders its witness ambiguous by its continued acceptance of special privileges from the state in the form of tax exemptions. Second, the state should know that it may not expect from the church in return for favors extended of its own free will, any *quid pro quo* in the form of a muting of the church's prophetic voice, nor should the state expect the church to accept the role of an uncritical instrument of support for the state's programs, or of any other conscious dilution of its supreme loyalty to Jesus Christ.

Special privileges for the clergy

It must be recognized that many special privileges are given to the clergy, but most of these fall within the realm of the traditional attitudes of the public concerning the clergy and do not directly concern the relationship between the church and state and thus are outside the mandate. The principal example of a special privilege granted by the state to the clergy consists of certain favorable tax treatment. Special tax exemptions for ministers are not different in principle from special tax exemptions for religious institutions.

The exemption of candidates for the ministry from military service, the relations of clergymen to the military service, and the problem of concientious objection

The right of the state to call citizens to, or defer them from, military duty for the good and freedom of the whole society is not here questioned. No class of citizens, as such, has an inherent right to claim exemption from this duty. The fact that a man serves God, or aspires to serve him, in a church vocation does not in itself excuse him from the responsibility shared by all citizens for the defense and security of the state. Ministers and candidates for the ministry, as citizens, have no grounds for claiming any special status from the state that differs from that of scientists, physicians, policemen, farmers, machinists, etc. The state may or may not choose to defer from military duty such groups of citizens on its judgment as to whether such deferment supports services essential to the welfare of the nation.

* * *

Perhaps the greatest single cause of confusion in debate of church-state problems arises from emotion-charged irrelevancies, particularly the challenging of a citizen's patriotism. Therefore, Presbyterians are urged to be alert to prevent diversion of attention from the concrete problem at hand, and to be insistent that the discussion be relevant to it.

If Presbyterians disagree with Roman Catholics or other identifiable groups on church-state problems, they ought not question the **personal** integrity of the spokesmen whose views they must dispute. Seldom does settlement come through discrediting of a personality; in any case, the issue itself must be adequately debated. This Committee urges that emotional and irrational arguments be renounced in favor of incisive and informed discussion of issues. In debate with fellow Christians it is imperative that a true sense of fellowship in Christ be encouraged.

Most particularly to be deprecated is the conversion of public discussion into a test of loyalty to democratic values. There can be no doubt that the kind of nation we shall be is at stake in the discussion of church-state relations since it touches upon a first principle of our Constitution. But it does not follow that those with whom we disagree are fascist or communist in their fundamental political commitments. The wisest assumption for us to make is that participants in debate will behave consistently with their true beliefs and that they will argue openly their actual commitments. The welfare of our Church and nation is not served by the introduction of extraneous charges.

Worst of all, from a church's point of view, is the confusing of the Christian's loyalty to Christ with other loyalties. Jesus Christ alone is Lord; the claims of family, state, and voluntary organizations are real to the Christian only in a pattern of life and thought established by the supremacy of Jesus Christ. Loyalty to Christ may on occasion put the Christian in clear opposition to certain demands of the state. If we allow the equivalence "a good American is a good Christian" to seize the public mind, we will soon find that the supremacy that belongs only to Christ will be usurped by the ebb and flow of opinion as to what is "American."

Richard L. Rubenstein

5. CHURCH AND STATE: THE JEWISH POSTURE

Richard L. Rubenstein was Director of the B'nai B'rith Hillel Foundations and Chaplain to Jewish Students at the University of Pittsburgh, Carnegie Institute of Technology, Chatham College, and Duquesne University. His discussion of this subject nicely represents the peculiar situation of the Jewish community in American society.

In modern times, Jewish equality of status within the political order has been possible only when and where official Christianity has ceased to be privileged. Where the special pre-eminence of the Christian church remained a relevant political fact, Jews have never been able to attain genuine equality of condition within that community. Jews have also fared best in multi-national and multi-ethnic political communities such as the old Austro-Hungarian Empire or contemporary America.

The fact that Jewish emancipation was largely the result of the temporary triumph of secular humanism in France does not necessarily mean that Jews have uniformly favored the underlying secular humanist ideology which produced the disestablishment of the church. Because Jews were among those who gained most visibly from the destruction of the old order, those who continued to oppose the French Revolution and its entailments tended to identify the Revolution in some sense with Jewish ends and purposes. This was strategically useful, in any event, because of the utility of the unpopular Jews as opponents. A similar identification of ends and ideology took place after the Russian Revolution. In neither upheaval was there a real coincidence of aim or interest between the Jewish com-

From *Religion and the Public Order*, ed. Donald A. Giannella (Chicago, 1964), pp. 150–169. Reprinted by permission of University of Chicago Press.

munity and its emancipators. Religious Jews of whatever bent could not and do not favor many of the tenets of the secular humanist ideology which led to Jewish emancipation. Those Jews who participated most wholeheartedly in the revolutionary movements were precisely those least concerned with the preservation of their identity as Jews.

The problem of theological anthropology, the religious doctrine of man [is] relevant to the problem of the separation of church and state. It is no accident that the American doctrine of separation was the product of a culture deeply Protestant in its ethos and influenced by Lockean deism and rationalism. Although it is difficult to make generalized statements about any of the major religious communities, it would seem that Protestantism has felt more decisively the tension and opposition between God and the world, the spirit and the flesh, and the religious and political orders than have either Judaism or Catholicism. Ernest Troeltsch's distinction between the church-type and the sect-type religious communities is very much to the point. Both Judaism and Catholicism are essentially church-type structures in that religious status is obligatory and hence proves nothing with regard to the member's virtue. The sect, defined by Max Weber as "a voluntary association of only those who are . . . religiously and morally qualified" is a more typically Protestant structure. Sects are founded by people who feel strongly the opposition between the political and the religious orders. They have despaired of the world and seek to maintain the community of the elect, undisturbed by the world's corruption. For members of sectarian religious communities, separation of the religious and political orders is absolutely necessary because of the incurable corruption of the political and social order.

Non-Christians who cannot accept the doctrine of the Incarnation are nevertheless frequently at one with its fundamental insight that there is an existential and an axiological continuum between the spirit and the flesh, between God and man. Those who affirm this continuum cannot really accept the separation of the religious and the political orders as their theological ideal. Nevertheless, it would be consistent with this position to suggest that the union of the two orders will only truly be achieved at the End of Time, the Time of the Messiah for Jews and the Parousia for Christians. In our imperfect and alienated world, the preponderant weight of social necessity favors separation.

I have attempted to stress a number of elements that arose out of religious and cultural perspectives most religious Jews do not and cannot entirely accept, but which were present in the culture which created Jewish emancipation in Europe and the First Amendment in America. In modern times there have been many attempts to identify Judaism largely or entirely with the culture of its neighbors. The identity of Judaism and "the German spirit" has understandably not stood the test of time. It has been supplanted by an assertion of the identity of Judaism and the roots of American democracy. There is undoubtedly far more reason to assert the latter identity than the former. Nevertheless, as we have seen, there are important areas in which the Enlightenment and sect-type Protestantism part company with fundamental Jewish convictions. There is nothing inherently sacred about the current American way of handling church-state problems. Under other circumstances other modes of dealing with the problem would be equally appropriate and suitable to Jewish needs.

There are, however, urgent *practical* reasons why there is near unanimity of opinion among Jews favoring the strongest possible guarantees of the separation of the religious and the political orders. As I have already suggested, the basic strategy of the Jewish community in modern times has been, wherever possible, withdrawal from Christian influence. Only in a society neutral to the practice of religion could Jews hope to attain that normalcy of life-situation which has eluded them for almost two thousand years. The ways in which Christian influence, perhaps unconsciously, excludes Jews from full participation in the national culture of even relatively secularized, contemporary France has been depicted by the French-Jewish-Tunisian novelist Albert Memmi in his *Portrait of a Jew*. As Memmi points out, Jews are alienated from the national culture at precisely those moments when the rest of the population is most strongly united in a shared community of aspiration and remembrance. Even the relatively formal and symbolic act of including prayers by rabbis as well as priests and ministers on public occasions is token of a legal equality in America which is unthinkable in Europe to this day.

Jews basically want nothing more than the opportunity to participate in American life under conditions of maximum equality with their fellow citizens. This is the simple practical basis for Jewish sentiment favoring separation of church and state in the United States. The Jewish community has had the experience of living as a minority for a very long time. Out of this experience, it has come to understand the incompatibility of any position other than absolute political neutrality in religious matters with the demands of equality. As has been indicated, nothing within Jewish tradition favors the separation of the religious and political orders. Nevertheless, everything within Jewish experience does. Were there none but Jews in America and were there a unanimity of Jewish assent on religious matters, there would probably be no such separation. Theologically speaking, one might describe the current situation as a concomitant of the confusion of tongues. I believe most responsible Jewish leaders would agree with Martin Marty's comment that "pluralism is a ground rule and not an altar." It is called for, not by our ideologies, but by the facticity of our concrete, limited situations. As long as America remains a multi-ethnic and multi-religious community, there can be no equitable alternative to political neutrality in religious affairs.

Even in an America agreed upon religious affirmation and affiliation, there would always be the question of the right of the atheist or the agnostic not to be forced to suffer the intrusion of an unwelcome religiosity in the public domain toward which he contributes his fair share. Although most Jewish leaders part company with secular humanist ideology, they most emphatically do *not* agree with those who assert that the American posture of religious neutrality excludes the irreligious. This position seems to occur more frequently among Catholic commentators on church-state affairs than among either their Protestant or their Jewish counterparts. If Jewish participants in the dialogue can not accept the Lockean conception of religion as a purely voluntary association, they do assert the practical necessity of acting *as if* the Lockean conception were true. Jewish law includes Jewish atheists in the Jewish religious community. Nevertheless, Jewish leaders would hardly insist, even had they the power so to do, upon a religious commitment from those who find such a commitment meaningless.

What I am suggesting is that Jewish concern for the individual goes beyond securing for him the opportunity to follow his own beliefs. It insists, particularly in a pluralistic society, that as far as possible his right to participate fully in the life of the community be recognized. Neutrality of the state toward religion is the only way to avoid excluding from full participation in community life the many secular humanists who share with the most devoted followers of any Western religion respect for human dignity and the worth of the individual. Recognition of this helps explain the position taken by Jews on many church-state issues.

America represents a new experiment for Jews. It offers the promise of an equality of condition which Jews have never known, even in the most advanced European nations. Like every human ideal, this promise cannot be extricated from the human context in which it is offered. The ideals implicit in law can never entirely be fulfilled. At best, they can be reasonably approximated. Jews do not really expect that the separation of the religious and political orders will ever be completely achieved. This would be possible only if the human beings who constitute the raw material of both orders were capable of an almost schizophrenic act of self-division. The absolute application of logic to human affairs leads not to justice but to murder, as the terror of the French Revolution and the rational terror of communism and nazism demonstrate. Nevertheless, historical Jewish experience has taught us that the ideal of a government neutral in religious matters offers the only hope for equality of condition for all men in a multi-ethnic and multi-religious community. Historical experience has also taught us that nothing is gained by the failure of the Jew to seek his rights under law when and where it is possible so to do. Finally, Jews are absolutely convinced that the decisions of our courts must be obeyed and respected. No insight is as deeply or as persistently present in Judaism as the conviction that society is radically imperiled when men assert a priority of personal inclination over the majesty of the law, for in Judaism God Himself is the Bestower and Teacher of the Law.

CHURCH AND STATE AS A POLITICAL ISSUE

6. CATHOLIC AND PATRIOT: GOVERNOR SMITH REPLIES

Al Smith was Democratic nominee for President in 1928. Having come up from lower Manhattan through Tammany Hall he became a distinguished and long term Governor of New York State. Although his religion was certainly a factor, it seems that his overwhelming defeat at the hands of Herbert Hoover probably reflected other issues more directly, among them his stand against prohibition, his very progressive record at Albany, etc. In April 1927 *The Atlantic Monthly* published "An Open Letter to The Honourable Alfred E. Smith" by Charles C. Marshall. Smith replied in the May issue with the help of Father Francis P. Duffy. This might be compared to John F. Kennedy's Houston Speech.

Charles C. Marshall, Esq.
Dear Sir:

In your open letter to me in the April *Atlantic Monthly* you "impute" to American Catholics views which, if held by them, would leave open to question the loyalty and devotion to this country and its Constitution of more than twenty million American Catholic citizens. I am grateful to you for defining this issue in the open and for your courteous expression of the satisfaction it will bring to my fellow citizens for me to give "a disclaimer of the convictions" thus imputed. Without mental res-

From Alfred E. Smith, "Governor Smith Replies," in *The Atlantic Monthly*, Vol. CXXXIX (May 1927), pp. 721–728. Reprinted by permission of *The Atlantic Monthly*.

ervation I can and do make that disclaimer. These convictions are held neither by me nor by any other American Catholic, as far as I know. . . .

Taking your letter as a whole and reducing it to commonplace English, you imply that there is conflict between religious loyalty to the Catholic faith and patriotic loyalty to the United States. Everything that has actually happened to me during my long public career leads me to know that no such thing as that is true. I have taken an oath of office in this State nineteen times. Each time I swore to defend and maintain the Constitution of the United States. All of this represents a period of public service in elective office almost continuous since 1903. I have never known any conflict between my official duties and my religious belief. No such conflict could exist. Certainly the people of this State recognize no such conflict. They have testified to my devotion to public duty by electing me to the highest office within their gift four times. You yourself do me the honor, in addressing me, to refer to "your fidelity to the morality you have advocated in public and private life and to the religion you have revered; your great record of public trusts successfully and honestly discharged." During the years I have discharged these trusts I have been a communicant of the Roman Catholic Church. If there were conflict, I, of all men, could not have escaped it, because I have not been a silent man, but a battler for social and political reform. These battles would in their very nature disclose this conflict if there were any.

But, wishing to meet you on your own ground, I address myself to your definite questions, against which I have thus far made only general statements. I must first call attention to the fact that you often divorce sentences from their context in such a way as to give them something other than their real meaning. I will specify. . . . You quote from the *Catholic Encyclopedia* that my Church "regards dogmatic intolerance,

not alone as her incontestable right, but as her sacred duty." And you say that these words show that Catholics are taught to be politically, socially, and intellectually intolerant of all other people. If you had read the whole of that article in the *Catholic Encyclopedia,* you would know that the real meaning of these words is that for Catholics alone the Church recognizes no deviation from complete acceptance of its dogma. These words are used in a chapter dealing with that subject only. The very same article in another chapter dealing with toleration toward non-Catholics contains these words: "The intolerant man is avoided as much as possible by every high-minded person. . . . The man who is tolerant in every emergency is alone lovable." The phrase "dogmatic intolerance" does not mean that Catholics are to be dogmatically intolerant of other people, but merely that inside the Catholic Church they are to be intolerant of any variance from the dogma of the Church.

Similar criticism can be made of many of your quotations. But, beyond this, by what right do you ask me to assume responsibility for every statement that may be made in any encyclical letter? As you will find in the *Catholic Encyclopedia* (Vol. V p. 414), these encyclicals are not articles of our faith. The Syllabus of Pope Pius IX, which you quote on the possible conflict between Church and State, is declared by Cardinal Newman to have "no dogmatic force." You seem to think that Catholics must be all alike in mind and in heart, as though they had been poured into and taken out of the same mould. You have no more right to ask me to defend as part of my faith every statement coming from a prelate than I should have to ask you to accept as an article of your religious faith every statement of an Episcopal bishop, or of your political faith every statement of a President of the United States. So little are these matters of the essence of my faith that I, a devout Catholic since childhood, never heard of them until I read your letter. Nor can you quote from the canons of our faith a syllable that would make us less good citizens than non-Catholics. . . .

Under our system of government the electorate entrusts to its officers of every faith the solemn duty of action according to the dictates of conscience. I may fairly refer once more to my own record to support these truths. No man, cleric or lay, has ever directly or indirectly attempted to exercise Church influence on my administration of any office I have ever held, nor asked me to show special favor to Catholics or exercise discrimination against non-Catholics.

It is a well-known fact that I have made all of my appointments to public office on the basis of merit and have never asked any man about his religious belief. In the first month of this year there gathered in the Capitol at Albany the first Governor's cabinet that ever sat in this State. It was composed, under my appointment, of two Catholics, thirteen Protestants, and one Jew. The man closest to me in the administration of the government of the State of New York is he who bears the title of Assistant to the Governor. He had been connected with the Governor's office for thirty years, in subordinate capacities, until I promoted him to the position which makes him the sharer with me of my every thought and hope and ambition in the administration of the State. He is a Protestant, a Republican, and a thirty-second-degree Mason. In my public life I have exemplified that complete separation of Church from State which is the faith of American Catholics to-day.

I summarize my creed as an American Catholic. I believe in the worship of God according to the faith and practice of the Roman Catholic Church. I recognize no power in the institutions of my Church to interfere with the operations of the Constitution of the United States or the enforcement of the law of the land. I believe in absolute freedom of conscience for all men and in equality of all churches, all sects, and all beliefs before the law as a matter of right and not as a matter of favor. I believe in the absolute separation of Church and State and in the strict enforcement of the provisions of the Constitution that Congress shall make no law respecting an establishment of religion or prohibiting the free exercise thereof. I believe that no tribunal of any church has any power to make any decree of any force in the law of the land, other than to establish the status of its own communicants within its own church. I believe in the support of the public school as one of the corner stones of American liberty. I believe in the right of every parent to choose whether his child shall be educated in the public school or in a religious school supported by those of his own faith. I believe in the principle of non-interference by this country in the internal affairs of other nations and that we should stand steadfastly against any such interference by whomsoever it may be urged. And I believe in the common brotherhood of man under the common fatherhood of God.

In this spirit I join with fellow Americans of all creeds in a fervent prayer that never again in this land will any public servant be challenged because of the faith in which he has tried to walk humbly with his God.

Very truly yours,
Alfred E. Smith

Paul Blanshard

7. THE CATHOLIC PLAN FOR AMERICA

> With his *American Freedom and Catholic Power* Paul Blanshard struck a respon-
> sive chord in many Americans after World War II who—consciously or not—
> had reservations about the political implications of growing Roman Catholic
> influence in American life. Mr. Blanshard has been an important figure in
> Protestants and Other Americans United—a lobbying group which has
> staunchly supported a rigorous separation of Church and State. A counter
> statement to Mr. Blanshard's may be found in *Catholicism and American Freedom*
> by James M. O'Neill (New York, 1952).

Back in the days of the most virulent anti-Catholic bigotry, when "The Menace" was a national institution and candidates for public office openly reviled the Pope, one dramatic question was frequently asked at anti-Catholic mass meetings: "What will become of American democracy if the United States is captured by the Papists?" That last word was usually hissed or whispered in a way to make shivers run up and down the spine.

The question was more reasonable than its source. In fact, the bigoted character of the source has tended to divert attention from a valid and important question. Many American liberals have been deterred from an honest analysis of the implications of Catholic rule by fear of being associated with anti-Catholic fanatics. They have allowed the Catholic hierarchy, unchallenged, to use American freedom as a cloak for the systematic cultivation of separatism and intolerance among the American Catholic people.

Recent developments in Europe and Latin America suggest that the future role of the Roman Catholic Church in American politics should be re-examined with some care. What would happen to American democracy if our alleged twenty-six million Catholics grew to be a majority in the population and followed the direction of their priests? Suppose that, on some magic carpet of time, we could pass over the next two centuries and find ourselves in a predominantly Catholic America. What would American democracy look like?

The democratic *form* of our leading institutions might not be altered very much. Probably the most striking effect of Catholic control would be apparent in the *spirit* of those institutions and the *use* to which they would be put. The Catholic hierarchy is perfectly willing to compromise with democratic forms of government so long as its own special areas of power are respected. In a Catholic America the principal institutions of American democracy might be permitted to continue if they were operated for Catholic objectives.

The most striking and immediate result of Catholic ascendancy in our democracy would be the transfer of control of education, religion and family relationships to the Catholic hierarchy. After Catholics had attained a majority in three-fourths of our states, this transfer could be accomplished by three comprehensive amendments to the United States Constitution. Let us draft them in outline.

The first Catholic amendment to the Constitution might be called, for educa-

From Paul Blanshard, *American Freedom and Catholic Power* (Boston, 1949), pp. 266–269. Reprinted by permission of the Beacon Press, Copyright © 1949, 1958 by Paul Blanshard.

tional purposes, the "Christian Commonwealth Amendment." In all likelihood, it would include all of the following statements:

1. The United States is a Catholic Republic, and the Catholic Apostolic and Roman religion is the sole religion of the nation.

2. The authority of the Roman Catholic Church is the most exalted of all authorities; nor can it be looked upon as inferior to the power of the United States government, or in any manner dependent upon it, since the Catholic Church as such is a sovereign power.

3. Priests and members of religious orders of the Roman Catholic Church who violate the law are to be tried by an ecclesiastical court of the Roman Catholic Church, and may, only with the consent of the competent Catholic authority, be tried by the courts of the United States or the states.

4. Apostate priests or those incurring the censure of the Roman Catholic Church cannot be employed in any teaching post or any office or employment in which they have immediate contact with the public.

5. Non-Catholic faiths are tolerated, but public ceremonies and manifestations other than those of the Roman Catholic religion will not be permitted.

6. The First Amendment to the Constitution of the United States is hereby repealed.

The second Catholic amendment to the Constitution of the United States might well be described for propaganda purposes as the "Christian Education Amendment." It could be expected with confidence to be phrased in forms like these:

1. American religious education belongs pre-eminently to the Roman Catholic Church, by reason of a double title in the supernatural order, conferred exclusively upon her by God Himself.

2. The Roman Catholic Church has the inalienable right to supervise the entire education of her children in all educational institutions in the United States, public or private, not merely in regard to the religious instruction given in such institutions, but in regard to every other branch of learning and every regulation in so far as religion and morality is concerned.

3. Compulsory education in public schools exclusively shall be unlawful in any state in the Union.

4. It shall be unlawful for any neutral or non-Catholic school to enroll any Catholic child without permission of the Church.

5. Since neutral schools are contrary to the fundamental principles of education, public schools in the United States are lawful only when both religious instruction and every other subject taught are permeated with Catholic piety.

6. The governments of the United States and of the states are permitted to operate their own schools for military and civic training without supervision by the Roman Catholic Church, provided they do not injure the rights of the said Church, and provided that only the Roman Catholic Church shall have power to impart any religious instructions in such schools.

7. With due regard to special circumstances, co-education shall be unlawful in any educational institution in the United States whose students have attained the age of adolescence.

8. The governments of the United States and the states shall encourage and assist the Roman Catholic Church by appropriate measures in the exercise of the Church's supreme mission as educator.

The third Catholic amendment to the Constitution of the United States might be called the "Christian Family Amendment," although, in the campaign for its adoption, the sanctity of womanhood and the defeat of communism would, doubtless, play a major part. The amendment probably would read:

1. The government of the United States, desirous of restoring to the institution of

matrimony, which is the basis of the family, that dignity conformable to the traditions of its people, assigns as civil effects of the sacrament of matrimony all that is attributed to it in the Canon Law of the Roman Catholic Church.

2. No matrimonial contract in the United States that involves a Catholic can be valid unless it is in accordance with the Canon Law of the Roman Catholic Church.

3. Marriages of non-Catholics are subject to the civil authority of the state, but all civil laws that contradict the Canon Law of the Roman Catholic Church on marriage are hereby declared null and void.

4. All marriages are indissoluble, and the divorce of all persons is prohibited throughout the territory of the United States: provided that nothing herein shall affect the right of annulment and remarriage in accordance with the Canon Law of the Roman Catholic Church.

5. Attempted mixed marriages or unions between members of the Roman Catholic Church and non-Catholics are null and void, and the children of such unions are illegitimate, unless a special dispensation is obtained from the ecclesiastical authority of the Catholic Church.

6. Birth control, or any act that deliberately frustrates the natural power to generate life, is a crime.

7. Direct abortion is murder of the innocent even when performed through motives of misguided pity when the life of a mother is gravely imperiled.

8. Sterilization of any human being is forbidden except as an infliction of grave punishment under the authority of the government for a crime committed.

I remember a verse from Job which is appropriate at this moment: "If I justify myself, mine own mouth shall condemn me." That is meant for Catholic liberals whose temperature has been rising while they have been reading these three amendments. As most of my readers have doubtless guessed, there is not an original thought and scarcely an original word in my entire three Catholic amendments. They are mosaics of official Catholic doctrine. *Every concept, almost every word and phrase, has been plagiarized line by line from Catholic documents.* The most important phrases are derived from the highest documents of Catholicism, the encyclicals of the Popes. The provisions on education come from Pius XI's *Christian Education of Youth,* and those on family life from his *Casti Connubii,* both of them accepted universally in the Catholic Church as the Bibles of present-day educational and family policy. A few provisions are taken directly from Canon Law, the recent laws of Catholic countries like Spain, and the 1929 Concordat between Mussolini and the Vatican, all of which have been publicly approved by Catholic authorities. Only place-names and enabling clauses have been added to give the Papal principles local application.

John F. Kennedy

8. REMARKS ON CHURCH AND STATE

John F. Kennedy, unlike Al Smith, who was reluctant to discuss it, confronted the "religious issue" both directly and often. This was so much the case that in the West Virginia primary, in which he ran against Hubert Humphrey, a vote for Humphrey became a vote for bigotry. He subsequently spoke directly to his clerical critics in Texas. From the encounter he gained their respect if not their votes. In spite of these efforts the issue remained in the 1960 campaign until the end.

I am grateful for your generous invitation to state my views.

While the so-called religious issue is necessarily and properly the chief topic here tonight, I want to emphasize from the outset that I believe that we have far more critical issues in the 1960 election: the spread of Communist influence, until it now festers only ninety miles off the coast of Florida—the humiliating treatment of our President and Vice-President by those who no longer respect our power—the hungry children I saw in West Virginia, the old people who cannot pay their doctor's bills, the families forced to give up their farms—an America with too many slums, with too few schools, and too late to the moon and outer space.

These are the real issues which should decide this campaign. And they are not religious issues—for war and hunger and ignorance and despair know no religious barrier.

But because I am a Catholic, and no Catholic has ever been elected President, the real issues in this campaign have been obscured—perhaps deliberately in some quarters less responsible than this. So it is apparently necessary for me to state once again—not what kind of church I believe in, for that should be important only to me, but what kind of America I believe in.

I believe in an America where the separation of church and state is absolute—where no Catholic prelate would tell the President (should he be a Catholic) how to act and no Protestant minister would tell his parishioners for whom to vote—where no church or church school is granted any public funds or political preference—and where no man is denied public office merely because his religion differs from the President who might appoint him or the people who might elect him.

I believe in an America that is officially neither Catholic, Protestant nor Jewish—where no public official either requests or accepts instructions on public policy from the Pope, the National Council of Churches or any other ecclesiastical source—where no religious body seeks to impose its will directly or indirectly upon the general populace or the public acts of its officials—and where religious liberty is so indivisible that an act against one church is treated as an act against all.

For while this year it may be a Catholic against whom the finger of suspicion is pointed, in other years it has been, and may someday be again, a Jew—or a Quaker—or a Unitarian—or a Baptist. It was Virginia's harassment of Baptist preachers, for example, that led to Jefferson's statute of religious freedom. Today, I may be the victim—but tomorrow it may be you—until the whole fabric of our har-

A transcript of Kennedy's statement along with the questions and answers which followed its delivery may be found in the *New York Times* of September 13, 1960, on page 22.

monious society is ripped apart at a time of great national peril.

Finally, I believe in an America where religious intolerance will someday end—where all men and all churches are treated as equal—where every man has the same right to attend or not attend the church of his choice—where there is no Catholic vote, no anti-Catholic vote, no bloc voting of any kind—and where Catholics, Protestants and Jews, both the lay and the pastoral level, will refrain from those attitudes of disdain and division which have so often marred their works in the past, and promote instead the American ideal of brotherhood.

That is the kind of America in which I believe. And it represents the kind of Presidency in which I believe—a great office that must be neither humbled by making it the instrument of any religious group, nor tarnished by arbitrarily withholding it, its occupancy, from the members of any 'religious group. I believe in a President whose views on religion are his own private affair, neither imposed upon him by the nation or imposed by the nation upon him as a condition to holding that office.

I would not look with favor upon a President working to subvert the First Amendment's guarantees of religious liberty (nor would our system of checks and balances permit him to do so). And neither do I look with favor upon those who would work to subvert Article VI of the Constitution by requiring a religious test—even by indirection—for if they disagree with that safeguard, they should be openly working to repeal it.

I want a Chief Executive whose public acts are responsible to all and obligated to none—who can attend any ceremony, service or dinner his office may appropriately require him to fulfill—and whose fulfillment of his Presidential office is not limited or conditioned by any religious oath, ritual or obligation.

This is the kind of America I believe in—and this is the kind of America I fought

for in the South Pacific and the kind my brother died for in Europe. No one suggested then that we might have a "divided loyalty," that we did "not believe in liberty" or that we belonged to a disloyal group that threatened "the freedoms for which our forefathers died."

And in fact this is the kind of America for which our forefathers did die when they fled here to escape religious test oaths, that denied office to members of less favored churches, when they fought for the Constitution, the Bill of Rights, the Virginia Statute of Religious Freedom—and when they fought at the shrine I visited today—the Alamo. For side by side with Bowie and Crockett died Fuentes and McCafferty and Bailey and Bedillio and Carey—but no one knows whether they were Catholics or not. For there was no religious test there.

I ask you tonight to follow in that tradition, to judge me on the basis of fourteen years in the Congress—on my declared stands against an ambassador to the Vatican, against unconstitutional aid to parochial schools, and against any boycott of the public schools (which I attended myself)—instead of judging me on the basis of these pamphlets and publications we have all seen that carefully select quotations out of context from the statements of Catholic Church leaders, usually in other countries, frequently in other centuries, and rarely relevant to any situation here—and always omitting, of course, that statement of the American bishops in 1948 which strongly endorsed church-state separation.

I do not consider these other quotations binding upon my public acts—why should you? But let me say, with respect to other countries, that I am wholly opposed to the state being used by any religious group, Catholic or Protestant, to compel, prohibit or persecute the free exercise of any other religion. And that goes for any persecution at any time, by anyone, in any country.

And I hope that you and I condemn with equal fervor those nations which deny their Presidency to Protestants and those which

191

deny it to Catholics. And rather than cite the misdeeds of those who differ, I would also cite the record of the Catholic Church in such nations as France and Ireland—and the independence of such statesmen as de Gaulle and Adenauer.

But let me stress again that these are my views—for, contrary to common newspaper usage, I am not the Catholic candidate for President. I am the Democratic Party's candidate for President, who happens also to be a Catholic.

I do not speak for my church on public matters—and the church does not speak for me.

Whatever issue may come before me as President, if I should be elected—on birth control, divorce, censorship, gambling, or any other subject—I will make my decision in accordance with these views, in accordance with what my conscience tells me to be in the national interest, and without regard to outside religious pressure or dictate. And no power or threat of punishment could cause me to decide otherwise.

But if the time should ever come—and I do not concede any conflict to be remotely possible—when my office would require me to either violate my conscience, or violate the national interest, then I would resign the office, and I hope any other conscientious public servant would do likewise.

But I do not intend to apologize for these views to my critics of either Catholic or Protestant faith, nor do I intend to disavow either my views or my church in order to win this election. If I should lose on the real issues, I shall return to my seat in the Senate, satisfied that I tried my best and was fairly judged.

But if this election is decided on the basis that 40,000,000 Americans lost their chance of being President on the day they were baptized, then it is the whole nation that will be the loser in the eyes of Catholics and non-Catholics around the world, in the eyes of history, and in the eyes of our own people.

But if, on the other hand, I should win this election, I shall devote every effort of mind and spirit to fulfilling the oath of the Presidency—practically identical, I might add, with the oath I have taken for fourteen years in the Congress. For, without reservation, I can, and I quote, "solemnly swear that I will faithfully execute the office of President of the United States and will to the best of my ability preserve, protect and defend the Constitution, so help me God."

James A. Pike

9. A ROMAN CATHOLIC IN THE WHITE HOUSE?

James A. Pike was Episcopal Bishop of California. Previous to his ordination he had legal training and taught law. He first published an article on this theme in the popular press as the Kennedy nomination seemed likely. He returned to give it more extensive consideration in a book from which the following selection is taken.

Because of the nature of the issue itself, there will be many who will dissent from one or another of the points made in this book. This is as it should be. But we devoutly hope that no reader will say to his friends that because of this book, he will not vote for a Roman Catholic for President. The most that he can honestly say, if he has read the book carefully, is that he has weighed into his total decision (along with important national and international issues which we have not in the least discussed in this book) the views of Presidential candidates on Church and State issues and that he is prepared to vote for or against a particular American citizen for the Presidency. Our greatest hope is that the reader will have been impressed, in relation to his responsible exercise of the ballot, with the following points:

1. No voter should vote against any candidate simply on the ground of his religion. This is bigotry.

2. So to vote would be to impose a "religious test" contrary to the spirit of the Constitutional prohibition.

3. But a man's religio-ethical outlook does—and should—have a bearing on his decision-making, and a holder of public office is no exception to this. Therefore his likely decisions—or announced policies—on particular questions which are affected by religious orientation, are worthy and suitable subjects for consideration by the electorate.

4. One of the most basic things about the American tradition, which operates in a pluralistic culture, is the relationship of Church and State. Most American citizens—including most Roman Catholics, we are sure—prefer an equal and free opportunity for all faiths, not only for private worship but for public worship, evangelism, and propagation. As to Protestants, Jews, or secularists who may be candidates, no one thinks of asking about this whole question—this tradition is so well established among them. The matter becomes evident and complicated only in the case of a Roman Catholic candidate.

5. There are two well-supported views within the Roman Catholic Church on this general question, and the question is not an abstract one. Those holding the "official view" maintain that "error has no rights" and that the government when it is feasible should protect the Roman Catholic Church by not allowing to non-Roman Catholics the right to propagandize their views. They would feel that ultimately the public schools should be vehicles of Roman Catholic teaching. Further, they are convinced that the Church—as soon as may be—should receive the official protection and support of public legislation and all the trappings of official status.

6. On the other hand, there is a strong tradition, which we hold the average American Roman Catholic follows consciously or unconsciously, to the contrary.

He is perfectly happy to see their Church operate in the "competitive market." They may take a theologically dim view of the rest of us but genially they wish us to have the same "breaks" as they have. Those of them who may know of the Vatican strictures to the contrary, regard them as "dated."

7. All of us have friends of the latter type. Whatever may be the internal inconsistencies of their position, we couldn't care less; that's their problem. But when it comes to the crucial question of the highest office in the nation, some of us can be reasonably concerned as to whether it is really possible for a Roman Catholic—when all the chips are down—to hold such genial views.

8. In this connection there are several collateral considerations. First, these same friends are not as disturbed as we are about the application (there you really see it in action) of the "official view" in countries in which their Church has pre-eminence, and some of them will even say, "What business have these Bible-thumping fellows down there in Colombia, anyway? The people are content with their religion." Second, members of this "liberal" group who are articulate in their position do not seem to plead for "the American way" as finally right but simply as a permissible position within Roman Catholic thought. The serious fact is that those taking the genial position (which we know they mean most sincerely) are running right up against official declarations of Popes, modern as well as medieval, and, as Roman Catholics they are committed to the doctrine of the infallibility of the Pope and of the necessity of external conformity and "internal assent" even to "noninfallible" declarations. It is not impossible that a Roman Catholic layman in so important a post as the Presidency might be reminded of this basic doctrine of his Church. True, Al Smith, when confronted with the force of certain encyclicals is reported to have said

with honest perplexity, "What the hell is an 'enkiklika?'" But it is just possible that had he assumed the office of the Presidency someone might have made it his business to provide the answer to his question.

9. All this is not just an abstract question merely suitable for theological seminars. The fact is that it bears on what are in the life of the country certain basic questions, on which voters may differ in terms of their individual conviction as to the right direction of national policy. Most recently, there has been the foreign aid-birth control issue; but still left as "unfinished business" are the matters of public aid to parochial schools, and diplomatic representation to the Vatican, the degree to which we encourage (through the use of our boundless national resources) foreign governments which practice repressive measures against our fellow Christians, and the role of the United States in the political fortunes of the Vatican vis-à-vis other nations.

10. Then there is the question of assessing to what degree a Roman Catholic President would be subject to various types of informal ecclesiastical pressures, and the degree to which a Roman Catholic President would really be able to enter into the occasions reflecting our pluralistic society—and other questions of a considerable variety, the specific nature of which one could hardly predict at the time one casts one's ballot. On the other hand, as important as all these questions are, there are other very important questions—foreign policy, the approach to the problem of nuclear weapons and their testing, and the corollary questions of general disarmament, the policy of taxation, the approach to labor relations, civil rights, including integration and the proper limits of Congressional investigations. The proportion of the problems we have raised as compared with these other questions will vary in the mind of each voter. But nevertheless the questions we have raised are *real* questions.

In the final analysis a voter faced with the question of casting his vote for a Roman Catholic candidate will have to weigh the degree of his own trust in not only the candidate but in the candidate's Church. He will first, of course, consider the candidate's verbalization as to the part that his religious faith will play in his official decisions. Then he should decide whether or not this position is a tenable one. And more importantly, he will have to decide for himself as to the likelihood of the candidate's real intentions to function in this manner and to be a President of "all the people." Too, he will have to consider the likelihood that his Church will allow him to carry out his own good intentions in this area. We, as outsiders, feel that it would be in the long-term interest of the Roman Catholic Church to allow him so to do within the limits of its doctrinal position; and it may well be that the hierarchy of the Church would appreciate this point.

So in answering the question which supplies the title of this book, we come back to the basic question of trust. This is not the only field in which a candidate's words are not the only criterion. No present Roman Catholic possibility—and we are sure none who will surface in the future—will fail to say, "I'm as good an American as anybody else," etc., etc. The degree to which we can trust such well-meant remarks obviously depends upon the man's record in regard to the issues in this area and on our general trust of him as a person; and, as we have indicated, it depends too on our trust of the Roman Catholic Church itself. And so, in closing, we will answer our initial question as best we can:

A Roman Catholic for President? *It depends.*

The asking of the question is not bigotry. It is the exercise of responsible citizenship.

CHURCH AND STATE AS A JURIDICIAL PROBLEM

10. CANTWELL v. CONNECTICUT

This first of the "Jehovah's Witness cases" concerned the conviction of Newton Cantwell and two sons under Connecticut statutes for proselytizing in a heavily Roman Catholic section of New Haven, Conn. "Cantwell" explicitly applies the religion clauses of the First Amendment to the States through the "due process clause" of the Fourteenth. Brief excerpts follow.

MR. JUSTICE ROBERTS DELIVERED
THE OPINION OF THE COURT.

First. We hold that the statute, as construed and applied to the appellants, deprives them of their liberty without due process of law in contravention of the Fourteenth Amendment. The fundamental concept of liberty embodied in that Amendment embraces the liberties guaranteed by the First Amendment. The First Amendment declares that Congress shall make no law respecting an establishment of religion or prohibiting the free exercise thereof. The Fourteenth Amendment has rendered the legislatures of the states as

310 U. S. 296 (1940).

incompetent as Congress to enact such laws. The constitutional inhibition of legislation on the subject of religion has a double aspect. On the one hand, it forestalls compulsion by law of the acceptance of any creed or the practice of any form of worship. Freedom of conscience and freedom to adhere to such religious organization or form of worship as the individual may choose cannot be restricted by law. On the other hand, it safeguards the free exercise of the chosen form of religion. Thus the Amendment embraces two concepts, —freedom to believe and freedom to act. The first is absolute but, in the nature of things, the second cannot be. Conduct remains subject to regulation for the protection of society. The freedom to act must have appropriate definition to preserve the enforcement of that protection. In every case the power to regulate must be so exercised as not, in attaining a permissible end, unduly to infringe the protected freedom. . . .

Nothing we have said is intended even remotely to imply that, under the cloak of religion, persons may, with impunity, commit frauds upon the public. Certainly penal laws are available to punish such conduct. Even the exercise of religion may be at some slight inconvenience in order that the state may protect its citizens from injury. . . .

Second. We hold that, in the circumstances disclosed, the conviction of Jesse Cantwell on the fifth count must be set aside. . . .

The offense known as breach of the peace embraces a great variety of conduct destroying or menacing public order and tranquility. It includes not only violent acts but acts and words likely to produce violence in others. No one would have the hardihood to suggest that the principle of freedom of speech sanctions incitement to riot

or that religious liberty connotes the privilege to exhort others to physical attack upon those belonging to another sect. When clear and present danger of riot, disorder, interference with traffic upon the public streets, or other immediate threat to public safety, peace, or order, appears, the power of the State to prevent or punish is obvious. Equally obvious is it that a State may not unduly suppress free communication of views, religious or other, under the guise of conserving desirable conditions. . . .

In the realm of religious faith, and in that of political belief, sharp differences arise. In both fields the tenets of one man may seem the rankest error to his neighbor. To persuade others to his own point of view, the pleader, as we know, at times, resorts to exaggeration, to vilification of men who have been, or are, prominent in church or state, and even to false statement. But the people of this nation have ordained in the light of history, that, in spite of the probability of excesses and abuses, these liberties are, in the long view, essential to enlightened opinion and right conduct on the part of the citizens of a democracy.

The essential characteristic of these liberties is, that under their shield many types of life, character, opinion and belief can develop unmolested and unobstructed. Nowhere is this shield more necessary than in our own country for a people composed of many races and of many creeds. There are limits to the exercise of these liberties. The danger in these times from the coercive activities of those who in the delusion of racial or religious conceit would incite violence and breaches of the peace in order to deprive others of their equal right to the exercise of their liberties, is emphasized by events familiar to all. These and other transgressions of those limits the States appropriately may punish.

11. WEST VIRGINIA STATE BOARD OF EDUCATION v. BARNETTE

The following are excerpts from a "Flag Salute Case." After the Gobitis decision (1940), on the basis of state legislation, the West Virginia State Board of Education required the flag salute in public schools. This decision, as the text makes clear, explicitly overturned the earlier ruling.

MR. JUSTICE JACKSON DELIVERED
THE OPINION OF THE COURT.

The Gobitis decision . . . assumed, as did the argument in that case and in this, that power exists in the State to impose the flag salute discipline upon school children in general. The Court only examined and rejected a claim based on religious beliefs of immunity from an unquestioned general rule. The question which underlies the flag salute controversy is whether such a ceremony so touching matters of opinion and political attitude may be imposed upon the individual by official authority under powers committed to any political organization under our Constitution. We examine rather than assume existence of this power and, against this broader definition of issues in this case, re-examine specific grounds assigned for the Gobitis decision.

1. It was said that the flag-salute controversy confronted the Court with "the problem which Lincoln cast in memorable dilemma: 'Must a government of necessity be too strong for the liberties of its people, or too weak to maintain its own existence?'" and that the answer must be in favor of strength.

We think these issues may be examined free of pressure or restraint growing out of such considerations.

It may be doubted whether Mr. Lincoln would have thought that the strength of government to maintain itself would be impressively vindicated by our confirming power of the state to expel a handful of children from school. Such oversimplification, so handy in political debate, often lacks the precision necessary to postulates of judicial reasoning. If validly applied to this problem, the utterance cited would resolve every issue of power in favor of those in authority and would require us to override every liberty thought to weaken or delay execution of their policies.

Government of limited power need not be anemic government. Assurance that rights are secure tends to diminish fear and jealousy of strong government, and by making us feel safe to live under it makes for its better support. Without promise of a limiting Bill of Rights it is doubtful if our Constitution could have mustered enough strength to enable its ratification. To enforce those rights today is not to choose weak government over strong government. It is only to adhere as a means of strength to individual freedom of mind in preference to officially disciplined uniformity for which history indicates a disappointing and disastrous end.

The subject now before us exemplifies this principle. Free public education, if faithful to the ideal of secular instruction and political neutrality, will not be partisan or enemy of any class, creed, party, or faction. If it is to impose any ideological discipline, however, each party or denomination must seek to control, or failing that, to weaken the influence of the educational system. Observance of the limitations of the Constitution will not weaken government in the field appropriate for its exercise.

319 U.S. 624 (1943).

2. It was also considered in the Gobitis case that functions of educational officers in states, counties and school districts were such that to interfere with their authority "would in effect make us the school board for the country."

The Fourteenth Amendment, as now applied to the States, protects the citizen against the State itself and all of its creatures—Boards of Education not excepted. These have, of course, important, delicate, and highly discretionary functions, but none that they may not perform within the limits of the Bill of Rights. That they are educating the young for citizenship is reason for scrupulous protection of Constitutional Freedoms of the individual, if we are not to strangle the free mind at its source and teach youth to discount important principles of our government as mere platitudes.

3. The Gobitis opinion reasoned that this is a field "where courts possess no marked and certainly no controlling competence," that it is committed to the legislatures as well as the courts to guard cherished liberties and that it is constitutionally appropriate to "fight out the wise use of legislative authority in the form of public opinion and before legislative assemblies rather than to transfer such a contest to the judicial arena," since all the "effective means of inducing political changes are left free."

The very purpose of a Bill of Rights was to withdraw certain subjects from the vicissitudes of political controversy, to place them beyond the reach of majorities and officials and to establish them as legal principles to be applied by the courts. One's right to life, liberty, and property, to free speech, a free press, freedom of worship and assembly, and other fundamental rights may not be submitted to vote; they depend on the outcome of no elections.

4. Lastly, and this is the very heart of the Gobitis opinion, it reasons that "National unity is the basis of national security," that the authorities have "the right to select appropriate means for its attainment," and hence reaches the conclusion that such compulsory measures toward "national unity" are constitutional. Upon the verity of this assumption depends our answer in this case.

National unity as an end which officials may foster by persuasion and example is not in question. The problem is whether under our Constitution compulsion as here employed is a permissible means for its achievement.

Struggle to coerce uniformity of sentiment in support of some end thought essential to their time and country have been waged by many good as well as by evil men. Nationalism is a relatively recent phenomenon but at other times and places the ends have been racial or territorial security, support of a dynasty or regime, and particular plans for saving souls. As first and moderate methods to attain unity have failed, those bent on its accomplishment must resort to an ever increasing severity. . . .

It seems trite but necessary to say that the First Amendment to our Constitution was designed to avoid these ends by avoiding these beginnings. There is no mysticism in the American concept of the State or of the nature or origin of its authority. We set up government by consent of the governed, and the Bill of Rights denies those in power any legal opportunity to coerce that consent. Authority here is to be controlled by public opinion, not public opinion by authority.

The case is made difficult not because the principles of its decision are obscure but because the flag involved is our own. Nevertheless, we apply the limitations of the Constitution with no fear that freedom to be intellectually and spiritually diverse or even contrary will disintegrate the social organization. To believe that patriotism will not flourish if patriotic ceremonies are voluntary and spontaneous instead of a compulsory routine is to make an unflattering estimate of the appeal of our institutions to free minds. We can have intellectual individualism and the rich cultural diversities that we owe to exceptional minds only at the price of occasional eccentricity and abnormal attitudes. When they are so harmless to others or to the State as those we deal with here, the price is not too great. But freedom to differ is not limited to things that do not matter much. That would be a mere shadow of freedom. The test of its substance is the right to differ as to things that touch the heart of the existing order.

If there is any fixed star in our constitutional constellation, it is that no official, high or petty, can prescribe what shall be orthodox in politics, nationalism, religion, or other matters of opinion or force citizens to confess by word or act their faith therein. If there are any circumstances which permit an exception, they do not now occur to us.

We think the action of the local authorities in compelling the flag salute and pledge transcends constitutional limitations on their power and invades the sphere of intellect and spirit which it is the purpose of the First Amendment to our Constitution to reserve from all official control.

The decision of this Court in Minersville School District v. Gobitis and the holdings of those few per curiam decisions which preceded and foreshadowed it are overruled, and the judgment enjoining enforcement of the West Virginia Regulation is affirmed.

Mr. Justice Roberts and Mr. Justice Reed adhere to the views expressed by the Court in Minersville School District v. Gobitis and are of the opinion that the judgment below should be reversed.

MR. JUSTICE FRANKFURTER, DISSENTING.

The essence of the religious freedom guaranteed by our Constitution is . . . this: no religion shall either receive the state's support or incur its hostility. Religion is outside the sphere of political government. This does not mean that all matters on which religious organizations or beliefs may pronounce are outside the sphere of government. Were this so, instead of the separation of church and state, there would be the subordination of the state on any matter deemed within the sovereignty of the religious conscience. Much that is the concern of temporal authority affects the spiritual interests of men. But it is not enough to strike down a non-discriminatory law that it may hurt or offend some dissident view. It would be too easy to cite numerous prohibitions and injunctions to which laws run counter if the variant interpretations of the Bible were made the tests of the obedience to law. The validity of secular laws cannot be measured by their conformity to religious doctrines. It is only in a theocratic state that ecclesiastical doctrines measure legal right or wrong.

An act compelling profession of allegiance to a religion, no matter how subtly or tenuously promoted, is bad. But an act promoting good citizenship and national allegiance is within the domain of governmental authority and is therefore to be judged by the same considerations of power and of constitutionality as those involved in the many claims of immunity from civil obedience because of religious scruples.

That claims are pressed on behalf of sincere religious convictions does not of itself establish their constitutional validity. Nor does waving the banner of religious freedom relieve us from examining the power we are asked to deny the states. Otherwise the doctrine of separation of church and state, so cardinal in the history of this nation and for the liberty of our people, would mean not the disestablishment of a state church but the establishment of all churches and of all religious groups.

The subjection of dissidents to the general requirement of saluting the flag, as a measure conducive to the training of children in good citizenship, is very far from being the first instance of exacting obedience to general laws that have offended deep religious scruples. Compulsory vaccination, compulsory medical treatment, these are but illustrations of conduct that has often been compelled in the enforcement of legislation of general applicability even though the religious consciences of particular individuals rebelled at the exaction.

Law is concerned with external behavior and not with the inner life of man. It rests in large measure upon compulsion. Socrates lives in history partly because he gave his life for the conviction that duty of obedience to secular law does not pre-suppose consent to its enactment or belief in its virtue. The consent upon which free government rests is the consent that comes from sharing in the process of making and unmaking laws. The state is not shut out from a domain because the individual conscience may deny the state's claim. The individual conscience may profess what faith it chooses. It may affirm and promote that faith—in the language of the Constitution, it may "exercise" it freely—but it cannot thereby restrict community action through political organs in matters of community concern, so long as the action is not asserted in a discriminatory way either openly or by stealth. One may have the right to practice one's religion and at the same time owe the duty of formal obedience to laws that run counter to one's beliefs.

12. EVERSON v. BOARD OF EDUCATION

This case concerned the practice of reimbursing parents of parochial school children (as well as those whose children attended public schools) for fares spent to reach their schools on regular busses of the public transportation system. Here the issue of "establishment" was openly confronted in a very close (5–4) decision.

MR. JUSTICE BLACK DELIVERED
THE OPINION OF THE COURT.

Since there has been no attack on the statute on the ground that a part of its language excludes children attending private schools operated for profit from enjoying state payment for their transportation, we need not consider this exclusionary language; it has no relevancy to any constitutional question here presented. . . .

The only contention here is that the State statute and the resolution, in so far as they authorized reimbursement to parents of children attending parochial schools, violate the Federal Constitution in these two respects, which to some extent, overlap. First. They authorize the State to take by taxation the private property of some and bestow it upon others, to be used for their own private purposes. This, it is alleged, violates the due process clause of the Fourteenth Amendment. Second. The statute and the resolution forced inhabitants to pay taxes to help support and maintain schools which are dedicated to, and which regularly teach, the Catholic Faith. This is alleged to be a use of State Power to sup-

330 U.S. 1 (1947).

port church schools contrary to the prohibition of the First Amendment which the Fourteenth Amendment made applicable to the states.

First. The due process argument that the State law taxes some people to help others carry out their private purposes is framed in two phases. The first phase is that a state cannot tax A to reimburse B for the cost of transporting his children to church schools. This is said to violate the due process clause because the children are sent to these church schools to satisfy the personal desires of their parents, rather than the public's interest in the general education of all children. This argument, if valid, would apply equally to prohibit state payment for the transportation of children to any non-public school, whether operated by a church, or any other non-government individual or group. But, the New Jersey legislature has decided that a public purpose will be served by using tax-raised funds to pay the bus fares of all school children, including those who attend parochial schools. The New Jersey Court of Errors and Appeals has reached the same conclusion. The fact that a state law, passed to satisfy a public need, coincides with the personal desires of the individuals most directly affected is certainly an inadequate reason for us to say that a legislature has erroneously appraised the public need.

Insofar as the second phase of the due process argument may differ from the first, it is by suggesting that taxation for transportation of children to church schools constitutes support of a religion by the State. But if the law is invalid for this reason, it is because it violates the First Amendment's prohibition against the establishment of religion by law. This is the exact question raised by appellant's second contention, to consideration of which we now turn.

Second. The New Jersey statute is challenged as a "law respecting an establishment of religion." The First Amendment, as made applicable to the states by the Fourteenth, commands that a state "shall make no law respecting an establishment of religion, or prohibiting the free exercise thereof." . . .

The meaning and scope of the First Amendment, preventing establishment of religion or prohibiting the free exercise thereof, in the light of its history and the evils it was designed forever to suppress, have been several times elaborated by the decisions of this Court prior to the application of the First Amendment to the states by the Fourteenth. The broad meaning given the Amendment by these earlier cases has been accepted by this Court in its decisions concerning an individual's religious freedom rendered since the Fourteenth Amendment was interpreted to make the prohibitions of the First applicable to state action abridging religious freedom. There is every reason to give the same application and broad interpretation to the "establishment of religion" clause. The interrelation of these complementary clauses was well summarized in a statement of the Court of Appeals of South Carolina, quoted with approval by this Court, in Watson v. Jones, "The structure of our government has, for the preservation of civil liberty, rescued the temporal institutions from religious interference. On the other hand, it has secured religious liberty from the invasions of the civil authority."

The "establishment of religion" clause of the First Amendment means at least this: Neither a state nor the Federal Government can set up a church. Neither can pass laws which aid one religion, aid all religions, or prefer one religion over another. Neither can force nor influence a person to go to or to remain away from church against his will or force him to profess a belief or disbelief in any religion. No person can be punished for entertaining or professing religious beliefs or disbeliefs, for church attendance or non-attendance. No tax in any amount, large or small, can be levied to support any religious activities or institutions, whatever they may be called, or whatever form they may adopt to teach or practice religion. Neither a state nor the Federal Government can, openly or secretly, participate in the affairs of any religious organizations or groups and vice versa. In the words of Jefferson, the clause against establishment of religion by law was intended to erect "a wall of separation between Church and State."

We must consider the New Jersey statute in accordance with the foregoing limitations imposed by the First Amendment. But we must not strike that state statute down if it is within the state's constitutional power even though it approaches the verge of that power. New Jersey cannot consistently with the "establishment of religion" clause of the First Amendment contribute tax-raised funds to the support of an institution which teaches the tenets and faith of any church. On the other hand, other language of the amendment commands that New Jersey cannot exclude individual Catholics, Lutherans, Mohammedans, Baptists, Jews, Methodists, Non-believers, Presbyterians, or the members of any other faith, because of their faith, or lack of it, from receiving the benefits of public welfare legislation. While we do not mean to intimate that a state could not provide transportation only to children attending public schools, we must be careful, in protecting the citizens of New Jersey against state-established churches, to be sure that we do not inadvertently prohibit New Jersey from extending its general State law benefits to all its citizens without regard to their religious belief.

Measured by these standards, we cannot say that the First Amendment prohibits New Jersey from spending tax-raised funds to pay the bus fares of parochial school pupils as a part of a general program under which it pays the fares of pupils attending public and other schools. It is undoubtedly true that children are helped to get to

church schools. There is even a possibility that some of the children might not be sent to the church schools if the parents were compelled to pay their children's bus fares out of their own pockets when transportation to a public school would have been paid for by the State. The same possibility exists where the state requires a local transit company to provide reduced fares to school children including those attending parochial schools, or where a municipally owned transportation system undertakes to carry all school children free of charge. Moreover, state-paid policemen, detailed to protect children going to and from church schools from the very real hazards of traffic, would serve much the same purpose and accomplish much the same result as state provisions intended to guarantee free transportation of a kind which the state deems to be best for the school children's welfare. And parents might refuse to risk their children to the serious danger of traffic accidents going to and from parochial schools, the approaches to which were not protected by policemen. Similarly, parents might be reluctant to permit their children to attend schools which the state had cut off from such general government services as ordinary police and fire protection, connections for sewage disposal, public highways and sidewalks. Of course, cutting off church schools from these services, so separate and so indisputably marked off from the religious function, would make it far more difficult for the schools to operate. But such is obviously not the purpose of the First Amendment. That Amendment requires the state to be a neutral in its relations with groups of religious believers and non-believers; it does not require the state to be their adversary. State power is no more to be used so as to handicap religions, than it is to favor them.

This Court has said that parents may, in the discharge of their duty under state compulsory education laws, send their children to a religious rather than a public school if the school meets the secular educational requirements which the state has power to impose. It appears that these parochial schools meet New Jersey's requirements. The State contributes no money to the schools. It does not suport them. Its legislation, as applied, does no more than provide a general program to help parents get their children, regardless of their religion, safely and expeditiously to and from accredited schools.

The First Amendment has erected a wall between church and state. That wall must be kept high and impregnable. We could not approve the slightest breach. New Jersey has not breached it here.

Affirmed.

MR. JUSTICE JACKSON, DISSENTING.

I find myself, contrary to first impressions, unable to join in this decision. I have a sympathy, though it is not ideological, with Catholic citizens who are compelled by law to pay taxes for public schools, and also feel constrained by conscience and discipline to support other schools for their own children. Such relief to them as this case involves is not in itself a serious burden to taxpayers and I had assumed it to be as little serious in principle. Study of this case convinces me otherwise. The Court's opinion marshals every argument in favor of state aid and puts the case in its most favorable light, but much of its reasoning confirms my conclusions that there are no good grounds upon which to support the present legislation. In fact the undertones of the opinion, advocating complete and uncompromising separation of Church from State, seem utterly discordant with its conclusion yielding support to their commingling in educational matters. The case which irresistibly comes to mind as the most fitting precedent is that of Julia who according to Byron's reports, "whispering 'I will ne'er consent,' — consented."

It seems to me that the basic fallacy in the Court's reasoning, which accounts for its failure to apply the principles it avows, is in ignoring the essentially religious test by which beneficiaries of this expenditure are selected. A policeman protects a Catholic, of course — but not because he is a Catholic, it is because he is a man and a member of our society. The fireman protects the Church school — but not because it is a Church school; it is because it is property, part of the assets of our society. Neither the fireman nor the policeman has to ask before he renders aid "Is this man or building identified with the Catholic Church?" But before these school authorities draw a check to reimburse for a student's fare they must ask just that question, and if the school is a Catholic one they may render aid because it is such, while if it is of any other faith or is run for profit, the help must be withheld. To consider the converse of the Court's reasoning will best disclose its fallacy. That there is no parallel between police and fire protection and this plan of reimbursement is apparent from the incongruity of the limitation of this Act if applied to police and fire service. Could we sustain an Act that said police shall protect pupils on the way to or from public schools and Catholic schools but not while going to and coming from other schools, and firemen shall extinguish a blaze in public or Catholic school buildings but shall not put out a blaze in Protestant Church schools or private schools operated for profit? That is the true analogy to the case we have before us and I should think it pretty plain that such a scheme would not be valid.

This policy of our Federal Constitution has never been wholly pleasing to most religious groups. They all are quick to invoke its protections; they all are irked when they feel its restraints. This Court has gone a long way, if not an unreasonable way, to hold that public business of such paramount importance as maintenance of public order, protection of the privacy of the home, and taxation may not be pursued by a state in a way that even indirectly will interfere with religious proselyting.

But we cannot have it both ways. Religious teaching cannot be a private affair when the state seeks to impose regulations which infringe on it indirectly, and a public affair when it comes to taxing citizens of one faith to aid another, or those of no faith to aid all. If these principles seem harsh in prohibiting aid to Catholic education, it must not be forgotten that it is the same Constitution that alone assures Catholics the right to maintain these schools at all when predominant local sentiments would forbid them. Nor should I think that those who have done so well without this aid would want to see this separation between Church and State broken down. If the state may aid these religious schools, it may therefore regulate them. Many groups have sought aid from tax funds only to find that it carried political controls with it. Indeed this Court has declared that "It is hardly lack of due process for the Government to regulate that which it subsidizes."

But in any event, the great purposes of the Constitution do not depend on the approval or convenience of those they restrain. I cannot read the history of the struggle to separate political from ecclesiastical affairs, well summarized in the opinion of Mr. Justice Rutledge in which I generally concur, without a conviction that the Court today is unconsciously giving the clock's hands a backward turn.

Mr. Justice Frankfurter joins in this opinion.

MR. JUSTICE RUTLEDGE, WITH WHOM
MR. JUSTICE FRANKFURTER, MR. JUSTICE
BURTON AGREE, DISSENTING.

Our constitutional policy . . . does not deny the value or the necessity for religious training, teaching or observance. Rather it secures their free exercise. But to that end it does deny that the state can undertake or sustain them in any form or degree. For this reason the sphere of religious activity, as distinguished from the secular intellectual liberties, has been given the twofold protection and, as the state cannot forbid, neither can it perform or aid in performing the religious function. The dual prohibition makes that function altogether private. It cannot be made a public one by legislative act. This was the very heart of Madison's Remonstrance, as it is of the Amendment itself.

It is not because religious teaching does not promote the public or the individual's welfare, but because neither is furthered when the state promotes religious education, that the Constitution forbids it to do so. Both legislatures and courts are bound by that distinction. In failure to observe it lies the fallacy of the "public function"-"social legislation" argument, a fallacy facilitated by easy transference of the argument's basing from due process unrelated to any religious aspect to the First Amendment.

By no declaration that a gift of public money to religious uses will promote the general or individual welfare, or the cause of education generally, can legislative bodies overcome the Amendment's bar. Nor may the courts sustain their attempts to do so by finding such consequences for appropriations which in fact give aid to or promote religious uses. Legislatures are free to make, and courts to sustain, appropriations only when it can be found that in fact they do not aid, promote, encourage or sustain religious teaching or observances, be the amount large or small. No such finding has been or could be made in this case. The Amendment has removed this form of promoting the public welfare from legislative and judicial competence to make a public function. It is exclusively a private affair.

The reasons underlying the Amendment's policy have not vanished with time or diminished in force. Now as when it was adopted the price of religious freedom is double. It is that the church and religion shall live both within and upon that freedom. There cannot be freedom of religion, safeguarded by the state, and intervention by the church or its agencies in the state's domain or dependency on its largesse. The great condition of religious liberty is that it be free from sustenance, as also from other interferences, by the state. For when it comes to rest upon that secular foundation it vanishes with the resting. Public money devoted to payment of religious costs, educational or other, brings the quest for more.

It brings too the struggle of sect against sect for the larger share or for any. Here one by numbers alone will benefit most, there another. That is precisely the history of societies which have had an established religion and dissident groups. It is the very thing Jefferson and Madison experienced and sought to guard against, whether in its blunt or in its more screened forms. The end of such strife cannot be other than to destroy the cherished liberty. The dominating group will achieve the dominant benefit; or all will embroil the state in their dissensions.

13. ILLINOIS EX REL. McCOLLUM v. BOARD OF EDUCATION

The McCollum Case dealt with a Champaign, Illinois "released time" plan.

MR. JUSTICE BLACK DELIVERED
THE OPINION OF THE COURT.

This case relates to the power of a state to utilize its tax-supported public school system in aid of religious instruction insofar as that power may be restricted by the First and Fourteenth Amendments to the Federal Constitution.

Although there are disputes between the parties as to various inferences that may or may not properly be drawn from the evidence concerning the religious program, the following facts are shown by the record without dispute. In 1940 interested members of the Jewish, Roman Catholic, and a few of the Protestant faiths formed a voluntary association called the Champaign Council on Religious Education. They obtained permission from the Board of Education to offer classes in religious instruction to public school pupils in grades four

to nine inclusive. Classes were made up of pupils whose parents signed printed cards requesting that their children be permitted to attend; they were held weekly, thirty minutes for the lower grades, forty-five minutes for the higher. The council employed the religious teachers at no expense to the school authorities, but the instructors were subject to the approval and supervision of the superintendent of schools. The classes were taught in three separate religious groups by Protestant teachers, Catholic priests, and a Jewish rabbi, although for the past several years there have apparently been no classes instructed in the Jewish religion. Classes were conducted in the regular classrooms of the school building for pursuit of their secular studies. On the other hand, students who were released from secular study for the religious instructions were required to be present at the religious classes. Reports of their pres-

333 U. S. 203 (1948).

ence or absence were to be made to their secular teachers.

The foregoing facts, without reference to others that appear in the record, show the use of tax-supported property for religious instruction and the close cooperation between the school authorities and the religious council in promoting religious education. The operation of the state's compulsory education system thus assists and is integrated with the program of religious instruction carried on by separate religious sects. Pupils compelled by law to go to school for secular education are released in part from their legal duty upon the condition that they attend the religious classes. This is beyond all question a utilization of the tax-established and tax-supported public school system to aid religious groups to spread their faith. And it falls squarely under the ban of the First Amendment (made applicable to the States by the Fourteenth) as we interpreted it in Everson v. Board of Education.

The majority in the Everson case, and the minority . . . agreed that the First Amendment's language, properly interpreted, had erected a wall of separation between Church and State. They disagreed as to the facts shown by the record and as to the proper application of the First Amendment's language to those facts.

Recognizing that the Illinois program is barred by the First and Fourteenth Amendments if we adhere to the views expressed both by the majority and the minority in the Everson case, counsel for the respondents challenge those views as dicta and urge that we reconsider and repudiate them. They argue that historically the First Amendment was intended to forbid only government preference of one religion over another, not an impartial governmental assistance of all religions. In addition they ask that we distinguish or overrule our holding in the Everson case that the Fourteenth Amendment made the "establishment of religion" clause of the First

Amendment applicable as a prohibition against the states. After giving full consideration to the arguments presented we are unable to accept either of these contentions.

To hold that a state cannot consistently with the First and Fourteenth Amendments utilize its public school system to aid any or all religious faiths or sects in the dissemination of their doctrines and ideals does not, as counsel urge, manifest a governmental hostility to religion or religious teachings. A manifestation of such hostility would be at war with our national tradition as embodied in the First Amendment's guaranty of the free exercise of religion. For the First Amendment rests upon the premise that both religion and government can best work to achieve their lofty aims if each is left free from the other within its respective sphere. Or, as we said in the Everson case, the First Amendment has erected a wall between Church and State which must be kept high and impregnable.

Here not only are the state's tax-supported public school buildings used for the dissemination of religious doctrines. The State also affords sectarian groups an invaluable aid in that it helps to provide pupils for their religious classes through use of the state's compulsory public school machinery. This is not separation of Church and State.

The cause is reversed and remanded to the State Supreme Court for proceedings not inconsistent with this opinion.

MR. JUSTICE FRANKFURTER
DELIVERED THE FOLLOWING OPINION,
IN WHICH MR. JUSTICE JACKSON,
MR. JUSTICE RUTLEDGE
AND MR. JUSTICE BURTON JOIN.

We dissented in Everson v. Board of Education, because in our view the Constitutional principle requiring separation of Church and State compelled invalidation of the ordinance sustained by the majority.

Illinois has here authorized the commingling of sectarian with secular instruction in the public schools. The Constitution of the United States forbids this.

Separation means separation, not something less. Jefferson's metaphor in describing the relation between Church and State speaks of a "wall of separation," not of a fine line easily overstepped. The public school is at once the symbol of our democracy and the most pervasive means for promoting our common destiny. In no activity of the State is it more vital to keep out divisive forces than in its schools. To avoid confusing, not to say fusing, what the Constitution sought to keep strictly apart. "The great American principle of eternal separation"—Elihu Root's phrase bears repetition—is one of the vital reliances of our Constitutional system for assuring unities among our people stronger than our diversities. It is the Court's duty to enforce this principle in its full integrity.

We renew our conviction that "we have staked the very existence of our country on the faith that complete separation between the state and religion is best for the state and best for religion." If nowhere else, in the relation between Church and State, "good fences make good neighbors."

MR. JUSTICE REED, DISSENTING.

This Court summarized the amendment's accepted reach into the religious field, as I understand its scope, in Everson v. Board of Education. The Court's opinion quotes the gist of the Court's reasoning in Everson. I agree as there stated that none of our governmental entities can "set up a church." I agree that they cannot "aid" all or any religions or prefer one "over another." But "aid" must be understood as a purposeful assistance directly to the church itself or to some religious group or organization doing religious work of such a character that it may fairly be said to be performing ecclesiastical functions. "Prefer" must give an advantage to one "over another." I agree that pupils cannot "be released in part from their legal duty" of school attendance upon condition that they attend religious classes. But as Illinois has held that it is within the discretion of the School Board to permit absence from school for religious instruction no legal duty of school attendance is violated . . . . Of course, no tax can be levied to support organizations intended "to teach or practice religion." I agree too that the state cannot influence one toward religion against his will or punish him for his beliefs. Champaign's religious education course does none of these things.

With the general statements in the opinions concerning the constitutional requirement that the nation and states, by virtue of the First and Fourteenth Amendments, may "make no law respecting an establishment of religion," I am in agreement. But, in the light of the meaning given to those words by the precedents, customs, and practices which I have detailed above, I cannot agree with the Court's conclusion that when pupils compelled by law to go to school for secular education are released from school so as to attend the religious classes, churches are unconstitutionally aided. Whatever may be the wisdom of the arrangement as to the use of the school buildings made with The Champaign Council of Religious Education, it is clear to me that past practice shows such cooperation between the schools and a nonecclesiastical body is not forbidden by the First Amendment. When actual church services have always been permitted on government property, the mere use of the school buildings by a non-sectarian group for religious education ought not to be condemned as an establishment of religion. For a non-sectarian organization to give the type of instruction here offered cannot be said to violate our rule as to the establishment of religion by the state. The prohibition of enactments respecting the establishment of religion do not bar every friendly gesture between church and state. It is not an absolute prohibition against every conceivable situation where the two may work together any more than the other provisions of the First Amendment—free speech, free press—are absolutes. If abuses occur such as the use of the instruction hour for sectarian purposes, I have no doubt . . . that Illinois will promptly correct them. If they are of a kind that tend to the establishment of a church or interfere with the free exercise of religion, this Court is open for a review of any erroneous decision. This Court cannot be too cautious in upsetting practices embedded in our society by many years of experience. A state is entitled to have great leeway in its legislation when dealing with the important social problems of its population. A definite violation of legislative limits must be established. The Constitution should not be stretched to forbid national customs in the way courts act to reach arrangements to avoid federal taxation. Devotion to the great principle of religious liberty should not lead us into a rigid interpretation of the constitutional guarantee that conflicts with accepted habits of our people. This is an instance where, for me, the history of past practices is determinative of the meaning of a constitutional clause not a decorous introduction to the study of its text. The judgment should be affirmed.

14. ZORACH v. CLAUSON

Within four years a similar case had reached the Supreme Court. The chief difference was that the pupils (who desired to be) were not released to receive religious instruction in a specified classroom but were dismissed from school to attend the class in church buildings. Both the dissenters on the bench and commentators have questioned the significance given to this circumstance in the decision of the Court.

MR. JUSTICE DOUGLAS DELIVERED THE OPINION OF THE COURT.

New York City has a program which permits its public schools to release students during the school day so that they may leave the school buildings and school grounds and go to religious centers for religious instruction or devotional exercises. A student is released on written request of his parents. Those not released stay in the classrooms. The churches make weekly reports to the schools, sending a list of children who have been released from public school but who have not reported for religious instruction.

This "released time" program involves neither religious instruction in public school classrooms nor the expenditure of public funds. All costs, including the application blanks, are paid by the religious organizations. The case is therefore unlike McCollum v. Board of Education which involved a "released time" program from Illinois. In that case the classrooms were turned over to religious instructors. We accordingly held that the program violated the First Amendment which (by reason of the Fourteenth Amendment) prohibits the states from establishing religion or prohibiting its free exercise.

Appellants, who are taxpayers and resi-

343 U. S. 306 (1952).

dents of New York City and whose children attend its public schools, challenge the present law, contending it is in essence not different from the one involved in the McCollum case. Their argument, stated elaborately in various ways, reduces itself to this: the weight and influence of the school is put behind a program for religious instruction; public school teachers police it, keeping tab on students who are released; the classroom activities come to a halt while the students who are released for religious instruction are on leave; the school is a crutch on which the churches are leaning for support in their religious training; without the cooperation of the schools this "released time" program, like the one in the McCollum case, would be futile and ineffective. The New York Court of Appeals sustained the law against this claim of unconstitutionality. The case is here on appeal.

Our problem reduces itself to whether New York by this system has either prohibited the "free exercise" of religion or has made a law "respecting an establishment of religion" within the meaning of the First Amendment.

It takes obtuse reasoning to inject any issue of the "free exercise" of religion into the present case. No one is forced to go to the religious classroom and no religious exercise or instruction is brought to the classrooms of the public schools. A student need not take religious instruction. He is left to his own desires as to the manner or time of his religious devotions, if any.

Moreover, apart from that claim of coercion, we do not see how New York by this type of "released time" program has made a law respecting an establishment of religion within the meaning of the First Amendment. There is much talk of the separation of Church and State in the history of the Bill of Rights and in the decisions clustering around the First Amendment. See Everson v. Board of Education; McCollum v. Board of Education. There cannot be the slightest doubt that the First Amendment reflects the philosophy that Church and State should be separated. And so far as interference with the "free exercise" of religion and an "establishment" of religion are concerned, the separation must be complete and unequivocal. The First Amendment within the scope of its coverage permits no exception; the prohibition is absolute. The First Amendment, however, does not say that in every and all respects there shall be a separation of Church and State. Rather it studiously defines the manner, the specific ways, in which there shall be no concert or union or dependency one on the other. That is the common sense of the matter. Otherwise the state and religion would [be] aliens to each other—hostile, suspicious, and even unfriendly. Churches could not be required to pay even property taxes. Municipalities would not be permitted to render police or fire protection to religious groups. Policemen who helped parishioners into their places of worship would violate the Constitution. Prayers in our legislative halls; the appeals to the Almighty in the messages of the Chief Executive; the proclamations making Thanksgiving Day a holiday; "so help me God" in our courtroom oaths—these and all other references to the Almighty that run through our laws, our public rituals, our ceremonies would be flouting the First Amendment. A fastidious atheist or agnostic could even object to the supplication with which the Court opens each session: "God save the United States and this Honorable Court."

We would have to press the concept of separation of Church and State to these extremes to condemn the present law on constitutional grounds. The nullification of this law would have wide and profound effects. A Catholic student applies to his teacher for permission to leave the school during hours on a Holy Day of Obligation to attend a mass. A Jewish student asks his teacher for permission to be excused for Yom Kippur. A Protestant wants the afternoon off for a family baptismal ceremony.

In each case the teacher requires parental consent in writing. In each case the teacher, in order to make sure the student is not a truant, goes further and requires a report from the priest, the rabbi, or the minister. The teacher in other words cooperates in a religious program to the extent of making it possible for her students to participate in it. Whether she does it occasionally for a few students, regularly for one, or pursuant to a systematized program designed to further the religious needs of all the students does not alter the character of the act.

We are a religious people whose institutions presuppose a Supreme Being. We guarantee the freedom to worship as one chooses. We make room for as wide a variety of beliefs and creeds as the spiritual needs of man deem necessary. We sponsor an attitude on the part of government that shows no partiality to any one group and that lets each flourish according to the zeal of its adherents and the appeal of its dogma. When the state encourages religious instruction or cooperates with religious authorities by adjusting the schedule of public events to sectarian needs, it follows the best of our traditions. For it then respects the religious nature of our people and accommodates the public service to their spiritual needs. To hold that it may not would be to find in the Constitution a requirement that the government show a callous indifference to religious groups. That would be preferring those who believe in no religion over those who do believe. Government may not finance religious groups nor undertake religious instruction nor blend secular and sectarian education nor use secular institutions to force one or some religion on any person. But we find no constitutional requirement which makes it necessary for government to be hostile to religion and to throw its weight against efforts to widen the effective scope of religious influence. The government must be neutral when it comes to competition between sects. It may not

thrust any sect on any person. It may not make a religious observance compulsory. It may not coerce anyone to attend church, to observe a religious holiday, or to take religious instruction. But it can close its doors or suspend its operations as to those who want to repair to their religious sanctuary for worship or instruction. No more than that is undertaken here.

This program may be unwise and improvident from an educational or a community viewpoint. That appeal is made to us on a theory, previously advanced, that each case must be decided on the basis of "our own prepossessions." See McCollum v. Board of Education. Our individual preferences, however, are not the constitutional standard. The constitutional standard is the separation of Church and State. The problem, like many problems in constitutional law, is one of degree.

In the McCollum case the classrooms were used for religious instruction and the force of the public school was used to promote that instruction. Here, as we have said, the public schools do no more than accommodate their schedules to a program of outside religious instruction. We follow the McCollum case. But we cannot expand it to cover the present released time program unless separation of Church and State means that public institutions can make no adjustment of their schedules to accommodate the religious needs of the people. We cannot read into the Bill of Rights such a philosophy of hostility to religion.

Affirmed.

MR. JUSTICE BLACK, DISSENTING.

I see no significant difference between the invalid Illinois system and that of New York here sustained. Except for the use of the school buildings in Illinois, there is no difference between the systems which I consider even worthy of mention. In the New York program, as in that of Illinois, the school authorities release some of the children on the condition that they attend the religious classes, get reports on whether they attend, and hold the other children in the school building until the religious hour is over. As we attempted to make categorically clear, the McCollum decision would have been the same if the religious classes had not been held in the school buildings. We said:

"Here not only are the State's tax-supported public school buildings used for the dissemination of religious doctrines. The State also affords sectarian groups an invaluable aid in that it helps to provide pupils for their religious classes through the use of the State's compulsory school machinery. This is not separation of Church and State." McCollum thus held that Illinois could not constitutionally manipulate the compelled classroom hours of its compulsory school machinery so as to channel children into sectarian classes. Yet that is exactly what the Court holds New York can do.

MR. JUSTICE JACKSON DISSENTING.

This released time program is founded upon a use of the State's power of coercion, which, for me, determines its unconstitutionality. Stripped to its essentials, the plan has two stages, first, that the State compel each student to yield a large part of his time for public secular education and, second, that some of it be "released" to him on condition that he devote it to sectarian religious purposes.

No one suggests that the Constitution would permit the State directly to require this "released" time to be spent "under the control of a duly constituted religious body." This program accomplishes that forbidden result by indirection. If public education were taking so much of the pupils' time as to injure the public or the student's welfare by encroaching upon their religious opportunity, simply shortening everyone's school day would facilitate voluntary and optional attendance at Church classes. But that suggestion is rejected upon the ground that if they are made free many students will not go to the Church. Hence, they must be deprived of freedom for this period, with Church attendance put to them as one of the two permissible ways of using it.

A number of Justices just short of a majority of the majority that promulgates today's passionate dialectics joined in answering them in Illinois ex rel. McCollum v. Board of Education. The distinction attempted between that case and this is trivial, almost to the point of cynicism, magnifying its nonessential details and disparaging compulsion which was the underlying reason for invalidity. A reading of the Court's opinion in that case along with its opinion in this case will show such difference of overtones and undertones as to make clear that the McCollum case has passed like a storm in a teacup. The wall which the Court was professing to erect between Church and State has become even more warped and twisted than I expected. Today's judgment will be more interesting to students of psychology and of the judicial processes than to students of constitutional law.

Philip Kurland

15. A DOCTRINE IN SEARCH OF AUTHORITY

Professor Kurland's proposed reading of the religion clauses of the first amendment has attracted a great deal of attention.

Like most commands of our Constitution, the religion clauses of the first amendment are not statements of abstract principles. History, not logic, explains their inclusion in the Bill of Rights; necessity, not merely morality, justifies their presence there. . . . Religious toleration, summed up in the second of the two clauses, was, . . . necessary to preserve the peace. Separation, represented by the first of the two clauses, was necessary to make such religious freedom a reality. But the separation clause had a greater function than the assurance of toleration of dissenting religious beliefs and practices. To suggest but two lessons of the evils resulting from the alliance of church and state, there was abundant evidence of the contributions of the churches to the warfare among nations as well as the conflict within them and equally obvious was the inhibition on scientific endeavor that followed from the acceptance by the state of church dogma. It is not necessary to suggest that the Francophiles in the American community were dedicated to the anti-clericalism that contributed to the French Revolution, but they certainly were not ignorant of the evils that aroused such violent reactions. For them toleration could hardly satisfy the felt needs; separation was a necessary concomitant. But admittedly separation was a new concept in practice. Toleration had a long English history; separation—conceived in the English writings of Roger Williams—had its beginnings as an historical fact only on the shores of this continent. It is justified in Williams' terms by the necessity for keeping the state out of the affairs of the church, lest the church be subordinated to the state; in Jeffersonian terms its function is to keep the church out of the business of government, lest the government be subordinated to the church. Limited powers of government were not instituted to expand the realm of power of religious organizations, but rather in favor of freedom of action and thought by the people.

Nor were these two concepts closed systems at the time of the adoption of the first amendment. The objectives of the provisions were clear, but the means of their attainment were still to be developed and, indeed, are still in the course of development. Thus, like the other great clauses of the Constitution, the religion clauses cannot now be confined to the application they might have received in 1789.

The utilization or application of these clauses in conjunction is difficult. For if the command is that inhibitions not be placed by the state on religious activity, it is equally forbidden the state to confer favors upon religious activity. These commands would be impossible of effectuation unless they are read together as creating a doctrine more akin to the reading of the equal protection clause than to the due process clause, *i.e.*, they must be read to mean that religion may not be used as a basis for classification for purposes of governmental action, whether that action be the conferring of rights or privileges or the imposition of duties or obligations. Or, to put it in

From *Religion and the Law: Of Church and State and the Supreme Court* by Philip B. Kurland, pp. 16–18. Copyright © 1961, 1962 by Philip B. Kurland, all rights reserved. Originally published by Aldine Publishing Company, republished by University of Chicago Press, 1978. Reprinted by permission.

Lord Bryce's terms: "It is accepted as an axiom by all Americans that the civil power ought to be not only neutral and impartial as between different forms of faith, but ought to leave these matters entirely on one side. . . ." It must be recognized, however, that this statement of the "neutral" principle of equality, that religion cannot supply a basis for classification of governmental action, still leaves many problems unanswered. Not the least of them flows from the fact that the actions of the state must be carefully scrutinized to assure that classifications that purport to relate to other matters are not really classifications in terms of religion. "[C]lassification in abstract terms can always be carried to the point at which, in fact, the class singled out consists only of particular known persons or even a single individual. It must be admitted that, in spite of many ingenious attempts to solve this problem, no entirely satisfactory criterion has been found that would always tell us what kind of classification is compatible with equality before the law."

It is the genius of the common law, and thus of American constitutional law, that its growth and principles are measured in terms of concrete factual situations, or at least with regard to factual situations as concrete as the deficiencies of our adversary system permit them to be. It remains then to examine the cases that have arisen and the rationales offered in their solution and to see how the suggested thesis would resolve them. Before doing so, however, it might be desirable to repeat two propositions. First, the thesis proposed here as the proper construction of the religion cláuses of the first amendment is that the freedom and separation clauses should be read as a single precept that government cannot utilize religion as a standard for action or inaction because these clauses prohibit classification in terms of religion either to confer a benefit or to impose a burden. Second, the principle offered is meant to provide a starting point for solutions to problems brought before the Court, not a mechanical answer to them.

Mark de Wolfe Howe

16. THE CONSTITUTIONAL QUESTION

Professor Howe was a highly respected authority on legal questions.

As the first step towards an analysis of law it seems important that the principal questions of history with which the Court has been concerned should be identified.

The questions are two. The first concerns the interpretation of the religious clause of the First Amendment: "Congress shall make no law respecting an establishment of religion, or prohibiting the free exercise

thereof . . ." The second—and in many ways more important—concerns the effect that adoption of the Fourteenth Amendment had on the power of the states. The relevant provisions of that Amendment are these: "No State shall make or enforce any law which shall abridge the privileges or immunities of citizens of the United States; nor shall any State deprive any person of

Reprinted from *Religion in a Free Society*, Santa Barbara, California, 1958. This is a pamphlet sponsored by the Center for the Study of Democratic Institutions.

life, liberty, or property, without due process of law; nor deny to any person within its jurisdiction the equal protection of the laws."

When Mr. Justice Rutledge [in his *Everson* dissent] sought to discover the intention of those who were responsible for the writing and enactment of the First Amendment, he chose, as others before him had chosen, to treat the opinions of Jefferson and Madison, as they had been formulated in Virginia's earlier struggle to safeguard religious liberty, as of predominant, if not controlling, importance. It is not my purpose either to contest this or to question the interpretation which Justice Rutledge gave to the views of Jefferson and Madison. I am willing to proceed on the assumption that the two Virginians sought in their own state not only to safeguard the individual's conscience but to oppose even those governmental aids to religion which did not appreciably infringe or endanger any individual's liberty. I shall also discuss the problems concerning the interpretation of the First Amendment on the more dubious assumption that Madison—and with him the American people—intended through that Amendment to impose upon the national government exactly those prohibitions which had successfully been imposed upon the Commonwealth of Virginia.

Having made these assumptions it will be well, I think, to emphasize their implications. The First Amendment thus interpreted would serve two purposes. In the first place, it would protect the individual's conscience from every form of Congressional violation, whether by means of legislation with respect to an establishment of religion or by more direct methods. In the second place, it would impose a disability upon the national government to adopt laws with respect to establishments whether or not their consequence would be to infringe individual rights of conscience.

To find this second purpose in the First Amendment involves, necessarily I think, the admission that the Amendment is something more than a charter of individual liberties. In making that admission one is emphasizing a fact which has too frequently been overlooked—that the Bill of Rights as a whole, and the First Amendment in particular, reflect not only a philosophy of freedom but a theory of federalism. We often forget that the framers were as much concerned with safeguarding the powers of the states as they were with protecting the immunities of the people. Some barriers to national power found their justification in theories of jurisdiction rather than in concepts of personal freedom. Yet it has been a tendency of judges and statesmen alike to read the Bill of Rights as if its provisions had no other purpose than to protect the citizen against the nation. The tendency may be usefully indicated by a reminder of the decision of the Supreme Court in *Cantwell* v. *Connecticut*, the first case of our time in which the Court indicated how the religious clauses of the First Amendment should be interpreted.

By this interpretation the sole purpose of the religious provisions in the First Amendment was to secure the liberty of individuals against national invasion. This interpretation contains no suggestion that national aid to religion or national recognition of religious interests is objectionable when the immunities of individuals are not significantly affected. There is not, in other words, any indication that the Court saw the non-establishment clause as a self-denying ordinance deriving some of its force from a theory of federalism rather than a philosophy of individual rights. To the extent that the Court in its *Cantwell* decision thus disregarded the possibility that the clause might outlaw legislation which does not concern the individual conscience it did not accept the Rutledge interpretation of Madisonian theory. By that rejection or neglect it would seem that Justice Roberts overlooked the aspects of a philosophy of federalism embodied in the First Amendment and the Bill of Rights.

In what I have said so far I have been willing to proceed on the assumption that the Rutledge court was substantially accurate when it described the views of Jefferson the Virginian and Madison the American. A similar assumption is less easily made when one turns to the other historical question which had critical importance to the disposition of the *McCollum* case.

When we remember that the Court which decided the *Cantwell* case, and for which Mr. Justice Roberts was speaking, had before it a case arising not under the First but under the Fourteenth Amendment, its failure to emphasize the principles of federalism is not surprising. . . . A few scholars and individual Justices of the Supreme Court have contended that the framers of the Fourteenth Amendment intended that its adoption should transform all the specific limitations on federal power found in the Bill of Rights into rigid limitations on state authority. If that interpretation were accepted it would mean, of course, that after 1868 no state could make a law "respecting an establishment of religion, or prohibiting the free exercise thereof." The prohibition would be enforced not because of the peculiar sanctity of the interests secured in the First Amendment but by virtue of the fact that the Amendment is a part of the Bill of Rights.

A majority of the Court has never been willing to accept such a mechanistic and revolutionary interpretation of the Fourteenth Amendment. Instead the Court has taken the view that though some of the specific prohibitions of the Bill of Rights have become applicable to the states, there are others which the states are not compelled to respect. The generalities which the Court has used for the classification of rights have served to separate those "immunities [that are] implicit in the concept of ordered liberty" (which the states must respect) from those which "are not so rooted in the traditions and conscience of our people as to be ranked as fundamental."

It is not surprising that the Supreme Court, after a period of some uncertainty, came to accept the view that the First Amendment's specific guarantee of freedom of speech and press had been made binding on the states by the Fourteenth Amendment. When that principle was settled it was clear that the free exercise of religion must enjoy similar protection — and it was given that protection with energetic vigor. When Mr. Justice Roberts in the *Cantwell* case found in the religious clauses of the First Amendment security for two religious freedoms, the one of belief, the other of action, he found it natural to assume that each had been rendered secure against state action by the adoption of the Fourteenth Amendment. It would, of course, have been absurd to say that though earlier decisions interpreting the Fourteenth Amendment had made good against the states the *relative* freedom of religious action the Court would not protect the *absolute* freedom of religious belief from state infringement. Surely if a freedom which the Court has classified as "relative" is considered essential to a scheme of ordered liberty the other freedom which it has described as "absolute" deserves no lower classification.

Had the Court in the *Everson* and *McCollum* cases done no more than apply the rule of incorporation enunciated by Mr. Justice Roberts seven years previously, its action might have been beyond criticism. It is the something more that happened which troubles many. By its re-examination of the purposes of the First Amendment the Court imposed, perhaps quite properly, special limitations on the powers of the national government which, as I have said, gain their strength from concepts of federalism rather than from principles of individual liberty. Yet it then proceeded, without discussion, to make those special, non-libertarian limitations on the national government effective against the states as if they were essential to the scheme of ordered liberty prescribed by the due process clause of the Fourteenth Amendment. The Court did not seem to be aware of the fact that some legislative enactments respecting an establishment of religion affect most remotely, if at all, the personal rights of religious liberty.

The Supreme Court of the United States has not yet re-examined its own interpretations of history either as they relate to the original meaning of the First Amendment or as they apply to the incorporation of the non-establishment clause of the Fourteenth. I find it hard to believe that a re-examination of the first matter is of critical importance. I would suggest, however, that public and judicial attention may well be directed to the second issue. If that effort should be made it seems to me that we might find ourselves generally satisfied with the resolution which a respect for history might compel us to adopt. We might find ourselves allowing the states to take such action in aid of religion as does not appreciably affect the religious or other constitutional rights of individuals while condemning all state action which unreasonably restricts the exercise and enjoyment of other constitutional rights. . . .

There is much evidence to support the belief that the framers of the First Amendment believed religious liberty was more important than other substantive rights to which they gave constitutional protection. To make that admission does not, however, involve a concession that all of the current demands which fly the colors of religious liberty are entitled to preferential respect. In particular, I think, it does not mean that government is under any affirmative responsibility to facilitate the fulfillment of a man's obligations to God. Yet this, I take it,

has been the conclusion to which some of those who assert the priority of religious liberty would seek to carry us.

For two reasons I reject the conclusion. In the first place, it seems to me to violate a theory of government which was fundamental in the minds of the framers of the Constitution and which still plays an important and legitimate role in its administration. As I read the original document and its Bill of Rights it seems to me to expound a political theory which is grounded in the belief that liberty is the by-product of limitations on governmental power, not the objective of its existence.

One may fairly say that the conception that liberty becomes effective when the boundaries of governmental power are clearly defined reflects the naiveté of the eighteenth century. One must, however, acknowledge that the naiveté survived with such vigor that it not only defined in the nineteenth century the scope of the Fourteenth Amendment but in the twentieth has measured the significance of the Supreme Court's decision in the Segregation Cases. Just as the framers of the Bill of Rights thought that they had done enough when they protected certain rights from governmental infringement, so the draftsmen of the Fourteenth Amendment believed that they had secured the Negro's essential liberties when they restricted the powers of the states. In 1954 the Supreme Court went no further in its segregation decisions than to say that the states could not constitutionally compel segregation on racial grounds. The Court did not hold that the Fourteenth Amendment requires that Negro and white pupils be given an integrated education.

These distinctions are of profound importance. When they are forgotten we begin to use the word "rights" and the phrase "civil liberty" in misleading ways. Our rights, as the framers conceived them, were essentially certain specified immunities. They were not claims on, but assurances against, the government. In my judgment one of the greatest dangers in saying that some of our civil liberties are "natural rights" is that by the introduction of Nature or God into the discussion we seem to be asserting that an immunity against governmental interference has been transformed into an affirmative claim on government. When churchmen or others who believe that because religious liberty enjoys a preferential position the government is bound to take action that will make it effective, they ask us to abandon or overlook a central principle in the political theory of the Republic.

It may be urged that there is no reason why the twentieth century should feel itself compelled to respect an outmoded principle of eighteenth century political theory. We have learned from experience that rights considered as mere immunities are limp and inadequate. This realization has led our governments to act affirmatively in making racial equality, freedom of speech, and the dignity of man political realities. Why, therefore, it may be asked, should not the government give to persons who feel an obligation to fulfill their duties to God equivalent aids and supports?

The answer seems to me to lie in the stubborn fact that in so far as religion is concerned, the political theory of the eighteenth century is codified in the non-establishment clause of the First Amendment. Without a constitutional amendment we are not free to exclude its policies from our living tradition. When the framers of the First Amendment guaranteed religious liberty they accompanied that guarantee with specific prohibition against Congress' enacting any laws respecting an establishment of religion. At the very least that prohibition seems to me to have made the eighteenth century theory of liberty controlling in the area of religion. May it not fairly be argued that it was precisely because the framers granted a preferred status to religious liberty that they saw the need

to minimize the consequences of that preference by making the central thesis of their political theory articulate in the non-establishment clause? . . .

The theses that I have offered for consideration are three.

First, I have urged that in so far as national power is concerned we are compelled by our respect for the intention of the framers to read the non-establishment clause of the First Amendment as a barrier not only to federal action which infringes religious and other liberties of individuals but as a prohibition of even those federal aids to religion which do not appreciably affect individual liberties.

Second, I have urged that when the limitations of the Fourteenth Amendment were imposed upon the states they lost not only the power directly to deny the free exercise of religion but to give any aid to religion which would significantly affect the secured liberties of individuals. In considering this problem I suggested that there is no justification for setting as high a barrier against state governments as must be recognized against the nation.

Third, I have suggested that the claim that religious liberty, either against the state or against the nation, has a more favorable status than other constitutional liberties is no longer justified. The denial of that preferential status seems to me to be required not only by the political theory on which our governments were founded but to be required by the policy of non-establishment, both as that policy has set limits to the power of the nation and as it has confined the authority of the states.

An added word of caution seems suitable in conclusion. There has been some tendency to assume that the dimensions of all interests relating to religion are dependent upon interpretations which the Supreme Court may give to the religious clauses of the First Amendment. This assumption is today mistaken, for as liberties and rights beyond the reach of that Amendment have secured recognition, the powers of government, as they relate to the interests and influence of religion, have necessarily been affected. Those persons who may be fearful of the possible consequences flowing from my suggestion that the states should be permitted to give more aid to religion than the nation is allowed to provide, may find real comfort, I suggest, in the fact that the equal protection clause of the Fourteenth Amendment sets limits to state power which did not exist when the First Amendment was adopted and which, perhaps, were not envisioned when the Fourteenth Amendment itself became binding on the states. A parallel expansion of constitutional rights against the federal government has significantly reduced the importance of the religious clauses of the First Amendment below the level they occupied in 1789. If those who demand for religious liberty today the same preferential status it enjoyed when the nation was founded will admit that their favorite liberty has been the beneficiary of an expanding constitutionalism, they might also be willing to surrender their outpost of intransigence. From the beginning of time men have found it difficult to live with each other. Reasonable men, however, have found it less difficult than have the impassioned.

Paul G. Kauper

17. CHURCH AND STATE

These excerpts are from a chapter in a book entitled *Civil Liberties and the Constitution.*

The Relevant Constitutional Limitations

"Separation of church and state" is the symbolic language so often used as a beginning point of discussion. Actually, this precise language does not have much relevancy to the American scene. It is borrowed from European history and tradition where the problem could be identified in terms of a single church and of a single state or in later years of a single state and two churches, namely, Catholic and Protestant. To speak of separation of church and state in the United States invites some difficulty in the use of terms, first, because we have a plurality of states including the federal government and the individual states, and, secondly, because we have a plurality of church bodies. Perhaps it would be more illuminating to identify the subject in terms of the problems arising out of the interrelationship of religious and political forces in the community. The term "state" denotes the politically organized community with its monopoly of coercive power. The church, on the other hand, is a voluntary association which must depend on noncoercive religious motivation and persuasion in making its impact upon the individual and the community.

The problems we are concerned with have a substantial legal significance since both the Constitution of the United States and the constitutions of the several states

From Paul C. Kauper, *Civil Liberties and the Constitution* (Ann Arbor, 1962), pp. 6–10, 26–30. Reprinted by permission of University of Michigan Press.

include provisions that deal with the church-state problem. The First Amendment to the Constitution provides that Congress shall make no law respecting an establishment of religion or prohibiting the free exercise thereof. Many of our state constitutions have provisions more explicit than this and designed, in many cases, to make clear that public property and public money shall not be used for religious or sectarian purposes or in aid of sectarian education. Moreover, the Supreme Court of the United States has said that the provisions of the First Amendment are made applicable to the states through the Fourteenth Amendment's Due Process Clause, so that as a matter of federal constitutional restriction, and in addition to or apart from the limitations imposed by its own constitution, each state must observe the limitation that it can make no law respecting an establishment of religion or prohibiting the free exercise thereof.

In any discussion of the constitutional aspects of church-state relations, it will be useful at the outset to turn to general ideas developed by the Supreme Court in the interpretation of the First Amendment in order to appreciate the legal questions underlying current developments. The emphasis will necessarily be upon the First Amendment, both for the reason that some of the most significant current questions have to do with the limitations on the federal government and for the further reason, as already mentioned, that the Supreme Court has said that this limitation is made applicable to the states through the Fourteenth Amendment. Indeed, we here have the curious situation that in order to find the meaning of the First Amendment as a restriction on Congress, we must look to recent decisions of the Court construing the Fourteenth Amendment, since in determining the limitations on the states under the Due Process Clause of the Fourteenth Amendment the Court has used the First Amendment as a controlling standard.

The First Amendment says nothing explicitly about separation of church and state. This term is not used in the federal constitution and, indeed, it is not used in American constitutions generally. This phrase is useful as a shorthand term for conveying a set of related ideas, but it is not a legal term, and certainly not a definitive constitutional term. What the First Amendment does say is that Congress shall make no law respecting an establishment of religion or prohibiting the free exercise thereof. Two different although related ideas are expressed in this opening clause of the First Amendment. Congress shall make no law respecting an establishment of religion, and Congress shall make no law prohibiting the free exercise of religion. Ordinarily, when people think of religious freedom they are thinking of the kind of freedom protected by this second part of the opening language of the First Amendment, namely, that Congress shall make no law prohibiting the free exercise of religion. Freedom to exercise one's religion is, indeed, a fundamental right protected under the Constitution. It embraces freedom of worship, freedom in the organization of religious associations, freedom in the propagation of the faith, freedom in the distribution of religious literature, freedom in the enjoyment of public facilities dedicated to the dissemination and propagation of ideas, freedom from discrimination on religious grounds in the enjoyment of rights and privileges. This encompasses a wide field.

The question may be raised whether the enjoyment of these freedoms is dependent on the separation of church and state. If, for instance, there is an established church, as in England, is this incompatible with the free exercise of religion? Some would say not and point to England as an example. The Anglican church is the established Church of England. But is there not complete freedom of religion in England? All nonconformist and dissenting religious groups are free to pursue their own ways.

219

No one's faith is coerced. This is not quite the case. The clergy and members of the Church of England are really not free to exercise their own religion since control of the Church is technically in the hands of Parliament. No established church subject to governmental control or dependent upon governmental support is really completely free. Moreover, members of independent churches are not completely free to propagandize their beliefs in the market place of ideas if they are competing with a religion enjoying a preferred status established and supported by law. Non-establishment as a rule requiring neutrality as between religions is then an important facet of the central concept of religious freedom. On the other hand, if nonestablishment means that government must be completely indifferent to religion and that it can do nothing which aids religion in any way, even though not preferential or discriminatory, the relationship of nonestablishment to the free exercise of religion becomes a more complicated matter. If the government without dictating or coercing belief on anyone's part recognizes the place of religion in the life of the community, and, without preferring one or more religious groups, accommodates its program and the use of its facilities to religious needs and supports activities in which the government and the churches have a concurrent interest and common concern, religious freedom is not placed in jeopardy. On the contrary, it may be argued that the government is thereby contributing to religious freedom and making it more meaningful. Some situations may arise when a choice must even be made between the nonestablishment principle as broadly conceived and the principle that the government may not discriminate on religious grounds.

It is evident then that the critical problems in respect to the separation of church and state turn on the interpretation given to the first phase of the opening clause of the First Amendment, namely, that Congress and, as interpreted, the states shall make no law respecting an establishment of religion.

As previously noted, the Constitution does not employ the term "separation of church and state," much less the terms "wall of separation" or "complete and permanent separation of church and state." These are all phrases that have been coined outside the constitutional language. The Supreme Court has said that the twin phrases of the First Amendment, proscribing laws respecting an establishment of religion or prohibiting the free exercise thereof, combine to require a separation of church and state.

Critique of the Separation Principle

In the light of these expressions of opinion and the holdings by the Court, what can be said about the meaning of nonestablishment and what is its relevancy to today's most urgent problems in this area?

In any critical examination of this general problem of church-state relations and more particularly of the nonestablishment limitation, it is useful to start with the elementary idea that the state and the church serve basically different functions and objectives. It is the state's business to operate the politically organized society and serve the community's civil needs. The business of the church is to minister to man's spiritual needs and to carry on activities appropriate to a sense of religious concern. It is not the business of the state to operate a church or to engage in the propagation of religious ideas. On the other hand, it is not the function of the churches to exercise the coercive authority of the politically organized community. This separation of function has its roots not simply in some theoretical conception of a convenient division of labor but is grounded more profoundly on the theory that the cause of human freedom is best served when religion and its institutions are grounded in voluntarism and not dependent upon political force.

The really important questions we face today, however, do not arise from any threat of formal confusion of functions or any attempt at formal institutional blending of the separate functions of the church and state. Rather they have to do with the practical problems of interrelationship involving questions of the recognition of the function of each and of the contribution that each makes to the total scheme of things.

Even though a separateness of function is recognized in regard to the primary purposes of politically organized society and religious institutions, it is clear that this abstract idea must be given practical meaning in the context of a social community where both the secular and religious societies draw on the same human resources. This is what introduces the perplexing aspects of our problem. We may speak of a duality of citizenship—an allegiance to both the secular and the spiritual realms. Or, in Luther's terms, we have the two kingdoms: the kingdom of the sword and the kingdom of the spirit. Yet they must necessarily operate within the same community. From this it follows that each must respect the other, and, indeed, each is dependent upon the other.

The state has a complete monopoly of coercive power with the result that the church is necessarily dependent upon the state for the maintenance of the elementary conditions of peace and order essential to the enjoyment of religious freedom and to the discharge of the church's functions, whether it be the maintenance of a house of worship, propagation of the faith, teaching the young, or ministering to the sick and needy. It is an idea well accepted in Christian theology and doctrine that the state itself occupies an important role in God's created order and that its primary function in punishing the wrongdoer and preserving the peace of the community is to make possible the conditions that will advance the kingdom of the spirit. The church as the community of believers, therefore, respects the state and looks to the state for protection of the peace of the community, for protection of its property, and for enjoyment of the public services rendered by the state. Already at this point it becomes evident that there is an interdependence which is not accurately portrayed by the wall of separation metaphor. The church is dependent upon the state in a very real way in order to maintain its functions. For this reason the church deems it appropriate that its members support the state, pay taxes, vote, and serve as magistrates and civil servants despite the radical views of a small group within the Christian communion who, in order to carry separation to a maximum, have divorced themselves from the political life of the community. It is appropriately the function of the state to provide police and fire protection and to give churches the benefit of the same services provided to other organizations and to individuals whether it be in the furnishing of utility service or whatever service the politically organized community renders. Obviously, the state in giving the religious community the benefit of these services is extending aid to religion in a very real sense. To suggest that this is distinguishable because this is not aid to religion as such is simply to use words to avoid the critical problem. When government makes its facilities available to protect organized religious groups and to make possible the system in which religion can flourish, it is giving the most important aid that a state can give to any group with respect to the performance of its functions. It is aid to religion but not the kind of aid forbidden by the Constitution. It is a benefit shared by the church with all the community, and the state in extending this benefit is not thereby using its power to promote or sanction religious belief.

As the church is dependent on the state and depends for its effective functioning and even survival on valuable services furnished by the state, so, in turn, the politically organized community expects to be served by the religious community. The tradition developed in English legal history that the Chancellor was the keeper of the King's conscience. This term epitomized the idea that the King counted on conceptions of equity developed by this ecclesiastical officer to liberalize the Common Law and to infuse it with moral conceptions of a basic religious orientation. This is simply another manifestation of the idea that the churches in the discharge of their separate functions — cultivating the spiritual lives of their parishioners and developing moral and ethical ideas founded on religious insight and motivation — make an important contribution to the politically organized community. The state in formulating policy and in fashioning the law must depend upon the moral sense and values of the community. It makes little difference whether we recognize the church's contribution to the legal order and to the conception of public policy in terms of a body of moral or natural law which serves as a guide or norm for the framing of positive law, or identify this contribution to the civic order both through the impact of religiously motivated citizens and public officers and the discharge by the church of a prophetic function in speaking of matters of public concern. In regard to such matters as disarmament, the use of nuclear weapons as war weapons, birth control, distribution of surplus foods to needy peoples, immigration policy, aid to education, aid for the aged, the churches do have a real, vital interest. These are matters of both religious and civic concern.

There are some who suggest that separation of church and state means that religion and politics must be kept separate. If by this is meant that the church, in deference to the separation idea, may minister only to the spiritual needs of its members and not exercise a prophetic function in speaking to the problems of our day, then we have a gross misconception of the separation principle. Indeed, a higher principle arises here in terms of religious freedom on the part of any person or group to express ideas that have religious significance and which are relevant also to current social, economic, and political problems. Criticism is often made of the Roman Catholic Church that it attempts to influence legislative policy in such matters, for instance, as birth control, sterilization, euthanasia, and obscenity in literature and the movies. On this matter it should be clear, first of all, that insofar as this is a separation problem it is not a constitutional problem, since it is part of the freedom of churches to propagandize and to use their efforts to influence legislative policy. The Constitution does prohibit giving to any church a formal place in the legislative process. But it does not prohibit the churches or their members from giving their opinions on matters of political concern or speaking in support of legislative proposals. This, indeed, is part of their function as religious bodies. The idea that a man's religion is irrelevant to his conduct as a citizen or as a public officer states a low view of religion and a sterile concept of the place of religion in influencing a man's conduct, attitudes, and motivations.

VII. *Dimensions of Inclusive Pluralism (1960-   )*

In the 1960's any lingering sense of Protestant hegemony gave way to recognition of pluralism as the American cultural reality. This pluralism extended well beyond the Protestant-Catholic-Jewish mainstream, giving considerable support to the rights of both nonbelievers and adherents of new or uncommon faiths. Thus, as the nation approached its bicentennial celebration, it appeared for the first time to be manifestly plural in religion and genuinely secular in government. Yet, just as this process seemed complete, religious and political groups seeking to reunite God and Country returned to the political arena with renewed vigor, challenging the movement toward religious pluralism and secular government as the creation of a godless nation.

These issues of cultural transformation have been shaped, in large part, by the resolution of Church-State issues in a variety of forums. For example, during the 1960'o, 1970's and 1980's, these has been a virtual explosion of judicial activity in the realm of Church-State affairs. During this period, many Americans have looked to the Supreme Court as the final arbiter of the American Church-State question. And so, a series of lawsuits, typically concerned with whether a particular state program contravened the establishment clause of the First Amendment, began to wind their way through the federal courts. Thus, the establishment clause that lay virtually dormant for its first 150 years has become a regular source of litigation in recent decades.

The tremors created by the Supreme Court's establishment clause decisions have been felt in the political arena. When the Court's opinions have challenged widespread beliefs, many people have turned to political action to restore the "American values" (or, perhaps, the republican Protestant values) they perceive as threatened or lost. For example, upon the Supreme Court's decision to strike down public school-sponsored prayer and Bible reading, the governors of all but one state called for a constitutional amendment to return prayer to the classroom. On the other hand, those opposed to official recognition of any consensus religiosity continue to fight to sever any remaining ties between Church and State.

Thus, although the Supreme Court may be the final arbiter of the Constitution's meaning, it will not always have the last word on Church-State questions. For over a century, legislators have periodically proposed a constitutional amendment acknowledging the sovereignty of Christ. And most recently, substantial political support has been mustered behind the amendment sponsored by President Reagan to legalize school-sponsored prayers.

The 1980's have also seen a resurgence of popular interest in the role of religion

223

in politics. The Church-State question figured prominently in the 1984 Reagan-Mondale presidential race, and a variety of religious groups leaped into the fray with theological pronouncements on political events ranging from abortion to the nuclear arms race. Thus, both the courtroom and the voting booth have provided forums for resolution of the contemporary Church-State question.

Additionally, scholars of religion have begun to inquire more deeply into the role played by religion in American culture. These studies, many of which were stimulated by Robert Bellah's celebrated article, "Civil Religion in America," show the manifold ways in which religion may be indelibly stamped upon the American character, and hence its political structures, no matter how much Church is formally and constitutionally separated from State. Whether there is a separate and distinct "civil religion" existing alongside the churches is debatable, and the debates over its existence may themselves be part of the effort to ensure that traditional values are not completely eradicated from American culture despite the upheavals of the recent decades. In any event, a vast number of Americans continue to see themselves as citizens of "one Nation under God." So long as this religious underpinning remains a part of our culture, the Church-State question will remain a challenge for scholars, judges, politicians, and, ultimately, the American people.

The following materials are organized into three levels of interaction between religion and government—institutional, social and cultural. The narrowest category is institutional interaction in which specific agencies of government, such as the Internal Revenue Service, deal with particular religious organizations. In other words, an organization representing the temporal authority structure is intersecting with an organization representing one branch of the spiritual authority structure. The second level of interaction, at the social level, involves the relationship of governmental institutions and religious activity. The best example of this is non-denominational prayers in public schools. Finally, the interaction is broadest at the cultural level. For many generations, the American dream has had religious connotations for a vast number of our citizens. This teleological link between America and the Kingdom of God can be heard in the rhetoric of virtually every president from George Washington to Ronald Reagan, and it shapes, in a fundamental way, the relationship of many Americans to their religions and their governments. In considering the relationship of Church and State in American history, especially in this most recent period, it is useful to view these three levels of interaction as they become increasingly broad and complex—from the basic institutional level to the broader social and ultimately to the even broader and more complex cultural level. In this period, however, we have chosen to begin with the level of social interaction since the Supreme Court's school prayer decisions have in many ways set the stage for the contemporary approach to the relationship of Church and State.

Religion in the Public Schools

1. ENGEL v. VITALE

The so-called Regents Prayer Case, when joined to the ruling that followed concerning Bible reading, meant that the neutrality required by the religion clauses of the First Amendment would no longer be satisfied by "non-denominational" Judeo-Christian exercises, at least in the public schools.

Mr. JUSTICE BLACK DELIVERED THE OPINION OF THE COURT.

The respondent Board of Education of Union Free School District No. 9, New Hyde Park, New York, acting in its official capacity under state law, directed the School District's principal to cause the following prayer to be said aloud by each class in the presence of a teacher at the beginning of each school day:

Almighty God, we acknowledge our dependence upon Thee, and we beg Thy blessings upon us, our parents, our teachers and our Country.

This daily procedure was adopted on the recommendation of the State Board of Regents, a governmental agency created by the State Constitution to which the New York Legislature has granted broad supervisory, executive, and legislative powers over the State's public school system. These state officials composed the prayer which they recommended and published as a part of their "Statement on Moral and Spiritual Training in the Schools," saying: "We believe that this Statement will be subscribed to by all men and women of good will, and we call upon all of them to aid in giving life to our program."

Shortly after the practice of reciting the Regents' prayer was adopted by the School District, the parents of ten pupils brought this action in a New York State Court insisting that use of this official prayer in the public schools was contrary to the beliefs, religions, or religious practices of both themselves and their children. Among other things, these parents challenged the constitutionality of both the state law authorizing the School District to direct the use of prayer in public schools and the School District's regulation ordering the recitation of this particular prayer on the ground that these actions of official governmental agencies violate that part of the First Amendment of the Federal Constitution which commands that "Congress shall make no law respecting an establishment of religion"—a command which was "made applicable to the State of New York by the Fourteenth Amendment of the said Constitution." . . .

We think that by using its public school system to encourage recitation of the Regents' prayer, the State of New York has adopted a practice wholly inconsistent with the Establishment Clause. There can, of course, be no doubt that New York's program of daily classroom invocation of God's blessings as prescribed in the Regents' prayer is a religious activity. It is a solemn avowal of divine faith and supplication for the blessings of the Almighty. The nature of such a prayer has always been religious, none of the respondents has denied this and the trial court expressly so found:

370 U.S. 421 (1962).

The religious nature of prayer was recognized by Jefferson and has been concurred in by theological writers, the United States Supreme Court and State courts and administrative officials, including New York's Commissioner of Education. A committee of the New York Legislature has agreed.

The Board of Regents as amicus curiae, the respondents and intervenors all concede the religious nature of prayer, but seek to distinguish this prayer because it is based on our spiritual heritage. . . .

The petitioners contend among other things that the state laws requiring or permitting use of the Regents' prayer must be struck down as a violation of the Establishment Clause because that prayer was composed by governmental officials as a part of a governmental program to further religious beliefs. For this reason, petitioners argue, the State's use of the Regents' prayer in its public school system breaches the constitutional wall of separation between Church and State. We agree with that contention since we think that the constitutional prohibition against laws respecting an establishment of religion must at least mean that in this country it is no part of the business of government to compose official prayers for any group of the American people to recite as a part of a religious program carried on by government.

It is a matter of history that this very practice of establishing governmentally composed prayers for religious services was one of the reasons which caused many of our early colonists to leave England and seek religious freedom in America. . . .

It is an unfortunate fact of history that when some of the very groups which had most strenuously opposed the established Church of England found themselves sufficiently in control of colonial governments in this country to write their own prayers into law, they passed laws making their own religion the official religion of their respective colonies. Indeed, as late as the time of the Revolutionary War, there were established

churches in at least eight of the thirteen former colonies and established religions in at least four of the other five. But the successful Revolution against English political domination was shortly followed by intense opposition to the practice of establishing religion by law. This opposition crystallized rapidly into an effective political force in Virginia where the minority religious groups such as Presbyterians, Lutherans, Quakers and Baptists had gained such strength that the adherents to the established Episcopal Church were actually a minority themselves. In 1785–1786, those opposed to the established Church, led by James Madison and Thomas Jefferson, who, though themselves not members of any of those dissenting religious groups, opposed all religious establishments by law on grounds of principle, obtained the enactment of the famous "Virginia Bill for Religious Liberty" by which all religious groups were placed on an equal footing so far as the State was concerned. Similar though less far-reaching legislation was being considered and passed in other States.

By the time of the adoption of the Constitution, our history shows that there was a widespread awareness among many Americans of the dangers of a union of Church and State. These people knew, some of them from bitter personal experience, that one of the greatest dangers to the freedom of the individual to worship in his own way lay in the Government's placing its official stamp of approval upon one particular kind of prayer or one particular form of religious services. They knew the anguish, hardship and bitter strife that could come when zealous religious groups struggled with one another to obtain the Government's stamp of approval from each King, Queen, or Protector that came to temporary power. The Constitution was intended to avert a part of this danger by leaving the government of this country in the hands of the people rather than in the hands of any monarch. But this safeguard was not enough. Our Founders were no more willing to let the content of their prayers and their privilege of praying whenever they pleased be influenced by the ballot box than they were to let these vital matters of personal conscience depend upon the succession of monarchs. The First Amendment was added to the Constitution to stand as a guarantee that neither the power nor the prestige of the Federal Government would be used to control, support or influence the kinds of prayer the American people can say—that the people's religions must not be subjected to the pressures of government for change each time a new political administration is elected to office. Under that Amendment's prohibition against governmental establishment of religion, as reinforced by the provisions of the Fourteenth Amendment, government in this country, be it state or federal, is without power to prescribe by law any particular form of prayer which is to be used as an official prayer in carrying on any program of governmentally sponsored religious activity.

There can be no doubt that New York's state prayer program officially establishes the religious beliefs embodied in the Regents' prayer. The respondents' argument to the contrary, which is largely based upon the contention that the Regents' prayer is "nondenominational" and the fact that the program, as modified and approved by state courts, does not require all pupils to recite the prayer but permits those who wish to do so to remain silent or be excused from the room, ignores the essential nature of the program's constitutional defects. Neither the fact that the prayer may be denominationally neutral nor the fact that its observance on the part of the students is voluntary can serve to free it from the limitations of the Establishment Clause, as it might from the Free Exercise Clause, of the First Amendment, both of which are operative against the States by virtue of the Fourteenth Amendment. Although these two clauses may in certain instances overlap, they forbid two quite different kinds of governmental

encroachment upon religious freedom. The Establishment Clause, unlike the Free Exercise Clause, does not depend upon any showing of direct governmental compulsion and is violated by the enactment of laws which establish an official religion whether those laws operate directly to coerce nonobserving individuals or not. This is not to say, of course, that laws officially prescribing a particular form of religious worship do not involve coercion of such individuals. When the power, prestige and financial support of government is placed behind a particular religious belief, the indirect coercive pressure upon religious minorities to conform to the prevailing officially approved religion is plain. But the purposes underlying the Establishment Clause go much further than that. Its first and most immediate purpose rested on the belief that a union of government and religion tends to destroy government and to degrade religion. The history of governmentally established religion, both in England and in this country, showed that whenever government had allied itself with one particular form of religion, the inevitable result had been that it had incurred the hatred, disrespect and even contempt of those who held contrary beliefs. That same history showed that many people had lost their respect for any religion that had relied upon the support of government to spread its faith. The Establishment Clause thus stands as an expression of principle on the part of the Founders of our Constitution that religion is too personal, too sacred, too holy, to permit its "unhallowed perversion" by a civil magistrate. Another purpose of the Establishment Clause rested upon an awareness of the historical fact that governmentally established religions and religious persecutions go hand in hand. . . . It was in large part to get completely away from . . . systematic religious persecution that the Founders brought into being our Nation, our Constitution, and our Bill of Rights with its prohibition against any governmental establishment of religion. The New York laws officially prescribing the Regents' prayer are inconsistent both with the purposes of the Establishment Clause and with the Establishment Clause itself.

It has been argued that to apply the Constitution in such a way as to prohibit state laws respecting an establishment of religious services in public schools is to indicate a hostility toward religion or toward prayer. Nothing, of course, could be more wrong. The history of man is inseparable from the history of religion. And perhaps it is not too much to say that since the beginning of that history many people have devoutly believed that "More things are wrought by prayer than this world dreams of." It was doubtless largely due to men who believed this that there grew up a sentiment that caused men to leave the cross-currents of officially established state religions and religious persecution in Europe and come to this country filled with the hope that they could find a place in which they could pray when they pleased to the God of their faith in the language they chose. And there were men of this same faith in the power of prayer who led the fight for adoption of our Constitution and also for our Bill of Rights with the very guarantees of religious freedom that forbid the sort of governmental activity which New York has attempted here. These men knew that the First Amendment, which tried to put an end to governmental control of religion and of prayer, was not written to destroy either. They knew rather that it was written to quiet well-justified fears which nearly all of them felt arising out of an awareness that governments of the past had shackled men's tongues to make them speak only the religious thoughts that government wanted them to speak and to pray only to the God that government wanted them to pray to. It is neither sacrilegious nor antireligious to say that each separate government in this country should stay out of the business of writing or sanctioning official prayers and leave that purely religious function to the people themselves and to those the people choose to look to for religious guidance.

It is true that New York's establishment of its Regents' prayer as an officially approved religious doctrine of that State does not amount to a total establishment of one particular religious sect to the exclusion of all others—that, indeed, the governmental endorsement of that prayer seems relatively insignificant when compared to the governmental encroachments upon religion which were commonplace 200 years ago. To those who may subscribe to the view that because the Regents' official prayer is so brief and general there can be no danger to religious freedom in its governmental establishment, however, it may be appropriate to say in the words of James Madison, the author of the First Amendment:

[I]t is proper to take alarm at the first experiment on our liberties. . . . Who does not see that the same authority which can establish Christianity, in exclusion of all other Religions, may establish with the same ease any particular sect of Christians, in exclusion of all other Sects? That the same authority which can force a citizen to contribute three pence only of his property for the support of any one establishment, may force him to conform to any other establishment in all cases whatsoever?

MR. JUSTICE STEWART, DISSENTING.

A local school board in New York has provided that those pupils who wish to do so may join in a brief prayer at the beginning of each school day, acknowledging their dependence upon God and asking His blessing upon them and upon their parents, their teachers, and their country. The court today decides that in permitting this brief nondenominational prayer the school board has violated the Constitution of the United States. I think this decision is wrong. . . .

With all respect, I think the Court has misapplied a great constitutional principle. I cannot see how an "official religion" is established by letting those who want to say a prayer say it. On the contrary, I think that to deny the wish of these school children to join in reciting this prayer is to deny them the opportunity of sharing in the spiritual heritage of our Nation. . . . We deal here not with the establishment of a state church, which would, of course, be constitutionally impermissible, but with whether school children who want to begin their day by joining in prayer must be prohibited from doing so. Moreover, I think that the Court's task, in this as in all areas of constitutional adjudication, is not responsibly aided by the uncritical invocation of metaphors like the "wall of separation," a phrase nowhere to be found in the Constitution. What is relevant to the issue here is . . . the history of the religious traditions of our people, reflected in countless practices of the institutions and officials of our government.

At the opening of each day's Session of this Court we stand, while one of our officials invokes the protection of God. Since the days of John Marshall our Crier has said, "God save the United States and this Honorable Court." Both the Senate and the House of Representatives open their daily Sessions with prayer. Each of our Presidents, from George Washington to John F. Kennedy, has upon assuming his office asked the protection and help of God.

The Court today says that the state and federal governments are without constitutional power to prescribe any particular form of words to be recited by any group of the American people on any subject touching religion. One of the stanzas of "The Star-Spangled Banner," made our National Anthem by Act of Congress in 1931, contains these verses:

Blest with victory and peace, may the heav'n rescued land
Praise the Pow'r that hath made and preserved us a nation!
Then conquer we must, when our cause it is just,
And this be our motto "In God is our Trust."

In 1954 Congress added a phrase to the Pledge of Allegiance to the Flag so that it now contains the words "one Nation *under God* indivisible, with liberty and justice for all." In 1952 Congress enacted legislation calling upon the President each year to proclaim a National Day of Prayer. Since 1865 the words "IN GOD WE TRUST" have been impressed on our coins.

Countless similar examples could be listed, but there is no need to belabor the obvious. It was all summed up by this Court just ten years ago in a single sentence: "We are a religious people whose institutions presuppose a Supreme Being."

I do not believe that this Court, or the Congress, or the President has by the actions and practices I have mentioned established an "official religion" in violation of the Constitution. And I do not believe the State of New York has done so in this case. What each has done has been to recognize and to follow the deeply entrenched and highly cherished spiritual traditions of our Nation—traditions which come down to us from those who almost two hundred years ago avowed their "firm Reliance on the Protection of divine Providence" when they proclaimed the freedom and independence of this brave new world.

I dissent.

229

2. SCHOOL DISTRICT OF ABINGTON TOWNSHIP v. SCHEMPP

The question of daily Bible readings as a part of opening school exercises finally reached the Supreme Court in a case which was argued during February of 1963 and decided on June 17th. Excerpts follow.

MR. JUSTICE CLARK DELIVERED
THE OPINION OF THE COURT.

Once again we are called upon to consider the scope of the provision of the First Amendment to the United States Constitution which declares that "Congress shall make no law respecting an establishment of religion, or prohibiting the free exercise thereof . . . ." These companion cases present the issues in the context of state action requiring that schools begin each day with readings from the Bible. While raising the basic questions under slightly different factual situations, the cases permit of joint treatment. In light of the history of the First Amendment and of our cases interpreting and applying its requirements, we hold that the practices at issue and the laws requiring them are unconstitutional under the Establishment Clause, as applied to the States through the Fourteenth Amendment.

* * *

It is true that religion has been closely identified with our history and government. As we said in *Engel* v. *Vitale*, "The history of man is inseparable from the history of religion. And . . . since the beginning of that history many people have devoutly believed that 'More things are wrought by prayer than this world dreams of.'" In *Zorach* V. *Clauson* we gave specific recognition to the proposition that "[w]e are a religious people whose institutions pre-suppose a Supreme Being." . . .

This is not to say, however, that religion has been so identified with our history and government that religious freedom is not likewise as strongly imbedded in our public and private life. Nothing but the most telling of personal experiences in religious persecution suffered by our forebears . . . could have planted our belief in liberty of religious opinion any more deeply in our heritage. . . .

Almost a hundred years ago in *Minor* v. *Board of Education of Cincinnati*, Judge Alphonso Taft, father of the revered Chief Justice, in an unpublished opinion stated the ideal of our people as to religious freedom as one of

absolute equality before the law, of all religious opinions and sects. . . .
The government is neutral, and, while protecting all, it prefers none, and it *disparages* none.

Before examining this "neutral" position in which the Establishment and Free Exercise Clauses of the First Amendment place our Government it is well that we discuss the reach of the Amendment under the cases of this Court.

First, this Court has decisively settled that the First Amendment's mandate that "Congress shall make no law respecting an establishment of religion, or prohibiting the free exercise thereof" has been made wholly applicable to the States by the Fourteenth Amendment. . . . In a series of cases since *Cantwell* the Court has repeatedly reaffirmed that doctrine, and we do so now.

Second, this Court has rejected unequivocally the contention that the Establishment Clause forbids only governmental preference of one religion over another. Al-

374 U. S. 203 (1963).

most 20 years ago in *Everson* the Court said that "[n]either a state nor the Federal Government can set up a church. Neither can pass laws which aid one religion, aid all religions, or prefer one religion over another." . . .

While none of the parties to either of these cases has questioned these basic conclusions of the Court, both of which have been long established, recognized and consistently reaffirmed, others continue to question their history, logic and efficacy. Such contentions, in the light of the consistent interpretation in cases of this Court, seem entirely untenable and of value only as academic exercises.

The interrelationship of the Establishment and the Free Exercise Clauses was first touched upon by Mr. Justice Roberts for the Court in *Cantwell* v. *Connecticut* where it was said that their "inhibition of legislation" had

a double aspect. On the one hand, it forestalls compulsion by law of the acceptance of any creed or the practice of any form of worship. Freedom of conscience and freedom to adhere to such religious organization or form of worship as the individual may choose cannot be restricted by law. On the other hand, it safeguards the free exercise of the chosen form of religion. Thus the Amendment embraces two concepts,—freedom to believe and freedom to act. The first is absolute but, in the nature of things, the second cannot be.

Finally, in *Engel* v. *Vitale*, only last year, these principles were so universally recognized that the Court, without the citation of a single case and over the sole dissent of Mr. Justice Stewart, reaffirmed them. The Court found the 22-word prayer used in "New York's program of daily classroom invocation of God's blessings as prescribed in the Regents' prayer . . . [to be] a religious activity." It held that "it is no part of the business of government to compose official prayers for any group of the American people to recite as a part of a religious program carried on by government." In discussing the reach of the Establishment and Free Exercise Clauses of the First Amendment the Court said:

Although these two clauses may in certain instances overlap, they forbid two quite different kinds of governmental encroachment upon religious freedom. The Establishment Clause, unlike the Free Exercise Clause, does not depend upon any showing of direct governmental compulsion and is violated by the enactment of laws which establish an official religion whether those laws operate directly to coerce nonobserving individuals or not. This is not to say, of course, that laws officially prescribing a particular form of religious worship do not involve coercion of such individuals. When the power, prestige and financial support of government is placed behind a particular religious belief, the indirect coercive pressure upon religious minorities to conform to the prevailing officially approved religion is plain.

And in further elaboration the Court found that the "first and most immediate purpose [of the Establishment Clause] rested on the belief that a union of government and religion tends to destroy government and to degrade religion." When government, the Court said, allies itself with one particular form of religion, the inevitable result is that it incurs "the hatred, disrespect and even contempt of those who held contrary beliefs."

The wholesome "neutrality" of which this Court's cases speak thus stems from a recognition of the teachings of history that powerful sects or groups might bring about a fusion of governmental and religious functions or a concert or dependency of one upon the other to the end that official support of the State or Federal Government would be placed behind the tenets of one or of all orthodoxies. This the Establishment Clause prohibits. And a further reason for neutrality is found in the Free Exercise Clause, which recognizes the value of religious training, teaching and observance and, more particularly, the right of every person to freely choose his own course with reference thereto, free of any

231

compulsion from the state. This the Free Exercise Clause guarantees. Thus, as we have seen, the two clauses may overlap. As we have indicated, the Establishment Clause has been directly considered by this Court eight times in the past score of years and, with only one Justice dissenting on the point, it has consistently held that the clause withdrew all legislative power respecting religious belief or the expression thereof. The test may be stated as follows: what are the purpose and the primary effect of the enactment? If either is the advancement or inhibition of religion then the enactment exceeds the scope of legislative power as circumscribed by the Constitution. That is to say that to withstand the strictures of the Establishment Clause there must be a secular legislative purpose and a primary effect that neither advances nor inhibits religion. The Free Exercise Clause, likewise considered many times here, withdraws from legislative power, state and federal, the exertion of any restraint on the free exercise of religion. Its purpose is to secure religious liberty in the individual by prohibiting any invasions thereof by civil authority. Hence it is necessary in a free exercise case for one to show the coercive effect of the enactment as it operates against him in the practice of his religion. The distinction between the two clauses is apparent — a violation of the Free Exercise Clause is predicated on coercion while the Establishment Clause violation need not be so attended.

Applying the Establishment Clause principles to the cases at bar we find that the States are requiring the selection and reading at the opening of the school day of verses from the Holy Bible and the recitation of the Lord's Prayer by the students in unison. These exercises are prescribed as part of the curricular activities of students who are required by law to attend school. They are held in the school buildings under the supervision and with the participation of teachers employed in those schools.

None of these factors, other than compulsory school attendance, was present in the program upheld in *Zorach* v. *Clauson.* The trial court in No. 142 has found that such an opening exercise is a religious ceremony and was intended by the State to be so. We agree with the trial court's finding as to the religious character of the exercises. Given that finding, the exercises and the law requiring them are in violation of the Establishment Clause.

There is no such specific finding as to the religious character of the exercises in No. 119, and the State contends (as does the State in No. 142) that the program is an effort to extend its benefits to all public school children without regard to their religious belief. Included within its secular purposes, it says, are the promotion of moral values, the contradiction to the materialistic trends of our times, the perpetuation of our institutions and the teaching of literature. The case came up on demurrer, of course, to a petition which alleged that the uniform practice under the rule had been to read from the King James version of the Bible and that the exercise was sectarian. The short answer, therefore, is that the religious character of the exercise was admitted by the State. But even if its purpose is not strictly religious, it is sought to be accomplished through readings, without comment, from the Bible. Surely the place of the Bible as an instrument of religion cannot be gainsaid, and the State's recognition of the pervading religious character of the ceremony is evident from the rule's specific permission of the alternative use of the Catholic Douay version as well as the recent amendment permitting nonattendance at the exercises. None of these factors is consistent with the contention that the Bible is here used either as an instrument for nonreligious moral inspiration or as a reference for the teaching of secular subjects.

The conclusion follows that in both cases the laws require religious exercises and such exercises are being conducted in direct violation of the rights of the appellees and petitioners. Nor are these required exercises mitigated by the fact that individual students may absent themselves upon parental request, for that fact furnishes no defense to a claim of unconstitutionality under the Establishment Clause. See *Engel v. Vitale.* Further, it is no defense to urge that the religious practices here may be relatively minor encroachments on the First Amendment. . . .

It is insisted that unless these religious exercises are permitted a "religion of secularism" is established in the schools. We agree of course that the State may not establish a "religion of secularism" in the sense of affirmatively opposing or showing hostility to religion, thus "preferring those who believe in no religion over those who do believe." *Zorach v. Clauson.* We do not agree, however, that this decision in any sense has that effect. In addition, it might well be said that one's education is not complete without a study of comparative religion or the history of religion and its relationship to the advancement of civilization. It certainly may be said that the Bible is worthy of study for its literary and historic qualities. Nothing we have said here indicates that such study of the Bible or of religion, when presented objectively as part of a secular program of education, may not be effected consistently with the First Amendment. But the exercises here do not fall into those categories. They are religious exercises, required by the States in violation of the command of the First Amendment that the Government maintain strict neutrality, neither aiding nor opposing religion.

Finally, we cannot accept that the concept of neutrality, which does not permit a State to require a religious exercise even with the consent of the majority of those affected, collides with the majority's right to free exercise of religion. While the Free Exercise Clause clearly prohibits the use of state action to deny the rights of free exercise to *anyone,* it has never meant that a majority could use the machinery of the State to practice its beliefs. Such a contention was effectively answered by Mr. Justice Jackson for the Court in *West Virginia Board of Education v. Barnette:*

> The very purpose of a Bill of Rights was to withdraw certain subjects from the vicissitudes of political controversy, to place them beyond the reach of majorities and officials and to establish them as legal principles to be applied by the courts. One's right to . . . freedom of worship . . . and other fundamental rights may not be submitted to vote; they depend on the outcome of no elections.

The place of religion in our society is an exalted one, achieved through a long tradition of reliance on the home, the church and the inviolable citadel of the individual heart and mind. We have come to recognize through bitter experience that it is not within the power of government to invade that citadel, whether its purpose or effect be to aid or oppose, to advance or retard. In the relationship between man and religion, the State is firmly committed to a position of neutrality. Though the application of that rule requires interpretation of a delicate sort, the rule itself is clearly and concisely stated in the words of the First Amendment. Applying that rule to the facts of these cases, we affirm the judgment in No. 142. In No. 119, the judgment is reversed and the cause remanded to the Maryland Court of Appeals for further proceedings consistent with this opinion.

It is so ordered.

3. EPPERSON v. ARKANSAS

The courtroom clash over Tennessee's "monkey law"—which prohibited the schools from teaching Darwin's theory of evolution—pitted famed advocates Clarence Darrow and William Jennings Bryan against one another in the 1927 case of *Scopes* v. *State*. The issue came alive again forty years later when a similiar Arkansas statute was challenged. Despite Darwin's triumph in this case, a debate continues to rage in some communities over whether the schools should teach "creation science" (generally based on the Genesis account) in addition to or instead of the theory of evolution.

MR. JUSTICE FORTAS DELIVERED
THE OPINION OF THE COURT.

This appeal challenges the constitutionality of the "anti-evolution" statute which the State of Arkansas adopted in 1928 to prohibit the teaching in its public schools and universities of the theory that man evolved from other species of life. The statute was a product of the upsurge of "fundamentalist" religious fervor of the twenties. The Arkansas statute was an adaptation of the famous Tennessee "monkey law" which that State adopted in 1925. The constitutionality of the Tennessee law was upheld by the Tennessee Supreme Court in the celebrated *Scopes* case in 1927.

The Arkansas law makes it unlawful for a teacher in any state-supported school or university "to teach the theory or doctrine that mankind ascended or descended from a lower order of animals," or "to adopt or use in any such institution a textbook that teaches" this theory. Violation is a misdemeanor and subjects the violator to dismissal from his position.

The present case concerns the teaching of biology in a high school in Little Rock. According to the testimony, until the events here in litigation, the official textbook furnished for the high school biology course did not have a section on the Darwinian Theory. Then, for the academic year 1965–1966, the school administration, on recommendation

of the teachers of biology in the school system, adopted and prescribed a textbook which contained a chapter setting forth "the theory about the origin . . . of man from a lower form of animal." . . .

Susan Epperson, a young woman who graduated from Arkansas' school system and then obtained her master's degree in zoology at the University of Illinois, was employed by the Little Rock school system in the fall of 1964 to teach 10th grade biology at Central High School. At the start of the next academic year, 1965, she was confronted by the new textbook (which one surmises from the record was not unwelcome to her). She faced at least a literal dilemma because she was supposed to use the new textbook for classroom instruction and presumably to teach the statutorily condemned chapter; but to do so would be a criminal offense and subject her to dismissal.

She instituted the present action in the Chancery Court of the State, seeking a declaration that the Arkansas statute is void and enjoining the State and the defendant officials of the Little Rock school system from dismissing her for violation of the statute's provisions.

Only Arkansas and Mississippi have such "anti-evolution" or "monkey" laws on their books. There is no record of any prosecutions in Arkansas under its statute. It is possible that the statute is presently more of a curiosity than a vital fact of life in these

393 U.S. 97 (1968).

States. Nevertheless, the present case was brought, the appeal is properly here, and it is our duty to decide the issues presented.

At the outset, it is urged upon us that the challenged statute is vague and uncertain and therefore within the condemnation of the Due Process Clause of the Fourteenth Amendment. . . .

[W]e do not rest our decision upon the asserted vagueness of the statute. On [any] interpretation of its language, Arkansas' statute cannot stand. It is of no moment whether the law is deemed to prohibit mention of Darwin's theory, or to forbid any or all of the infinite varieties of communication embraced within the term "teaching." Under either interpretation, the law must be stricken because of its conflict with the constitutional prohibition of state laws respecting an establishment of religion or prohibiting the free exercise thereof. The overriding fact is that Arkansas' law selects from the body of knowledge a particular segment which it proscribes for the sole reason that it is deemed to conflict with a particular religious doctrine; that is, with a particular interpretation of the Book of Genesis by a particular religious group.

The antecedents of today's decision are many and unmistakable. They are rooted in the foundation soil of our Nation. They are fundamental to freedom.

Government in our democracy, state and national, must be neutral in matters of religious theory, doctrine, and practice. It may not be hostile to any religion or to the advocacy of no-religion; and it may not aid, foster, or promote one religion or religious theory against another or even against the militant opposite. The First Amendment mandates governmental neutrality between religion and religion, and between religion and nonreligion. . . .

There is and can be no doubt that the First Amendment does not permit the State to require that teaching and learning must be tailored to the principles or prohibitions of any religious sect or dogma. In *Everson* v. *Board of Education*, this Court, in upholding a state law to provide free bus service to school children, including those attending parochial schools, said: "Neither [a State nor the Federal Government] can pass laws which aid one religion, aid all religions, or prefer one religion over another." . . .

While study of religions and of the Bible from a literary and historic viewpoint, presented objectively as part of a secular program of education, need not collide with the First Amendment's prohibition, the State may not adopt programs or practices in its public schools or colleges which "aid or oppose" any religion. This prohibition is absolute. It forbids alike the preference of a religious doctrine or the prohibition of theory which is deemed antagonistic to a particular dogma. . . .

The State's undoubted right to prescribe the curriculum for its public schools does not carry with it the right to prohibit, on pain of criminal penalty, the teaching of a scientific theory or doctrine where that prohibition is based upon reasons that violate the First Amendment. . . .

In the present case, there can be no doubt that Arkansas has sought to prevent its teachers from discussing the theory of evolution because it is contrary to the belief of some that the Book of Genesis must be the exclusive source of doctrine as to the origin of man. No suggestion has been made that Arkansas' law may be justified by considerations of state policy other than the religious views of some of its citizens. It is clear that fundamentalist sectarian conviction was and is the law's reason for existence. Its antecedent, Tennessee's "monkey law," candidly stated its purpose: to make it unlawful "to teach any theory that denies the story of the Divine Creation of man as taught in the Bible, and to teach instead that man has descended from a lower order of animals." Perhaps the sensational publicity attendant upon the *Scopes* trial induced Arkansas to

235

adopt less explicit language. It eliminated Tennessee's reference to "the story of the Divine Creation of man" as taught in the Bible, but there is no doubt that the motivation for the law was the same: to suppress the teaching of a theory which, it was thought, "denied" the divine creation of man.

Arkansas' law cannot be defended as an act of religious neutrality. Arkansas did not seek to excise from the curricula of its schools and universities all discussion of the origin of man. The law's effort was confined to an attempt to blot out a particular theory because of its supposed conflict with the Biblical account, literally read. Plainly, the law is contrary to the mandate of the First, and in violation of the Fourteenth, Amendment to the Constitution.

4. STONE v. GRAHAM

Between *School District of Abington Township* v. *Schempp* in 1963 and *Stone* v. *Graham* in 1980, the Supreme Court developed a three-part test for establishment clause cases. Often referred to as the *Lemon* test (because it was first crystalized in *Lemon* v. *Kurtzman* in 1971), this tripartite test was applied in *Stone* v. *Graham* to a Kentucky law requiring that the Ten Commandments be posted in every public school classroom.

PER CURIAM OPINION.

A Kentucky statute requires the posting of a copy of the Ten Commandments, purchased with private contributions, on the wall of each public classroom in the State. Petitioners, claiming that this statute violates the Establishment and Free Exercise Clauses of the First Amendment, sought an injunction against its enforcement. The state trial court upheld the statute, finding that its "avowed purpose" was "secular and not religious," and that the statute would "neither advance nor inhibit any religion or religious group" nor involve the State excessively in religious matters. . . . We reverse.

This Court has announced a three-part test for determining whether a challenged state statute is permissible under the Establishment Clause of the United States Constitution:

First, the statute must have a secular legislative purpose; second, its principal or primary effect must be one that neither advances nor inhibits religion . . . ; finally the statute must not foster "an excessive government entanglement with religion."

If a statute violates any of these three principles, it must be struck down under the Establishment Clause. We conclude that Kentucky's statute requiring the posting of the Ten Commandments in public schoolrooms had no secular legislative purpose, and is therefore unconstitutional.

The Commonwealth insists that the statute in question serves a secular legislative purpose, observing that the legislature required the following notation in small print at the bottom of each display of the Ten Commandments: "The secular application of the Ten Commandments is clearly seen in its adoption as the fundamental legal code of Western Civilization and the Common Law of the United States." . . .

449 U.S. 39 (1980).

The trial court found the "avowed" purpose of the statute to be secular, even as it labeled the statutory declaration "self-serving." Under this Court's rulings, however, such an "avowed" secular purpose is not sufficient to avoid conflict with the First Amendment. In *School District of Abington Township* v. *Schempp* this Court held unconstitutional the daily reading of Bible verses and the Lord's Prayer in the public schools, despite the school district's assertion of such secular purposes as "the promotion of moral values, the contradiction to the materialistic trends of our times, the perpetuation of our institutions and the teaching of literature." . . .

The pre-eminent purpose for posting the Ten Commandments on schoolroom walls is plainly religious in nature. The Ten Commandments is undeniably a sacred text in the Jewish and Christian faiths, and no legislative recitation of a supposed secular purpose can blind us to that fact. The Commandments do not confine themselves to arguably secular matters, such as honoring one's parents, killing or murder, adultery, stealing, false witness, and covetousness. See Exodus 20:12–17; Deuteronomy 5:16–21. Rather, the first part of the Commandments concerns the religious duties of believers: worshipping the Lord God alone, avoiding idolatry, not using the Lord's name in vain, and observing the sabbath day. See Exodus 20:1–11; Deuteronomy 5:6–15.

This is not a case in which the Ten Commandments are integrated into the school curriculum, where the Bible may constitutionally be used in an appropriate study of history, civilization, ethics, comparative religion, or the like. . . . Posting of religious texts on the wall serves no such educational function. If the posted copies of the Ten Commandments are to have any effect at all, it will be to induce the school children to read, meditate upon, perhaps to venerate and obey, the Commandments. However desirable this might be as a matter of private devotion, it is not a permissible state objective under the Establishment Clause.

It does not matter that the posted copies of the Ten Commandments are financed by voluntary private contributions, for the mere posting of the copies under the auspices of the legislature provides the "official support of the State . . . Government" that the Establishment Clause prohibits. Nor is it significant that the Bible verses involved in this case are merely posted on the wall, rather than read aloud as in *Schempp* and *Engel*, for "it is no defense to urge that the religious practices here may be relatively minor encroachments on the First Amendment." . . . We conclude that K.R.S. 158.178 violates the first part of the [three-part] test, and thus the Establishment Clause of the Constitution.

5. **WIDMAR v. VINCENT**

Yet another approach to religion in the public schools is called "equal access." Under an equal access approach, public schools having extracurricular activities must provide equal opportunity for both religious and secular organizations. In *Widmar* v. *Vincent* the Supreme Court upheld the constitutionality of the equal access approach in the context of a public university. The constitutional issue remains unresolved at the elementary and secondary school levels. Several federal appellate courts have held the practice unconstitutional, yet the United States Congress has recently mandated equal access in public schools receiving federal funds. Equal access in the public schools will undoubtedly reach the Supreme Court in the near future. Although the Court's decision in *Widmar* v. *Vincent* is based on the free speech clause of the First Amendment, some commentators have seen equal access as an example of the inherent conflict within the religion clauses of the First Amendment. Students seeking equal access for religious groups rest their claims on free exercise (and free speech) grounds, while opponents argue that the establishment clause bars religious groups from meeting on school property.

JUSTICE POWELL DELIVERED THE OPINION OF THE COURT.

This case presents the question whether a state university, which makes its facilities generally available for the activities of registered student groups, may close its facilities to a registered student group desiring to use the facilities for religious worship and religious discussion.

It is the stated policy of the University of Missouri at Kansas City to encourage the activities of student organizations. The University officially recognizes over 100 student groups. It routinely provides University facilities for the meetings of registered organizations. Students pay an activity fee of $41 per semester (1978–1979) to help defray the costs to the University.

From 1973 until 1977 a registered religious group named Cornerstone regularly sought and received permission to conduct its meetings in University facilities. In 1977, however, the University informed the group that it could no longer meet in University build-ings. The exclusion was based on a regulation, adopted by the Board of Curators in 1972, that prohibits the use of University buildings or grounds "for purposes of religious worship or religious teaching."

Eleven University students, all members of Cornerstone, brought suit to challenge the regulation in Federal District Court for the Western District of Missouri. They alleged that the University's discrimination against religious activity and discussion violated their rights to free exercise of religion, equal protection, and freedom of speech under the First and Fourteenth Amendments to the Constitution of the United States. . . .

Through its policy of accommodating their meetings, the University has created a forum generally open for use by student groups. Having done so, the University has assumed an obligation to justify its discriminations and exclusions under applicable constitutional norms. The Constitution forbids a State to enforce certain exclusions from a forum generally open to the public, even if

454 U.S. 263 (1981).

it was not required to create the forum in the first place. . . .

The University's institutional mission, which it describes as providing a *"secular* education" to its students, does not exempt its actions from constitutional scrutiny. With respect to persons entitled to be there, our cases leave no doubt that the First Amendment rights of speech and association extend to the campuses of state universities. . . .

Here the University of Missouri has discriminated against student groups and speakers based on their desire to use a generally open forum to engage in religious worship and discussion. These are forms of speech and association protected by the First Amendment. . . .

In order to justify discriminatory exclusion from a public forum based on the religious content of a group's intended speech, the University must therefore satisfy the standard of review appropriate to content-based exclusions. It must show that its regulation is necessary to serve a compelling state interest and that it is narrowly drawn to achieve that end. . . .

In this case the University claims a compelling interest in maintaining strict separation of church and State. It derives this interest from the "Establishment Clauses" of both the Federal and Missouri Constitutions.

The University first argues that it cannot offer its facilities to religious groups and speakers on the terms available to other groups without violating the Establishment Clause of the Constitution of the United States. We agree that the interest of the University in complying with its constitutional obligations may be characterized as compelling. It does not follow, however, that an "equal access" policy would be incompatible with this Court's Establishment Clause cases. Those cases hold that a policy will not offend the Establishment Clause if it can pass a three-pronged test: "First, the [governmental policy] must have a secular legislative purpose; second, its principal or primary effect must be one that neither ad-

vances nor inhibits religion . . . ; finally, the [policy] must not foster 'an excessive government entanglement with religion.' " . . .

In this case two prongs of the test are clearly met. . . . [But] the University argues here, that allowing religious groups to share the limited public forum would have the "primary effect" of advancing religion.

The University's argument misconceives the nature of this case. The question is not whether the creation of a religious forum would violate the Establishment Clause. The University has opened its facilities for use by student groups, and the question is whether it can now exclude groups because of the content of their speech. In this context we are unpersuaded that the primary effect of the public forum, open to all forms of discourse, would be to advance religion.

We are not oblivious to the range of an open forum's likely effects. It is possible—perhaps even foreseeable—that religious groups will benefit from access to University facilities. But this Court has explained that a religious organization's enjoyment of merely "incidental" benefits does not violate the prohibition against the "primary advancement" of religion. . . .

We are satisfied that any religious benefits of an open forum at UMKC would be "incidental" within the meaning of our cases. Two factors are especially relevant.

First, an open forum in a public university does not confer any imprimatur of State approval on religious sects or practices. As the Court of Appeals quite aptly stated, such a policy "would no more commit the University . . . to religious goals," than it is "now committed to the goals of the Students for a Democratic Society, the Young Socialist Alliance," or any other group eligible to use its facilities.

Second, the forum is available to a broad class of non-religious as well as religious speakers; there are over 100 recognized student groups at UMKC. The provision of benefits to so broad a spectrum of groups is an important index of secular effect. . . . If the

Establishment Clause barred the extension of general benefits to religious groups, "a church could not be protected by the police and fire departments, or have its public sidewalk kept in repair." . . . At least in the absence of empirical evidence that religious groups will dominate UMKC's open forum, we agree with the Court of Appeals that the advancement of religion would not be the forum's "primary effect."

Our holding in this case in no way undermines the capacity of the University to establish reasonable time, place, and manner regulations. Nor do we question the right of the University to make academic judgments as to how best to allocate scarce resources or "to determine for itself on academic grounds who may teach, what may be taught, how it shall be taught, and who may be admitted to study." . . . Finally, we affirm the continuing validity of cases . . . that recognize a University's right to exclude even First Amendment activities that violate reasonable campus rules or substantially interfere with the opportunity of other students to obtain an education.

The basis for our decision is narrow. Having created a forum generally open to student groups, the University seeks to enforce a content-based exclusion of religious speech. Its exclusionary policy violates the fundamental principle that a state regulation of speech should be content-neutral, and the University is unable to justify this violation under applicable constitutional standards. . . .

6. WALLACE v. JAFFREE

> The moment of silence has emerged as a potential way to return religion to the public school day. Defended as an entirely secular opportunity for students to start the day with a quiet moment, opponents (and some proponents) have seen it as a thinly disguised attempt to circumvent the prohibition of school-sponsored prayer in *Engel* v. *Vitale*. In this case, the Supreme Court held Alabama's moment of silence law unconstitutional, but a majority of the justices suggested that other moments of silence might pass muster. Also of note is Justice Rehnquist's call to the Court to abandon its entire approach to the establishment clause.

JUSTICE STEVENS DELIVERED
THE OPINION OF THE COURT.

At an early stage of this litigation, the constitutionality of three Alabama statutes was questioned: (1) § 16–1–20, enacted in 1978, which authorized a one-minute period of silence in all public schools "for meditation"; (2) § 16–1–20.1, enacted in 1981, which authorized a period of silence "for meditation or voluntary prayer"; and (3) § 16–1–20.2, enacted in 1982, which authorized teachers to lead "willing students" in a prescribed prayer to "Almighty God . . . the Creator and Supreme Judge of the world." [The trial court] held that [the second two statutes] were constitutional because, in its opinion, Alabama has the power to establish a state religion if it chooses to do so.

The Court of Appeals . . . held them both unconstitutional. We have already affirmed the Court of Appeals' holding with respect to § 16–1–20.2. Moreover, appellees have not questioned the holding that § 16–1–20 [authorizing a moment of silence "for medita-

U.S. (1985).

tion"] is valid. Thus, the narrow question for decision is whether § 16–1–20.1, which authorizes a period of silence for "meditation or voluntary prayer," is a law respecting the establishment of religion within the meaning of the First Amendment.

Appellee Ishmael Jaffree is a resident of Mobile County, Alabama. On May 28, 1982, he filed a complaint on behalf of three of his minor children; two of them were second-grade students and the third was then in kindergarten. . . . The complaint . . . alleged that two of the children had been subjected to various acts of religious indoctrination "from the beginning of the school year in September, 1981"; that the defendant teachers had "on a daily basis" led their classes in saying certain prayers in unison; that the minor children were exposed to ostracism from their peer group class members if they did not participate; and that Ishmael Jaffree had repeatedly but unsuccessfully requested that the devotional services be stopped. The original complaint made no reference to any Alabama statute. [Later,] the appellees challenged the constitutionality of three Alabama statutes: §§ 16–1–20, 16–1–20.1, and 16–1–20.2.

[T]he District Court reviewed a number of opinions of this Court interpreting the Establishment Clause of the First Amendment, and then embarked on a fresh examination of the question whether the First Amendment imposes any barrier to the establishment of an official religion by the State of Alabama. After reviewing at length what it perceived to be newly discovered historical evidence, the District Court concluded that "the establishment clause of the first amendment to the United States Constitution does not prohibit the state from establishing a religion."

Our unanimous affirmance of the [reversal by the Court of Appeals of the District Court's decision] concerning § 16–1–20.2 makes it unnecessary to comment at length on the District Court's remarkable conclu-

sion that the Federal Constitution imposes no obstacle to Alabama's establishment of a state religion. Before analyzing the precise issue that is presented to us, it is nevertheless appropriate to recall how firmly embedded in our constitutional jurisprudence is the proposition that the several States have no greater power to restrain the individual freedoms protected by the First Amendment than does the Congress of the United States.

As is plain from its text, the First Amendment was adopted to curtail the power of Congress to interfere with the individual's freedom to believe, to worship, and to express himself in accordance with the dictates of his own conscience. Until the Fourteenth Amendment was added to the Constitution, the First Amendment's restraints on the exercise of federal power simply did not apply to the States. But when the Constitution was amended to prohibit any State from depriving any person of liberty without due process of law, that Amendment imposed the same substantive limitations on the States' power to legislate that the First Amendment had always imposed on the Congress' power. This Court has confirmed and endorsed this elementary proposition of law time and time again.

Just as the right to speak and the right to refrain from speaking are complimentary [sic] components of a broader concept of individual freedom of mind, so also the individual's freedom to choose his own creed is the counterpart of his right to refrain from accepting the creed established by the majority. At one time it was thought that this right merely proscribed the preference of one Christian sect over another, but would not require equal respect for the conscience of the infidel, the atheist, or the adherent of a non-Christian faith such as Mohammedism or Judaism. But when the underlying principle has been examined in the crucible of litigation, the Court has unambiguously concluded that the individual freedom of conscience protected by the First Amendment embraces the right to select any religious faith or none at all. This conclusion derives support not only from the interest in respecting the individual's freedom of conscience, but also from the conviction that religious beliefs worthy of respect are the product of free and voluntary choice by the faithful, and from recognition of the fact that the political interest in forestalling intolerance extends beyond intolerance among Christian sects—or even intolerance among "religions"—to encompass intolerance of the disbeliever and the uncertain. . . . The State of Alabama, no less than the Congress of the United States, must respect that basic truth.

When the Court has been called upon to construe the breadth of the Establishment Clause, it has examined the criteria developed over a period of many years. Thus, in *Lemon* v. *Kurtzman* we wrote:

Every analysis in this area must begin with consideration of the cumulative criteria developed by the Court over many years. Three such tests may be gleaned from our cases. First, the statute must have a secular legislative purpose; second, its principal or primary effect must be one that neither advances nor inhibits religion; finally, the statute must not foster "an excessive government entanglement with religion."

It is the first of these three criteria that is most plainly implicated by this case. . . . [E]ven though a statute that is motivated in part by a religious purpose may satisfy the first criterion, the First Amendment requires that a statute must be invalidated if it is entirely motivated by a purpose to advance religion.

In applying the purpose test, it is appropriate to ask "whether government's actual purpose is to endorse or disapprove of religion." In this case, the answer to that question is dispositive. For the record not only provides us with an unambiguous affirmative answer, but it also reveals that the enactment of § 16–1–20.1 was not motivated by any clearly secular purpose—indeed, the statute had *no* secular purpose.

The sponsor of the bill that became § 16–1–20.1, Senator Donald Holmes, inserted into the legislative record—apparently without dissent—a statement indicating that the legislation was an "effort to return voluntary prayer" to the public schools. Later Senator Holmes confirmed this purpose before the District Court. In response to the question whether he had any purpose for the legislation other than returning voluntary prayer to public schools, he stated, "No, I did not have no other purpose in mind." The State did not present evidence of *any* secular purpose. . . .

The legislative intent to return prayer to the public schools is, of course, quite different from merely protecting every student's right to engage in voluntary prayer during an appropriate moment of silence during the school day. The 1978 statute already protected that right, containing nothing that prevented any student from engaging in voluntary prayer during a silent minute of meditation. Appellants have not identified any secular purpose that was not fully served by § 16–1–20 before the enactment of § 16–1–20.1. . . .

The Legislature enacted § 16–1–20.1 despite the existence of § 16–1–20 for the sole purpose of expressing the State's endorsement of prayer activities for one minute at the beginning of each school day. The addition of "or voluntary prayer" indicates that the State intended to characterize prayer as a favored practice. Such an endorsement is not consistent with the established principle that the Government must pursue a course of complete neutrality toward religion.

The importance of that principle does not permit us to treat this as an inconsequential case involving nothing more than a few words of symbolic speech on behalf of the political majority. For whenever the State itself speaks on a religious subject, one of the questions that we must ask is "whether the Government intends to convey a message of endorsement or disapproval of religion." . . . Keeping in mind, as we must, "both the fundamental place held by the Establishment Clause in our constitutional scheme and the myriad, subtle ways in which Establishment Clause values can be eroded," we conclude that § 16–1–20.1 violates the First Amendment.

JUSTICE REHNQUIST, DISSENTING.

Thirty-eight years ago this Court, in *Everson* v. *Board of Education*, summarized its exegesis of Establishment Clause doctrine thus:

In the words of Jefferson, the clause against establishment of religion by law was intended to erect "a wall of separation between church and State."

It is impossible to build sound constitutional doctrine upon a mistaken understanding of constitutional history, but unfortunately the Establishment Clause has been expressly freighted with Jefferson's misleading metaphor for nearly forty years. Thomas Jefferson was of course in France at the time the constitutional amendments known as the Bill of Rights were passed by Congress and ratified by the states. His letter to the Danbury Baptist Association was a short note of courtesy, written fourteen years after the amendments were passed by Congress. He would seem to any detached observer as a less than ideal source of contemporary history as to the meaning of the Religion Clauses of the First Amendment.

Jefferson's fellow Virginian James Madison, with whom he was joined in the battle for the enactment of the Virginia Statute of Religious Liberty of 1786, did play as large a part as anyone in the drafting of the Bill of Rights. He had two advantages over Jefferson in this regard: he was present in the United States, and he was a leading member of the First Congress. But when we turn to the record of the proceedings in the First Congress leading up to the adoption of the Establishment Clause of the Constitution, including Madison's significant contributions thereto, we see a far different picture of its purpose than the highly simplified "wall of separation between church and State."

During the debates in the thirteen colonies over ratification of the Constitution, one of the arguments frequently used by opponents of ratification was that without a Bill of Rights guaranteeing individual liberty the new general government carried with it a potential for tyranny. The typical response to this argument on the part of those who favored ratification was that the general government established by the Constitution had only delegated powers, and that these delegated powers were so limited that the government would have no occasion to violate individual liberties. This response satisfied some, but not others, and of the eleven colonies which ratified the Constitution by early 1789, five proposed one or another amendments guaranteeing individual liberty. Three—New Hampshire, New York, and Virginia—included in one form or another a declaration of religious freedom. Rhode Island and North Carolina flatly refused to ratify the Constitution in the absence of amendments in the nature of a Bill of Rights. Virginia and North Carolina proposed identical guarantees of religious freedom.

On June 8, 1789, James Madison rose in the House of Representatives and "reminded the House that this was the day that he had heretofore named for bringing forward amendments to the Constitution." . . .

On the basis of the record of [the] proceedings in the House of Representatives, James Madison was undoubtedly the most important architect among the members of the House of the amendments which became the Bill of Rights, but it was James Madison speaking as an advocate of sensible legislative compromise, not as an advocate of incorporating the Virginia Statute of Religious Liberty into the United States Constitution. During the ratification debate in the Virginia Convention, Madison had actually opposed the idea of any Bill of Rights. His sponsorship of the amendments in the House was obviously not that of a zealous believer in the necessity of the Religion Clauses, but of one who felt it might do some good, could do no harm, and would satisfy those who had ratified the Constitution on the condition that Congress propose a Bill of Rights. His original language "nor shall any national religion be established" obviously does not conform to the "wall of separation" between church and State idea which latter day commentators have ascribed to him. His explanation on the floor of the meaning of his language—"that Congress should not establish a religion, and enforce the legal observation of it by law" is of the same ilk. When he replied to Huntington in the debate over the proposal which came from the Select Committee of the House, he urged that the language "no religion shall be established by law" should be amended by inserting the word "national" in front of the word "religion."

It seems indisputable from these glimpses of Madison's thinking, as reflected by actions on the floor of the House in 1789, that he saw the amendment as designed to prohibit the establishment of a national religion, and perhaps to prevent discrimination among sects. He did not see it as requiring neutrality on the part of government between religion and irreligion. Thus the Court's opinion in Everson—while correct in bracketing Madison and Jefferson together in their exertions in their home state leading to the enactment of the Virginia Statute of Religious Liberty— is totally incorrect in suggesting that Madison carried these views onto the floor of the United States House of Representatives when he proposed the language which would ultimately become the Bill of Rights.

The repetition of this error in the Court's opinion in [Illinois v. McCollum and Engel v. Vitale] does not make it any sounder historically. Finally, in Abington School District v. Schempp, the Court made the truly remarkable statement that "the views of Madison and Jefferson, preceded by Roger Williams

came to be incorporated not only in the Federal Constitution but likewise in those of most of our States." On the basis of what evidence we have, this statement is demonstrably incorrect as a matter of history. And its repetition in varying forms in succeeding opinions of the Court can give it no more authority than it possesses as a matter of fact; stare decisis may bind courts as to matters of law, but it cannot bind them as to matters of history.

None of the other Members of Congress who spoke during the August 15th debate expressed the slightest indication that they thought the language before them from the Select Committee, or the evil to be aimed at, would require that the Government be absolutely neutral as between religion and irreligion. The evil to be aimed at, so far as those who spoke were concerned, appears to have been the establishment of a national church, and perhaps the preference of one religious sect over another; but it was definitely not concern about whether the Government might aid all religions evenhandedly. . . .

There is simply no historical foundation for the proposition that the Framers intended to build the "wall of separation" that was constitutionalized in Everson.

Notwithstanding the absence of an historical basis for this theory of rigid separation, the wall idea might well have served as a useful albeit misguided analytical concept, had it led this Court to unified and principled results in Establishment Clause cases. The opposite, unfortunately, has been true; in the 38 years since Everson our Establishment Clause cases have been neither principled nor unified. Our recent opinions, many of them hopelessly divided pluralities, have with embarrassing candor conceded that the "wall of separation" is merely a "blurred, indistinct, and variable barrier," which "is not wholly accurate" and can only be "dimly perceived." . . .

The "wall of separation between church and State" is a metaphor based on bad history, a metaphor which has proved useless as a guide to judging. It should be frankly and explicitly abandoned.

The Court has more recently attempted to add some mortar to *Everson's* wall through the three-part test of *Lemon* v. *Kurtzman,* which served at first to offer a more useful test for purposes of the Establishment Clause than did the "wall" metaphor. Generally stated, the *Lemon* test proscribes state action that has a sectarian purpose or effect, or causes an impermissible governmental entanglement with religion.

[D]ifficulties arise because the *Lemon* test has no more grounding in the history of the First Amendment than does the wall theory upon which it rests. The three-part test represents a determined effort to craft a workable rule from an historically faulty doctrine; but the rule can only be as sound as the doctrine it attempts to service. The three-part test has simply not provided adequate standards for deciding Establishment Clause cases, as this Court has slowly come to realize. . . .

The true meaning of the Establishment Clause can only be seen in its history. . . . As drafters of our Bill of Rights, the Framers inscribed the principles that control today. Any deviation from their intentions frus-

trates the permanence of that Charter and will only lead to the type of unprincipled decisionmaking that has plagued our Establishment Clause cases since *Everson.*

The Framers intended the Establishment Clause to prohibit the designation of any church as a "national" one. The Clause was also designed to stop the Federal Government from asserting a preference for one religious denomination or sect over others. Given the "incorporation" of the Establishment Clause as against the States via the Fourteenth Amendment in *Everson,* States are prohibited as well from establishing a religion or discriminating between sects. As its history abundantly shows, however, nothing in the Establishment Clause requires government to be strictly neutral between religion and irreligion, nor does that Clause prohibit Congress or the States from pursuing legitimate secular ends through nondiscriminatory sectarian means. . . .

The State surely has a secular interest in regulating the manner in which public schools are conducted. Nothing in the Establishment Clause of the First Amendment, properly understood, prohibits any such generalized "endorsement" of prayer. I would therefore reverse the judgment of the Court of Appeals in *Wallace* v. *Jaffree.*

7. SCHOOL PRAYER AMENDMENT

After the Supreme Court's decisions in *Engel* v. *Vitale* and *School District of Abington Township* v. *Schempp,* the governors of forty-nine states called for a constitutional amendment to overturn the Court's rulings. No amendment was adopted at that time, but the effort has been revitalized from time to time. The following school prayer amendment, introduced with President Reagan's support, received serious attention from the Congress in 1984.

Nothing in this Constitution shall be construed to prohibit individual or group prayer in public schools or other public institutions.

No person shall be required by the United States or by any State to participate in prayer.

245

James E. Wood, Jr.

8. RELIGIOUS FUNDAMENTALISM AND THE NEW RIGHT

Professor Wood, a minister of the Southern Baptist convention, is the Director of J. M. Dawson Studies in Church and State at Baylor University and Editor of the *Journal of Church and State,* where the following first appeared as an editorial. In this essay, Professor Wood describes the intense political activity of the Moral Majority and other groups mixing conservative Protestant theology with conservative political action.

The symbiosis of religious fundamentalism and the political New Right must be viewed as a major feature of this election year in the United States. Perhaps, no other feature in American politics in 1980 has attracted more attention from the electronic media or elicited more coverage in the press throughout the nation. . . . Aided particularly by fundamentalist Christian evangelists with vast television audiences and orchestrated primarily by quasi-religious organizations with an avowed political purpose, the movement has sought to unite right-wing conservative faith with right-wing conservative politics, largely around a dozen or so key issues. While the impact of this movement on the elections in 1980 may not be measurable for some time to come, the alliance of religious fundamentalism with the political New Right during the past year is a phenomenon not to be taken lightly. Clearly, fundamentalist Christians are forming a burgeoning new force in American politics and are shifting away from their traditional view that "religion and politics don't mix." . . .

The recent emergence of Christian fundamentalism as a new political force in American life, however, both as to its extent and its character, is significantly unlike earlier examples of the role played by organized religion in American politics. Primarily spearheaded by television evangelists, largely without denominational identity or denominational support, the New Religious Right generally identifies its adherents as "ultraconservative evangelical Christians." Whether as fundamentalists or ultraconservative evangelicals, they see themselves as reacting against the "liberalism" of the mainline religious denominations, the National Council of Churches, and the World Council of Churches, particularly in the areas of social concerns and public affairs. This stance is, in turn, transferred to one of reaction against the "liberalism" to be found also in the political establishment, particularly in areas of public policy bearing on civil liberties and civil rights, national defense, and foreign affairs. While lacking formal support from even traditionally conservative religious denominations, the political arm of fundamentalism has found a growing and devoted constituency from among virtually all denominations. Almost overnight a large constituency has been built by means of access to and skillful use of the mass media, sophisticated mass mailing lists, highly developed public relations techniques, and well-organized lobbies in Washington, in state capitals, and in city halls. Fundamentalists are clearly being led out of the pews and into the polls.

Impetus for the New Religious Right movement may be attributable to a variety

Originally published in *Journal of Church and State,* Vol. XXII, Autumn 1980, 409–421. Used by permission.

of causes, all of which have had a cumulative effect of mounting concern within fundamentalism, principally the outlawing of prayer in the public schools, the legalization of abortion, the spread of pornography, and the 1978 attempt by the Internal Revenue Service to deny tax-exempt status to church schools which failed to meet the agency's racial guidelines. Meanwhile, Richard A. Viguerie, direct mail fund raiser and reputed founder of the New Right, has credited veteran political organizers of the political far-right with taking the initiative in recruiting fundamentalist leaders, such as television evangelists Jerry Falwell and James Robison, to support right-wing political causes and the election of Ronald Reagan as President. . . .

The politicization of Christian fundamentalism is a very recent phenomenon. It has found institutional expression in a variety of organizations, but three are particularly worthy of note during this election year: Christian Voice, Moral Majority, and The Roundtable (formerly Religious Roundtable). Each was organized less than two years ago, in 1979, and each has become an important political force of the New Right during the past year. While each was organized on avowedly ultraconservative religious principles, each exists to serve a political purpose in the 1980 elections and beyond through the mobilization of the New Religious Right. Each is passionately and unswervingly dedicated to advance the New Right in American politics, and each is aligned in one way or another through its leaders with right-wing political groups, such as the Committee for the Survival of a Free Congress, Conservative Caucus, Heritage Foundation, and National Conservative Political Action. Neither Christian Voice nor Moral Majority, both of which are action-oriented for the implementation of a political agenda, is tax-exempt. Although by law no more than $5,000 may be contributed to a candidate's campaign for any single election, independent groups such as Christian Voice and Moral Majority may spend unlimited funds for a political candidate since they are not officially a part of the candidate's campaign organization.

In the vanguard of the fundamentalist organizations dedicated to the New Right is Christian Voice, with national headquarters in Pasadena, California. Formed in January 1979 as a national political lobby, it claims to represent the Christian community—to have enlisted more than thirty-seven thousand ministers, both Catholic and Protestant, and to have enrolled more than one hundred eighty-seven thousand members. It has an annual budget in 1980 of $3 million and maintains a registered lobby in Washington, D.C. . . . Ultraconservative members of Congress, all of whom are viewed as members of the New Right, serve on the organization's advisory committee. . . .

The purpose of Christian Voice is to mobilize "evangelical Christians" into effective political action. The head of Christian Voice, Robert Grant, a tourist agent and veteran activist against gay rights, declared earlier this year in a meeting held in the Russell Senate Office Building in Washington, "If Christians unite, we can do anything. We can pass any law or any amendment. And that is exactly what we intend to do." Meanwhile, issues such as school busing, the ban on public school prayers, the right of choice in abortion, and the civil rights of homosexuals are viewed, according to Grant, as "just a fraction of a master plan to destroy everything that is good and moral here in America."

The organization implements its program through a political action committee which provides funds and trained volunteers to elect candidates for public office and by mass distribution of congressional voting records with respect to the organization's special list of "moral issues." Early in 1980, Christian Voice launched a nationwide campaign, which included state primaries, to elect Ronald Reagan and other candidates for public office identified with the New Right and to sweep approximately fifty "liberal" members of the Ninety-sixth Congress out of office. Through the Christian Communications Network, much free time has been given Christian Voice by Pat Robertson, television host of "The 700 Club."

A major part of Christian Voice's strategy is to rate all members of Congress on a "morality scale." Those members of Congress who fail to pass the ratings test are then targeted for defeat by a network of ministers and lay members of Christian Voice. Earlier this year, it released its congressional "Report Card," with the results of its "morality ratings" for the 1979 session of Congress. According to Christian Voice, the ratings were based on "14 key House and Senate votes which have important, moral significance to the Christian community." These issues included the elimination of forced school busing, opposition to the creation of the Department of Education, termination of sanctions against Zimbabwe Rhodesia, prohibition of federal funds for abortion, support of prayer in public schools, support of military defense of Taiwan, opposition to SALT II, and opposition to racial and sexual quotas in education and employment, all of which required a "moral" or Christian vote of "yes." As would be expected, the results were far from a "morality rating," as claimed by Christian Voice, but rather a rating of members of Congress according to their political leanings to the New Right. . . .

Organized in June 1979 and with headquarters in Washington, D.C., Moral Majority has become the largest of the fundamentalist organizations dedicated to the New Right. Moral Majority was cofounded by Jerry Falwell, who also serves as president, a television evangelist with a weekly audience of more than 25 million and an annual budget of almost $60 million. It boasts of a network of seventy-two thousand pastors and four hundred thousand lay members. Twice a month, the organization publishes a sixteen-page newspaper, *Moral Majority Report*. Robert Billings, cofounder and former executive director, recently re-

signed in order to serve in the Reagan campaign as coordinator for Christian interest groups. As in the case of Christian Voice, Moral Majority vigorously opposes ERA and civil rights for homosexuals and strongly supports government prohibition of abortion, prayer in the public schools, a strong national defense, and, as Falwell says, "anything else that relates to the sovereignty of this country." . . .

While many critics of Moral Majority, both from pulpits and in the mass media, have been unwilling to concede that the organization represents either morality or a majority, its gains in membership and its impact on local elections and the Republican Party platform have certainly been impressive. Whatever its political impact, whether lasting or not, Moral Majority is permeated with a triumphalism in its crusade for the soul of the nation. The political takeover, it is believed, will inevitably come through the mobilization of fundamentalists who are committed to vote pro-God, pro-family, and pro-America in politics. As Pat Robertson expressed it, "We have enough votes to run the country. And when the people say, 'We've had enough,' we are going to take over." The mix of religion and politics has been well expressed by Jerry Falwell in outlining the three goals of Moral Majority: "First, get them converted; second, get them baptized; and third, get them registered to vote." It remains to be seen whether the dream of Moral Majority represents any sort of wave of the future in view of the increasingly pluralistic character of American society and the growing complexities in national and international affairs requiring highly sophisticated political decisions. In the meantime, Moral Majority shows little awareness of the disparity between religious vision and political reality in a democratic society. . . .

As noted earlier, the involvement of organized religion in politics is by no means new to the American experience, but has long been an important dimension of the nation's political and religious history. There are, however, certain basic differences to be found in the present configuration of the fundamentalist political movement from earlier patterns of religion and politics. First and foremost is the politicization of fundamentalism, which is itself a new and significant phenomenon. It is, of course, much too early to tell how widespread or how lasting this political movement will be within fundamentalism, let alone in the nation. To be sure, there have been earlier political expressions of fundamentalism, such as its vigorous opposition to the teaching of evolution in the public schools during the twenties (and now recently revived), but such isolated excursions by fundamentalism were narrowly confined to single issue politics and were not a part of a comprehensive political agenda for action. Rather, in the past fundamentalism has been fond of arguing, especially against the political and social concerns of the mainline religious denominations, that a moral society could not be created by legislation, but only by changing the hearts of individuals. Therefore, political involvement was traditionally viewed as incompatible with the primary task of fundamentalist religion.

Second, the political crusade being conducted by fundamentalism is neither a call to mere single issue politics nor to Christians simply for political involvement, but rather a call to a political ideology, a political agenda, and to partisan political action. The partisan politics being advanced is the inevitable result of an alliance between religious fundamentalism and the New Right— the religious far-right joined with the political far-right. This has been translated into a particular brand of party politics, to be implemented at the local, state, and national levels. It has also meant, at the practical level, identification with the Republican Party in 1980—both its platform, which the political fundamentalists helped to formulate, and its politically ultraconservative candidates. This development is in marked contrast to the tradition of mainline religious denominations—Catholic, Protestant, and Jewish—which have, by and large, generally seen their role in the political process to be one of advocacy of ideas in the formulation of public policy and not the advancement of partisan politics or the election of particular candidates. Again, in contrast to the general pattern of religion and politics, the fundamentalist political movement has transformed political issues into moral absolutes and thereby has sought to define *the* Christian position on a wide range of issues in domestic and international affairs.

Finally, the massive attempt at political mobilization of one segment of organized religion, aimed at the implementation of a broad range of political objectives and, eventually, a political takeover, is on a scale unprecedented in the nation's history. One must avoid, of course, the tendency to over estimate the political strength of the fundamentalist political movement, but one cannot ignore the enormous influence exerted by the movement through the mass media. . . .

The reasons behind the emergence of the fundamentalist political movement are not difficult to understand. Many ills attend American society, and the movement is no doubt meeting genuinely felt needs and frustrations of multitudes of people. Millions of Americans, having lost their political innocence in the sixties culminating in the tragedy of Watergate, have experienced growing distrust of government and the political establishment. Meanwhile, the social revolution of recent decades has resulted in placing a severe strain on moral and religious values and in posing severe threats to family life throughout the nation. The eroding patterns of authority and the growing permissiveness of an increasingly pluralistic society have had a frightening effect on millions of Americans. Understandably, there is a nativist longing for the certainties of the past that the New Religious Right readily seeks to fill, albeit with highly simplistic answers to extremely complex questions and through a mythologizing of America's past. These answers

249

and this mythology have not been seen by the New Religious Right as forthcoming from the mainline religious denominations or the official voices of the religious community. As a consequence, the political arm of fundamentalism sees itself as offering the moral and political answers to the nation's ills, as furnishing a virtual blueprint for the reordering of American society.

If, however, the reasons for the New Religious Right are explainable, the dangers and defects of the movement should be equally evident. There is, of course, the danger of religion's simply being used by politicians and religionists alike for the accomplishment of political ends. History is replete with examples of this, whereby religion is profaned to serve less than moral ends in the struggle for political power, the maintenance of the status quo, or the advance of nationalism—such as Iran and South Africa today or Shinto Japan earlier. As Martin Marty observed in this regard, "The echoes of the Iranian militants are loud and clear." By confusing moral absolutes with public policy, anyone who dissents is identified with immorality and is in conflict with the will of God. The pluralism of America's faiths, not to mention the almost 80 million persons who remain without any religious affiliation, is ignored as well as the essential safeguards of a free society. The religious vision of the nation held by the New Religious Right may be in harmony with America's theocrats, past and present, but it is out of character with the founding of this nation and the guarantees of the First Amendment.

To identify any nation with God is to distort the prophetic role of religion and to deny the fundamental basis of a free and democratic society by making an idol of the state.

Fortunately, many Americans have a strong bias, for both historical and theological reasons, against the blending of religion and politics. The temptation of religious leaders to use political means for the accomplishment of religious ends is no less dangerous than the temptation of public officials to use religion for political ends.

In the final analysis, it is not a question of the right of fundamentalists to be involved in politics that is the real issue, either for the religious or the political community, but rather the *nature* of that involvement which is at issue. Not only does the New Religious Right presume to make political issues into moral absolutes and moral absolutes into political issues, but it holds forth a political agenda which must be ruled as both morally and politically deficient. With all of its espousal of morality in public policy, one looks in vain for the movement's concerns with the sins of injustice, poverty, bigotry, racism, and war. Thus many religious leaders and civil libertarians have been profoundly, and rightly, concerned with the potentially far-reaching implications of this political phenomenon both with respect to religion and politics. The present resurgence of America's theocrats, with their enculturation of a particular and strident form of religious faith, is an ominous sign of the times which does not bode well for the prophetic role of religion, the separation of church and state, or a pluralistic and free society. Reinhold Niebuhr perceptively warned some years ago, "The temper and integrity with which the political fight is waged is more important for the health of a society than any particular [public] policy." The truth is one worth remembering for the future course of religion and politics in America.

9. NATIONAL CONFERENCE OF CATHOLIC BISHOPS ON RELIGION AND POLITICS

In the 1980's, the American Roman Catholic bishops have become increasingly vocal on political issues. They issued a pastoral letter titled "Peace in the Modern World: Religious Perspectives and Principles" as well as a pastoral letter on the American economy. Additionally, individual bishops have made strong public statements on issues such as abortion. The following is a 1984 statement of Bishop James W. Mallone on behalf of the National Conference of Catholic Bishops.

The Administrative Board of the United States Catholic Conference . . . asked that I issue a statement reaffirming the Conference's position on the question of religion and politics. I am pleased to do so, since your pluralistic society should welcome discussion of the moral dimensions of public policy and thoughtful examination of the relationship of religious bodies to the political order.

As a nation we are constitutionally committed to the separation of church and state but not to the separation of religious and moral values from public life. The genius of the American political tradition lies in preserving religious freedom for all—but not at the price of excluding religious and moral content from discussions of domestic and foreign policy.

The question therefore is not whether we should discuss the relationship of religion, morality, and politics but how to discuss the relationship. While responsibility for the quality and character of this discussion rests with all citizens, it rests especially with religious leaders, political leaders, and the media.

[W]e do not take positions for or against particular parties or individual candidates.

Bishops are teachers in the Catholic Church entrusted with the responsibility of communicating the content of Catholic moral teaching and illustrating its relevance to social and political issues. We do not seek the formation of a voting bloc nor do we preempt the right and duty of individuals to decide conscientiously whom they will support for public office. Rather, having stated our positions, we encourage members of our own Church and all citizens to examine the positions of candidates on issues and decide who will best contribute to the common good of society.

The content of Catholic teaching leads us to take positions on many public issues; we are not a one-issue Church. . . .

[Our] concerns range from protecting human life from the attack of abortion, to safeguarding human life from the devastation of nuclear war; they extend to the enhancement of life through promoting human rights and satisfying human needs like nutrition, education, housing and health care, especially for the poor. We emphasize that the needs of the poor must be adequately addressed if we are to be considered a just and compassionate society. Attention to the least among us is the test of our moral vision, and it should be applied to candidates at every level of our government. . . .

[I]n speaking of human dignity and the sanctity of life, we give special emphasis to two issues today. They are the prevention of nuclear war and the protection of unborn human life.

These issues pertaining to the sanctity of human life itself are and cannot help but be matters of public morality. Evident in the case of war and peace, this is no less true in the case of abortion, where the human right to life of the unborn and society's interest in

Excerpts from statement of Bishop James W. Mallone, President, United States Catholic Conference on Relevance of Moral Values to Public Issues, October 14, 1984, used with permission.

251

protecting it necessarily make this a matter of public, not merely private, morality.

On questions such as these, we realize that citizens and public officials may agree with our moral arguments while disagreeing with us and among themselves on the most effective legal and policy remedies. The search for political and public policy solutions to such problems as war and peace and abortion may well be long and difficult, but a prudential judgment that political solutions are not now feasible does not justify failure to undertake the effort.

Whether the issue be the control, reduction, and elimination of nuclear arms or the legal protection of the unborn, the task is to work for the feasibility of what may now be deemed unfeasible. The pursuit of complex objectives like these ought not to be set aside because the goals may not be immediately reachable. In debating such matters, there is much room for dialogue about what constitutes effective, workable responses; but the debate should not be about whether a response in the political order is needed.

None of these issues will be resolved quickly. All will extend far beyond the present political campaign. The discussion of religion and politics will also be pursued long after the campaign. Let us conduct our immediate dialogue with reason and civility, so that the resources of religious and moral vision and the method of rational political debate will be sustained and enhanced in our public life.

10. NATIONAL COUNCIL OF CHURCHES ON RELIGION AND POLITICS

In 1984 the National Council of the Churches of Christ in the United States issued the following guidelines, which it described as a drawing together of "long-standing positions" on the issue of religion and politics.

The continual controversy over religion and politics revolves around several points of confusion which could be clarified by reference to history.

1. *Religion, Morality and Law.* One of the purposes of law is to define and punish unacceptable behavior. Determining what behavior is unacceptable is the province of morality, which is essential to all civilized societies. Religion is one important source of moral insights, but it is not the only one. The legal tradition going back to the Codes of Hammurabi and Justinian is another source, as is the philosophical tradition going back to Socrates, Plato and Aristotle, and the medical tradition going back to Hippocrates and Galen. Every voice urging greater recognition and implementation of morality in this nation is entitled to respect and consideration, religion no less than any other. Not all voices will agree on the definition of morality, however, and not all forms of immorality need be, or can be, made punishable by law, so it is equally important that all voices urging the embodiment of morality in law be subject to debate and criticism, religion no less than any other. That is part of the essential public dialogue of a democracy.

2. *"Separation of Church and State."* It is not a violation of the separation of church and state for religious groups or their leaders to proclaim what they believe to be the right course for the nation, to try to persuade others to their point of view, to try to get laws passed which will advance what they believe is right, and to support candidates who will enact and enforce such laws. That is the right and duty of every citizen, and none are to be disqualified because of their religious commitments or convictions, but neither are

they to be immune from criticism or opposition because of their religious commitments or convictions.

Preachers in their pulpits are entitled to exhort their followers and anyone else who will listen to work for the kind of public policy that will advance what they believe to be the right and moral course for the nation. That is what preachers are *supposed* to do, and so doing is not "imposing" their religious views on anyone because people can disregard their counsel—and often do— even if they declare that they are proclaiming the will of God or that those who disagree are sinful, pagan or bound for perdition. Preachers have done so throughout the history of the nation, and such activity is not only well within the bounds of freedom of speech and the free exercise of religion but is an important contribution to the shaping of the nation's public policy.

Preachers may even run for public office and serve if elected. The last state law banning clergy from civil office was struck down by a unanimous Supreme Court in 1978. . . . If clergy cannot be [banned] from candidacy for public office, how much less can they be [banned] from preaching on public issues or their followers be [banned] from acting on them politically.

However, a church which chooses to support or oppose specific candidates for public office runs the risk of losing its tax exemption, since Section 501(c)(3) of the Internal Revenue Code prohibits non-profit charitable organizations—including churches— from intervening in "any political campaign on behalf of any candidate for public office." That does not mean that it is illegal or unconstitutional to do so, but that there may be adverse tax consequences of so doing, which a church may in exceptional circumstances be willing to risk when it believes that its duty to God and humankind requires.

3. *Religion and the Candidate and Office Holder*. The Constitution forbids any religious test for public office. Therefore, a candidate's religious affiliation cannot disqualify him or her for election or appointment to public office in the United States. By the same token, a candidate's religion should not be show-cased as though it were a qualification or credential for public office. . . .

This view of the proper role of religion does not require the office-holder to be silent about his or her religious views when pertinent; far from it. The office-holder should seek in every way to advance what he or she believes the common good requires, and if that understanding of the common good derives in whole or in part from religious teaching or doctrine all the better! But others are not obliged to agree. Public policy proposals consonant with the office-holder's religious convictions should be neither accepted nor rejected for that reason, but should be debated on their secular merits and effects, like any others. If they do commend themselves to a majority as desirable public policy and are enacted into law, they are no more "imposed" on others than are any other laws duly enacted by the will of the majority.

What the office-holder should not do is to use the powers of office to advance the institutional interests of his or her faith-group at the expense of others or of religion at the expense of non-adherents of religion. Likewise, the office-holder should not seek to implement in public policy the doctrinal teachings or tenets of her or his religion unless and to the extent they coincide with the secular common good. And candidates, though entitled to express their religious views while campaigning, should be wary of the temptation, if elected, to consider that they have somehow gained a "mandate" to advance those views as public policy without explicit authorization from the electorate. The office-holder (or candidate) should also avoid stigmatizing critics or opponents as irreligious or sinful just because they disagree.

By and large, the Presidents of the United States through more than two centuries of history have generally observed these principles in practice, and in this respect have set a good example for public servants at all levels.

11. NATIONAL JEWISH COMMUNITY RELATIONS ADVISORY COUNCIL ON RELIGION AND POLITICS

In 1985 the following statement on the role of religion and religious groups in the political process was adopted by the National Jewish Community Relations Advisory Council (NJCRAC). This council includes eleven national and over one hundred local organizations representing Orthodox, Conservative and Reform Jewish groups.

We have long held that it is legitimate, indeed desirable, for religious groups and clergy to advocate policies that would shape society in ways that those faith communities view as fulfilling their ideal of the "good society." They have a Constitutional right not only to advocate their views on public-policy issues, but also to question candidates on their positions on those issues, to make their views known to their constituents and to the public at large, and to seek to build a community consensus in support of their positions. We would hope that religion, and religious groups, would speak to the ethics and morality of society in the public marketplace of ideas. We believe that all issues may be put on the table for discussion in the marketplace of ideas, but the manner of advocacy should respect our tradition of church-state separation, free of any hint of coercion or verbal violence. In the debate of public-policy issues, it is desirable that the focus be on the public good. These principles have guided Jewish organizations as we have spoken out on a wide array of public-policy issues.

Our concern grows out of what we perceive as growing dangerous tendencies in the political process which attempt to convert political parties into sectarian instruments and raise religious tests for public office. We witnessed in the 1984 election campaign such activities as a call by a candidate in a Congressional race against a Jewish member of Congress to "put a Christian in Congress"; questions addressed by a journalist in a nationally televised debate of the presidential candidates as to whether the

presidential candidates were "born-again Christians," whether they attended church regularly, and whether they believed that abortion was a sin; a statement by the President that those who are against school prayer are "intolerant of religion"; clergy pressing members of their faith to subordinate to church beliefs their mandate as public officials to uphold the law and the Constitution; and, in Minnesota, some local political organizations demanding that school board candidates meet a religious test.

When church and synagogue officials command that their adherents who hold public office act in accordance with religious teaching inconsistent with responsibilities imposed by law, they threaten the very existence of a democracy whose citizens belong to a wide variety of faiths, or none. Such conduct goes well beyond the legitimate exercise of public advocacy. And while churches and synagogues have the right to judge whether their members' conduct meets the demands of the faith, the exercise of that right against public officials for actions taken in furtherance of their official duties is highly divisive.

The knowledge of the ravages of religious wars and religious persecution was what led the Founding Fathers, high-minded moralists, but also pragmatists, to erect, through the Bill of Rights, the wall of separation of church and state as part of the fundamental law of this land. It is important to recall that the Constitution specifically proscribes religious tests for public office. These guarantees not only have protected the rights of religious minorities, but also have fostered a society in which religious pluralism and freedom of religious expression have flourished and prospered.

Religious groups, as all groups in American society, have wide latitude in seeking to achieve their moral imperatives in the public arena. They can properly raise any issue for public debate; they can properly seek the redress of any government decision including, of course, decrees of the United States Supreme Court. The debate of public policy does not require the compromise of fundamental beliefs, including religious imperatives. It does require acting on the recognition that all the participants of the debate have that same right. It further requires respect for those whose views are bitterly opposed. The American democratic process benefits from public debate of differing views among people of good will, but is endangered when national debates degenerate into mortal combat between the forces of good and the forces of evil.

We recognize that religious groups in their hierarchies of social concern may feel a greater intensity about some issues than others, and they will act accordingly. While groups may legitimately coalesce around a single issue, the nation as a whole needs to respond wisely to the totality of needs of the American people.

While we believe that any issue may be debated in the marketplace of ideas under the rules of fair play, the Jewish community relations field will continue to assert vigorously our profound belief that there are issues that must be beyond the reach of government. We stand with Roger Williams, Jefferson, Madison, and those who followed, up to and including Justice William Brennan,

in contending that the well-being of American society requires the inviolate protection of belief, and the sanctity of religious belief above all. They are beyond the jurisdiction of government. Even in areas like abortion, the Supreme Court has held that the Constitution requires limits on government intervention. We believe that in the uncertain area between private and public morality, the vindication of one religious tradition can come only at the expense of another. However, we do not deny the right of others to challenge these views in debates, but we urge that such advocacy be marked by civility and mutual respect.

The separation of religious dogma from politics is incumbent upon not only religious groups and their spokesmen, but also upon public officials, candidates for public office, and political parties. They, too, are called upon to avoid entangling the religious and political mainstreams of American life. They must stand guard against any who would identify American party politics with any brand of religious view. In conflicts over public policy, the determinant should be the public good rather than theological dogma. We look to them to reject categorically the pernicious notion that only one brand of politics or religion meets with God's approval and that others are necessarily evil. We look to them to recommit the major political parties of this nation to the spirit of religious tolerance and religious forbearance that is indispensable to a free society. Above all, we look to political and religious bodies to oppose any and all efforts, whether direct or subtle, to tamper with the First Amendment, the very foundation of American liberties.

12. McGOWAN v. MARYLAND

In the nation's early history, state statutes often mandated various kinds of religious observances. James Madison, for example, introduced a bill in Virginia (originally drafted by Thomas Jefferson) that would punish "Sabbath-breakers." Similar laws have remained on the books of many states, and the Supreme Court in *McGowan* v. *Maryland* was faced with the issue of whether Sunday closing laws are an unconstitutional establishment of religion.

MR. CHIEF JUSTICE WARREN DELIVERED THE OPINION OF THE COURT.

The issues in this case concern the constitutional validity of Maryland criminal statutes, commonly known as Sunday Closing Laws or Sunday Blue Laws. These statutes, with exceptions to be noted hereafter, generally proscribe all labor, business and other commercial activities on Sunday. The questions presented are whether the classifications within the statutes bring about a denial of equal protection of the law, whether the laws are so vague as to fail to give reasonable notice of the forbidden conduct and therefore violate due process, and whether the statutes are laws respecting an establishment of religion or prohibiting the free exercise thereof.

Appellants are seven employees of a large discount department store located on a highway in Anne Arundel County, Maryland. They were indicted for the Sunday sale of a three-ring loose-leaf binder, a can of floor wax, a stapler and staples, and a toy submarine in violation of Md. Ann. Code, Art. 27, § 521. Generally, this section prohibited, throughout the State, the Sunday sale of all merchandise except the retail sale of tobacco products, confectioneries, milk, bread, fruits, gasoline, oils, greases, drugs and medicines, and newspapers and periodicals.

. . .

The essence of appellants' "establish-ment" argument is that Sunday is the Sabbath day of the predominant Christian sects; that the purpose of the enforced stoppage of labor on that day is to facilitate and encourage church attendance; that the purpose of setting Sunday as a day of universal rest is to induce people with no religion or people with marginal religious beliefs to join the predominant Christian sects; that the purpose of the atmosphere of tranquility created by Sunday closing is to aid the conduct of church services and religious observance of the sacred day. In substantiating their "establishment" argument, appellants rely on the wording of the present Maryland statutes, on earlier versions of the current Sunday laws and on prior judicial characterizations of these laws by the Maryland Court of Appeals. Although only the constitutionality of § 521, the section under which appellants have been convicted, is immediately before us in this litigation, inquiry into the history of Sunday Closing Laws in our country, in addition to an examination of the Maryland Sunday closing statutes in their entirety and of their history, is relevant to the decision of whether the Maryland Sunday law in question is one respecting an establishment of religion. There is no dispute that the original laws which dealt with Sunday labor were motivated by religious forces. But what we must decide is whether present Sunday legislation, having undergone exten-

366 U.S. 420 (1961).

sive changes from the earliest forms, still retains its religious character.

Sunday Closing Laws go far back into American history, having been brought to the colonies with a background of English legislation dating to the thirteenth century. In 1237, Henry III forbade the frequenting of markets on Sunday; the Sunday showing of wools at the staple was banned by Edward III in 1354; in 1409, Henry IV prohibited the playing of unlawful games on Sunday [etc.] . . . The law of the colonies to the time of the Revolution and the basis of the Sunday laws in the States was 29 Charles II, c. 7 (1677). It provided, in part:

For the better observation and keeping holy the Lord's day, commonly called Sunday: be it enacted . . . that all the laws enacted and in force concerning the observation of the day, *and repairing to the church thereon*, be carefully put in execution; and that all and every person and persons whatsoever shall upon every Lord's day apply themselves to the observation of the same, by exercising themselves thereon in the duties of piety and true religion, publicly and privately; and that no tradesman, artificer, workman, laborer, or other person whatsoever, *shall do or exercise any worldly labor or business or work* of their ordinary callings upon the Lord's day, or any part thereof (works of necessity and charity only excepted); . . . and that no person or persons whatsoever shall publicly cry, show forth, or expose for sale any wares, merchandise, fruit, herbs, goods, or chattels, whatsoever, upon the Lord's day, or any part thereof. . . . (Emphasis added.)

Observation of the above language, and of that of the prior mandates, reveals clearly that the English Sunday legislation was in aid of the established church.

The American colonial Sunday restrictions arose soon after settlement. Starting in 1650, the Plymouth Colony proscribed servile work, unnecessary travelling, sports, and the sale of alcoholic beverages on the Lord's day and enacted laws concerning church attendance. The Massachusetts Bay Colony and the Connecticut and New Haven Colonies enacted similar prohibitions, some even

earlier in the seventeenth century. The religious orientation of the colonial statutes was equally apparent. For example, a 1629 Massachusetts Bay instruction began, "And to the end the Sabbath may be celebrated in a religious manner. . . ." A 1653 enactment spoke of Sunday activities "which things tend much to the dishonor of God, the reproach of religion, and the profanation of his holy Sabbath, the sanctification whereof is sometimes put for all duties immediately respecting the service of God. . . ." These laws persevered after the Revolution and, at about the time of the First Amendment's adoption, each of the colonies had laws of some sort restricting Sunday labor. . . .

But, despite the strong religious origin of these laws, beginning before the eighteenth century, nonreligious arguments for Sunday closing began to be heard more distinctly and the statutes began to lose some of their totally religious flavor. In the middle 1700's, Blackstone wrote, "[T]he keeping one day in the seven holy, as a time of relaxation and refreshment as well as for public worship, is of admirable service to a state considered merely as a civil institution. It humanizes, by the help of conversation and society, the manners of the lower classes; which would otherwise degenerate into a sordid ferocity and savage selfishness of spirit; it enables the industrious workman to pursue his occupation in the ensuing week with health and cheerfulness." . . . A 1788 English work dealing with chimney sweeps . . . in addition to providing for their Sunday religious affairs, also regulated their hours of work. The preamble to a 1679 Rhode Island enactment stated that the reason for the ban on Sunday employment was that "persons being evil minded, have presumed to employ in servile labor, more than necessity requireth, their servants. . . ." The New York law of 1788 omitted the term "Lord's day" and substituted "the first day of the week commonly called Sunday." Similar changes marked the Maryland statutes, discussed below. With the advent of the First Amendment, the colonial provisions requiring church attendance were soon repealed. . . .

More recently, further secular justifications have been advanced for making Sunday a day of rest, a day when people may recover from the labors of the week just passed and may physically and mentally prepare for the week's work to come. In England, during the First World War, a committee investigating the health conditions of munitions workers reported that "if the maximum output is to be secured and maintained for any length of time, a weekly period of rest must be allowed. . . . On economic and social grounds alike this weekly period of rest is best provided on Sunday."

The proponents of Sunday closing legislation are no longer exclusively representatives of religious interests. . . .

Throughout the years, state legislatures have modified, deleted from and added to their Sunday statutes. Almost every State in our country presently has some type of Sunday regulation and over forty possess a relatively comprehensive system. Thus have Sunday laws evolved from the wholly religious sanctions that originally were enacted. . . .

In light of the evolution of our Sunday Closing Laws through the centuries, and of their more or less recent emphasis upon secular considerations, it is not difficult to discern that as presently written and administered, most of them, at least, are of a secular rather than of a religious character, and that presently they bear no relationship to establishment of religion as those words are used in the Constitution of the United States.

Throughout this century and longer, both the federal and state governments have oriented their activities very largely toward improvement of the health, safety, recreation and general well-being of our citizens. Numerous laws affecting public health, safety factors in industry, laws affecting hours and conditions of labor of women and children, week-end diversion at parks and beaches, and cultural activities of various kinds, now

point the way toward the good life for all. Sunday Closing Laws, like those before us, have become part and parcel of this great governmental concern wholly apart from their original purposes or connotations. The present purpose and effect of most of them is to provide a uniform day of rest for all citizens; the fact that this day is Sunday, a day of particular significance for the dominant Christian sects, does not bar the State from achieving its secular goals. To say that the States cannot prescribe Sunday as a day of rest for these purposes solely because centuries ago such laws had their genesis in religion would give a constitutional interpretation of hostility to the public welfare rather than one of mere separation of church and State.

We now reach the Maryland statutes under review. The title of the major series of sections of the Maryland Code dealing with Sunday closing—Art. 27, §§ 492–534C—is "Sabbath Breaking"; § 492 proscribes work or bodily labor on the "Lord's day," and forbids persons to "profane the Lord's day" by gaming, fishing et cetera; § 522 refers to Sunday as the "Sabbath day." As has been mentioned above, many of the exempted Sunday activities in the various localities of the State may only be conducted during the afternoon and late evening; most Christian church services, of course, are held on Sunday morning and early Sunday evening. Finally, as previously noted, certain localities do not permit the allowed Sunday activities to be carried on within one hundred yards of any church where religious services are being held. This is the totality of the evidence of religious purpose which may be gleaned from the face of the present statute and from its operative effect.

The predecessors of the existing Maryland Sunday laws are undeniably religious in origin. . . .

Considering the language and operative effect of the current statutes, we no longer find the blanket prohibition against Sunday work or bodily labor. To the contrary, we find that § 521 of Art. 27, the section which appellants violated, permits the Sunday sale of tobaccos and sweets and a long list of sundry articles which we have enumerated above; we find that § 509 of Art. 27 permits the Sunday operation of bathing beaches, amusement parks and similar facilities; we find that Art. 2B, § 28, permits the Sunday sale of alcoholic beverages, products strictly forbidden by predecessor statutes; we are told that Anne Arundel County allows Sunday bingo and the Sunday playing of pin ball machines and slot machines, activities generally condemned by prior Maryland Sunday legislation. Certainly, these are not works of charity or necessity. Section 521's current stipulation that shops with only one employee may remain open on Sunday does not coincide with a religious purpose. These provisions, along with those which permit various sports and entertainments on Sunday, seem clearly to be fashioned for the purpose of providing a Sunday atmosphere of recreation, cheerfulness, repose and enjoyment. Coupled with the general proscription against other types of work, we believe that the air of the day is one of relaxation rather than one of religion. . . .

13. MARSH v. CHAMBERS

Colonial legislatures often commenced with a prayer, and the Continental Congress took up the practice in 1774. The tradition continues in the United States Congress and many state legislative halls. In *Marsh* v. *Chambers* the Supreme Court discussed the constitutionality of having a chaplain paid with tax dollars deliver an invocation prior to each session of the Nebraska legislature. This case also gave the Court the opportunity to elaborate further on its view of the concept of "neutrality" embodied in the First Amendment.

CHIEF JUSTICE BURGER DELIVERED
THE OPINION OF THE COURT.

The Nebraska Legislature begins each of its sessions with a prayer offered by a chaplain who is chosen biennially by the Executive Board of the Legislative Council and paid out of public funds. Robert E. Palmer, a Presbyterian minister, has served as chaplain since 1965 at a salary of $319.75 per month for each month the legislature is in session. . . .

The opening of sessions of legislative and other deliberative public bodies with prayer is deeply embedded in the history and tradition of this country. From colonial times through the founding of the Republic and ever since, the practice of legislative prayer has coexisted with the principles of disestablishment and religious freedom. In the very courtrooms in which the United States District Judge and later three Circuit Judges heard and decided this case, the proceedings opened with an announcement that concluded, "God save the United States and this Honorable Court." The same invocation occurs at all sessions of this Court.

The tradition in many of the Colonies was, of course, linked to an established church, but the Continental Congress, beginning in 1774, adopted the traditional procedure of opening its sessions with a prayer offered by a paid chaplain. . . . Although prayers were not offered during the Constitutional Convention, the First Congress, as one of its early items of business, adopted the policy

463 U.S. 783 (1983).

of selecting a chaplain to open each session with prayer. Thus, on April 7, 1789, the Senate appointed a committee "to take under consideration the manner of electing Chaplains." On April 9, 1789, a similar committee was appointed by the House of Representatives. On April 25, 1789, the Senate elected its first chaplain, [and] the House followed suit on May 1, 1789. A statute providing for the payment of these chaplains was enacted into law on September 22, 1789.

On September 25, 1789, three days after Congress authorized the appointment of paid chaplains, final agreement was reached on the language of the Bill of Rights. Clearly the men who wrote the First Amendment Religion Clause did not view paid legislative chaplains and opening prayers as a violation of that Amendment, for the practice of opening sessions with prayer has continued without interruption ever since that early session of Congress. It has also been followed consistently in most of the states, including Nebraska, where the institution of opening legislative sessions with prayer was adopted even before the State attained statehood. . . .

Standing alone, historical patterns cannot justify contemporary violations of constitutional guarantees, but there is far more here than simply historical patterns. . . .

. . . No more is Nebraska's practice of over a century, consistent with two centuries of national practice, to be cast aside. It can hardly be thought that in the same week Members of the First Congress voted to appoint and to pay a chaplain for each House and also voted to approve the draft of the First Amendment for submission to the states, they intended the Establishment Clause of the Amendment to forbid what they had just declared acceptable. In applying the First Amendment to the states through the Fourteenth Amendment, it would be incongruous to interpret that Clause as imposing more stringent First Amendment limits on the states than the draftsmen imposed on the Federal Government.

This unique history leads us to accept the interpretation of the First Amendment draftsmen who saw no real threat to the Establishment Clause arising from a practice of prayer similar to that now challenged. We conclude that legislative prayer presents no more potential for establishment than the provision of school transportation . . . beneficial grants for higher education . . . or tax exemptions for religious organizations. . . .

Respondent . . . argues that we should not rely too heavily on "the advice of the Founding Fathers" because the messages of history often tend to be ambiguous and not relevant to a society far more heterogeneous than that of the Framers. . . . Respondent also points out that John Jay and John Rutledge opposed the motion to begin the first session of the Continental Congress with prayer. . . .

We do not agree that evidence of opposition to a measure weakens the force of the historical argument; indeed it infuses it with power by demonstrating that the subject was considered carefully and the action not taken thoughtlessly, by force of long tradition and without regard to the problems posed by a pluralistic society. Jay and Rutledge specifically grounded their objection on the fact that the delegates to the Congress "were so divided in religious sentiments . . . that [they] could not join in the same act of worship." Their objection was met by Samuel Adams, who stated that "he was no bigot, and could hear a prayer from a gentleman of piety and virtue, who was at the same time a friend to his country." . . .

This interchange emphasizes that the delegates did not consider opening prayers as a proselytizing activity or as symbolically placing the government's "official seal of approval on one religious view." Rather, the Founding Fathers looked at invocations as "conduct whose . . . effect . . . harmonize[d] with the tenets of some or all religions." The Establishment Clause does not always bar a state from regulating conduct simply because it "harmonizes with religious canons." Here, the individual claiming injury by the practice is an adult, presumably not readily susceptible to "religious indoctrination."

In light of the unambiguous and unbroken history of more than 200 years, there can be no doubt that the practice of opening legislative sessions with prayer has become part of the fabric of our society. To invoke Divine guidance on a public body entrusted with making the laws is not, in these circumstances, an "establishment" of religion or a step toward establishment; it is simply a tolerable acknowledgment of beliefs widely held among the people of this country. As Justice Douglas observed, "[w]e are a religious people whose institutions presuppose a Supreme Being." . . .

We turn then to the question of whether any features of the Nebraska practice violate the Establishment Clause. Beyond the bare fact that a prayer is offered, three points have been made: first, that a clergyman of only one denomination—Presbyterian—has been selected for 16 years; second, that the chaplain is paid at public expense; and third, that the prayers are in the Judeo-Christian tradition. Weighed against the historical background, these factors do not serve to invalidate Nebraska's practice.

The Court of Appeals was concerned that Palmer's long tenure has the effect of giving preference to his religious views. We cannot, any more than Members of the Congresses of this century, perceive any suggestion that choosing a clergyman of one denomination advances the beliefs of a particular church. To the contrary, the evidence indicates that Palmer was reappointed because his performance and personal qualities were acceptable to the body appointing him. Palmer was not the only clergyman heard by the legislature; guest chaplains have officiated at the request of various legislators and as substitutes during Palmer's absences. Absent proof that the chaplain's reappointment stemmed from an impermissible motive, we conclude that his long tenure does not in itself conflict with the Establishment Clause.

Nor is the compensation of the chaplain from public funds a reason to invalidate the Nebraska Legislature's chaplaincy; remuneration is grounded in historic practice initiated, as we noted earlier, by the same Congress that drafted the Establishment Clause of the First Amendment. . . . The content of the prayer is not of concern to judges where, as here, there is no indication that the prayer opportunity has been exploited to proselytize or advance any one, or to disparage any other, faith or belief. That being so, it is not for us to embark on a sensitive evaluation or to parse the content of a particular prayer.

We do not doubt the sincerity of those, who like respondent, believe that to have prayer in this context risks the beginning of the establishment the Founding Fathers feared. But this concern is not well founded, for as Justice Goldberg [has] aptly observed . . . :

It is of course true that great consequences can grow from small beginnings, but the measure of constitutional adjudication is the ability and willingness to distinguish between real threat and mere shadow.

The unbroken practice for two centuries in the National Congress, for more than a century in Nebraska and in many other states, gives abundant assurance that there is no real threat "while this Court sits." . . .

JUSTICE BRENNAN,
WITH WHOM JUSTICE MARSHALL JOINS,
DISSENTING.

The Court today has written a narrow and, on the whole, careful opinion. In effect, the Court holds that officially sponsored legislative prayer, primarily on account of its "unique history," is generally exempted from the First Amendment's prohibition against "an establishment of religion." The Court's opinion is consistent with dictum in at least one of our prior decisions, and its limited rationale should pose little threat to

the overall fate of the Establishment Clause.
. . .

The Court makes no pretense of subjecting Nebraska's practice of legislative prayer to any of the formal "tests" that have traditionally structured our inquiry under the Establishment Clause. That it fails to do so is, in a sense, a good thing, for it simply confirms that the Court is carving out an exception to the Establishment Clause rather than reshaping Establishment Clause doctrine to accommodate legislative prayer. For my purposes, however, I must begin by demonstrating what should be obvious: that, if the Court were to judge legislative prayer through the unsentimental eye of our settled doctrine, it would have to strike it down as a clear violation of the Establishment Clause.
. . .

That the "purpose" of legislative prayer is pre-eminently religious rather than secular seems to me to be self-evident. "To invoke Divine guidance on a public body entrusted with making the laws," is nothing but a religious act. Moreover, whatever secular functions legislative prayer might play—formally opening the legislative session, getting the members of the body to quiet down, and imbuing them with a sense of seriousness and high purpose—could so plainly be performed in a purely nonreligious fashion that to claim a secular purpose for the prayer is an insult to the perfectly honorable individuals who instituted and continue the practice.

The "primary effect" of legislative prayer is also clearly religious. As we said in the context of officially sponsored prayers in the public schools, "prescribing a particular form of religious worship," even if the individuals involved have the choice not to participate, places "indirect coercive pressure upon religious minorities to conform to the prevailing officially approved religion. . . ." More importantly, invocations in Nebraska's legislative halls explicitly link religious belief and observance to the power and prestige of the State. "[T]he mere appearance of a joint exercise of legislative authority by Church and State provides a significant symbolic benefit to religion in the minds of some by reason of the power conferred."

Finally, there can be no doubt that the practice of legislative prayer leads to excessive "entanglement" between the State and religion. . . . In the case of legislative prayer, the process of choosing a "suitable" chaplain, whether on a permanent or rotating basis, and insuring that the chaplain limits himself or herself to "suitable" prayers, involves precisely the sort of supervision that agencies of government should if at all possible avoid.

[E]xcessive "entanglement" might [also] arise out of "the divisive political potential" of a state statute or program.

Ordinarily political debate and division, however vigorous or even partisan, are normal and healthy manifestations of our democratic system of government, but political division along religious lines was one of the principal evils against which the First Amendment was intended to protect. The potential divisiveness of such conflict is a threat to the normal political process.

In this case, this second aspect of entanglement is also clear. The controversy between Senator Chambers and his colleagues, which had reached the stage of difficulty and rancor long before this lawsuit was brought, has split the Nebraska Legislature precisely on issues of religion and religious conformity. The record in this case also reports a series of instances, involving legislators other than Senator Chambers, in which invocations by Reverend Palmer and others led to controversy along religious lines. And in general, the history of legislative prayer has been far more eventful—and divisive—than a hasty reading of the Court's opinion might indicate. . . .

The principles of "separation" and "neutrality" implicit in the Establishment Clause serve many purposes. Four of these are particularly relevant here.

The first, which is most closely related to

the more general conceptions of liberty found in the remainder of the First Amendment, is to guarantee the individual right to conscience. The right to conscience, in the religious sphere, is not only implicated when the government engages in direct or indirect coercion. It is also implicated when the government requires individuals to support the practices of a faith with which they do not agree.

The second purpose of separation and neutrality is to keep the state from interfering in the essential autonomy of religious life, either by taking upon itself the decision of religious issues, or by unduly involving itself in the supervision of religious institutions or officials.

The third purpose of separation and neutrality is to prevent the trivialization and degradation of religion by too close an attachment to the organs of government. The Establishment Clause "stands as an expression of principle on the part of the Founders of our Constitution that religion is too personal, too sacred, too holy, to permit its 'unhallowed perversion' by a civil magistrate."

Finally, the principles of separation and neutrality help assure that essentially religious issues, precisely because of their importance and sensitivity, not become the occasion for battle in the political arena. . . . With regard to most issues, the government may be influenced by partisan argument and may act as a partisan itself. In each case, there will be winners and losers in the political battle, and the losers' most common recourse is the right to dissent and the right to fight the battle again another day. With regard to matters that are essentially reli-

gious, however, the Establishment Clause seeks that there should be no political battles, and that no American should at any point feel alienated from his government because that government has declared or acted upon some "official" or "authorized" point of view on a matter of religion.

The imperatives of separation and neutrality are not limited to the relationship of government to religious institutions or denominations, but extend as well to the relationship of government to religious beliefs and practices. . . .

Legislative prayer clearly violates the principles of neutrality and separation that are embedded within the Establishment Clause. It is contrary to the fundamental message of *Engel* and *Schempp*. It intrudes on the right to conscience by forcing some legislators either to participate in a "prayer opportunity," with which they are in basic disagreement, or to make their disagreement a matter of public comment by declining to participate. It forces all residents of the State to support a religious exercise that may be contrary to their own beliefs. It requires the State to commit itself on fundamental theological issues. It has the potential for degrading religion by allowing a religious call to worship to be intermeshed with a secular call to order. And it injects religion into the political sphere by creating the potential that each and every selection of a chaplain, or consideration of a particular prayer, or even reconsideration of the practice itself, will provoke a political battle along religious lines and ultimately alienate some religiously identified group of citizens. . . .

263

Christmas is a holiday laden with both sacred and secular meanings. In *Lynch* v. *Donnelly*, residents of Pawtucket, Rhode Island challenged a traditional practice involving a "Seasons Greetings" display, sponsored by the city on private property, that included a nativity scene along with secular symbols of the holiday season. This case, combined with the decision in *Marsh* v. *Chambers*, suggests that in recent years the Court has moved toward a "benevolent neutrality" approach to Church and State and away from the "strict separation" approach evident in the early school prayer cases.

One year later, the Court was asked to consider whether the establishment clause would prohibit the Village of Scarsdale, New York from displaying a privately owned crèche in a public park. The Court split evenly (one justice not participating) and thus automatically affirmed the appellate court's decision holding that the Constitution does not forbid such a display.

CHIEF JUSTICE BURGER DELIVERED
THE OPINION OF THE COURT.

We granted certiorari to decide whether the Establishment Clause of the First Amendment prohibits a municipality from including a crèche, or Nativity scene, in its annual Christmas display.

Each year, in cooperation with the downtown retail merchants' association, the city of Pawtucket, R. I., erects a Christmas display as part of its observance of the Christmas holiday season. The display is situated in a park owned by a nonprofit organization and located in the heart of the shopping district. The display is essentially like those to be found in hundreds of towns or cities across the Nation—often on public grounds—during the Christmas season. The Pawtucket display comprises many of the figures and decorations traditionally associated with Christmas, including, among other things, a Santa Claus house, reindeer pulling Santa's sleigh, candy-striped poles, a Christmas tree, carolers, cutout figures representing such characters as a clown, an elephant, and a teddy bear, hundreds of colored lights, a large banner that reads "SEASONS GREET-

INGS," and the crèche at issue here. All components of this display are owned by the city.

The crèche, which has been included in the display for 40 or more years, consists of the traditional figures, including the Infant Jesus, Mary and Joseph, angels, shepherds, kings, and animals, all ranging in height from 5" to 5'. In 1973, when the present crèche was acquired, it cost the city $1,365; it now is valued at $200. The erection and dismantling of the crèche costs the city about $20 per year; nominal expenses are incurred in lighting the crèche. No money has been expended on its maintenance for the past 10 years.

Respondents, Pawtucket residents and individual members of the Rhode Island affiliate of the American Civil Liberties Union, and the affiliate itself, brought this action in the United States District Court for Rhode Island, challenging the city's inclusion of the crèche in the annual display. The District Court held that the city's inclusion of the crèche in the display violates the Establishment Clause. . . .

This Court has explained that the purpose of the Establishment and Free Exercise Clauses of the First Amendment is

465 U.S. 668 (1984).

to prevent, as far as possible, the intrusion of either [the church or the state] into the precincts of the other.

At the same time, however, the Court has recognized that

total separation is not possible in an absolute sense. Some relationship between government and religious organizations is inevitable.

In every Establishment Clause case, we must reconcile the inescapable tension between the objective of preventing unnecessary intrusion of either the church or the state upon the other, and the reality that, as the Court has so often noted, total separation of the two is not possible.

The Court has sometimes described the Religion Clauses as erecting a "wall" between church and state. The concept of a "wall" of separation is a useful figure of speech probably deriving from views of Thomas Jefferson. The metaphor has served as a reminder that the Establishment Clause forbids an established church or anything approaching it. But the metaphor itself is not a wholly accurate description of the practical aspects of the relationship that in fact exists between church and state.

No significant segment of our society and no institution within it can exist in a vacuum or in total or absolute isolation from all the other parts, much less from government. "It has never been thought either possible or desirable to enforce a regime of total separation. . . ." Nor does the Constitution require complete separation of church and state; it affirmatively mandates accommodation, not merely tolerance, of all religions, and forbids hostility toward any. Anything less would require the "callous indifference" we have said was never intended by the Establishment Clause. Indeed, we have observed, such hostility would bring us into "war with our national tradition as embodied in the First Amendment's guaranty of the free exercise of religion."

The Court's interpretation of the Establishment Clause has comported with what history reveals was the contemporaneous understanding of its guarantees. A significant example of the contemporaneous understanding of that Clause is found in the events of the first week of the First Session of the First Congress in 1789. In the very week that Congress approved the Establishment Clause as part of the Bill of Rights for submission to the states, it enacted legislation providing for paid chaplains for the House and Senate. . . .

The interpretation of the Establishment Clause by Congress in 1789 takes on special significance in light of the Court's emphasis that the First Congress

was a Congress whose constitutional decisions have always been regarded, as they should be regarded, as of the greatest weight in the interpretation of that fundamental instrument.

It is clear that neither the 17 draftsmen of the Constitution who were Members of the First Congress, nor the Congress of 1789, saw any establishment problem in the employment of congressional Chaplains to offer daily prayers in the Congress, a practice that has continued for nearly two centuries. It would be difficult to identify a more striking example of the accommodation of religious belief intended by the Framers.

There is an unbroken history of official acknowledgment by all three branches of government of the role of religion in American life from at least 1789. Seldom in our opinions was this more affirmatively expressed than in Justice Douglas' opinion for the Court validating a program allowing release of public school students from classes to attend off-campus religious exercises. Rejecting a claim that the program violated the Establishment Clause, the Court asserted pointedly:

We are a religious people whose institutions presuppose a Supreme Being.

Our history is replete with official references to the value and invocation of Divine guidance in deliberations and pronouncements of the Founding Fathers and contemporary leaders. Beginning in the early colonial period long before Independence, a day of Thanksgiving was celebrated as a religious holiday to give thanks for the bounties of Nature as gifts from God. President Washington and his successors proclaimed Thanksgiving, with all its religious overtones, a day of national celebration and Congress made it a National Holiday more than a century ago. That holiday has not lost its theme of expressing thanks for Divine aid any more than has Christmas lost its religious significance.

Executive Orders and other official announcements of Presidents and of the Congress have proclaimed both Christmas and Thanksgiving National Holidays in religious terms. And, by Acts of Congress, it has long been the practice that federal employees are released from duties on these National Holidays, while being paid from the same public revenues that provide the compensation of the Chaplains of the Senate and the House and the military services. Thus, it is clear that Government has long recognized—indeed it has subsidized—holidays with religious significance.

Other examples of reference to our religious heritage are found in the statutorily prescribed national motto "In God We Trust," which Congress and the President mandated for our currency, and in the language "One nation under God," as part of the Pledge of Allegiance to the American flag. That pledge is recited by many thousands of public school children—and adults—every year.

Art galleries supported by public revenues display religious paintings of the 15th and 16th centuries, predominantly inspired by one religious faith. The National Gallery in Washington, maintained with Government support, for example, has long exhibited masterpieces with religious messages, notably the Last Supper, and paintings depicting the Birth of Christ, the Crucifixion, and the Resurrection, among many others with explicit Christian themes and messages. The very chamber in which oral arguments on this case were heard is decorated with a notable and permanent—not seasonal—symbol of religion: Moses with the Ten Commandments. Congress has long provided chapels in the Capitol for religious worship and meditation.

There are countless other illustrations of the Government's acknowledgment of our religious heritage and governmental sponsorship of graphic manifestations of that heritage. Congress has directed the President to proclaim a National Day of Prayer each year "on which [day] the people of the United States may turn to God in prayer and meditation at churches, in groups, and as individuals." Our Presidents have repeatedly issued such Proclamations. Presidential Proclamations and messages have also [been] issued to commemorate Jewish Heritage Week, and the Jewish High Holy Days. One cannot look at even this brief résumé without finding that our history is pervaded by expressions of religious beliefs such as are found in *Zorach*. Equally pervasive is the evidence of accommodation of all faiths and all forms of religious expression, and hostility toward none. Through this accommodation, as Justice Douglas observed, governmental action has "follow[ed] the best of our traditions" and "respect[ed] the religious nature of our people." . . .

This history may help explain why the Court consistently has declined to take a rigid, absolutist view of the Establishment Clause. We have refused "to construe the Religion Clauses with a literalness that would undermine the ultimate constitutional objective as *illuminated by history*." In our modern, complex society, whose traditions and constitutional underpinnings rest on and encourage diversity and pluralism in all areas, an absolutist approach in applying the

266

Establishment Clause is simplistic and has been uniformly rejected by the Court.

Rather than mechanically invalidating all governmental conduct or statutes that confer benefits or give special recognition to religion in general or to one faith—as an absolutist approach would dictate—the Court has scrutinized challenged legislation or official conduct to determine whether, in reality, it establishes a religion or religious faith, or tends to do so. . . .

In each case, the inquiry calls for line-drawing; no fixed, per se rule can be framed. The Establishment Clause like the Due Process Clauses is not a precise, detailed provision in a legal code capable of ready application. The purpose of the Establishment Clause "was to state an objective, not to write a statute." The line between permissible relationships and those barred by the Clause can no more be straight and unwavering than due process can be defined in a single stroke or phrase or test. The Clause erects a "blurred, indistinct, and variable barrier depending on all the circumstances of a particular relationship."

In the line-drawing process we have often found it useful to inquire whether the challenged law or conduct has a secular purpose, whether its principal or primary effect is to advance or inhibit religion, and whether it creates an excessive entanglement of government with religion. But, we have repeatedly emphasized our unwillingness to be confined to any single test or criterion in this sensitive area. . . . In two cases, the Court did not even apply [this] "test." We did not, for example, consider that analysis relevant in Marsh v. Chambers. . . .

In this case, the focus of our inquiry must be on the crèche in the context of the Christmas season. . . . In [Stone v. Graham,] for example, we invalidated a state statute requiring the posting of a copy of the Ten Commandments on public classroom walls. But the Court carefully pointed out that the Commandments were posted purely as a religious admonition, not "integrated into the

school curriculum, where the Bible may constitutionally be used in an appropriate study of history, civilization, ethics, comparative religion, or the like." Similarly, in Abington, although the Court struck down the practices in two States requiring daily Bible readings in public schools, it specifically noted that nothing in the Court's holding was intended to "indicat[e] that such study of the Bible or of religion, when presented objectively as part of a secular program of education, may not be effec:ed consistently with the First Amendment." Focus exclusively on the religious component of any activity would inevitably lead to its invalidation under the Establishment Clause.

The Court has invalidated legislation or governmental action on the ground that a secular purpose was lacking, but only when it has concluded there was no question that the statute or activity was motivated wholly by religious considerations. . . .

When viewed in the proper context of the Christmas Holiday season, it is apparent that, on this record, there is insufficient evidence to establish that the inclusion of the crèche is a purposeful or surreptitious effort to express some kind of subtle governmental advocacy of a particular religious message. In a pluralistic society a variety of motives and purposes are implicated. The city, like the Congresses and Presidents, however, has principally taken note of a significant historical religious event long celebrated in the Western World. The crèche in the display depicts the historical origins of this traditional event long recognized as a National Holiday. . . .

The narrow question is whether there is a secular purpose for Pawtucket's display of the crèche. The display is sponsored by the city to celebrate the Holiday and to depict the origins of that Holiday. These are legitimate secular purposes. . . .

Comparisons of the relative benefits to religion of different forms of governmental support are elusive and difficult to make. But to conclude that the primary effect of including the crèche is to advance religion in violation of the Establishment Clause would require that we view it as more beneficial to and more an endorsement of religion, for example, than expenditure of large sums of public money for textbooks supplied throughout the country to students attending church-sponsored schools; expenditure of public funds for transportation of students to church-sponsored schools; federal grants for college buildings of church-sponsored institutions of higher education combining secular and religious education; noncategorical grants to church-sponsored colleges and universities; and the tax exemptions for church properties sanctioned in *Walz* v. *Tax Comm'n.* It would also require that we view it as more of an endorsement of religion than the Sunday Closing Laws upheld in *McGowan* v. *Maryland;* the release program for religious training in *Zorach* v. *Clauson;* and the legislative prayers upheld in *Marsh* v. *Chambers.*

We are unable to discern a greater aid to religion deriving from inclusion of the crèche than from these benefits and endorsements previously held not violative of the Establishment Clause. . . .

We are satisfied that the city has a secular purpose for including the crèche, that the city has not impermissibly advanced religion, and that including the crèche does not create excessive entanglement between religion and government. . . .

Of course the crèche is identified with one religious faith but no more so than the examples we have set out from prior cases in which we found no conflict with the Establishment Clause. . . . It would be ironic, however, if the inclusion of a single symbol of a particular historic religious event, as part of a celebration acknowledged in the Western World for 20 centuries, and in this country by the people, by the Executive Branch, by the Congress, and the courts for 2 centuries, would so "taint" the city's exhibit as to render it violative of the Establishment Clause. To forbid the use of this one passive symbol—the crèche—at the very time people are taking note of the season with Christmas hymns and carols in public schools and other public places, and while the Congress and legislatures open sessions with prayers by paid chaplains would be a stilted overreaction contrary to our history and to our holdings. If the presence of the crèche in this display violates the Establishment Clause, a host of other forms of taking official note of Christmas, and of our religious heritage, are equally offensive to the Constitution.

The Court has acknowledged that the "fears and political problems" that gave rise to the Religion Clauses in the 18th century are of far less concern today. We are unable to perceive the Archbishop of Canterbury, the Bishop of Rome, or other powerful religious leaders behind every public acknowledgment of the religious heritage long officially recognized by the three constitutional branches of government. Any notion that these symbols pose a real danger of establishment of a state church is farfetched indeed. . . .

Taxation and Regulation

15. WALZ v. TAX COMMISSION

Walz v. Tax Commission provided the Supreme Court with its first opportunity to consider whether tax exemptions for religious organizations run afoul of the Constitution's proscription of the establishment of religion. In upholding the tax exemption, the Court considered the effect of history on its interpretation of the First Amendment.

MR. CHIEF JUSTICE BURGER DELIVERED THE OPINION OF THE COURT.

Appellant, owner of real estate in Richmond County, New York, sought an injunction in the New York courts to prevent the New York City Tax Commission from granting property tax exemptions to religious organizations for religious properties used solely for religious worship. The exemption from state taxes is authorized by Art. 16, § 1, of the New York Constitution, which provides in relevant part:

Exemptions from taxation may be granted only by general laws. Exemptions may be altered or repealed except those exempting real or personal property used exclusively for religious, educational or charitable purposes as defined by law and owned by any corporation or association organized or conducted exclusively for one or more of such purposes and not operating for profit.

The essence of appellant's contention was that the New York City Tax Commission's grant of an exemption to church property indirectly requires the appellant to make a contribution to religious bodies and thereby violates provisions prohibiting establishment of religion under the First Amendment which under the Fourteenth Amendment is binding on the States. . . .

[F]or the men who wrote the Religion Clauses of the First Amendment the "establishment of a religion connoted sponsorship, financial support, and active involvement of the sovereign in religious activity. In England, and in some Colonies at the time of the separation in 1776, the Church of England was sponsored and supported by the Crown as a state, or established, church; in other countries "establishment" meant sponsorship by the sovereign of the Lutheran or Catholic Church. . . .

The Establishment and Free Exercise Clauses of the First Amendment are not the most precisely drawn portions of the Constitution. The sweep of the absolute prohibitions in the Religion Clauses may have been calculated; but the purpose was to state an objective not to write a statute. In attempting to articulate the scope of the two Religion Clauses, the Court's opinions reflect the limitations inherent in formulating general principles on a case-by-case basis. The considerable internal inconsistency in the opinions of the Court derives from what, in retrospect, may have been too sweeping utterances on aspects of these clauses that seemed clear in relation to the particular cases but have limited meaning as general principles.

The Court has struggled to find a neutral course between the two Religion Clauses, both of which are cast in absolute terms, and either of which, if expanded to a logical extreme, would tend to clash with the other. . . .

The course of constitutional neutrality in this area cannot be an absolutely straight

397 U.S. 664 (1970).

line; rigidity could well defeat the basic purpose of these provisions, which is to insure that no religion be sponsored or favored, none commanded, and none inhibited. The general principle deducible from the First Amendment and all that has been said by the Court is this: that we will not tolerate either governmentally established religion or governmental interference with religion. Short of those expressly proscribed governmental acts there is room for play in the joints productive of a benevolent neutrality which will permit religious exercise to exist without sponsorship and without interference.

Each value judgment under the Religion Clauses must therefore turn on whether particular acts in question are intended to establish or interfere with religious beliefs and practices or have the effect of doing so. Adherence to the policy of neutrality that derives from an accommodation of the Establishment and Free Exercise Clauses has prevented the kind of involvement that would tip the balance toward government control of churches or governmental restraint on religious practice. . . .

In *Everson* the Court declined to construe the Religion Clauses with a literalness that would undermine the ultimate constitutional objective as illuminated by history. Surely, bus transportation and police protection to pupils who receive religious instruction "aid" that particular religion to maintain schools that plainly tend to assure future adherents to a particular faith by having control of their total education at an early age. No religious body that maintains schools would deny this as an affirmative if not dominant policy of church schools. But if as in *Everson* buses can be provided to carry and policemen to protect church school pupils, we fail to see how a broader range of police and fire protection given equally to all churches, along with nonprofit hospitals, art galleries, and libraries receiving the same tax exemption, is different for purposes of the Religion Clauses.

Similarly, making textbooks available to pupils in parochial schools in common with public schools was surely an "aid" to the sponsoring churches because it relieved those churches of an enormous aggregate cost for those books. Supplying of costly teaching materials was not seen either as manifesting a legislative purpose to aid or as having a primary effect of aid contravening the First Amendment. . . . In so holding the Court was heeding both its own prior decisions and our religious tradition.

With all the risks inherent in programs that bring about administrative relationships between public education bodies and church-sponsored schools, we have been able to chart a course that preserved the autonomy and freedom of religious bodies while avoiding any semblance of established religion. This is a "tight rope" and one we have successfully traversed.

The legislative purpose of a property tax exemption is neither the advancement nor the inhibition of religion; it is neither sponsorship nor hostility. New York, in common with the other States, has determined that certain entities that exist in a harmonious relationship to the community at large, and that foster its "moral or mental improvement," should not be inhibited in their activities by property taxation or the hazard of loss of those properties for nonpayment of taxes. It has not singled out one particular church or religious group or even churches as such; rather, it has granted exemption to all houses of religious worship within a broad class of property owned by non-profit, quasi-public corporations which include hospitals, libraries, playgrounds, scientific, professional, historical, and patriotic groups. The State has an affirmative policy that considers these groups as beneficial and stabilizing influences in community life and finds this classification useful, desirable, and in the public interest. Qualification for tax exemption is not perpetual or immutable; some tax-exempt groups lose that status when their activities take them outside the classification and new entities can come into being and qualify for exemption.

Governments have not always been tolerant of religious activity, and hostility toward religion has taken many shapes and forms —economic, political, and sometimes harshly oppressive. Grants of exemption historically reflect the concern of authors of constitutions and statutes as to the latent dangers inherent in the imposition of property taxes; exemption constitutes a reasonable and balanced attempt to guard against those dangers. The limits of permissible state accommodation to religion are by no means co-extensive with the noninterference mandated by the Free Exercise Clause. To equate the two would be to deny a national heritage with roots in the Revolution itself. . . . We cannot read New York's statute as attempting to establish religion; it is simply sparing the exercise of religion from the burden of property taxation levied on private profit institutions.

We find it unnecessary to justify the tax exemption on the social welfare services or "good works" that some churches perform for parishioners and others—family counselling, aid to the elderly and the infirm, and to children. Churches vary substantially in the scope of such services; programs expand or contract according to resources and need. As public-sponsored programs enlarge, private aid from the church sector may diminish. The extent of social services may vary, depending on whether the church serves an urban or rural, a rich or poor constituency. To give emphasis to so variable an aspect of the work of religious bodies would introduce an element of governmental evaluation and standards as to the worth of particular social welfare programs, thus producing a kind of continuing day-to-day relationship which the policy of neutrality seeks to minimize. Hence, the use of a social welfare yardstick as a significant element to qualify for tax exemption could conceivably give rise to confrontations that could escalate to constitutional dimensions.

Determining that the legislative purpose of tax exemption is not aimed at establishing, sponsoring, or supporting religion does not end the inquiry, however. We must also be sure that the end result—the effect—is not an excessive government entanglement with religion. The test is inescapably one of degree. Either course, taxation of churches or exemption, occasions some degree of involvement with religion. Elimination of exemption would tend to expand the involvement of government by giving rise to tax valuation of church property, tax liens, tax foreclosures, and the direct confrontations and conflicts that follow in the train of those legal processes.

Granting tax exemptions to churches necessarily operates to afford an indirect economic benefit and also gives rise to some, but yet a lesser, involvement than taxing them. In analyzing either alternative the questions are whether the involvement is excessive, and whether it is a continuing one calling for official and continuing surveillance leading to an impermissible degree of entanglement. Obviously a direct money subsidy would be a relationship pregnant with involvement and, as with most governmental grant programs, could encompass sustained and detailed administrative relationships for enforcement of statutory or administrative standards, but that is not this case. The hazards of churches supporting government are hardly less in their potential than the hazards of government supporting churches; each relationship carries some involvement rather than the desired insulation and separation. We cannot ignore the instances in history when church support of government led to the kind of involvement we seek to avoid.

The grant of a tax exemption is not sponsorship since the government does not transfer part of its revenue to churches but simply abstains from demanding that the church support the state. No one has ever suggested that tax exemption has converted libraries, art galleries, or hospitals into arms of the state or put employers "on the public payroll." There is no genuine nexus between tax exemption and establishment of religion. As Mr. Justice Holmes commented in a related context "a page of history is worth a volume of logic." The exemption creates only a minimal and remote involvement between church and state and far less than taxation of churches. It restricts the fiscal relationship between church and state, and tends to complement and reinforce the desired separation insulating each from the other.

Separation in this context cannot mean absence of all contact; the complexities of modern life inevitably produce some contact and the fire and police protection received by houses of religious worship are no more than incidental benefits accorded all persons or institutions within a State's boundaries, along with many other exempt organizations. . . .

All of the 50 States provide for tax exemption of places of worship, most of them doing so by constitutional guarantees. For so long as federal income taxes have had any potential impact on churches—over 75 years—religious organizations have been expressly exempt from the tax. Such treatment is an "aid" to churches no more and no less in principle than the real estate tax exemption granted by States. Few concepts are more deeply embedded in the fabric of our national life, beginning with pre-Revolutionary colonial times, than for the government to exercise at the very least this kind of benevolent neutrality toward churches and religious exercise generally so long as none was favored over others and none suffered interference.

It is significant that Congress, from its earliest days, has viewed the Religion Clauses of the Constitution as authorizing statutory real estate tax exemption to religious bodies. In 1802 the 7th Congress enacted a taxing statute for the County of Alexandria, adopting the 1800 Virginia statutory pattern which provided tax exemptions for churches. As early as 1813 the 12th Congress refunded import duties paid by religious societies on the importation of religious articles. During this period the City Council of Washington, D.C., acting under congressional authority, enacted a series of real and personal property assessments that uniformly exempted church property. In 1870 the Congress specifically exempted all churches in the District of Columbia and appurtenant grounds and property "from any and all taxes or assessments, national, municipal, or county." . . .

It is obviously correct that no one acquires a vested or protected right in violation of the Constitution by long use, even when that span of time covers our entire national existence and indeed predates it. Yet an unbroken practice of according the exemption to churches, openly and by affirmative state action, not covertly or by state inaction, is not something to be lightly cast aside. . . .

Nothing in this national attitude toward religious tolerance and two centuries of uninterrupted freedom from taxation has given the remotest sign of leading to an established church or religion and on the contrary it has operated affirmatively to help guarantee the free exercise of all forms of religious belief. Thus, it is hardly useful to suggest that tax exemption is but the "foot in the door" or the "nose of the camel in the tent" leading to an established church. Any move that realistically "establishes" a church or tends to do so can be dealt with "while this Court sits." . . .

It is interesting to note that while the precise question we now decide has not been directly before the Court previously, the broad question was discussed by the Court in relation to real estate taxes assessed nearly a century ago on land owned by and adjacent to a church in Washington, D.C. At that time Congress granted real estate tax exemptions to buildings devoted to art, to institutions of public charity, libraries, cemeteries, and "church buildings, and grounds actually occupied by such buildings." In denying tax exemption as to land owned by but not used for the church, but rather to produce income, the Court concluded:

> In the exercise of this [taxing] power, Congress, like any state legislature unrestricted by constitutional provisions, may, at its discretion, wholly exempt certain classes of property from taxation, or may tax them at a lower rate than other property. . . .

It appears that at least up to 1885 this Court, reflecting more than a century of our history and uninterrupted practice, accepted without discussion the proposition that federal or state grants of tax exemption to churches were not a violation of the Religion Clauses of the First Amendment. As to the New York statute, we now confirm that view.

16. BOB JONES UNIVERSITY v. UNITED STATES

Taxation not only produces revenue for the government, it provides a method for the state to enforce its policies. In the *Bob Jones University* case, the controversy arose from a challenge to the tax-exempt status of a religious school that had racially discriminatory admissions standards.

CHIEF JUSTICE BURGER DELIVERED
THE OPINION OF THE COURT.

We granted certiorari to decide whether petitioners, nonprofit private schools that prescribe and enforce racially discriminatory admissions standards on the basis of religious doctrine, qualify as tax-exempt organizations under § 501(c)(3) of the Internal Revenue Code of 1954.

No. 81-3, Bob Jones University v. United States

Bob Jones University is a nonprofit corporation located in Greenville, South Carolina. Its purpose is "to conduct an institution of learning . . . , giving special emphasis to the Christian religion and the ethics revealed in the Holy Scriptures." The corporation operates a school with an enrollment of approximately 5,000 students, from kindergarten through college and graduate school. Bob Jones University is not affiliated with any religious denomination, but is dedicated to the teaching and propagation of its fundamentalist Christian religious beliefs. It is both a religious and educational institution. Its teachers are required to be devout Christians, and all courses at the University are taught according to the Bible. Entering students are screened as to their religious beliefs, and their public and private conduct is strictly regulated by standards promulgated by University authorities.

The sponsors of the University genuinely believe that the Bible forbids interracial dating and marriage. To effectuate these views, Negroes were completely excluded until 1971. From 1971 to May 1975, the University accepted no applications from unmarried Negroes, but did accept applications from Negroes married within their race.

Following the decision of the United States Court of Appeals for the Fourth Circuit in *McCrary* v. *Runyon*, prohibiting racial exclusion from private schools, the University revised its policy. Since May 29, 1975, the University has permitted unmarried Negroes to enroll; but a disciplinary rule prohibits interracial dating and marriage. . . .

461 U.S. 574 (1983).

No. 81-1, Goldsboro Christian Schools, Inc. v. *United States*

Goldsboro Christian Schools is a nonprofit corporation located in Goldsboro, North Carolina. Like Bob Jones University, it was established "to conduct an institution of learning . . . , giving special emphasis to the Christian religion and the ethics revealed in the Holy scriptures." The school offers classes from kindergarten through high school, and since at least 1969 has satisfied the State of North Carolina's requirements for secular education in private schools. The school requires its high school students to take Bible-related courses, and begins each class with prayer.

Since its incorporation in 1963, Goldsboro Christian Schools has maintained a racially discriminatory admissions policy based upon its interpretation of the Bible. Goldsboro has for the most part accepted only Caucasians. On occasion, however, the school has accepted children from racially mixed marriages in which one of the parents is Caucasian.

Goldsboro never received a determination by the IRS that it was an organization entitled to tax exemption under § 501(c)(3). Upon audit of Goldsboro's records for the years 1969 through 1972, the IRS determined that Goldsboro was not an organization described in § 501(c)(3), and therefore was required to pay taxes under the Federal Insurance Contribution Act and the Federal Unemployment Tax Act. . . .

[T]he IRS [has] formalized the policy first announced in 1970, that . . . to qualify for a tax exemption pursuant to § 501(c)(3), an institution must show, first, that it falls within one of the eight categories expressly set forth in that section, and second, that its activity is not contrary to settled public policy.

Section 501(c)(3) provides that "[c]orporations . . . organized and operated exclusively for religious, charitable . . . or educational purposes" are entitled to tax exemption. Petitioners argue that the plain language of the statute guarantees them tax-exempt status. They emphasize the absence of any language in the statute expressly requiring all exempt organizations to be "charitable" in the common law sense, and they contend that the disjunctive "or" separating the categories in § 501(c)(3) precludes such a reading. Instead, they argue that if an institution falls within one or more of the specified categories it is automatically entitled to exemption, without regard to whether it also qualifies as "charitable." . . .

It is a well-established canon of statutory construction that a court should go beyond the literal language of a statute if reliance on that language would defeat the plain purpose of the statute. . . .

Section 501(c)(3) therefore must be analyzed and construed within the framework of the Internal Revenue Code and against the background of the Congressional purposes. Such an examination reveals unmistakable evidence that, underlying all relevant parts of the Code, is the intent that entitlement to tax exemption depends on meeting certain common law standards of charity—namely, that an institution seeking tax-exempt status must serve a public purpose and not be contrary to established public policy. . . .

We are bound to approach these questions with full awareness that determinations of public benefit and public policy are sensitive matters with serious implications for the institutions affected; a declaration that a given institution is not "charitable" should be made only where there can be no doubt that the activity involved is contrary to a fundamental public policy. But there can no longer be any doubt that racial discrimination in education violates deeply and widely accepted views of elementary justice. . . .

An unbroken line of cases following *Brown* v. *Board of Education* establishes beyond doubt this Court's view that racial discrimination in education violates a most fundamental national public policy, as well as rights of individuals. . . .

Few social or political issues in our history have been more vigorously debated and more extensively ventilated than the issue of racial discrimination, particularly in education. Given the stress and anguish of the history of efforts to escape from the shackles of the "separate but equal" doctrine, it cannot be said that educational institutions that, for whatever reasons, practice racial discrimination, are institutions exercising "beneficial and stabilizing influences in community life," or should be encouraged by having all taxpayers share in their support by way of special tax status. . . . Whatever may be the rationale for such private schools' policies, and however sincere the rationale may be, racial discrimination in education is contrary to public policy. Racially discriminatory educational institutions cannot be viewed as conferring a public benefit within the "charitable" concept discussed earlier, or within the Congressional intent underlying § 170 and § 501(c)(3). . . .

Petitioners contend that, even if the Commissioner's policy is valid as to nonreligious private schools, that policy cannot constitutionally be applied to schools that engage in racial discrimination on the basis of sincerely held religious beliefs. As to such schools it is argued that the IRS construction of § 170 and § 501(c)(3) violates their free exercise rights under the Religion Clauses of the First Amendment. This contention presents claims not heretofore considered by this Court in precisely this context.

This Court has long held the Free Exercise Clause of the First Amendment an absolute prohibition against governmental regulation of religious beliefs. . . . As interpreted by this Court, moreover, the Free Exercise Clause provides substantial protection for lawful conduct grounded in religious belief. . . . However, "[n]ot all burdens on religion are unconstitutional. . . . The state may justify a limitation on religious liberty by showing that it is essential to accomplish an overriding governmental interest."

On occasion this Court has found certain governmental interests so compelling as to allow even regulations prohibiting religiously based conduct. In *Prince* v. *Massachusetts,* for example, the Court held that neutrally cast child labor laws prohibiting sale of printed materials on public streets could be applied to prohibit children from dispensing religious literature. The Court found no constitutional infirmity in "excluding [Jehovah's Witness children] from doing there what no other children may do." . . . Denial of tax benefits will inevitably have a substantial impact on the operation of private religious schools, but will not prevent those schools from observing their religious tenets.

The governmental interest at stake here is compelling. As discussed [above] the Government has a fundamental, overriding interest in eradicating racial discrimination in education*—discrimination that prevailed, with official approval, for the first 165 years of this Nation's history. That governmental interest substantially outweighs whatever burden denial of tax benefits places on petitioners' exercise of their religious beliefs. The interests asserted by petitioners cannot be accommodated with that compelling governmental interest . . . and no "less restrictive means" . . . are available to achieve the governmental interest.**

---

*We deal here only with religious *schools*— not with churches or other purely religious institutions; here, the governmental interest is in denying public support to racial discrimination in education. As noted earlier, racially discriminatory schools "exer[t] a pervasive influence on the entire educational process," outweighing any public benefit that they might otherwise provide.

**Bob Jones University also contends that denial of tax exemption violates the Establishment Clause by preferring religions whose tenets do not require racial discrimination over those which believe racial intermixing is forbidden. It is well settled that neither a State nor the Federal Government may pass laws which "prefer one religion over another," but "[i]t is equally true" that a regulation does not violate the Establishment Clause merely because it "happens to coincide or harmonize with the tenets of some or all religions." The IRS policy at issue here is founded on a "neutral, secular basis," and does not violate the Establishment Clause. In addition, as the Court of Appeals noted, "the uniform application of the rule to all religiously operated schools *avoids* the necessity for a potentially entangling inquiry into whether a racially restrictive practice is the result of sincere religious belief."

17. LARSON v. VALENTE

> Despite the First Amendment's establishment and free exercise clauses, states periodically seek to regulate religious organizations that do not conform to the pattern set by mainstream religions. *Larson* v. *Valente* involves regulations and reporting requirements for religious organizations that receive most of their contributions from non-members.

JUSTICE BRENNAN DELIVERED
THE OPINION OF THE COURT.

The principal question presented by this appeal is whether a Minnesota statute, imposing certain registration and reporting requirements upon only those religious organizations that solicit more than fifty per cent of their funds from non-members, discriminates against such organizations in violation of the Establishment Clause of the First Amendment.

Appellants are John R. Larson, Commissioner of Securities, and Warren Spannaus, Attorney General, of the State of Minnesota. They are, by virtue of their offices, responsible for the implementation and enforcement of the Minnesota's charitable solicitations Act. This Act, in effect since 1961, provides for a system of registration and disclosure respecting charitable organizations, and is designed to protect the contributing public and charitable beneficiaries against fraudulent practices in the solicitation of contributions for purportedly charitable purposes. A charitable organization subject to the Act must register with the Minnesota Department of Commerce before it may solicit contributions within the State. . . .

From 1961 until 1978, all "religious organizations" were exempted from the requirements of the Act. But effective March 29, 1978, the Minnesota Legislature amended the Act so as to include a "fifty per cent rule" in the exemption provision covering religious organizations. This fifty per cent rule provided that only those religious organizations that received more than half of their total contributions from members or affiliated organizations would remain exempt from the registration and reporting requirements of the Act.

Shortly after the enactment of § 309.515–1(b), the Department notified appellee Holy Spirit Association for the Unification of World Christianity (Unification Church) that it was required to register under the Act because of the newly enacted provision. Appellees Valente, Barber, Haft, and Korman, claiming to be followers of the tenets of the Unification Church, responded by bringing the present action in the United States District Court for the District of Minnesota. Appellees sought a declaration that the Act, on its face and as applied to them through § 309.515–1(b)'s fifty per cent rule, constituted an abridgment of their First Amendment rights of expression and free exercise of religion, as well as a denial of their right to equal protection of the laws, guaranteed by the Fourteenth Amendment; appellees also sought temporary and permanent injunctive relief. Appellee Unification Church was later joined as a plaintiff by stipulation of the parties. . . .

The clearest command of the Establishment Clause is that one religious denomination cannot be officially preferred over another. Before the Revolution, religious establishments of differing denominations were common throughout the Colonies. But the Revolutionary generation emphatically disclaimed that European legacy, and "ap-

456 U.S. 228 (1982).

plied the logic of secular liberty to the condition of religion and the churches:" If Parliament had lacked the authority to tax unrepresented colonists, then by the same token the newly independent States should be powerless to tax their citizens for the support of a denomination to which they did not belong. The force of this reasoning led to the abolition of most denominational establishments at the state level by the 1780s, and led ultimately to the inclusion of the Establishment Clause in the First Amendment in 1791.

This constitutional prohibition of denominational preferences is inextricably connected with the continuing vitality of the Free Exercise Clause. Madison once noted that "Security for civil rights must be the same as that for religious rights; it consists in the one case in a multiplicity of interests and in the other in a multiplicity of sects." Madison's vision—freedom for all religion being guaranteed by free competition between religions—naturally assumed that every denomination would be equally at liberty to exercise and propagate its beliefs. But such equality would be impossible in an atmosphere of official denominational preference. Free exercise thus can be guaranteed only when legislators—and voters—are required to accord to their own religions the very same treatment given to small, new, or unpopular denominations. As Justice Jackson noted in another context, "there is no more effective practical guaranty against arbitrary and unreasonable government than to require that the principles of law which officials would impose upon a minority must be imposed generally." . . .

Since *Everson* v. *Board of Education* this Court has adhered to the principle, clearly manifested in the history and logic of the Establishment Clause, that no State can "pass laws which aid one religion" or that "prefer one religion over another." This principle of denominational neutrality has been restated on many occasions. . . . In short, when we are presented with a state law granting a denominational preference,

our precedents demand that we treat the law as suspect and that we apply strict scrutiny in adjudging its constitutionality.

The fifty per cent rule of § 309.515–1(b) clearly grants denominational preferences of the sort consistently and firmly deprecated in our precedents. Consequently, that rule must be invalidated unless it is justified by a compelling governmental interest . . . and unless it is closely fitted to further that interest. . . .

[After discussion, the Court concluded] that the fifty per cent rule in § 309.515–1(b) [was not] "closely fitted" to further a "compelling governmental interest."

In *Lemon* v. *Kurtzman*, we announced three "tests" that a statute must pass in order to avoid the prohibition of the Establishment Clause.

First, the statute must have a secular legislative purpose; second, its principal or primary effect must be one that neither advances nor inhibits religion . . . ; finally, the statute must not foster "an excessive governmental entanglement with religion."

[T]he *Lemon* v. *Kurtzman* "tests" are intended to apply to laws affording a uniform benefit to *all* religions, and not to provisions, like § 309.515–1(b)'s fifty per cent rule, that discriminate *among* religions. Although application of the *Lemon* tests is not necessary to the disposition of the case before us, those tests do reflect the same concerns that warranted the application of strict scrutiny to § 309.515–1(b)'s fifty per cent rule. . . . We view the third of those tests as most directly implicated in the present case. Justice Harlan well described the problems of entanglement in his separate opinion in *Walz*, where he observed that governmental involvement in programs concerning religion

may be so direct or in such degree as to engender a risk of politicizing religion. . . . [R]eligious groups inevitably represent certain points of view and not infrequently assert them in the political arena, as evidenced by the continuing debate respecting birth control and abortion laws. Yet history cautions that political fragmentation on sectarian lines must be guarded against. . . . [G]overnment participation in certain programs, whose very nature is apt to entangle the state in details of administration and planning, may escalate to the point of inviting undue fragmentation.

The Minnesota statute challenged here is illustrative of this danger. By their "very nature," the distinctions drawn by § 309.515–1(b) and its fifty per cent rule "engender a risk of politicizing religion"—a risk, indeed, that has already been substantially realized.

It is plain that the principal effect of the fifty per cent rule in § 309.515–1(b) is to impose the registration and reporting requirements of the Act on some religious organizations but not on others. . . . We do not suggest that the burdens of compliance with the Act would be intrinsically impermissible if they were imposed evenhandedly. But this statute does not operate evenhandedly, nor was it designed to do so: The fifty per cent rule of § 309.515–1(b) effects the *selective* legislative imposition of burdens and advantages upon particular denominations. The "risk of politicizing religion" that inheres in such legislation is obvious, and indeed is confirmed by the provision's legislative history. For the history of § 309.515–1(b)'s fifty per cent rule demonstrates that the provision was drafted with the explicit intention of including particular religious denominations and excluding others. For example, the second sentence of an early draft of § 309.515–1(b) read, "A religious society or organization which solicits from its religious affiliates who are qualified under this subdivision and who are represented in a body or convention *that elects and controls the governing board of the religious society or organization* is exempt from the requirements of . . . Sections 309.52 and 309.53." The legislative history discloses that the legislators perceived that the italicized language would bring a Roman Catholic archdiocese within the Act, that the legislators did not want the amendment to have that effect, and that an amendment deleting the italicized clause was passed in committee for the sole purpose of exempting the archdiocese from the provisions of the Act. . . . On the other hand, there were certain religious organizations that the legislators did not want to exempt from the Act. One state senator explained that the fifty per cent rule was "an attempt to deal with the religious organizations which are soliciting on the street and soliciting by direct mail, but who are not substantial religious institutions in . . . our state." Another senator said, "what you're trying to get at here is the people that are running around airports and running around streets and soliciting people and you're trying to remove them from the exemption that normally applies to religious organizations." Still another senator, who apparently had mixed feelings about the proposed provision, stated, "I'm not sure why we're so hot to regulate the Moonies anyway."

In short, the fifty per cent rule's capacity—indeed, its express design—to burden or favor selected religious denominations led the Minnesota legislature to discuss the characteristics of various sects with a view towards "religious gerrymandering." As THE CHIEF JUSTICE stated in *Lemon*, "This kind of state inspection and evaluation of the religious content of a religious organization is fraught with the sort of entanglement that the Constitution forbids. It is a relationship pregnant with dangers of excessive government direction . . . of churches."

In sum, we conclude that the fifty per cent rule of § 309.515–1(b) is not closely fitted to the furtherance of any compelling governmental interest asserted by appellants, and that the provision therefore violates the Establishment Clause. Indeed, we think that § 309.515–1(b)'s fifty per cent rule sets up precisely the sort of official denominational preference that the Framers of the First Amendment forbade. Accordingly, we hold that appellees cannot be compelled to register and report under the Act on the strength of that provision. . . .

William P. Thompson

18. GOVERNMENT INTERVENTION IN RELIGIOUS AFFAIRS

In 1981 a conference was convened to discuss "Government Intervention in Religious Affairs." The sponsors included a variety of Protestant organizations, the National Council of Churches, the Synagogue Council of America, the U.S. Catholic Conference and the General Conference of the Seventh-day Adventists. The chairperson was William P. Thompson, then Stated Clerk of the United Presbyterian Church in the United States and former President of the National Council of Churches. His introductory remarks included the following list of governmental activities about which the religious groups were concerned.

It is my privilege to welcome you to this important conference on Government Intervention in Religious Affairs. It is "important" for several reasons:

1. It brings together representatives of more than ninety percent of the adherents of organized religion in the United States, making it possibly the most inclusive such gathering in American history!

2. It gathers up a constellation of concerns that have been increasingly troubling this wide range of religious groups during the past decade; and

3. It has elicited the leadership of some of the outstanding thinkers and actors in the arena of church-state and First Amendment law to help us analyze the problems we confront and seek solutions to them. . . .

The Planning Committee agreed on these purposes for this gathering:

a. To review the data collected in the preceding years of study and to explore their implications for religious bodies;

b. To develop and utilize preparatory materials, conference papers and other resources suitable for use by religious bodies;

c. To analyze alternate modes of response by religious bodies in such situations; and

d. To acquaint regional and local leadership of religious bodies with the problems and their ramifications.

What are the problems that so exercised the sponsoring bodies? They were troubled about the following actions by state and federal governmental agencies:

1. Efforts to regulate fund-raising solicitations by religious bodies;

2. Efforts to require religious groups to register with and report to government officials if they engage in any efforts to influence legislation (so-called "lobbying disclosure" laws);

3. Efforts by the National Labor Relations Board to supervise elections for labor representation by lay teachers in Roman Catholic parochial schools (which have since been halted by the U.S. Supreme Court);

4. Internal Revenue Service's definition of "integrated auxiliaries" that tends to separate church-related colleges and hospitals from the churches that sponsor them;

5. State departments of education's attempts to regulate the curriculum content and teachers' qualifications in Christian schools (which have since been halted by state courts in Ohio, Vermont and Kentucky);

6. Attempts by federal and state departments of labor to collect unemployment compensation taxes from church-related agencies that hitherto were exempt, as churches are;

Reprinted from *Government Intervention in Religious Affairs*, ed. Dean M. Kelley (New York: Pilgrim Press, 1982) by permission of the National Council of Churches of Christ in the U.S.A. and Dean M. Kelley, Editor.

7. Imposition by the then Department of Health, Education and Welfare of requirements of coeducational sports, hygiene instruction, dormitory and off-campus residence facilities at church-related colleges (such as Brigham Young University) which had religious objections to mingling of the sexes in such ways;

8. Efforts by several federal agencies (Civil Rights Commission, Equal Employment Opportunities Commission, Department of Health and Human Services and Department of Education) to require church-related agencies and institutions, including theological seminaries, to report their employment and admissions statistics by race, sex and religion, even though they received no government funds, with threats to cut off such funds to students attending such schools unless they hired faculty, for instance, from other religious adherences;

9. Sampling surveys by the Bureau of the Census of churches and church agencies, requiring them to submit voluminous reports, though the Bureau admitted it had no authority to do so;

10. Grand jury interrogation of church workers about internal affairs of churches;

11. Use by intelligence agencies of clergy as informants;

12. Subpoenas of ecclesiastical records by plaintiffs and defendants in civil and criminal suits;

13. Placing of a church in receivership because of allegations of financial mismanagement made by dissident members;

14. Granting by courts of conservatorship orders to parents to obtain physical custody of (adult) children from unpopular religious movements for purposes of forcing them to abandon their adherence thereto;

15. Withdrawal of tax exemption from various religious groups for failure to comply with "public policy";

16. Determination by IRS of what is "religious ministry" by clergy to qualify for exclusion of cash housing allowance from taxable income (often in contradiction to the religious body's own definition of "ministry");

17. Redefinition by the courts of ecclesiastical polity, so that hierarchical bodies are in effect rendered congregational in polity, and dispersed "connectional" bodies are deemed to be hierarchical, contrary to their own self-definition.

No one of these developments, taken by itself, is sufficiently alarming to necessitate a convocation like this, and indeed some of them might be thought by some people to be justified. But the *pattern* that they form when viewed *together* is an alarming one, and that is why we are here. . . .

We are not called together in a spirit of panic or desperation. We do not propose that the way to deal with this problem is to launch a militant counter-attack against all government on every front.

Indeed, we do not see the situation as one of automatic confrontation at all. We do not discern a calculated conspiracy in governmental circles to stamp out religion or religious bodies. We are not sounding a mindless battle cry, "Leave us alone!" as though there were never grounds for justifiable governmental action. Our final paper, in fact, suggests that governmental intervention is sometimes legitimate.

Rather, what we hope to do is to analyze the situation, suggest various forces and factors at work, and hear proposals about various kinds of responses that have been or can be made, and the advantages and disadvantages of each. Then the sponsoring bodies can reach their own conclusions about the course they severally may wish to follow.

19. LEMON v. KURTZMAN

Lemon v. *Kurtzman* is not only an important discussion of the constitutional limits on aid to religious schools, but it also formally introduced the concept that "political divisiveness" may be part of the "entanglement" test.

MR. CHIEF JUSTICE BURGER DELIVERED
THE OPINION OF THE COURT.

These two appeals raise questions as to Pennsylvania and Rhode Island statutes providing state aid to church-related elementary and secondary schools. Both statutes are challenged as violative of the Establishment and Free Exercise Clauses of the First Amendment and the Due Process Clause of the Fourteenth Amendment.

Pennsylvania has adopted a statutory program that provides financial support to nonpublic elementary and secondary schools by way of reimbursement for the cost of teachers' salaries, textbooks, and instructional materials in specified secular subjects. Rhode Island has adopted a statute under which the State pays directly to teachers in nonpublic elementary schools a supplement of 15% of their annual salary. Under each statute state aid has been given to church-related educational institutions. We hold that both statutes are unconstitutional. . . .

In *Everson* v. *Board of Education,* this Court upheld a state statute that reimbursed the parents of parochial school children for bus transportation expenses. There MR. JUSTICE BLACK, writing for the majority, suggested that the decision carried to "the verge" of forbidden territory under the Religion Clauses. Candor compels acknowledgment, moreover, that we can only dimly perceive the lines of demarcation in this extraordinarily sensitive area of constitutional law.

The language of the Religion Clauses of the First Amendment is at best opaque, particularly when compared with other portions of the Amendment. Its authors did not simply prohibit the establishment of a state church or a state religion, an area history shows they regarded as very important and fraught with great dangers. Instead they commanded that there should be "no law *respecting* an establishment of religion." A law may be one "respecting" the forbidden objective while falling short of its total realization. A law "respecting" the proscribed result, that is, the establishment of religion, is not always easily identifiable as one violative of the Clause. A given law might not *establish* a state religion but nevertheless be one "respecting" that end in the sense of being a step that could lead to such establishment and hence offend the First Amendment.

In the absence of precisely stated constitutional prohibitions, we must draw lines with reference to the three main evils against which the Establishment Clause was intended to afford protection: "sponsorship, financial support, and active involvement of the sovereign in religious activity." . . .

Every analysis in this area must begin with consideration of the cumulative criteria developed by the Court over many years. Three such tests may be gleaned from our cases. First, the statute must have a secular legislative purpose; second, its principal or primary effect must be one that neither advances nor inhibits religion . . . ; finally, the statute must not foster "an excessive government entanglement with religion."

Inquiry into the legislative purposes of the Pennsylvania and Rhode Island statutes affords no basis for a conclusion that the leg-

403 U.S. 602 (1971).

islative intent was to advance religion. On the contrary, the statutes themselves clearly state that they are intended to enhance the quality of the secular education in all schools covered by the compulsory attendance laws. There is no reason to believe the legislatures meant anything else. A State always has a legitimate concern for maintaining minimum standards in all schools it allows to operate. . . . The legislatures of Rhode Island and Pennsylvania have concluded that secular and religious education are identifiable and separable. In the abstract we have no quarrel with this conclusion.

The two legislatures, however, have also recognized that church-related elementary and secondary schools have a significant religious mission and that a substantial portion of their activities is religiously oriented. They have therefore sought to create statutory restrictions designed to guarantee the separation between secular and religious educational functions and to ensure that State financial aid supports only the former. All these provisions are precautions taken in candid recognition that these programs approached, even if they did not intrude upon, the forbidden areas under the Religion Clauses. We need not decide whether these legislative precautions restrict the principal or primary effect of the programs to the point where they do not offend the Religion Clauses, for we conclude that the cumulative impact of the entire relationship arising under the statutes in each State involves excessive entanglement between government and religion.

In *Walz* v. *Tax Commission* . . . the Court upheld state tax exemptions for real property owned by religious organizations and used for religious worship. That holding, however, tended to confine rather than enlarge the area of permissible state involvement with religious institutions by calling for close scrutiny of the degree of entanglement involved in the relationship. The objective is

to prevent, as far as possible, the intrusion of either into the precincts of the other.

Our prior holdings do not call for total separation between church and state; total separation is not possible in an absolute sense. Some relationship between government and religious organizations is inevitable. . . . Fire inspections, building and zoning regulations, and state requirements under compulsory school-attendance laws are examples of necessary and permissible contacts. Indeed, under the statutory exemption before us in *Walz*, the State had a continuing burden to ascertain that the exempt property was in fact being used for religious worship. Judicial caveats against entanglement must recognize that the line of separation, far from being a "wall," is a blurred, indistinct, and variable barrier depending on all the circumstances of a particular relationship.

This is not to suggest, however, that we are to engage in a legalistic minuet in which precise rules and forms must govern. A true minuet is a matter of pure form and style, the observance of which is itself the substantive end. Here we examine the form of the relationship for the light that it casts on the substance.

In order to determine whether the government entanglement with religion is excessive, we must examine the character and purposes of the institutions that are benefited, the nature of the aid that the State provides, and the resulting relationship between the government and the religious authority. . . .

Rhode Island Program

The church schools involved in the program are located close to parish churches. This understandably permits convenient access for religious exercises since instruction in faith and morals is part of the total educational process. The school buildings contain identifying religious symbols such as crosses on the exterior and crucifixes, and religious paintings and statues either in the classrooms or hallways. Although only approximately 30 minutes a day are devoted to direct religious instruction, there are religiously oriented extracurricular activities. Approximately two-thirds of the teachers in these schools are nuns of various religious orders. Their dedicated efforts provide an atmosphere in which religious instruction and religious vocations are natural and proper parts of life in such schools. Indeed the role of teaching nuns in enhancing the religious atmosphere has led the parochial school authorities to attempt to maintain a one-to-one ratio between nuns and lay teachers in all schools rather than to permit some to be staffed almost entirely by lay teachers.

. . .

The substantial religious character of these church-related schools gives rise to entangling church-state relationships of the kind the Religion Clauses sought to avoid. Although the District Court found that concern for religious values did not inevitably or necessarily intrude into the content of secular subjects, the considerable religious activities of these schools led the legislature to provide for careful governmental controls and surveillance by state authorities in order to ensure that state aid supports only secular education.

The dangers and corresponding entanglements are enhanced by the particular form of aid that the Rhode Island Act provides. Our decisions have permitted the States to provide church-related schools with secular, neutral, or nonideological services, facilities, or materials. Bus transportation, school lunches, public health services, and secular textbooks supplied in common to all students were not thought to offend the Establishment Clause. . . .

We cannot . . . refuse here to recognize that teachers have a substantially different ideological character from books. In terms of potential for involving some aspect of faith or morals in secular subjects, a textbook's content is ascertainable, but a teacher's handling of a subject is not. We cannot ignore the danger that a teacher under religious control and discipline poses to the separation of the religious from the purely secular aspects of pre-college education. The conflict of functions inheres in the situation.

In our view the record shows these dangers are present to a substantial degree. The Rhode Island Roman Catholic elementary schools are under the general supervision of the Bishop of Providence and his appointed representative, the Diocesan Superintendent of Schools. In most cases, each individual parish, however, assumes the ultimate financial responsibility for the school, with the parish priest authorizing the allocation of parish funds. With only two exceptions, school principals are nuns appointed either by the Superintendent or the Mother Provincial of the order whose members staff the school. By 1969 lay teachers constituted more than a third of all teachers in the parochial elementary schools, and their number is growing. They are first interviewed by the superintendent's office and then by the school principal. The contracts are signed by the parish priest, and he retains some discretion in negotiating salary levels. Religious authority necessarily pervades the school system.

The schools are governed by the standards set forth in a "Handbook of School Regulations," which has the force of synodal law in the diocese. It emphasizes the role and importance of the teacher in parochial schools: "The prime factor for the success or the failure of the school is the spirit and personality, as well as the professional competency, of the teacher. . . ." The Handbook also states that: "Religious formation is not confined to formal courses; nor is it restricted to a single subject area." Finally, the Handbook advises teachers to stimulate interest in religious vocations and missionary work. Given the mission of the church school, these instructions are consistent and logical. . . .

We need not and do not assume that teachers in parochial schools will be guilty of bad faith or any conscious design to evade the limitations imposed by the statute and the First Amendment. We simply recognize that a dedicated religious person, teaching in a school affiliated with his or her faith and operated to inculcate its tenets, will inevitably experience great difficulty in remaining religiously neutral. Doctrines and faith are not inculcated or advanced by neutrals. With the best of intentions such a teacher would find it hard to make a total separation between secular teaching and religious doctrine. What would appear to some to be essential to good citizenship might well for others border on or constitute instruction in religion. Further difficulties are inherent in the combination of religious discipline and the possibility of disagreement between teacher and religious authorities over the meaning of the statutory restrictions.

We do not assume, however, that parochial school teachers will be unsuccessful in their attempts to segregate their religious beliefs from their secular educational responsibilities. But the potential for impermissible fostering of religion is present. The Rhode Island Legislature has not, and could not, provide state aid on the basis of a mere assumption that secular teachers under religious discipline can avoid conflicts. The State must be certain, given the Religion Clauses, that subsidized teachers do not inculcate religion—indeed the State here has undertaken to do so. To ensure that no trespass occurs, the State has therefore carefully conditioned its aid with pervasive restrictions. An eligible recipient must teach only those courses that are offered in the public schools and use only those texts and materials that are found in the public schools. In addition the teacher must not engage in teaching any course in religion.

A comprehensive, discriminating, and continuing state surveillance will inevitably be required to ensure that these restrictions are obeyed and the First Amendment otherwise respected. Unlike a book, a teacher cannot be inspected once so as to determine the extent and intent of his or her personal beliefs and subjective acceptance of the limitations imposed by the First Amendment. These prophylactic contacts will involve excessive and enduring entanglement between state and church.

There is another area of entanglement in the Rhode Island program that gives concern. The statute excludes teachers employed by nonpublic schools whose average per-pupil expenditures on secular education equal or exceed the comparable figures for public schools. In the event that the total expenditures of an otherwise eligible school exceed this norm, the program requires the government to examine the school's records in order to determine how much of the total expenditures is attributable to secular education and how much to religious activity. This kind of state inspection and evaluation of the religious content of a religious organization is fraught with the sort of entanglement that the Constitution forbids. It is a relationship pregnant with dangers of excessive government direction of church schools and hence of churches. The Court noted "the hazards of government supporting churches" in *Walz* v. *Tax Commission*, and we cannot ignore here the danger that pervasive modern governmental power will ultimately intrude on religion and thus conflict with the Religion Clauses.

[The Court then conducted a similar analysis of the Pennsylvania program.]

A broader base of entanglement of yet a different character is presented by the divisive political potential of these state programs. In a community where such a large number of pupils are served by church-related schools, it can be assumed that state assistance will entail considerable political activity. Partisans of parochial schools, understandably concerned with rising costs and sincerely dedicated to both the religious and secular educational missions of their schools, will inevitably champion this cause and promote political action to achieve their goals. Those who oppose state aid, whether for constitutional, religious, or fiscal reasons, will inevitably respond and employ all of the usual political campaign techniques to prevail. Candidates will be forced to declare and voters to choose. It would be unrealistic to ignore the fact that many people confronted with issues of this kind will find their votes aligned with their faith.

Ordinarily political debate and division, however vigorous or even partisan, are normal and healthy manifestations of our democratic system of government, but political division along religious lines was one of the principal evils against which the First Amendment was intended to protect. . . . The potential divisiveness of such conflict is a threat to the normal political process. . . . To have States or communities divide on the issues presented by state aid to parochial schools would tend to confuse and obscure other issues of great urgency. We have an expanding array of vexing issues, local and national, domestic and international, to debate and divide on. It conflicts with our whole history and tradition to permit questions of the Religion Clauses to assume such importance in our legislatures and in our elections that they could divert attention from the myriad issues and problems that confront every level of government. The highways of church and state relationships are not likely to be one-way streets, and the Constitution's authors sought to protect religious worship from the pervasive power of government. The history of many countries attests to the hazards of religion's intruding into the political arena or of political power intruding into the legitimate and free exercise of religious belief.

Of course, as the Court noted in *Walz*, "[a]dherents of particular faiths and individual churches frequently take strong positions on public issues." We could not expect otherwise, for religious values pervade the fabric of our national life. But in *Walz* we dealt with a status under state tax laws for the benefit of all religious groups. Here we are confronted with successive and very likely permanent annual appropriations that benefit relatively few religious groups. Political fragmentation and divisiveness on religious lines are thus likely to be intensified.

The potential for political divisiveness related to religious belief and practice is aggravated in these two statutory programs by the need for continuing annual appropriations and the likelihood of larger and larger demands as costs and populations grow. The Rhode Island District Court found that the parochial school system's "monumental and deepening financial crisis" would "inescapably" require larger annual appropriations subsidizing greater percentages of the salaries of lay teachers. Although no facts have been developed in this respect in the Pennsylvania case, it appears that such pressures for expanding aid have already required the state legislature to include a portion of the state revenues from cigarette taxes in the program.

In *Walz* it was argued that a tax exemption for places of religious worship would prove to be the first step in an inevitable progression leading to the establishment of state churches and state religion. That claim could not stand up against more than 200 years of virtually universal practice imbedded in our colonial experience and continuing into the present.

The progression argument, however, is more persuasive here. We have no long history of state aid to church-related educational institutions comparable to 200 years of tax exemption for churches. Indeed, the state programs before us today represent something of an innovation. We have already noted that modern governmental programs have self-perpetuating and self-expanding propensities. These internal pressures are only enhanced when the schemes involve institutions whose legitimate needs are growing and whose interests have substantial political support. Nor can we fail to see that in constitutional adjudication some steps, which when taken were thought to approach "the verge," have become the platform for yet further steps. A certain momentum develops in constitutional theory and it can be a "downhill thrust" easily set in motion but difficult to retard or stop. Development by momentum is not invariably bad; indeed, it is the way the common law has grown, but it is a force to be recognized and reckoned with. The dangers are increased by the difficulty of perceiving in advance exactly where the "verge" of the precipice lies. As well as constituting an independent evil against which the Religion Clauses were intended to protect, involvement or entanglement between government and religion serves as a warning signal.

Finally, nothing we have said can be construed to disparage the role of church-related elementary and secondary schools in our national life. Their contribution has been and is enormous. Nor do we ignore their economic plight in a period of rising costs and expanding need. Taxpayers generally have been spared vast sums by the maintenance of these educational institutions by religious organizations, largely by the gifts of faithful adherents.

The merit and benefits of these schools, however, are not the issue before us in these cases. The sole question is whether state aid to these schools can be squared with the dictates of the Religion Clauses. Under our system the choice has been made that government is to be entirely excluded from the area of religious instruction and churches excluded from the affairs of government. The Constitution decrees that religion must be a private matter for the individual, the family, and the institutions of private choice, and that while some involvement and entanglement are inevitable, lines must be drawn. . . .

20. MUELLER v. ALLEN

Mueller v. *Allen* is one of the more recent Supreme Court cases on aid to religious schools. It has been attacked and lauded, depending on the speaker's perspective, as permitting unprecedented support for parochial schools.

JUSTICE REHNQUIST DELIVERED
THE OPINION OF THE COURT.

Minnesota allows taxpayers, in computing their state income tax, to deduct certain expenses incurred in providing for the education of their children. . . .

Minnesota, like every other state, provides its citizens with free elementary and secondary schooling. It seems to be agreed that about 820,000 students attended this school system in the most recent school year. During the same year, approximately 91,000 elementary and secondary students attended some 500 privately supported schools located in Minnesota, and about 95% of these students attended schools considering themselves to be sectarian.

Minnesota, by a law originally enacted in 1955 and revised in 1976 and again in 1978, permits state taxpayers to claim a deduction from gross income for certain expenses incurred in educating their children. The de-

463 U.S. 388 (1983).

duction is limited to actual expenses incurred for the "tuition, textbooks and transportation" of dependents attending elementary or secondary schools. A deduction may not exceed $500 per dependent in grades K through six and $700 per dependent in grades seven through twelve. . . .

Petitioners—certain Minnesota taxpayers—sued in the United States District Court for the District of Minnesota claiming that § 290.09(22) violated the Establishment Clause by providing financial assistance to sectarian institutions. . . .

Today's case is no exception to our oft-repeated statement that the Establishment Clause presents especially difficult questions of interpretation and application. It is easy enough to quote the few words comprising that clause—"Congress shall make no law respecting an establishment of religion." It is not at all easy, however, [to] apply this Court's various decisions construing the Clause to governmental programs of financial assistance to sectarian schools and the parents of children attending those schools. Indeed, in many of these decisions "we have expressly or implicitly acknowledged that 'we can only dimly perceive the lines of demarcation in this extraordinarily sensitive area of constitutional law.' " . . .

One fixed principle in this field is our consistent rejection of the argument that "any program which in some manner aids an institution with a religious affiliation" violates the Establishment Clause. . . . For example, it is now well-established that a state may reimburse parents for expenses incurred in transporting their children to school and that it may loan secular textbooks to all schoolchildren within the state. . . . [O]ur decisions also have struck down arrangements resembling, in many respects, [programs we have upheld.] In this case we are asked to decide whether Minnesota's tax deduction bears greater resemblance to those types of assistance to parochial schools we have approved, or to those we have struck down. Petitioners place particular reliance on our

decision in *Committee for Public Education* v. *Nyquist* where we held invalid a New York statute providing public funds for the maintenance and repair of the physical facilities of private schools and granting thinly disguised "tax benefits," actually amounting to tuition grants, to the parents of children attending private schools. As explained below, we conclude that § 290.09(22) bears less resemblance to the arrangement struck down in *Nyquist* than it does to assistance programs upheld in our prior decisions and those discussed with approval in *Nyquist*.

The general nature of our inquiry in this area has been guided, since the decision in *Lemon* v. *Kurtzman*, by the "three-part" test laid down in that case:

First, the statute must have a secular legislative purpose; second, its principle or primary effect must be one that neither advances nor inhibits religion . . . ; finally the statute must not foster "an excessive government entanglement with religion."

While this principle is well settled, our cases have also emphasized that it provides "no more than [a] helpful signpost" in dealing with Establishment Clause challenges. With this *caveat* in mind, we turn to the specific challenges raised against § 290.09(22) under the *Lemon* framework.

Little time need be spent on the question of whether the Minnesota tax deduction has a secular purpose. Under our prior decisions, governmental assistance programs have consistently survived this inquiry even when they have run afoul of other aspects of the *Lemon* framework. This reflects, at least in part, our reluctance to attribute unconstitutional motives to the states particularly when a plausible secular purpose for the state's program may be discerned from the face of the statute.

A state's decision to defray the cost of educational expenses incurred by parents—regardless of the type of schools their children attend—evidences a purpose that is both secular and understandable. An educated populace is essential in the political and economic health of any community, and a state's efforts to assist parents in meeting the rising cost of educational expenses plainly serves this secular purpose of ensuring that the state's citizenry is well-educated. Similarly, Minnesota, like other states, could conclude that there is a strong public interest in assuring the continued financial health of private schools, both sectarian and non-sectarian. By educating a substantial number of students such schools relieve public schools of a correspondingly great burden—to the benefit of all taxpayers. In addition, private schools may serve as a benchmark for public schools, in a manner analogous to the "TVA yardstick" for private power companies. As JUSTICE POWELL has remarked:

Parochial schools, quite apart from their sectarian purpose, have provided an educational alternative for millions of young Americans; they often afford wholesome competition with our public schools; and in some States they relieve substantially the tax burden incident to the operation of public schools. The State has, moreover, a legitimate interest in facilitating education of the highest quality for all children within its boundaries, whatever school their parents have chosen for them. . . .

All these justifications are readily available to support § 290.09(22), and each is sufficient to satisfy the secular purpose inquiry of *Lemon.*

We turn therefore to the more difficult but related question whether the Minnesota statute has "the primary effect of advancing the sectarian aims of the nonpublic schools." . . . In concluding that it does not, we find several features of the Minnesota tax deduction particularly significant. First, an essential feature of Minnesota's arrangement is the fact that § 290.09(22) is only one among many deductions—such as those for medical expenses. Minn. Stat. § 290.09(10) and charitable contributions, Minn. Stat. § 290.21— available under the Minnesota tax laws. Our decisions consistently have recognized that traditionally "[l]egislatures have especially broad latitude in creating classifications and

distinctions in tax statutes," in part because the "familiarity with local conditions" enjoyed by legislators especially enables them to "achieve an equitable distribution of the tax burden." Under our prior decisions, the Minnesota legislature's judgment that a deduction for educational expenses fairly equalizes the tax burden of its citizens and encourages desirable expenditures for educational purposes is entitled to substantial deference.

Other characteristics of § 290.09(22) argue equally strongly for the provision's constitutionality. Most importantly, the deduction is available for educational expenses incurred by *all* parents, including those whose children attend public schools and those whose children attend non-sectarian private schools or sectarian private schools. Just as in *Widmar* v. *Vincent* where we concluded that the state's provision of a forum neutrally "open to a broad class of nonreligious as well as religious speakers" does not "confer any imprimatur of State approval," so here: "the provision of benefits to so broad a spectrum of groups is an important index of secular effect."

In this respect, as well as others, this case is vitally different from the scheme struck down in *Nyquist.* There, public assistance amounting to tuition grants, was provided only to parents of children in *nonpublic* schools. This fact had considerable bearing on our decision striking down the New York statute at issue; we explicitly distinguished both *Allen* and *Everson* on the grounds that "In both cases the class of beneficiaries included *all* schoolchildren, those in public as well as those in private schools." Moreover, we intimated that "public assistance (*e.g.,* scholarships) made available generally without regard to the sectarian-nonsectarian or public–non-public nature of the institution benefited" might not offend the Establishment Clause. We think the tax deduction adopted by Minnesota is more similar to this latter type of program than it is to the arrangement struck down in *Nyquist.* Unlike the assistance at issue in *Nyquist,* § 290.09(22) permits *all* parents—whether their children attend public school or private—to deduct their childrens' educational expenses. As *Widmar* and our other decisions indicate, a program, like § 290.09(22), that neutrally provides state assistance to a broad spectrum of citizens is not readily subject to challenge under the Establishment Clause.

We also agree with the Court of Appeals that, by channeling whatever assistance it may provide to parochial schools through individual parents, Minnesota has reduced the Establishment Clause objections to which its action is subject. It is true, of course, that financial assistance provided to parents ultimately has an economic effect comparable to that of aid given directly to the schools attended by their children. It is also true, however, that under Minnesota's arrangement public funds become available only as a result of numerous, private choices of individual parents of school-age children. For these reasons, we recognized in *Nyquist* that the means by which state assistance flows to private schools is of some importance: we said that "the fact that aid is disbursed to parents rather than to . . . schools" is a material consideration in Establishment Clause analysis, albeit "only one among many to be considered." It is noteworthy that all but one of our recent cases invalidating state aid to parochial schools have involved the direct transmission of assistance from the state to the schools themselves. The exception, of course, was *Nyquist*, which, as discussed previously is distinguishable from this case on other grounds. Where, as here, aid to parochial schools is available only as a result of decisions of individual parents [that] no "imprimatur of State approval," can be deemed to have been conferred on any particular religion, or on religion generally.

We find it useful in the light of the foregoing characteristics of § 290.09(22), to compare the attenuated financial benefits flowing to parochial schools from the section to the evils against which the Establishment Clause was designed to protect. These dangers are well-described by our statement that "what is at stake as a matter of policy [in Establishment Clause cases] is preventing that kind and degree of government involvement in religious life that, as history teaches us, is apt to lead to strife and frequently strain a political system to the breaking point." It is important, however, to "keep these issues in perspective":

At this point in the 20th century we are quite far removed from the dangers that prompted the Framers to include the Establishment Clause in the Bill of Rights. The risk of significant religious or denominational control over our democratic processes—or even of deep political division along religious lines—is remote, and when viewed against the positive contributions of sectarian schools, and such risk seems entirely tolerable in light of the continuing oversight of this Court.

The Establishment Clause of course extends beyond prohibition of a state church or payment of state funds to one or more churches. We do not think, however, that its prohibition extends to the type of tax deduction established by Minnesota. The historic purposes of the clause simply do not encompass the sort of attenuated financial benefit, ultimately controlled by the private choices of individual parents, that eventually flows to parochial schools from the neutrally available tax benefit at issue in this case. . . .

Thus, we hold that the Minnesota tax deduction for educational expenses satisfies the primary effect inquiry of our Establishment Clause cases.

Turning to the third part of the *Lemon* inquiry, we have no difficulty in concluding that the Minnesota statute does not "excessively entangle" the state in religion. The only plausible source of the "comprehensive, discriminating, and continuing state surveillance" necessary to run afoul of this standard would be in the fact that state officials must determine whether particular textbooks qualify for a deduction. In making this decision, state officials must disallow deductions taken from "instructional books and materials used in the teaching of religious tenets, doctrines or worship, the purpose of which is to inculcate such tenets, doctrines or worship." Making decisions such as this does not differ substantially from making the types of decisions approved in earlier opinions of this Court. In *Board of Education* v. *Allen*, for example, the Court upheld the loan of secular textbooks to parents or children attending nonpublic schools; though state officials were required to determine whether particular books were or were not secular, the system was held not to violate the Establishment Clause. . . . The same result follows in this case. . . .

John Courtney Murray, S.J.

21. REMARKS ON AID TO PAROCHIAL SCHOOLS

Father Murray was Professor of Theology at Woodstock College and a member of the Society of Jesus. His influential writings on the Church-State question from the perspective of American Catholics include the following brief defense of government support for religious schools.

[This is] the argument that has been made by Catholics in this country for more than a century with regard to the distribution of tax funds for the support of the school system. The structure of the argument is not complex. Its principle is that the canons of distributive justice ought to control the action of government in allocating funds that it coercively collects from all the people in pursuance of its legitimate interest in universal compulsory schooling. The fact is that these canons are presently not being observed. The "solution" to the School Question reached in the nineteenth century reveals injustice, and the legal statutes that establish the injustice are an abuse of power. So, in drastic brevity, runs the argument. For my part, I have never heard a satisfactory answer to it.

This is a fairly serious situation. When a large section of the community asserts that injustice is being done, and makes a reasonable argument to substantiate the assertion, either the argument ought to be convincingly refuted and the claim of injustice thus disposed of, or the validity of the argument ought to be admitted and the injustice remedied. As a matter of fact, however, the argument customarily meets a blank stare, or else it is "answered" by varieties of the fallacy known as *ignoratio elenchi*. At the extreme, from the side of the more careerist type of anti-Catholic, the rejoinder takes this form, roughly speaking (sometimes the rejoinder is roughly spoken): "We might be willing to listen to this argument about the rights of Catholic schools if we believed that Catholic schools had any rights at all. But we do not grant that they have any rights, except to tolerance. Their existence is not for the advantage of the public; they offend against the integrity of the democratic community, whose warrant is fidelity to Protestant principle (or secularist principle, as the case may be)." This "answer" takes various forms, more or less uncomplimentary to the Catholic Church, according to the temper of the speaker. But this is the gist of it. . . .

Reprinted from "America's Four Conspiracies" in *Religion in America*, ed. John Cogley (Cleveland, Ohio: World Publishing Company, 1958), pp. 221–222.

22. **THE PEOPLE SPEAK: PAROCHIAID AND THE VOTERS**

Edd Doerr's attack on government funding for parochial schools represented a position of Americans United for the Separation of Church and State, an organization that is devoted to maintaining a strict separation between Church and State, especially in education. Americans United (originally Protestants and Other Americans United) has often participated as a party or friend of the court in major cases involving the Establishment Clause.

Parochiaid—any form of direct or indirect tax aid for sectarian private schools from any level of government—has been a controversial political issue in the United States since the early nineteenth century. Generally speaking, however, the policy followed throughout the country until the present has been one of confining public support to public schools, usually on the ground that parochiaid would violate the constitutional principle of separation of church and state and would damage public education.

Since World War II controversies have raged over parochiaid in Congress and most state legislatives, in the courts, and in the arena of public opinion. Most parochiaid plans were defeated in the legislative process, while those which were enacted were challenged in the courts by Americans United and other organizations. All but the most minor and peripheral forms of parochiaid have been struck down as unconstitutional by the courts, particularly in a remarkable series of U.S. Supreme Court rulings beginning in 1971.

Advocates of parochiaid have tried to win over public opinion but their efforts proved to be ineffective. Between 1966 and 1978 twelve statewide referenda dealt with parochiaid in one form or another. In every case the parochiaiders lost. These referendum elections, then, shed a great deal of light on how the American people view proposals to provide public aid to denominational schools. . . .

As these . . . referenda . . . make clear, the American people are solidly opposed to any form of public aid for parochial and private schools. By inference they support the Supreme Court and lower court rulings which have ruled unconstitutional all but minor and peripheral forms of parochiaid.

The referenda were won by church-state separationists, incidentally, despite the fact that they were outspent in every political campaign by the advocates of parochiaid. In a number of the referenda, such as the one in Michigan in 1970, political and business leaders flocked to the parochiaid banner, though to no avail. In most of the referendum states, separationists formed formal or informal coalitions representing religious, teachers, parents, civil rights, and a variety of other groups. Americans United for Separation of Church and State was active in all of the referenda, often playing a key advisory role in view of its many years of experience in dealing with the parochiaid issue.

Americans oppose parochiaid for a variety of reasons. The most salient are probably these: It is unconstitutional. It means forcing all citizens to contribute involuntarily to the support of religious institutions. It would harm the public education system that enrolls 90% of American children. It would use public funds to divide children by creed, class, race, and in other ways. It would endanger the freedom and independence of religious private schools.

The lesson for politicians is obvious. Most

Americans support the constitutional principle of separation of church and state as essential to the preservation of religious liberty and other democratic values. There is rarely any real gain for politicians in moving against this main stream.

A. E. Dick Howard

23. UP AGAINST THE WALL: THE UNEASY SEPARATION OF CHURCH AND STATE

A. E. Dick Howard is Professor of Law at the University of Virginia and was Executive Director of the commission that wrote Virginia's most recent constitution. In the following excerpts from his essay titled "Up against the Wall," Professor Howard discusses the numerous complicated Supreme Court cases dealing with aid to religious schools. Note the difference in treatment between higher education on the one hand and primary and secondary education on the other.

Aid to Church-Related Education

In his first term on the Court, the new Chief Justice [Burger] wrote *Walz* v. *Tax Commission*, a near-unanimous decision (only Douglas dissenting) upholding property tax exemptions for religious property. Noting that all fifty states provide for tax exemptions for places of worship, Burger saw the First Amendment as permitting "benevolent neutrality" by government toward religion. Burger found "deeply embedded in the fabric of our national life" the principle that government could fashion policies grounded in benevolent neutrality towards religion "so long as none was favored over others and none suffered interference." Tax exemptions, he reasoned, did not constitute sponsorship as the government does not transfer revenue to churches "but simply abstains from demanding that the church support the state."

The Court's 1968 *Allen* opinion, permitting New York to lend textbooks to parochial schoolchildren, had fired the hopes of proponents of more general aid to church-related schools. Burger's *Walz* opinion, two years later, stirred those hopes even further. Concerned about the flagging finances of parochial schools, Catholic educators and parents saw in the language of "benevolent neutrality" the opportunity to carry *Everson's* general welfare legislation notion quite beyond such narrow aids as bus transportation or textbooks. Indeed, even before *Walz*, in the late sixties state legislatures had begun to enact significant programs of aid to private education—among them supplements to teachers' salaries, money to pay for textbooks and instructional materials, appropriations for maintenance and repair of schools, tuition grants to parents, and income tax credits. Opponents of such aid promptly went to court, and the stage was set in the early seventies for a major round of Supreme Court decisions on aid to church-related schools.

In 1971, in *Lemon* v. *Kurtzman*, the Court passed on aid programs from Rhode Island and Pennsylvania. Rhode Island's statute provided for a 15% salary supplement to be paid to teachers in nonpublic schools. Pennsylvania's act authorized the "purchase" of "secular" educational services from private schools, reimbursing those schools for teachers' salaries, textbooks, and instructional materials. Both states, conscious of the sensitive First Amendment questions raised by such aid, had laced the programs about with safeguards and restrictions. For example, Pennsylvania required that reimbursement be limited to courses in specified secular subjects, that textbooks and materials must be approved by the state, and that payment was not to be made for any course having religious content.

The safeguards proved the programs' undoing. To the purpose and effect test of establishment used in the 1963 prayer cases, Burger in *Walz* had added a third test—that a program not result in an "excessive governmental entanglement with religion." The property tax exemptions in *Walz* had passed that test, but the Pennsylvania and Rhode Island school aid programs in *Lemon* failed it. The very fact that the state had "carefully conditioned its aid with pervasive restrictions" meant that "comprehensive, discriminating, and continuing state surveillance" would be necessary to ensure that the schools honored the restrictions; the result would be "excessive and enduring entanglement between state and church."

The Chief Justice had yet another ground for striking down the Pennsylvania and Rhode Island programs—their "divisive political potential." Burger saw political division along religious lines one of the principal evils against which the First Amendment was directed. State programs channeling money to a relatively few religious groups— Roman Catholics were the overwhelming beneficiaries of the challenged programs— would, Burger thought, intensify political demands along religious lines.

Undaunted, the proponents of parochaid kept trying. The result was another round of major Supreme Court decisions, in June 1973. In the principal case, *Committee for Public Education & Religious Liberty* v. *Nyquist*, a divided Court struck down three New York programs—direct grants to private schools for "maintenance and repair" of facilities and equipment, a tuition reimbursement plan for low-income parents of children in private schools, and tax deductions for parents who did not qualify for tuition reimbursement. In the 1971 decisions, it had been "entanglement" that proved fatal for the Pennsylvania and Rhode Island programs. In 1973 it was the "effect" test that was fatal; the three programs were found to have the effect of advancing religion. Justice Powell, who wrote the majority opinion in *Nyquist*, found it unnecessary to consider whether the New York program would result in entanglement of state and religion. He did, however, bolster his opinion by invoking the political entanglement argument—that the programs carried a "potentially divisive political effect."

Nyquist brought a new lineup on the Court. The justices had been nearly unanimous in *Lemon;* only Justice White would have permitted the kinds of aid there struck down. In *Nyquist* the Court was more divided, three justices dissenting in whole or part. The case split the four Nixon appointees; Blackmun joined Powell's majority opinion, while Burger—hitherto the spokesman for the Court in every religion case— and Rehnquist dissented in part (they would have upheld the tuition grant and tax credit statutes). Burger thought "simple equity" supported aid to parents who sent their children to private schools; moreover, to give such aid would promote a "wholesome diversity" in education.

Since 1973, the Court has decided yet other parochaid cases, but the course has been largely charted by *Lemon* and *Nyquist*. In *Meek* v. *Pittenger* (1975), the Court reviewed three Pennsylvania programs—the loan of textbooks to students in private schools, the loan to the schools themselves of instructional equipment and materials, and provision of "auxiliary" services, such as counseling, testing, speech and hearing therapy, and similar services. Only the textbook program passed muster—and even that dispensation largely on the strength of the precedent set by *Allen.* Effect, entanglement, political divisiveness—all figured in the Court's opinion. The loan of instructional material was found to have the effect of advancing religion, while provision of auxiliary services raised the spectre of excessive entanglement in order to police the program, as well as the opportunity for divisive conflict along religious lines. As in 1973, Burger, White, and Rehnquist would have allowed more aid to church-related schools than permitted by the majority.

The Court relaxed the barriers somewhat, but only slightly, in *Wolman* v. *Walter* (1977). Reviewing several Ohio programs, the Court refused to permit the state to lend instructional materials and equipment for use in sectarian schools or to pay for field trips. The Court did, however, permit the state to provide specialized diagnostic, guidance, and other services to students in nonpublic schools, as the services were not performed on school premises.

The majority's continuing suspicion of any form of aid to sectarian schools at the primary and secondary level stands in sharp contrast to the Court's more deferential posture on aid to church-related colleges. The same day that the Court ruled against parochaid in *Lemon* v. *Kurtzman,* the justices upheld federal construction grants to four church-related colleges in Connecticut. The federal statute placed limits on the purposes for which grants could be used, among them the exclusion of facilities to be used for sectarian instruction or religious worship. Writing for a five-man majority, Chief Justice Burger in *Tilton* v. *Richardson* concluded that the grant program satisfied all the Court's establishment tests—purpose, effect, entanglement, and political divisiveness. Key to the decision were the differences Burger noted between higher education and primary and secondary schools. College stu-

dents, he thought, are less impressionable and less susceptible to religious indoctrination than younger students. Moreover, other forces, such as traditions of academic freedom, operate to create a more open climate at the college level.

All four of the Connecticut colleges were controlled by religious orders, and the faculty and student body at each were predominantly Catholic. Nevertheless, Burger noted that non-Catholics were admitted as students and were given faculty appointments. None of the colleges required students to attend religious services. Although all four schools required students to take theology courses, it was stipulated that the courses covered a range of religious experience and were not limited to Catholicism. In fact, some of the required courses at two of the colleges were taught by rabbis. In short, Burger was able to conclude that, although the colleges had "admittedly religious functions," their predominant educational mission was to provide their students with a secular education.

The Court has continued to maintain a sharp distinction between aid to sectarian primary and secondary schools and aid at the level of higher education. The justices' consistent rebuffs to parochaid in all its forms have been matched on the other side by a relaxed posture on aid to church-related colleges and their students. In 1973, in *Hunt* v. *McNair,* the Court rejected First Amendment challenges to the issuance by a South Carolina state authority of revenue bonds to help a Baptist college borrow money for capital improvements. No state money was involved, but having the authority's backing enabled the college to borrow money at more favorable interest rates. Justice Powell, who wrote the majority opinion, noted that the college's board of trustees was elected by the South Carolina Baptist Convention, that its charter could be amended only by the Convention, and that the Convention's approval was required for certain financial transactions. But Powell concluded that the college was not "pervasively sectarian" and that South Carolina had laid down sufficient safeguards to ensure that aid did not flow to religious activities.

Yet another case, decided in 1976, reflects the majority's ability to be more permissive toward aid to church-related colleges than to primary and secondary education. In that decision, *Roemer* v. *Board of Public Works*, the Court upheld Maryland's appropriation, on an annual basis, of noncategorical grants to private colleges, some of them with religious affiliations. For each fulltime student (not including seminary and theology students), a college received an amount equal to 15% of the state's appropriation for fulltime students in the state college system. At issue were appropriations to four Roman Catholic colleges. The district court had concluded that the four colleges were not "pervasively sectarian," and Justice Blackmun, reviewing findings as to curriculum, faculty, and other factors, held that the lower court's conclusion was not "clearly erroneous." Moreover, Maryland's system operated to ensure that aid would go only to "the secular side" of the colleges' activities. Nor, finally, was there "excessive entanglement" between government and religion.

GOD AND COUNTRY: CULTURAL ISSUES

Robert N. Bellah

24. CIVIL RELIGION IN AMERICA

Robert N. Bellah is Professor of Sociology and Comparative Studies at the University of California, Berkeley. When his essay titled "Civil Religion" first appeared in 1967, it touched off two decades of scholarly discussion and debate. The question addressed by Professor Bellah is, Does there exist "alongside of and rather clearly differentiated from the churches an elaborate and well-institutionalized civil religion in America"?

While some have argued that Christianity is the national faith, and others that church and synagogue celebrate only the generalized religion of "the American Way of Life," few have realized that there actually exists alongside of and rather clearly differentiated from the churches an elaborate and well-institutionalized civil religion in America. This article argues not only that there is such a thing, but also that this religion—or perhaps better, this religious dimension—has its own seriousness and integrity and requires the same care in understanding that any other religion does. . . .

The Idea of a Civil Religion

The phrase "civil religion" is, of course, Rousseau's. In . . . *The Social Contract*, he outlines the simple dogmas of the civil religion: the existence of God, the life to come, the reward of virtue and the punishment of vice, and the exclusion of religious intolerance. All other religious opinions are outside the cognizance of the state and may be freely

Reprinted, with permission, from "Religion in America," *Daedalus* (Journal of the American Academy of Arts and Sciences, Boston, Massachusetts), Winter 1967.

held by citizens. While the phrase *civil religion* was not used, to the best of my knowledge, by the founding fathers, and I am certainly not arguing for the particular influence of Rousseau, it is clear that similar ideas, as part of the cultural climate of the late-eighteenth century, were to be found among the Americans. For example, Franklin writes in his autobiography,

I never was without some religious principles. I never doubted, for instance, the existence of the Deity; that he made the world and govern'd it by his Providence; that the most acceptable service of God was the doing of good to men; that our souls are immortal; and that all crime will be punished, and virtue rewarded either here or hereafter. These I esteemed the essentials of every religion; and, being to be found in all the religions we had in our country, I respected them all, tho' with different degrees of respect, as I found them more or less mix'd with other articles, which, without any tendency to inspire, promote or confirm morality, serv'd principally to divide us, and make us unfriendly to one another.

It is easy to dispose of this sort of position as essentially utilitarian in relation to religion. . . . But there is every reason to believe that religion, particularly the idea of God, played a constitutive role in the thought of the early American statesmen. . . .

There are four references to God [in the Declaration of Independence.] The first speaks of the "Laws of Nature and of Nature's God" which entitle any people to be independent. The second is the famous statement that all men "are endowed by their Creator with certain inalienable Rights." Here Jefferson is locating the fundamental legitimacy of the new nation in a conception of "higher law" that is itself based on both classical natural law and Biblical religion. The third is an appeal to "the Supreme Judge of the world for the rectitude of our intentions," and the last indicates "a firm reliance on the protection of divine Providence." In these last two references, a Biblical God of history who stands in judgment over the world is indicated.

The intimate relation of these religious notions with the self-conception of the new Republic is indicated by the frequency of their appearance in early official documents. For example, we find in Washington's first inaugural address of 30 April 1789:

It would be peculiarly improper to omit in this first official act my fervent supplications to that Almighty Being who rules over the universe, who presides in the councils of nations, and whose providential aids can supply every defect, that His benediction may consecrate to the liberties and happiness of the people of the United States a Government instituted by themselves for these essential purposes, and may enable every instrument employed in its administration to execute with success the functions allotted to his charge.

No people can be bound to acknowledge and adore the Invisible Hand which conducts the affairs of man more than those of the United States. Every step by which we have advanced to the character of an independent nation seems to have been distinguished by some token of providential agency. . . .

The propitious smiles of Heaven can never be expected on a nation that disregards the eternal rules of order and right which Heaven itself has ordained. . . . The preservation of the sacred fire of liberty and the destiny of the republican model of government are justly considered, perhaps, as *deeply*, as *finally*, staked on the experiment intrusted to the hands of the American people.

Nor did these religious sentiments remain merely the personal expression of the president. At the request of both Houses of Congress, Washington proclaimed on October 3 of that same first year as president that November 26 should be "a day of public thanksgiving and prayer," the first Thanksgiving Day under the Constitution.

The words and acts of the founding fathers, especially the first few presidents, shaped the form and tone of the civil religion as it has been maintained ever since. Though much is selectively derived from Christianity, this religion is clearly not itself Christianity. For one thing, neither Washington nor Adams nor Jefferson mentions Christ in his inaugural address; nor do any of the subsequent presidents, although not one of them fails to mention God. The God of the civil religion is not only rather "unitarian," he is also on the austere side, much more related to order, law, and right than to salvation and love. Even though he is somewhat deist in cast, he is by no means simply a watchmaker God. He is actively interested and involved in history, with a special concern for America. Here the analogy has much less to do with natural law than with ancient Israel; the equation of America with Israel in the idea of the "American Israel" is not infrequent. What was implicit in the words of Washington already quoted becomes explicit in Jefferson's second inaugural when he said: "I shall need, too, the favor of that Being in whose hands we are, who led our fathers, as Israel of old, from their native land and planted them in a country flowing with all the necessaries and comforts of life." Europe is Egypt; America, the promised land. God has led his people to establish a new sort of social order that shall be a light unto all the nations.

This theme, too, has been a continuous one in the civil religion. . . . We find it again in President Johnson's inaugural address:

They came here—the exile and the stranger, brave but frightened—to find a place where a man could be his own man. They made a covenant with this land. Conceived in justice, written in liberty, bound in union, it was meant one day to inspire the hopes of all mankind; and it binds us still. If we keep its terms, we shall flourish.

What we have, then, from the earliest years of the republic is a collection of beliefs, symbols, and rituals with respect to sacred things and institutionalized in a collectivity. This religion—there seems no other word for it—while not antithetical to, and indeed sharing much in common with, Christianity, was neither sectarian nor in any specific sense Christian. At a time when the society was overwhelmingly Christian, it seems unlikely that this lack of Christian reference was meant to spare the feelings of the tiny non-Christian minority. Rather, the civil religion expressed what those who set the precedents felt was appropriate under the circumstances. It reflected their private as well as public views. Nor was the civil religion simply "religion in general." While generality was undoubtedly seen as a virtue by some, as in the quotation from Franklin above, the civil religion was specific enough when it came to the topic of America. Precisely because of this specificity, the civil religion was saved from empty formalism and served as a genuine vehicle of national religious self-understanding.

But the civil religion was not, in the minds of Franklin, Washington, Jefferson, or other leaders, with the exception of a few radicals like Tom Paine, ever felt to be a substitute for Christianity. There was an implicit but quite clear division of function between the civil religion and Christianity. Under the doctrine of religious liberty, an exceptionally wide sphere of personal piety and voluntary social action was left to the churches. But the churches were neither to control the state nor to be controlled by it. The national magistrate, whatever his private religious views, operates under the rubrics of the civil religion as long as he is in his official capacity. . . . This accommodation was undoubtedly the product of a particular historical moment and of a cultural background dominated by Protestantism of several varieties and by the Enlightenment, but it has survived despite subsequent changes in the cultural and religious climate.

Civil War and Civil Religion

Until the Civil War, the American civil religion focused above all on the event of the Revolution, which was seen as the final act of the Exodus from the old lands across the waters. The Declaration of Independence and the Constitution were the sacred scriptures and Washington the divinely appointed Moses who led his people out of the hands of tyranny. The Civil War, which Sidney Mead calls "the center of American history," was the second great event that involved the national self-understanding so deeply as to require expression in the civil religion. . . . Not only did the Civil War have the tragic intensity of fratricidal strife, but it was one of the bloodiest wars of the nineteenth century; the loss of life was far greater than any previously suffered by Americans.

The Civil War raised the deepest questions of national meaning. The man who not only formulated but in his own person embodied its meaning for Americans was Abraham Lincoln. For him the issue was not in the first instance slavery but "whether that nation, or any nation so conceived, and so dedicated, can long endure." . . . The phrases of Jefferson constantly echo in Lincoln's speeches. His task was, first of all, to save the Union—not for America alone but for the meaning of America to the whole world so unforgettably etched in the last phrase of the Gettysburg Address. . . .

With the Civil War, a new theme of death, sacrifice, and rebirth enters the civil religion. It is symbolized in the life and death of Lincoln. . . . With the Christian archetype in the background, Lincoln, "our martyred president," was linked to the war dead, those who "gave the last full measure of devotion." The theme of sacrifice was indelibly written into the civil religion.

The new symbolism soon found both physical and ritualistic expression. The great number of the war dead required the establishment of a number of national cemeteries [including Gettysburg and Arlington, in particular]. Memorial Day, which grew out of the Civil War, gave ritual expression to the themes we have been discussing. . . . [T]he Memorial Day observance, especially in the towns and smaller cities of America, is a major event for the whole community involving a rededication to the martyred dead, to the spirit of sacrifice, and to the American vision. Just as Thanksgiving Day . . . serves to integrate the family into the civil religion, so Memorial Day has acted to integrate the local community into the national cult. Together

with the less overtly religious Fourth of July and the more minor celebrations of Veterans Day and the birthdays of Washington and Lincoln, these two holidays provide an annual ritual calendar for the civil religion. The public-school system serves as a particularly important context for the cultic celebration of the civil rituals.

The Civil Religion Today

. . . [T]he civil religion at its best is a genuine apprehension of universal and transcendent religious reality as seen in or, one could almost say, as revealed through the experience of the American people. Like all religions, it has suffered various deformations and demonic distortions. At its best, it has neither been so general that it has lacked incisive relevance to the American scene nor so particular that it has placed American society above universal human values.

The American civil religion was never anticlerical or militantly secular. On the contrary, it borrowed selectively from the religious tradition in such a way that the average American saw no conflict between the two. In this way, the civil religion was able to build up without any bitter struggle with the church powerful symbols of national solidarity and to mobilize deep levels of personal motivation for the attainment of national goals.

Such an achievement is by no means to be taken for granted. It would seem that the problem of a civil religion is quite general in modern societies and that the way it is solved or not solved will have repercussions in many spheres. One needs only to think of France to see how differently things can go. The French Revolution was anticlerical to the core and attempted to set up an anti-Christian civil religion. . . .

American civil religion is still very much alive. Just three years ago we participated in a vivid re-enactment of the sacrifice theme in connection with the funeral of our assassinated president. The American Israel theme is clearly behind both Kennedy's New

Frontier and Johnson's Great Society. Let me give just one recent illustration of how the civil religion serves to mobilize support for the attainment of national goals. On 15 March 1965 President Johnson went before Congress to ask for a strong voting-rights bill. Early in the speech he said:

Rarely are we met with the challenge, not to our growth or abundance, or our welfare or our security—but rather to the values and the purposes and the meaning of our beloved nation.

The issue of equal rights for American Negroes is such an issue. And should we defeat every enemy, and should we double our wealth and conquer the stars and still be unequal to this issue, then we will have failed as a people and as a nation.

For with a country as with a person, "What is a man profited, if he shall gain the whole world, and lose his own soul?"

And in conclusion he said:

Above the pyramid on the great seal of the United States it says in Latin, "God has favored our undertaking."

God will not favor everything that we do. It is rather our duty to divine his will. I cannot help but believe that He truly understands and that He really favors the undertaking that we begin here tonight.

The civil religion has not always been invoked in favor of worthy causes. On the domestic scene, an American-Legion type of ideology that fuses God, country, and flag has been used to attack non-conformist and liberal ideas and groups of all kinds. Still, it has been difficult to use the words of Jefferson and Lincoln to support special interests and undermine personal freedom. The defenders of slavery before the Civil War came to reject the thinking of the Declaration of Independence. Some of the most consistent of them turned against not only Jeffersonian democracy but Reformation religion; they dreamed of a South dominated by medieval chivalry and divine-right monarchy. For all the overt religiosity of the radical right today, their relation to the civil religious consensus

is tenuous, as when the John Birch Society attacks the central American symbol of Democracy itself.

With respect to America's role in the world, the dangers of distortion are greater and the built-in safeguards of the tradition weaker. The theme of the American Israel was used, almost from the beginning, as a justification for the shameful treatment of the Indians so characteristic of our history. It can be overtly or implicitly linked to the idea of manifest destiny which has been used to legitimate several adventures in imperialism since the early-nineteenth century. Never has the danger been greater than today [in light of the Viet-Nam war]. . . .

The civil religion is obviously involved in the most pressing moral and political issues of the day. But it is also caught in another kind of crisis, theoretical and theological, of which it is at the moment largely unaware. "God" has clearly been a central symbol in the civil religion from the beginning and remains so today. This symbol is just as central to the civil religion as it is to . . . Judaism or Christianity. In the late-eighteenth century this posed no problem; even Tom Paine, contrary to his detractors, was not an atheist. From left to right and regardless of church or sect, all could accept the idea of God. But today, as even *Time* has recognized, the meaning of the word *God* is by no means so clear or so obvious. There is no formal creed in the civil religion. We have had a Catholic president; it is conceivable that we could have a Jewish one. But could we have an agnostic president? Could a man with conscientious scruples about using the word *God* . . . be elected chief magistrate of our country? If the whole God symbolism requires reformulation, there will be obvious consequences for the civil religion, consequences perhaps of liberal alienation and of fundamentalist ossification that have not so far been prominent in this realm. The civil religion has been a point of articulation between the profoundest commitments of the Western religious and philosophical tradition and the common beliefs of ordinary Americans. It is not too soon to consider how the deepening theological crisis may affect the future of this articulation.

The Third Time of Trial

In conclusion it may be worthwhile to relate the civil religion to the most serious situation that we as Americans now face, what I call the third time of trial. The first time of trial had to do with the question of independence, whether we should or could run our own affairs in our own way. The second time of trial was over the issue of slavery, which in turn was only the most salient aspect of the more general problem of the full institutionalization of democracy within our country. The second problem we are still far from solving though we have some notable successes to our credit. But we have been overtaken by a third great problem which has led to a third great crisis, in the midst of which we stand. This is the problem of responsible action in a revolutionary world, a world seeking to attain many of the things, material and spiritual, that we have already attained. Americans have, from the beginning, been aware of the responsibility and the significance our republican experiment has for the whole world. . . .

Without an awareness that our nation stands under higher judgment, the tradition of the civil religion would be dangerous indeed. Fortunately, the prophetic voices have never been lacking. . . . The spirit of civil disobedience that is alive today in the civil rights movement and the opposition to the Viet-Nam war was already clearly outlined by Henry David Thoreau when he wrote, "If the law is of such a nature that it requires you to be an agent of injustice to another, then I say, break the law." . . .

Out of the first and second times of trial have come, as we have seen, the major symbols of the American civil religion. There seems little doubt that a successful negotiation of this third time of trial—the attainment of some kind of viable and coherent world order—would precipitate a major new set of symbolic forms. . . . It would necessitate the incorporation of vital international symbolism into our civil religion, or, perhaps a better way of putting it, it would result in American civil religion becoming simply one part of a new civil religion of the world. It is useless to speculate on the form such a civil religion might take, though it obviously would draw on religious traditions beyond the sphere of Biblical religion alone. Fortunately, since the American civil religion is not the worship of the American nation but an understanding of the American experience in the light of ultimate and universal reality, the reorganization entailed by such a new situation need not disrupt the American civil religion's continuity. A world civil religion could be accepted as a fulfillment and not a denial of American civil religion. Indeed, such an outcome has been the eschatological hope of American civil religion from the beginning. To deny such an outcome would be to deny the meaning of America itself. . . .

John F. Wilson

25. THE CIVIL RELIGION PROPOSAL AS A REVITALIZATION MOVEMENT IN AMERICAN CULTURE

John F. Wilson is Professor of Religion at Princeton University and an editor of this volume. The following are excerpts from the last chapter of his book *Public Religion in American Culture* in which he reviews the evidence for and against a well-institutionalized and differentiated civil religion in America. In the following discussion, Professor Wilson sees the proposals about civil religion as themselves an attempt to revitalize American society.

[Recently,] discussion of public religion has entered a new stage in the proposal that it be understood as a differentiated and institutionalized positive religious tradition, as in "Civil Religion in America." That thesis [can be] reviewed as a construction put upon the data, but brief consideration of it from another point of view is [also] appropriate. This is to ask several questions in the framework of religious analysis: How may we interpret the development of the proposal that there is a civil religion in America? What significance should we assign to the emergence of a religious movement based upon such a proposal?

Elaboration of religiously grounded claims frequently entails an explicit historical trajectory set out in terms of origin and destiny. Under Robert Bellah's construct, the American civil religion is believed to point toward a world order; its destiny is to become transformed into a global civil religion. The religion of the republic, the construction proposed by Sidney Mead, is thought to carry the burden of a cultural revolution originating with the Enlightenment. This event, possibly the most momentous cultural event in history, is believed to reach fullest expression in the ideal of the American republic. Thus, each of these particular constructs includes a historical interpretation placed upon public religion cast in terms of universalistic claims. When viewed with some detach-

ment, however, both of these proposals appear to be highly ethnocentric. In the framework of a critical approach to religious movements, the logically necessary question is how such worldviews function as social constructions. How might we understand the appeal of civil religion, or the religion of the republic, as the basis for a social movement?

One of the conditions under which religious movements appear to develop is that of rapid social change, especially when an older and possibly waning culture is threatened by a newer and dynamic one. . . . Anthony F. C. Wallace has suggested an analytical model of the revitalization movement as a means of conceptualizing how a beleaguered society reaches for religious self-understanding out of the past, in terms which are familiar from the tradition at hand. This is a means of coping with an uncertain present and a threatening future. In this most general framework, revitalization movements are interpreted as attempts to recover, heighten, and strenuously advocate adherence to the religious legacy believed to be the center of the particular endangered culture. The anticipated outcome is preservation of that culture, possibly including the achievement of a more perfect embodiment of its central commitments. Of course, in a critical perspective, the recovered or revitalized culture is actually different from the older one. It has undergone a selective adaptation. In that process, elements have been dampened or heightened and the whole reorganized, usually in response to particular interest groups in the society.

If we seek an interpretation of the recent proposals about public religion in America in terms available from critical studies of religious movements, we can probably do no better than to view them as potential revitalization movements occasioned by widespread loss of internal confidence in American society and changed external cultural relationships. It is obvious that subcultures, such as those of black Americans or Spanish-speaking Americans (and a host of others), have become ethnically self-conscious enough to call into question the viability of traditional American society. This is in part because a broadly Protestant hegemony is experienced as alien and oppressive. Those sensitive to this situation have responded in different ways. One kind of response to this perceived condition has been resonance to the call for recovery of a civil religion or religion of the republic. While the manifest symbols of these proposals may be universal and global, the latent basis for interest in and support of them has more likely been a concern that the old familiar ways are directly challenged and severely threatened.

Interestingly enough, from this perspective, the ideological contents of revitalization movements turn out to be culturally specific versions of American Protestant Christianity, more classical than modern, which have been given a content of broadly political symbols and events. These constructs, in line with accepted critical interpretations of such movements, probably have more currency as reconceptualizations of past ideologies than as direct continuations of them.

Why should an idealized past be so prominent in these proposals? Partly because particular versions of Protestantism have repeatedly proved to be divisive, especially in the American setting. But at least as impor-

tant, the latent strategy of a revitalization movement is to counter a threat to the whole social fabric and, generally, to enlist Americans under more inclusive symbols and commitments than the narrower inherited construction would permit. In some respects, then, it may be helpful to interpret the civil religion phenomenon more properly as a latent political revitalization movement than as a manifestly religious one. At one level, this is because politics is the realm in which consensus is achieved in modern societies in spite of other divergent opinions. But at another level, the perceived threat may be that politics as a means of governing communities is proving to be anachronistic; societies seem less readily subject to control through classical political means. If this is the felt threat, the culture threatened is one in which the political process is taken seriously as a means of significantly affecting society. . . .

If by suggesting that the American civil religion proposal may be identified as the ideological core of a revitalization movement, we have seemed to diminish its significance (by associating it with the Ghost Dance movement, as an example), that is unfortunate. Better parallels to it might be found in such religio-social movements as pietism in the German Lands (and others) in the eighteenth century, or Stuart Puritanism in seventeenth-century England. Versions of millenarianism in nineteenth-century America may provide a yet closer parallel, even antecedent. The point is that in each case an older culture was deeply challenged by new social conditions, and its existence seemed to be threatened. As a cultural strategy, it moved to consolidate and reexpress what it took to be its essential commitments. Usually through a prophet or a cadre of leaders, the movement worked to conserve the old in the face of social change. So the civil religion proposal, or the advocacy of a religion of the republic, might be seen, finally, as the attempt, through a variety of particular forms, to distill the old political culture of the United

States which was supported by a broadly Protestant establishment. The purpose is to conserve that culture even as it, and the associated establishment, is threatened from within and without. . . .

Robert Bellah suggested that "Civil Religion in America" had gone undetected precisely because a western concept of religion as differentiated had prevented observers from recognizing something so obvious. Americans resist acknowledging in their own culture, he thought, something as obvious as Shinto in a foreign culture. But the further irony may be that emphasis upon civil religion itself betrays the other side of that same impulse—namely, to conceive of religion as developed and institutionalized. The materials [of public religion] . . . seem not to require that interpretation, but are better understood as aspects of an incredibly rich and internally complex culture.

Suggestions for Further Reading

For readers who seek further information on the time period discussed in each chapter, we have included below a short list of books pertinent to the designated chapters. We then list additional works dealing more broadly with Church and State in American history. The reader should note that these works often are (explicitly or implicitly) designed to foster a particular perspective on the Church-State question. Accordingly, no one work (whether or not cited here) should be taken as the final word on any aspect of politics, history, or religion. Thus, the "suggestions for further reading" have not been selected because they are necessarily the "best" works on a subject but because they are useful texts or are representative of one or more schools of thought present in the literature.

CHAPTER I

Davidson, Elizabeth H. *The Establishment of the English Church in Continental American Colonies* (1936).

Haskins, G. L. *Law and Authority in Early Massachusetts* (1949).

Miller, Perry. *Errand into the Wilderness* (1965).

———. *Roger Williams: His Contribution to the American Tradition* (1953).

Morgan, Edmund S. *Puritan Political Ideas, 1588–1794* (1964).

———. *Roger Williams: The Church and the State* (1967).

CHAPTER II

Bridenbaugh, Carl. *Mitre and Sceptre: Transatlantic Faiths, Ideas, Personalities and Politics, 1689–1775* (1962).

Cobb, Sanford H. *The Rise of Religious Liberty in America* (1902).

Curran, Francis X. *Catholics in Colonial Law* (1963).

Gaustad, Edwin S. *The Great Awakening in New England* (1957).

Greene, M. Louise. *The Development of Religious Liberty in Connecticut* (1905).

McLoughlin, William G. *New England Dissent, 1630–1833: The Baptists and the Separation of Church and State* (1971).

———, ed. *Isaac Backus on Church, State and Calvinism: Pamphlets, 1754–1789* (1968).

CHAPTER III

Alley, Robert, ed. *James Madison: A Free Conscience in a Secular Republic* (1985).

Antieu, Chester James, A. T. Downey, and E. C. Roberts. *Freedom from Federal Establishment: Formation and History of the First Amendment Religion Clauses* (1964).

Antieu, Chester James, P. M. Carroll, and T. C. Burke. *Religion under the State Constitutions* (1965).

Eckenrode, H. J. *Separation of Church and State in Virginia* (1910).

Hatch, Nathan O. *The Sacred Cause of Liberty: Republican Thought and the Millennium in Rev-olutionary New England* (1977).
Healey, Robert M. *Jefferson on Religion in Public Education* (1962).
Howe, Mark DeWolfe. *The Garden and the Wilderness: Religion and Government in American Constitutional History* (1965).
Kinney, Charles B., Jr. *Church and State: The Struggle for Separation in New Hampshire* (1955).
Malbin, Michael J. *Religion and Politics: The Intentions of the Authors of the First Amendment* (1978).
Meyer, Jacob C. *Church and State in Massachusetts, 1750–1833* (1930).
Moehlman, Conrad H. *The American Constitutions and Religion* (1938).
Niebuhr, Reinhold, and Alan Heimart. *A Nation So Conceived* (1963).
Wood, Gordon, *The Creation of the American Republic, 1776–1787* (1972).

CHAPTER IV

Billington, Ray Allen. *The Protestant Crusade, 1800–1860* (1938).
Bodo, John R. *The Protestant Clergy and Public Issues: 1812–1848* (1954).
Culver, Raymond B. *Horace Mann and Religion in the Massachusetts Public Schools* (1929).
Handy, Robert. *A Christian America: Protestant Hopes and Historical Realities* (1971).
Hudson, Winthrop, ed. *Nationalism and Religion in America: Concepts of American Identity and Mission* (1970).
Marty, Martin E. *Righteous Empire: The Protestant Experience in America* (1970).
Niebuhr, H. Richard. *The Social Sources of Denominationalism* (1954).
Story, Joseph. *Commentaries on the Constitution* (1833).

CHAPTER V

Cross, Robert D. *The Emergence of Liberal Catholicism in America* (1958).
Michaelson, Robert. *Piety in the Public School: Trends and Issues in Relationship between Religion and the Public Schools in the United States* (1970).
Moorhead, James H. *American Apocalypse: Yankee Protestants and the Civil War, 1860–1969* (1978).
Schaff, Philip. *Church and State in the United States* (1888).
Smith, Timothy L. *Revivalism and Social Reform: American Protestantism on the Eve of the Civil War* (1957).
Spear, Samuel T. *Religion and the State* (1876).
Strong, Josiah. *Our Country: Its Possible Future and Its Present Crises* (1885).

CHAPTER VI

Bennett, John C. *Christians and the State* (1958).
Blanshard, Paul. *American Freedom and Catholic Power* (1949).
Giannella, Donald A., ed. *Religion and the Public Order, No. 5* (1969).
Herberg, Will. *Protestant—Catholic—Jew: An Essay in American Religious Sociology* (1955).
Kauper, Paul. *Civil Liberties and the Constitution* (1962).
Kurland, Philip. *Religion and the Law: Of Church and State and the Supreme Court* (1962).
Lenski, Gerhard. *The Religious Factor* (1960).
Murray, John Courtney. *We Hold These Truths: Catholic Reflections on the American Proposition* (1964).

Regan, R. J. *American Pluralism and the Catholic Conscience* (1963).

Ryan, J. A., and M. F. X. Millar, eds. *The State and the Church* (1922).

Chapter VII

Bellah, Robert N. *The Broken Covenant: American Civil Religion in Time of Trial* (1975).

Boles, D. E. *The Bible, Religion and the Public Schools* (1964).

Dolbeare, Kenneth M., and Philip E. Hammond. *The School Prayer Decisions: From Court Policy to Local Practice* (1971).

Miller, Robert T., and Ronald B. Flowers. *Toward Benevolent Neutrality: Church, State and the Supreme Court* (1977).

Moehlman, Conrad H. *The Wall of Separation between Church and State: An Historical Study of Recent Criticism of the Religious Clauses of the First Amendment* (1951).

Morgan, Richard E. *The Supreme Court and Religion* (1972).

Muir, William K., Jr. *Prayer in the Public Schools: Law and Attitude Change* (1967).

Neuhaus, Richard John. *The Naked Public Square: Religion and Democracy in America* (1984).

Oaks, Dallin, ed. *The Wall between Church and State* (1963).

O'Neill, James M. *Religion and Education under the Constitution* (1949).

Richey, Russell E., and Donald G. Jones, eds. *American Civil Religion* (1974).

Wilson, John F. *Public Religion in American Culture* (1979).

General

Ahlstrom, Sydney, E. *A Religious History of the American People* (1972).

Bercovitch, Sacvan. *The Puritan Origins of the American Self* (1975).

Beth, Loren P. *The American Theory of Church and State* (1958).

Clebsch, William A. *From Sacred to Profane America: The Role of Religion in American History* (1968).

Cuninggim, Merrimon. *Freedom's Holy Light* (1955).

Dawson, Joseph M. *America's Way in Church, State and Society* (1953).

Drinan, Robert F. *Religion, the Courts and Public Policy* (1963).

Johnson, Alvin N., and F. H. Yost. *Separation of Church and State in the United States* (1948).

Kerwin, Jerome G. *The Catholic Viewpoint on Church and State* (1960).

Littell, Franklin H. *From State Church to Pluralism: A Protestant Interpretation of Religion in American History* (1971).

McLoughlin, William. *Revivals, Awakenings and Reform: An Essay on Religion and Social Change in America, 1607–1977* (1979).

Mead, Sidney. *The Lively Experiment: The Shaping of Christianity in America* (1963).

Morgan, Richard E. *The Politics of Religious Conflict: Church and State in America* (1968).

Niebuhr, H. Richard. *The Kingdom of God in America* (1937).

Pfeffer, Leo. *Church, State and Freedom* (1967).

Sanders, Thomas G. *Protestant Concepts of Church and State* (1964).

Sorauf, Frank J. *The Wall of Separation: The Constitutional Politics of Church and State* (1976).

Stokes, Anson Phelps. *Church and State in the United States* (1950).

Strout, Cushing. *The New Heavens and New Earth: Political Religion in America* (1974).

Thomas, John L. *Religion and the American People* (1963).

Index

Adams, Jasper, 80
Adams, John, 65–66, 82, 170, 296
Adenauer, Konrad, 192
Aid to religious schools, 281–95
Alison, Francis, 56, 61–62, 64, 65
Allen, Ethan, 86
American Civil Liberties Union, 264
American Historical Association, 151
American Historical Review, 3
American Philosophical Society, 85
American Protective Association
  (A.P.A.), 132, 133, 136, 139, 155
American Revolution, 63, 65, 87, 88
American Sunday-School Union, 117,
  119
Americans United for the Separation of
  Church and State, 291
American Tract Society, 120
Anabaptists, 28, 35, 38, 87
Andover Seminary, 110
Andrews, M. P., *The Founding of Mary-
  land*, 14
Anglican Church. *See* Church of
  England
Anglo-Saxon civilization, America as
  embodiment of Christian, 136–38
Antinomians, 28
Articles of Capitulation, 17
Atlantic Monthly, The, 184
Augustine, St., 141–42; *Confessions*, 23
Avery, John, 37

Backus, Issac, 89
Bacon, Leonard, 51
Baltimore, Lord, 14–15, 143, 145
Baptists, 34, 50, 57, 87–88, 117, 120, 135,
  173, 174, 175; Danbury, 78, 243; Mas-
  sachusetts Bay's banishment of, 13;
  varieties of, 45, 46
Barry, William, 146
Baylor University, 246
Bayne, Peter, 22
Beecher, Lyman, 94–95, 112–13, 114,
  115, 116, 118, 120; *A Plea for the West*,
  100–101
Bellah, Robert N., "Civil Religion in
  America," 224, 295–300, 301, 303
Bennett, John C., *Christians and the State*,
  173–76

Bible, reading of, in schools, 121–31,
  225, 230–33. *See also* Schools, religion
  in public
Billings, Robert, 248
Bill of Rights, 75, 87–89, 144, 198, 209,
  210, 214, 215, 216, 243–45; religion
  clauses of, 92–93
Birth control, 177
Black, Justice Hugo, 200–3, 205–6,
  210–11, 225–28, 281
Blackmun, Justice Harry A., 293, 295
Blanshard, Paul, *American Freedom and
  Catholic Power*, 187–89
Board of Education v. *Allen*, 290, 292, 294
Bob Jones University v. *United States*,
  273–75
Boorstin, Daniel J., *The Lost World of
  Thomas Jefferson*, 82–85
Boston Gazette, 48
Bradford, William, 21
Brady, Edward B., 139–42, 145
Brainerd, David, 49
Brennan, Justice William J., Jr., 261–63,
  276–78
Bridenbaugh, Carl. *Mitre and Sceptre*,
  64–67
Brigham Young University, 280
Brooks, Phillips, 148
Brown v. *Board of Education*, 274
Bryan, William Jennings, 234
Bryce, James (Lord), 122; *The American
  Commonwealth*, 154–57
Bureau of the Census, 280
Burger, Chief Justice Warren E., 259–61,
  269–75, 281–86, 292, 293, 294
Burke, Edmund, 47; *Conciliation with
  America*, 46
Burton, Justice Harold H., 204, 206

Calder, I. M., 3
Calhoun, John, 169
California, University of (Berkeley), 295
Calvinism, 2, 57, 90
Cambridge Platform, 49
Cantwell v. *Connecticut*, 195–96, 214, 215,
  230, 231
Carlyle, Thomas, 24–25, 168
Carnegie Institute of Technology, 181
Carolina, 18–19, 33

Carr, Peter, 83
Catholic Conference, U.S., 279
Catholic Encyclopedia, 185
Catholicism, 43, 45–46, 51, 57, 93, 100,
  101, 121, 122, 138; and Americanism,
  142–43, 161; in Canada, 157; and
  church and state, 139–42, 161, 163–67;
  crusade against, 132–35, 154–55; in
  Maryland, 14; and non-Catholic state,
  143–47; and passing Protestant era in
  America, 148; as political issue, 184–95
Catholic University of America, 163
Catholic World, 146
Chambers, Senator, 262
Chandler, Thomas Bradbury, 64; *An Ap-
  peal to the Public in Behalf of the Church
  of England in America,* 52, 53–56, 62;
  colonial criticism of appeal of, 56–61
  passim
Channing, William Ellery, 105–9, 114
Charles II, King, 16, 136
Charleston College, 80
Chatham College, 181
Chesterton, G. K., 24, 171
Christian Communications Network, 248
Christian History, 48
Christianity and Crisis, 173
Christian Voice, 247–48
Churches, and clergy, 154–57
Churches of Christ, 3–4
Church of England, 16, 27, 28, 34, 41,
  42, 47, 90, 219–20, 226. *See also* Estab-
  lishment, Anglican
Civil religion, 295–303
Civil Rights Commission, 280
Civil War, 121, 147, 156, 297–98
Clark, Justice Tom C., 230–33
Clarke, John, 16, 87
Clarke, Richard, 145, 146
Clergy, churches and, 154–57
Coke, Sir Edward, 169
College of New Jersey (Princeton), 38,
  86
College of Philadelphia, 61, 62
Colton, Calvin, 110–12
Committee for Public Education v. *Nyquist,*
  287, 288–89, 293
Committee for the Survival of a Free
  Congress, 247
Confession of Faith (Mennonites), 35–36
Congregationalism, 37, 53, 57, 87, 94,
  105, 113, 120; and Great Awakening,
  47, 49, 50; and Plan of Union, 117
Connecticut, 13, 26, 34, 37–38, 50–51;
  Beecher on disestablishment in,
  94–95, 112–13

Conservative Caucus, 247
Constitution, United States, 75, 133,
  143, 147, 169, 170, 171, 173, 177; Arti-
  cle VI of, 191
Continental Congress, 259, 260
Cooley, Thomas McIntyre, 122, 152–53,
  154; *A Treatise on the Constitutional
  Limitations Which Rest upon the Legisla-
  tive Power of the States of the American
  Union,* 157–60
Cooper, William, 48
Cotton, John, 3–7, 8, 11, 21, 26, 28–29,
  53, 169; *Abstract of the Laws of New
  England,* 23
Crispi, Francesco, 144
Cromwell, Oliver, 23
Cross, Arthur L., *The Anglican Episcopate
  and the American Colonies,* 61–63
Cross, Robert D., *The Emergence of Liberal
  Catholicism in America,* 143–47
Cultural issues, and God and country,
  295–303
Cutler, Timothy, 53

Dale, Sir Thomas, 11
"Dale's Laws," 11
Darrow, Clarence, 234
Dartmouth College, 49
Darwin, Charles, 234, 235
Davenport, John, 3, 30–31
Davies, Samuel, 38–42
Declaration of Independence, 86, 296,
  299
de Gaulle, Charles, 192
Delaware, Lord, 11
Dickinson, John, 56, 62; *The Farmer's
  Letters,* 62
Doddridge, Philip, 38
Dodge, Nehemiah, 78
Doerr, Edd, 291–92
Dongan, Thomas, 46
Douglas, Justice William, 208–10, 261,
  265
Duffy, Francis P., 184
Dunkers, 45, 46
Duquesne University, 181
Dutch, 20
Dutch Reformed Church, 44, 99, 117
Dwight, Timothy, 94, 113, 115, 120

Education, Department of, 280
Edwards, Jonathan, 49, 51
Edwards, Pierrepont, 94
Ely, Ezra Stiles, 96–100, 120
Emmons, Nathanael, 51

Engel v. *Vitale,* 225–29, 230, 231, 233, 237, 240, 244, 245, 263
Enlightenment, 86, 87, 118, 182, 301
Episcopalians, 86, 93, 117
Epperson v. *Arkansas,* 234–36
Equal access approach, 238–40
Equal Employment Opportunities Commission, 280
Erastus, 5
Establishment, Anglican: Jefferson and Madison on issue of, 68–89; threat of, 53–67. *See also* Church of England
Establishment clause. *See* First Amendment
Evangelicalism, 110–12, 117–20, 149–50
Everson v. *Board of Education,* 162, 206, 207, 209, 231, 270, 277, 281, 288, 292; discussion of, 200–205; and *Epperson* v. *Arkansas,* 235; Howe on, 214, 215; and *Wallace* v. *Jaffree,* 243, 244, 245

Falwell, Jerry, 247, 248
Federalist #10, 52
Ferry, Jules, 144
Finney, Charles G., 90
First Amendment, 75, 85–86, 87, 88, 170, 173, 175, 182, 219; concept of neutrality in, 259–63; establishment clause of, 223, 225, 227–28, 230–33, 236–37, 238, 241–45, 264–68, 269, 276–78, 281, 287–90, 291; and *Everson* case, 201–3, 204; free exercise clause of, 227, 230–33, 236, 264–65, 269, 275, 276, 277, 281; free speech clause of, 238; Howe on, 213–18; JFK on, 191; and *McCollum* case, 205–8; religion clauses of, 161, 171, 195, 212–13, 225, 238, 269–70, 273, 275, 281; and *Walz* v. *Tax Commission,* 269–73; and *West Virginia State Board of Education* v. *Barnette,* 198, 199; and *Zorach* v. *Clauson,* 208–9
Fiske, John, 136
"Flag Salute Case," 197–200
Fletcher, Reuben, 50
Fortas, Justice Abe, 234–36
Foster, Charles I., *An Errand of Mercy,* 117–20
Fourteenth Amendment, 173, 195–96, 198, 201, 205–7, 213–18; due process clause of, 195, 200, 219, 235, 281
Fox, George, *Journal,* 23
Frankfurter, Justice Felix, 199–200, 204, 206–7
Franklin, Benjamin, 296, 297

Free exercise clause. *See* First Amendment
French Revolution, 117, 181, 184, 298
Fundamental Constitutions, 18–19
Fundamentalism, religious, and New Right, 246–50
Fundamental Order, 13

Gates, Sir Thomas, 11
Gaustad, Edwin S., *The Great Awakening in New England,* 47–51
George, Henry, *Progress and Poverty,* 146
Gibbons, James Cardinal, 144, 145–46, 147
Gladden, Washington, 122, 132–35
Gladstone, William, 145
Gobitis decision, 197, 198, 199
Goldberg, Justice Arthur J., 261
Goldsboro Christian Schools, Inc. v. *United States,* 274
Governmental activity, religion and, 256–68
Grant, Robert, 247
Great Awakening, 33, 87, 90, 149; institutional effects of, 47–51

Handy, Robert T., *A Christian America,* 85; on religious freedom in America, 85–89
Harlan, Justice John M., 277–78
Hayes, Carlton, 170
Health, Education and Welfare, Department of, 280
Health and Human Services, Department of, 280
Hecker, Isaac T., 146, 147
Heritage Foundation, 247
Hewit, Augustine F., 144
Hobart, John Henry, 120
Holmes, Donald, 242
Holmes, Justice Oliver W., 272
Hooker, Thomas, 2, 13, 30; *Survey of the Summe of Church Discipline,* 23
Hoover, Herbert, 184
Howard, A. E. Dick, 292–95
Howe, Mark DeWolfe, 88; *Religion in a Free Society,* 213–18
Hudson, Winthrop, *American Protestantism,* 148–50
Humphrey, Heman, 115
Humphrey, Hubert, 190
Hunt v. *McNair,* 294

Immigrants, churches of, 42–45
Immigration, 32–33
Independent, The, 129

Indians, American, 1, 16, 21, 49
Inglis, Charles, 66–67
Institutional issues, and church and state, 269–95
Internal Revenue Service (IRS), 224, 247, 274, 275, 279, 280
Ireland, John, 142–43, 146–47

Jackson, Andrew, 102
Jackson, Justice Robert H., 197, 203–4, 206, 211, 233, 277
James I, King, 11
Jay, John, 260
Jefferson, Thomas, 26, 52, 92, 169, 205, 256; his Bill for Establishing Religious Freedom, 68, 73–74, 83, 86, 190, 226, 243, 244; and civil religion, 296–99 *passim*; death of, 115; on issue of establishment, 68–89 *passim*; letters of, 78–80; *Notes on Virginia*, 84; Rutledge court's interpretation of, 214–15; and separation of church and state, 28–29, 91, 168; his "wall of separation," 53, 173, 207, 265
Jehovah's Witness cases, 195
John Birch Society, 299
Johnson, Andrew, 297
Johnson, Lyndon B., 299
Johnson, Richard M., 102–5
Journal of Church and State, 246
Judaism, 60, 93, 254–55; and church-state issue, 161, 174–75, 181–84
Juridicial problem, church and state as, 195–222

Kauper, Paul G., *Civil Liberties and the Constitution*, 218–22
Keane, Bishop, 145
Kedroff case, 172
Kennedy, John F., 161, 184, 190–92, 193, 229, 298–99
Kurland, Philip, *Religion and the Law*, 212–13

La Guardia, Fiorello, 174
Lane Theological Seminary, 100
Larson, John R., 276
Larson v. *Valente*, 276–78
Leland, John, 87, 112, 116
Lemon test, 236, 245, 277
Lemon v. *Kurtzman*, 236, 242, 245, 277, 278, 287, 288, 289, 292–94; discussion of, 281–86
Leo XIII, Pope, 132, 140, 141, 163, 164, 166, 170
Lincoln, Abraham, 298, 299

Littell, Franklin H., *The Anabaptist View of the Church*, 35
Livingston, William, 44, 52, 56, 61, 64, 65
Locke, John, 18
Louis XVIII, King, 145
Luther, Martin, 41, 43, 221
Lutherans, 41, 46, 57
Lynch v. *Donnelly*, 264–68

McCollum v. *Board of Education*, 205–8, 209, 210, 211, 215, 244
McCrary v. *Runyon*, 273
McGlynn, Edward, 145, 146
McGowan v. *Maryland*, 256–59, 268
Maclear, James F., 112–16
Madison, James, 52, 53, 92, 205, 226, 228, 243–44, 256, 277; on issue of establishment, 68–89 *passim*; letters of, 80–82; *Memorial and Remonstrance*, 68–72, 73, 86, 169, 204; Rutledge court's interpretation of, 214–15; and separation of church and state, 91
Mallone, James W., 251–52
Manning, Henry Cardinal, 145
Marshall, Charles C., 184
Marshall, John, 229
Marshall, Justice Thurgood, 261
Marsh v. *Chambers*, 259–63, 264, 267, 268
Marty, Martin, 183, 250
Mary, Queen, 34
Maryland, 14–15, 46, 88, 143, 157, 256–59
Mason, George, 68
Mason, J. M., 118
Massachusetts, 89
Massachusetts Bay Colony, 2, 3, 8, 13, 26, 28, 29, 34, 51
Massachusetts Bay Company, 2
Mather, Cotton, 28, 169
Mather, Increase, 28
Mead, Sidney, 297–98, 301
Meek v. *Pittenger*, 293–94
Memmi, Albert, *Portrait of a Jew*, 183
Mennonites, 33, 35–36, 45, 46, 87
Mercersburg Seminary, 151
Methodists, 117, 119
Michigan, University of, 157
Miller, Perry, 25–31; *Errand into the Wilderness*, 25; *The New England Mind*, 25
Milnor, James, 120
Minorities, religious, in colonies, 45–47
Minor v. *Board of Education of Cincinnati*, 230
Mondale, Walter, 224
"Monkey law," 234, 235

Moral Majority, 246, 247, 248
Moral Majority Report, 248
Moravians, 33, 46
Moulart, Father, 167
Mueller v. *Allen*, 286–90
Murray, John Courtney, 290; *We Hold These Truths*, 168–72
Mussolini, Benito, 189

National Conference of Catholic Bishops, 251–52
National Conservative Political Action, 247
National Council of Churches, 190, 246, 252–53, 279
National Jewish Community Relations Advisory Council (NJCRAC), 254–55
National Labor Relations Board, 279
Nelson, Stephen S., 78
New Hampshire, 49
New Haven Colony, 3
New Jersey, 33, 49, 56
Newman, Cardinal John Henry, 185
New Netherland, 17
New Right, religious fundamentalism and, 246–50
Newton, Sir Isaac, 24
New York, 20, 46
New York Gazette, 56, 60–61, 62
Nicholas, George, 68
Niebuhr, H. Richard: *The Kingdom of God in America*, 20–25; *The Social Sources of Denominationalism*, 42–45
Niebuhr, Reinhold, 173
Nixon, Richard M., 293

O'Gorman, Thomas, 145
O'Neill, James M., *Catholicism and American Freedom*, 187

Paine, Solomon, 50
Paine, Tom, 86, 297, 299
Palmer, Robert E., 259, 261, 262
Paul, Saint, 17, 35, 140
Penn, William, 17–18, 20, 21, 22, 87, 143
Pennington, Isaac, 22, 23
Pennsylvania, 17, 20, 33, 35, 46, 143, 281–82, 284, 285
Pennsylvania Journal, 56–60, 61
Pfeffer, Leo, *Church, State and Freedom*, 172
Pike, James A., *A Roman Catholic in the White House*, 193–95
Pilgrims, 20, 21, 22, 24
Pittsburgh, University of, 181
Pius IX, Pope, 166–67; *Syllabus*, 139, 185

Pius XI, Pope: *Casti Connubii*, 189; *Christian Education of Youth*, 189
Pius XII, Pope, 171
Plymouth, 20
Pohle, Father, 165, 166–67
Political issue, church and state as, 184–85
Politics, religion and, 246–55
Powell, Justice Lewis F., Jr., 238–40, 288, 293, 294–95
Presbyterianism, 44, 45–46, 50–51, 57, 62, 110, 120, 134; and Plan of Union, 117; report of, on church and state, 176–81; Scotch-Irish, 20, 33; in Virginia, 38–42
Priestley, Joseph, 84–85
Princeton University, 301
Prince v. *Massachusetts*, 275
Protestantism, 14, 20–25, 33, 43; and anti-Catholic crusade, 132–35; and church-state issue, 161, 173; passing of era of, in America, 148–50; republican, 90–120 *passim*, 121, 136
Protestants and Other Americans United, 187, 291
Providence Plantations, 16
Puritan(s), 1, 3, 14, 20, 22, 23, 24, 87, 88; and church-state separation, 112–15; state and society, 25–31

Quakers, 17, 20, 27, 34, 38, 45, 46, 50, 57, 87; Niebuhr on, 22–25

Randolph, John, 82
Reagan, Ronald, 223, 224, 245, 247, 248
Reed, Justice Stanley F., 199, 207–8
Reformation, 87, 88, 164
Reformed churches, 46
Regulation, taxation and, 269–80
Rehnquist, Justice William H., 240, 243–45, 286–90, 293, 294
Religious liberty (freedom): constitutional limitations regarding, 157–60; Jefferson's Bill for Establishing, 68, 73–74, 83, 86, 190, 226, 243, 244
Religious perspectives, church and state in, 163–84
Rhode Island, 2, 8, 16, 20, 93, 281–85
Robbins, Ephraim, 78
Roberts, Justice Owen J., 195–96, 199, 214–15, 231
Robertson, Pat, 248
Robison, James, 247
Roemer v. *Board of Public Works*, 295
Root, Elihu, 207
Roundtable, The, 247

Rousseau, Jean Jacques, *The Social Contract*, 295–96
Rubenstein, Richard L., *Religion and the Public Order*, 181–84
Rush, Benjamin, 82, 84
Russian Revolution, 181
Rutledge, John, 260
Rutledge, Justice Wiley B., Jr., 204–5, 206, 214, 215
Ryan, John A., 163–67
Ryan, Stephen, 144, 146

Savoy Declaration, 22–23
Saybrook Platform, 34, 37, 50, 51
Schaff, Philip, 122, 154; "Church and State in the United States," 151–53
School District of Abington Township v. *Schempp*, 230–33, 236, 237, 244, 245, 263, 267
Schools: aid to religious, 281–95; religion in public, 121–31, 224, 225–45
Schwenkfelders, 46
Scopes v. *State*, 234, 235–36
Seccombe, Joseph, 48
Second Awakening, 113
Serle, Ambrose, 66–67
Seventh-day Adventists, General Conference of, 279
Shea, John Gilmary, 146
Silence, moment of, in schools, 240–41, 242
Simons, Menno, 35
Smith, Adam, 84
Smith, Al, 161, 184–86, 190, 194
Smith, William, 62, 65
Spalding, Bishop, 144–45
Spannaus, Warren, 276
Spear, Samuel T., *Religion and the State*, 129–31
Stamp Act, 66
Stevens, Justice John P., 240–43
Stewart, Justice Potter, 228–29, 231
Stiles, Ezra, 50, 51, 64
Stone v. *Graham*, 236–37, 267
Storer, Judge, 123–26
Story, Joseph, *Commentaries on the Constitution*, 92–93
Stritch, Samuel Cardinal, 148
Strong, Josiah, 122, 139; *Our Country*, 136–138
Stuart, Moses, 114
Sunday closing laws, 256–59
Supreme Court, U.S., 161–62, 172, 173, 177, 223, 279; on aid to religious schools, 281–90, 291, 292–95; church

and state before, 195–222; on religion and governmental activity, 256–68; on religion in public schools, 224, 225–45; on taxation and regulation, 269–78
Sweet, William Warren, *Religion in Colonial America*, 45–47
Synagogue Council of America, 279

Taft, Alphonso, 230
Tardivel, Jules, 146
Taxation and regulation, 269–80
Taylor, Nathaniel W., 113, 115–16
Temperance movement, 110
Ten Commandments, posting of, in classroom, 236–37
Theocracy, 20, 31
Thompson, William P., 279–80
Thoreau, Henry David, 300
Tilton v. *Richardson*, 294
Tocqueville, Alexis de, 90, 170
Toleration, Act of, 14, 34, 38, 40, 41, 46, 50, 152
Townshend Acts, 64
Tracy, Joseph, 145
Trinity College (Hartford, CT), 110
Troeltsch, Ernest, 182

Unification Church, 276
Union, Act of, 32
Union Theological Seminary, 85, 173
Unitarianism, 105
Utopianism, 20, 21

Van Buren, Martin, 102
Viguerie, Richard A., 247
Virginia, 1, 2, 11–13, 14, 90; issue of Anglican establishment in, 52, 53, 68, 73–74; Presbyterianism in, 38–42
Virginia, University of, 292
Virginia Company, 2, 11

Wallace, Anthony F. C., 301
Wallace v. *Jaffree*, 240–45
Walz v. *Tax Commission*, 268, 269–73, 277, 282, 284, 285, 292, 293
Ward, Nathaniel, 27
Warren, Chief Justice Earl, 256–59
Washington, George, 224, 229, 266, 296, 297
Watson v. *Jones*, 201
Webb, John, 48
Weber, Max, 182
Webster, Daniel, 114–15
Webster, Judge, 126–28
Westminster Assembly, 8
Westminster Confession, 22

Westphalia Treaty, 152
West Virginia State Board of Education v.
 Barnette, 197–200, 233
Wheelock, Eleazar, 49
White, Justice Byron R., 293, 294
Whitefield, George, 33
Widmar v. *Vincent*, 238–40, 288, 289
Willard, Samuel, 28
William, King, 34
Williams, Roger, 11, 16, 17, 20, 22, 23,
 28, 87, 170, 244; Mather on, 169; *Quer-*
 ies of Highest Consideration, 8–10; on
 state corruption of church, 168
Wilson, John F., *Public Religion in Ameri-*
 can Culture, 301–3

Winthrop, John, 22; *Conclusions for the*
 Plantation of New England, 21
Wise, John, 51
Witherspoon, John, 86
Wolman v. *Walter*, 294
Wood, James E., Jr., 246–50
Woodstock College, 168, 290
World Council of Churches, 246
World War I, 121
World War II, 174

Yale University, 53, 56, 94, 110

Zorach v. *Clauson*, 208–11, 230, 232, 233,
 268